P9-BYE-886

SEA

NORWEGIAN SEA

FINNMARK

Vadsø
Kirkenes

● Tromsø

NORTHERN NORWAY

TROMS

NORTHERN NORWAY AND SVALBARD
See pp202–221

● Bodø

NORDLAND

TRØNDELAG
See pp188–201

NORD-
TRØNDELAG

EASTERN NORWAY
See pp126–143

AKERSHUS

VESTFOLD

ØSTFOLD

AROUND OSLOFJORDEN
See pp112–125

0 kilometres   200

0 miles   100

EYEWITNESS TRAVEL

NORWAY

MAIN CONTRIBUTOR: SNORRE EVENSBERGET

LONDON, NEW YORK,
MELBOURNE, MUNICH AND DELHI
www.dk.com

PRODUCED FOR DORLING KINDERSLEY BY
Streiffert Förlag AB, Stockholm

SENIOR EDITOR & DESIGN Bo Streiffert
PROJECT EDITOR Guy Engström

MAIN CONTRIBUTOR Snorre Evensberget

OTHER CONTRIBUTORS Alf G. Andersen, Hans-Erik Hansen,
Tine Flinder-Nyquist, Annette Mürer

PHOTOGRAPHERS Jørn Bøhmer-Olsen, Frits Solvang, Rolf Sørensen

CARTOGRAPHER Stig Söderlind

ILLUSTRATORS Richard Bonson, Gary Cross,
Claire Littlejohn, John Woodcock

ENGLISH TRANSLATION Fiona Harris

Dorling Kindersley Limited
EDITOR Jane Hutchings
SENIOR DTP DESIGNER Jason Little
PRODUCTION Sarah Dodd

Reproduced in Singapore by Colourscan
Printed and bound by L. Rex Printing Company Limited, China

First American edition 2003

10 11 12 13 10 9 8 7 6 5 4 3 2

Published in the United States by DK Publishing,
375 Hudson Street, New York, NY 10014

Reprinted with revisions 2008, 2010

Copyright © 2003, 2010 Dorling Kindersley Limited, London
A Penguin Company

ALL RIGHTS RESERVED. WITHOUT LIMITING THE RIGHTS UNDER COPYRIGHT RESERVED
ABOVE, NO PART OF THIS PUBLICATION MAY BE REPRODUCED, STORED IN OR
INTRODUCED INTO A RETRIEVAL SYSTEM, OR TRANSMITTED, IN ANY FORM, OR BY ANY
MEANS (ELECTRONIC, MECHANICAL, PHOTOCOPYING, RECORDING, OR OTHERWISE),
WITHOUT THE PRIOR WRITTEN PERMISSION OF BOTH THE COPYRIGHT OWNER AND
THE ABOVE PUBLISHER OF THIS BOOK.

PUBLISHED IN GREAT BRITAIN BY DORLING KINDERSLEY LIMITED

A CATALOG RECORD FOR THIS BOOK IS AVAILABLE FROM THE LIBRARY OF CONGRESS

ISSN 1542-1554

ISBN 978-0-7566-6146-5

FLOORS ARE REFERRED TO THROUGHOUT IN ACCORDANCE WITH EUROPEAN
USAGE; IE THE "FIRST FLOOR" IS THE FLOOR ABOVE GROUND LEVEL

*Front cover main image: Geiranger Fjord and
Seven Sisters waterfall*

MIX
Paper from
responsible sources
FSC™ C018179
www.fsc.org

**The information in this
Dorling Kindersley Travel Guide is checked regularly.**
Every effort has been made to ensure that this book is as up-to-date
as possible at the time of going to press. Some details, however,
such as telephone numbers, opening hours, prices, gallery hanging
arrangements and travel information are liable to change. The
publishers cannot accept responsibility for any consequences arising
from the use of this book, nor for any material on third party
websites, and cannot guarantee that any website address in this
book will be a suitable source of travel information. We value the
views and suggestions of our readers very highly. Please write to:
Publisher, DK Eyewitness Travel Guides, Dorling Kindersley,
80 Strand, London, WC2R 0RL, Great Britain.

View of Geirangerfjorden

CONTENTS

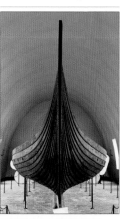

Gokstad ship, a 1,000-year-old
Viking vessel *(see pp84–5)*

◁ Nærøyfjorden, an arm of Aurlandsfjorden, surrounded by steep-sided mountains

Bridal crown from Hallingdal *(see pp24–5)*

Geitost and Jarlsberg cheeses

Skiers taking a break at a cabin in Trysil, Eastern Norway

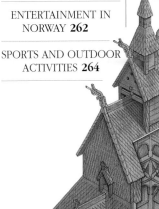

Borgund Stav-kirke *(see p183)*

HOW TO USE THIS GUIDE

This guide helps you to get the most from your visit to Norway by providing detailed practical information and expert recommendations. *Introducing Norway* maps the country and sets it in its historical and cultural context. The Oslo section and the six regional chapters describe

important sights using maps, photographs and illustrations. Restaurant and hotel recommendations can be found in *Travellers' Needs,* while the *Survival Guide* has tips on everything from making a telephone call to using local transportation, as well as information on money, etiquette and safety.

OSLO

The centre of the capital is divided into three areas, each with its own chapter which opens with a list of the sights to be covered. A fourth chapter, *Further Afield,* covers the peripheral areas of Bogstad, Frogner and Toyen. All sights are numbered and plotted on each chapter's area map. Information on each sight is easy to locate as the entries follow the numbering used on the map.

Sights at a Glance lists the chapter's sights by category: Churches, Museums and Galleries, Historic Buildings, Parks and Gardens.

All pages relating to Oslo have red thumb tabs.

A locator map shows you where you are in relation to other areas in the city centre.

1 Area Map
For easy reference, sights are numbered and located on a map. The central sights are also marked on the Oslo Street Finder maps on pages 104–109.

2 Street-by-Street Map
This gives a bird's eye view of the key areas covered in each chapter.

Stars indicate the sights that no visitor should miss.

Walking routes are shown in red.

3 Detailed Information
City sights are described individually. Addresses, phone numbers and opening times are given, as well as admission charges, wheelchair access, guided tours and transport.

Story boxes talk about subjects of interest linked to the sights.

1 Introduction
The landscape, history and character of each area is described here, along with an account of how the area has developed and what it has to offer the visitor.

NORWAY AREA BY AREA
Apart from Oslo, Norway has been divided into six areas, each of which has a separate chapter. The most interesting towns and sights in each region are located on a *Regional Map* at the beginning of each chapter.

Each area of Norway can be quickly identified by its colour-coded thumb tags *(see inside front cover).*

2 Regional Map
This map shows the most important roads and gives an illustrated overview of each area. Interesting places to visit are numbered, and there are useful tips on getting around the region by car and train.

Sights at a Glance shows all sights covered in the chapter.

3 Detailed Information
All the main towns and places to visit are described individually. Listed in order, they follow the numbering on the Regional Map. *Within each town or city, there is detailed information on important buildings and other sights.*

A Visitors' Checklist provides the practical information you will need to plan your visit.

4 Norway's Top Sights
National parks have maps showing places of interest. Illustrations reveal the interiors of historic buildings. Museums and galleries have floorplans. Large towns have maps showing selected sights.

INTRODUCING
NORWAY

DISCOVERING NORWAY

Norway was dealt a winning hand by Mother Nature, and few countries offer as many opportunities to get up and close to the great outdoors, with an abundance of fjords, glaciers, mountains, steppes and a bevy of winsome harbour-side towns splayed about its seemingly endless coastline. There's something here for everyone, from skiing and swimming to open-air museums and whale-watching tours out in the fjords, not to mention the beguiling Arctic Northern Lights. The country also scores points culturally, with some of Europe's best museums and cultural activities, including great displays of modern and classical art, grand Viking ships, beautiful medieval stave churches and alluring café and nightlife scenes.

Polar bear in Svalbard

OSLO AND OSLOFJORD

- **Vibrant shopping and nightlife district**
- **First class museums**
- **Spectacular forests and beaches**

Oslo has excellent museums, wonderful parks, great shopping and a lively nightlife. At the heart of the city is **Karl Johans Gate** *(see p48)*, which has a variety of cafés, bars and restaurants as well as a great selection of boutiques, perfect for whiling away an afternoon. **The National Gallery** *(see p52)* is one of Europe's best art museums, with the **Munch Museum** *(see p93)* and the **Viking Ships museum** *(see p84)* similarly impressive. But don't forget to escape the city, to visit the stunning Oslofjord and its pine-forested islands and sandy beaches.

EASTERN NORWAY

- **Hiking in spectacular national parks**
- **Winter sports at Lillehammer**
- **Atmospheric forest walks**

Eastern Norway is a diverse region offering a range of outdoor activities, including skiing, sailing, hiking and canoeing. The national parks at **Dovrefjell** *(see p138)*, **Rondane** *(see p138)* and, most spectacularly, **Jotunheimen** *(see p140)* offer some of the best hiking in Europe, as well as some of the world's finest fly fishing. The long **Gudbrandsdalen valley** *(see p133)* is great for touring the 18th-century farmsteads that run south all the way to the Winter Olympic city of **Lillehammer** *(see p136)*, which offers skiing and snow-boarding. **Hedmark**

Bustling Karl Johans Gate in the centre of Oslo

(see p127), near the Swedish border, is great for walks in the area's thick forests.

SØRLANDET & TELEMARK

- **The popular resort town of Kristiansand**
- **Sørlandet's charming clapboard houses**
- **Bracing outdoor pursuits in Lyngør**

Norway's southern regions are made up of islands, fells and lakes that are great for day trips out from the capital. **Kristiansand** *(see p152)* is known as "the summer city", and is made up of colourful houses. Norway's finest beach, the Sjøsanden, is just nearby in **Mandal** *(see p150)*, a town filled with tiny alleyways. Along the south-eastern coast are a number of clapboard resort towns

The stunningly beautiful Jotunheimen national park in eastern Norway

◁ *The Bridal Procession by A Tidemand and H Gude, 1848*

such as **Kragerø** *(see p149)*, **Risør** *(see p149)* and **Grimstad** *(see p150)*.

Lyngør *(see p149)* is a beguiling village spread across four islands, regularly considered to be one of the best-preserved hamlets in Europe. It is a haven for sailing aficionados, while inland hiking, canoeing and rock climbing is available.

VESTLANDET

- **Hanseatic town of Bergen**
- **Breathtaking fjords**
- **Awesome Jostedalsbreen glacier**

One of Norway's famed fjords in the Vestlandet region

Norway's southwestern coast is the most enchanting part of the country, a place to experience the true grandeur of the fjords. **Stavanger** *(see p164)* is a lovely wharfside town, but the fjords are best toured from **Bergen** *(see p170)*, a modern city that retains the feel of a Hanseatic fishing town. From here, travel along the plummeting **Flåmsbana railway** *(see p182)* towards the valleys of the verdant, alpine **Sognefjord** *(see p180)*, Norway's deepest and longest fjord. North of

Colourful water-front buildings in Trondheim

the towns of **Balestrand** and **Aurland** *(p182)* is the impressive **Jostedalsbreen** glacier *(see p184)*. Bergen is also a good place to join the **Hurtigruten** *(see p268)*, the coastal steamer that runs along Norway's coast all the way to the Russian border.

TRØNDELAG

- **Medieval Nidaros cathedral**
- **UNESCO World Heritage town of Røros**
- **Salmon-fishing at Namsos**

Trondheim's **Nidaros cathedral** *(see p199)* is the most stunning medieval structure in Norway. The city also proffers the regal **Stiftsgården** *(see p198)*, the largest wooden building in Scandinavia, as well as the atmospheric **Bryggen** *(see p197)* wharf area. A large student population gives Trondheim a lively nightlife, set in the cool district of **Bakklandet** *(see p198)*. The nearby mining town of **Røros** *(see p192)* contains timbered homes that are on the UNESCO World Heritage list. Trøndelag's coastline is well known for its salmon filled rivers, where the fishing is best at **Namsos** *(see p201)*. For great summer bathing, head to the island of **Munkholmen** *(see p193)*.

NORTHERN NORWAY

- **Reindeer-herding Sámi**
- **Spectacular midnight sun and Northern Lights**
- **Polar bears in their natural habitat in Svalbard**

The area north of the Arctic circle is the most remote part of Norway. Tranquil coastal towns like **Svolvær** *(see p210)* and **Andenes** *(see p209)* in the Lofoten and Vesterålen islands are perfect for fishing, bird- and whale-watching. Inland, the nomadic Sámi people still live a largely traditional way of life, herding reindeer and breeding huskies in towns such as **Karasjok** and **Kautokeino** *(see p215)*. **Nordkapp** *(see p218)* is Europe's northernmost point and the best place to take in the midnight sun. Some 650 km (400 miles) north of here in the Arctic Ocean, the island of **Svalbard** *(see p220)* offers a brave few the opportunity to witness polar bears in their native habitat. In winter, the gorgeous **Northern Lights** *(see p205)*, or *Aurora Borealis*, are visible across the sky.

The Northern Lights in the Norwegian winter sky

Putting Norway on the Map

The kingdom of Norway is one of the largest
countries in Europe, covering 324,219 sq km
(125,148 sq miles). The most southerly point,
Lindersnes, lies at about the same latitude as
Aberdeen in Scotland, and the northernmost tip,
near the North Cape, is at latitude 71°11'8" N.
The coastline bordering the Skagerrak, the North
Sea, the Norwegian Sea and the Arctic Ocean
measures 20,000 km (12,400 miles). Much of the
country is habitable thanks to the warming
effects of the Gulf Stream. The country has
around 4.8 million inhabitants, 500,000 of
whom live in the capital, Oslo.

SVALBARD

Kvitøya

Nordaustlandet

Kong Karls land

Spitsbergen

Barentsøya

Longyearbyen

Edge-øya

BARENTS SEA

Hopen

0 kilometres   250

0 miles   150

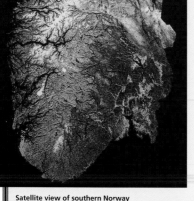

Satellite view of southern Norway

0 kilometres   250

0 miles   150

NORWEGIAN SEA

NORWAY

Namsos

Steinkjer

Trondheimsl...

Trondheim

Kristiansund

Molde

Ålesund

Andalsnes

Røros

Alvdal

Dombås

Idre

Florø

Otta

Sognefjorden

Lillehammer

Fagernes

Elverum

Bergen

Hamar

Mjøsa

Odda

Rjukan

Drammen

OSLO

Haugesund

Tønsberg

Moss

Sandefjord

Stavanger

Skien

Fredrikstad

Evje

Larvik

Strömstad

Egersund

Arendal

Väne...

Kristiansand

SKAGERRAK

Shetland Islands

Lerwick

(UK)

Torshavn

Aberdeen

Newcastle

Harwich

NORTH SEA

Amsterdam

Gothenburg

Hirtshals

Frederikshavn

DENMARK

Hanstholm

KEY

✈ International airport

☒ Domestic airport

⚓ Ferry port

▬ Motorway

▬ Major road

— Train line

–·– International border

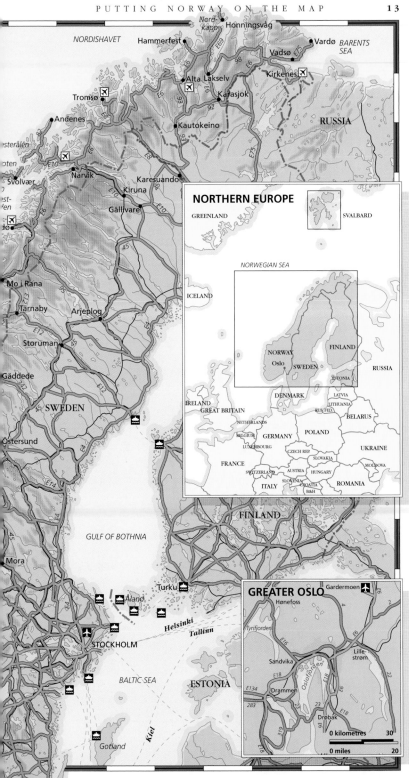

A PORTRAIT OF NORWAY

Norway's magnificent scenery and untamed nature have long captivated visitors. Spectacular fjords indent the rugged coastline, mountains rise above tranquil valleys. This is a country where music, art and literature are part of its soul, where sports such as skiing and football are actively pursued, and current affairs are hotly debated. It is also the home of the Nobel Peace Prize.

Wrapped around northwestern Scandinavia like a protective bastion against the North Sea, Norway is one of the most scenically beautiful places in Europe. The country stretches an incredible 1,752 km (1,089 miles), from southernmost Lindesnes across the Arctic Circle to the North Cape. It is barely 430 km (267 miles) at its widest point, and only 6 km (4 miles) at its narrowest.

A puffin

Geological processes such as the land rising, the Ice Age and erosion have created a remarkably varied landscape. Deep fjords penetrate the coastal mountain ranges, their glassy green waters extending far inland to waterside towns and settlements. More than 75,000 islands lie offshore, providing sheltered harbours and passageways for the numerous ferries, cruise ships and fishing boats that ply the coast.

The capital, Oslo, is a vibrant city centred round a harbour and guarded by a castle. It is an eclectic place of traditional timber houses, stately Neo-Classical buildings and the latest in ultra-modern architecture, with a thriving café-life that spills outdoors in summer. Around Oslofjorden – a summer playground teeming with boats – evidence of Norway's Viking heritage abounds. The Vikings were a warrior-like maritime race whose voyages took them as far as America in one direction and the Caspian Sea in

Fishermen at the former trading post of Sund in the Lofoten Islands

◁ Woman dressed in a traditional *bunad* playing folk music

Pumping riches from the bottom of the sea on the Ekofisk oil field

the other, and whose raiding parties inspired terror in the coastal communities of Northern Europe. Fascinating archaeological finds from this time, including 9th-century sailing vessels, are on show in museums such as Oslo's Viking Ship Museum.

Northeast of the capital, fertile farmland and forests give way to lofty mountains with peaks reaching 2,500 m (8,200 ft) and long, slender valleys with lakes and rivers. The south coast is lined with silver-sand beaches set against a backdrop of the 1,400-m (4,593-ft) high mountain plateau of Hardangervidda. Vestlandet, on the west coast, with the fishing port of Bergen and Norway's "oil capital", Stavanger, is picturesque fjord country.

NORTHERN LIGHTS

Pilgrims in days of old would make the treacherous journey north across the mountains to the sacred Nidaros Cathedral in Trondheim. Here lie the remains of the country's patron saint, Olav Haraldsson. The northernmost point in Norway, the North Cape, is a place of pilgrimage for modern-day travellers, its precipitous cliffs standing proud against the Barents Sea.

Northern Norway is the land of the midnight sun and shimmering Northern Lights. In the height of summer it basks in daylight around the clock; in winter the sun disappears altogether

National coat of arms

and its rearrival in the New Year is marked by joyous festivities.

CLIMATE

It is possible to live so far north in Norway because of the warming effects of the Gulf Stream. On the west coast this results in warm winters and cool summers. The south and west of the country have the highest average temperatures: 22° C (72° F) in Oslo in July. The coldest temperatures can be found in the mountains, particularly Finnmarksvidda, where −51.4° C (−60.5° F) was recorded in December 1886.

RICHES OF THE LAND AND SEA

Fishing, particularly herring, and the timber industry have formed the backbone of the Norwegian economy. This has always been a seafaring country, renowned for shipbuilding, and foreign trade has played an important role in its development. Industrialization gathered momentum in the 19th century; small sawmills and factories gave way to larger enterprises powered by hydro-electricity. In the 20th century, Norway made its fortune in offshore oil production, creating one of the world's richest countries. How the oil revenue should be spent has been the subject of much political controversy. The state of the environment is also a matter of fierce debate. Top of the list of concerns are pollution of the waterways, high energy consumption and which type of power stations should be built.

KING AND GOVERNMENT

Norway is a constitutional, hereditary monarchy. The current monarch is King Harald V, who succeeded to the throne in 1991. He is married to Queen Sonja, a commoner, and their two children, Crown Prince Haakon Magnus and Princess Märtha Louise, are also both married to commoners. Most Norwegians are traditionally fiercely proud of their royal family, who in turn are close to their people and are seen as modern, down-to-earth monarchs.

A Sami wedding party, Kautokeino, Finnmark

According to the constitution, the executive power rests with the king, but in practice it is the Council of State which governs. The Norwegian Parliament (Stortinget) has the decisive power when it comes to the management of the country. Elections to the 165-representative parliament are held every four years. Of the six principal parties jostling for power, the Labour Party held the majority from 1945–61; since then there have been both socialist and non-socialist governments.

The main political aims have been welfare, social stability and equality.

The Equal Opportunities Act of 1978 established a series of principles aiming to improve the balance of men and women in the workplace and ensuring equal pay for equal work. As a result, women entered political life in large numbers, and when Gro Harlem Brundtland formed her government in 1986, 44.4 per cent of the ministers were women, which caused an international sensation.

THE PEOPLE

Norwegians are hospitable people who will, more often than not, go out of their way to welcome a guest in their home and offer cake and a drink. This is a tradition that has its roots in the remote rural settlements of old when visitors needed sustenance after an arduous journey. Major investment in road-building, tunnels and bridges has meant that few communities are so isolated today, but old traditions live on.

The Norwegians are a deeply patriotic race, as can be seen on National Day (17 May), when young and old dress in folk costume (the *bunad, see pp24–5*) and parade through the streets. Yet this nationalistic outlook does not prevent them from accepting refugees and immigrants.

On the one hand Norwegians are regarded as a liberal, tolerant people, but on the other they still adhere to

The marriage of Crown Prince Haakon Magnus and Mette-Marit in Oslo Cathedral, 2001

laws that hark back to a bygone era. The sale of alcohol, for instance, is restricted to government-owned shops known as Vinmonopolet.

Norway was a Catholic country until the Reformation in 1537, when the state church became Evangelical-Lutheran by royal decree.

LANGUAGE

Norway has had vigorous and at times heated discussions over the status of its two languages, *bokmål* ("book language"), which is a derivation of Danish, and *nynorsk*, an amalgamation of the many Norwegian dialects nationwide.

Both *bokmål* and *nynorsk* have had equal official status since 1885. *Nynorsk* is most widely spoken in the west of the country (Vestlandet) and in the central valleys to the south and east. Norway's oldest minority language, Sami, is spoken by some 20,000 people *(see p215)*.

A NATION OF AVID READERS

Norwegians read more newspapers than anyone else in the world. On average, each household buys a remarkable 1.7 newspapers a day.

Sales of books are also high. The most popular volume today is Thor Heyerdahl's *The Kon-Tiki Expedition*, which has been published in nearly 70 languages and has sold millions of copies worldwide. Jostein Gaarder's *Sophie's World* was the world's best-selling book in 1996; Herbjørg Wassmo's *Tora-trilogy* has been translated into 22 languages, and several recent Norwegian crime novels have been published in as many as 30 countries.

Jubliant crowds on Holmenkoll Sunday for the ski-jumping highlight of the annual skiing festival

Thor Heyerdahl's best-selling book, *The Kon-Tiki Expedition*.

ART, MUSIC AND DRAMA

The 19th-century passion for National Romanticism in Norway laid the foundations for what has become a rich heritage of visual arts, music and literature. Artists working at this time, such as Adolf Tidemand and Hans Gude, captured the countryside and its people in their paintings. Edvard Munch followed with his deeply emotional Expressionist works. In music, the violinist Ole Bull and the pianist and composer Edvard Grieg looked to Norwegian folk songs for inspiration. The playwrights Bjørnstjerne Bjørnson and Henrik Ibsen put Norwegian issues firmly centre stage in their dramas.

The importance of traditions is obvious in the country's many open-air museums. It seems that no town is complete without its own collection of rustic timber buildings representing local building style and crafts such as wood-carving and decorative painting (known as *rosemaling*).

Folk music is rooted in the country's ancient songs and sagas, and musicians can often be heard playing the Hardanger fiddle, particularly at festivals. A multitude of school brass bands form a happy and harmonious part of the children's

National Day parade on 17 May and other festive occasions.

SPORTS AND THE OUTDOORS

Renowned as the cradle of skiing, during the 2002 Winter Olympics in Salt Lake City, USA, Norway won 11 gold medals and came third in the overall competition. The country has hosted two Winter Olympics: in Oslo in 1952 and Lillehammer in 1994.

Skier taking a break at a hut in Rondane National Park during Easter holidays

Skiing is a popular winter pastime and with the first snowfalls, trails are prepared and people of all ages venture out on skis. Events such as the Holmenkollen Ski Festival attract thousands of spectators.

Football has a strong following with 1,800 clubs throughout the country. In other fields, the women's handball and football teams have had great successes, followed closely by the whole nation on TV.

The nature-loving Norwegians still spend much of their spare time outdoors, by the sea, sailing, fishing or walking in the forests and mountains, where a network of mountain huts *(hytte)* provides overnight accommodation.

NORWAY AND THE WORLD

A member of NATO since 1949, Norway has remained a nation with a strong sense of "self". The referenda for joining the European Union (in 1972 and 1994) both resulted in a "no" vote; the latter with 52.2 per cent against and 47.8 per cent in favour. Opinion polls today indicate the same standpoint.

When it comes to international welfare and peace issues, however, Norway plays a central role. In relation to its gross national product, Norway is the world's largest donor. It has also sent nearly 60,000 soldiers to take part in United Nations peace-keeping missions, and awards the Nobel Peace prize every year.

Norway is becoming more dependent on the outside world, and there are concerns about the future and what will happen when its oil supplies run out.

It remains to be seen if the country's international involvement will increase after the next referendum on EU membership.

The annual award ceremony for the Nobel Peace Prize in the main hall of Oslo Town Hall

The Fjords

Among the world's most spectacular geological formations, the Norwegian fjords are long, narrow inlets stretching deep into the surrounding mountains. At their innermost reaches, their depth often matches the height of the cliffs above, while shallower waters connect them to the sea. They were created by a gradual process of glacier erosion during the last Ice Age (around 110,000 to 13,000 BC) when enormous glaciers crept through the valleys, gouging steep-sided crevices into the landscape, often far below the surface of the sea. When the glaciers melted, sea water burst in and filled the hollows left by the ice.

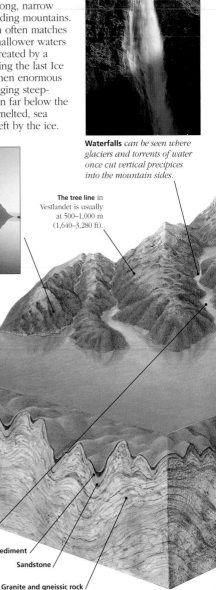

Waterfalls *can be seen where glaciers and torrents of water once cut vertical precipices into the mountain sides.*

The tree line in Vestlandet is usually at 500–1,000 m (1,640–3,280 ft).

Where the fjords *meet the sea on the west coast of Norway, the tree-covered mountains rise steeply. Spruce and birch are the most common species. In the north, the cliff faces are often bare all the way down to the shore.*

The threshold between the fjord and the sea often has a depth of just one-tenth of the fjord at its deepest point.

Sediment

Sandstone

Granite and gneissic rock

THE STRUCTURE OF A FJORD

This cut-away artwork shows a typical fjord, with a threshold of shallow water at the mouth falling steeply to great depths further inland, and inlets radiating from the main fjord. The sea bed, like the surrounding mountains, consists of granite and gneiss with sediment on top.

Fruit and vegetable *cultivation is a thriving industry at the inner reaches of the southern fjords. Here the climate is more favourable than by the coast.*

Glaciers *such as Jostedalsbreen (see p178) gouged out the fjords. Toward the end of the last Ice Age, the glaciers covered all of what was to become Sognefjorden. As the ice melted, the seawater forced its way into the basin.*

The mountain peaks *can reach as high as 1,500 m (4,900 ft) just a short distance from the shore. In inner Sognefjorden, the mountains rise to 2,000 m (6,560 ft).*

The inner arms of the fjord can extend 200 km (124 miles) from its mouth.

Small villages have developed in sheltered bays where the soil is good for fruit-growing and farming.

The inlets *can be very long and often branch into several tributaries. The glaciers carved through the rock wherever the surface was weak.*

A fjord's depth can be more than 1,200 m (3,930 ft).

ROAD TUNNELS UNDER THE FJORDS

Communications along the Atlantic coast of Norway have always been a challenge, with fjords cutting long clefts into the land and the risk of avalanches and the mountains themselves creating other obstacles. In recent years great improvements to the infrastructure have been made possible thanks to the riches from the North Sea oil fields. Using modern engineering techniques, huge tunnels have been driven through mountain ranges and under fjords, making transport easier between the small communities.

Car ferries *criss-cross the fjords at many points. Although not as quick an alternative as road tunnels and bridges, they remain a popular choice for the scenic views they offer.*

The 24.5-km (15-mile) long Lærdal Tunnel *(see p176)*

Landscape and Wildlife

Norway has an immensely varied landscape. The plains and rolling hills of the southwest give way to rounded mountains cut by rivers and lakes where Arctic char, salmon and trout can be fished. Reindeer inhabit the high plateaus; elk, wolf and roe deer the forests. Further north the terrain becomes more rugged. This is the habitat of bear, lynx and Arctic fox. Polar bears can be seen on the islands of Svalbard *(see pp220–1)*. The coast is punctuated by fjords where seals and even whales may be spotted. Skerries and islands provide ideal nesting sites for some of the country's 250 species of birds. Out to sea the waters are rich in cod, coley, mackerel and herring.

The brown bear *was once found throughout the country, but today lives in limited numbers in the far north.*

THE ATLANTIC COAST
The nesting cliffs of Runde, near Ålesund, Lofoten, Troms, Finnmark and Svalbard are home to several hundred thousand birds. Species include white-breasted guillemot, kittiwake, auk and puffin. Northern fulmar and northern gannet can also be seen in fewer numbers.

THE FORESTS
Half of Norway's land area is forest, creating a natural habitat for elk and roe deer, hare, fox and squirrel. It is possible to witness a capercaillie mating game or the migration of woodcock, or even hear the call of the black grouse and the cry of the common crane from the marshes.

Puffins, *"the parrots of the nesting cliffs", can be found in large numbers in northern Norway. The population varies according to feeding conditions.*

The elk *is Norway's largest member of the deer family, which includes wild reindeer, red deer and roe deer. It is found throughout the country.*

White-tailed eagles *nest high on coastal mountain shelves. Other predatory birds include the golden eagle, osprey, goshawk, buzzard and gyrfalcon.*

The lynx *prowls the area north from Trøndelag. Of the large predators, Norway also has bear and wolverine. The wolf, now an endangered species, inhabits the southeast.*

SEA MAMMALS

The killer whale is a relatively frequent visitor to the coast, especially to Tysfjord in northern Norway. Those people who take part in a whale and seal safari off Andøya *(see p207)* may be lucky to spot a sperm whale, which can be up to 18-m (60-ft) long. The Greenland whale occasionally appears off Svalbard. Porpoises swim close to the Norwegian shore and six species of seals live along the coast. Herds of walruses can be seen around Svalbard.

The killer whale *is one of the ocean's feared predators. It eats vast quantities of seals and fish, especially herring, and will attack other whales.*

The grey seal (fjordkobbe) *and the common seal* (steinkobbe) *are found off mainland Norway. Four other species can be seen on the islands of Svalbard.*

FJORDS AND MOUNTAINS

Red deer is the biggest game animal to be seen in the coastal areas and around the fjords. Reindeer rule the mountain plateaus, where the willow grouse lives in copses and willow thickets. The common ptarmigan is found on higher ground. The wolverine thrives in the mountains.

Wild reindeer *roam Hardangervidda, in the mountains of Dovrefjell and Rondane, and in the Bykle and Setesdal bills. The population fluctuates at around 70,000 animals.*

Musk oxen *can be found mainly in the Arctic, but a population has existed on the Dovrefjell plateau since 1932.*

THE FAR NORTH

Animals associated with the high mountains and forests, as well as Arctic species, are found in the far north of Norway. Wildlife on Svalbard is relatively limited, but Svalbard reindeer, Arctic fox and the polar bear in particular have adjusted well to the harsh environment. Bird life along the northern coast is particularly rich.

The Arctic fox, *or polar fox, was close to extinction in 1920 when it became an officially protected species. The population is growing, but is still very vulnerable.*

The common ptarmigan *has pure white winter plumage, apart from near its eyes and beak. It may nest as high as 1,650 m (5,400 ft) above sea level.*

The Norwegian Bunad

National Day on 17 May draws crowds of Norwegians on to the streets dressed either in traditional folk costumes or in the national dress, known as *bunad*. The two outfits differ: folk costumes have long-standing traditions in the regions, whereas the *bunad* is a more recent version of the traditional outfits. The large migration of rural people to the towns has made the *bunad* a symbol of their identity and for many an important link with their roots. Its use for festive occasions is becoming increasingly popular.

Silver filigree brooch, Nordland

BUNAD FROM VESTFOLD ①

The Vestfold *bunad* was recreated piece-by-piece. It was first presented in its final form in 1956. Vestfold's lively foreign trade probably led to the garments being made in lighter, imported materials, rather than thick homespun fabric, but these disintegrated more easily and no complete costumes have survived. There are two versions of the Vestfold *bunad (see left)*.

Silver-buckled woollen belt

Bonnet worn with the *bunad*

HALLINGDAL BUNAD ②

The traditional *bunad* in Hallingdal consists of a black, sometimes layered skirt, a floral apron and a black cloth bodice embroidered with wool. It has a white shirt with white-work embroidery on the neckband and wristbands, just like the exquisite bridal *bunad (see left)*, which is on display in Hallingdal District Museum in Nesbyen.

Bridal crown in red woollen broadcloth

The bridal bodice in luxurious cream brocade

AMLI BUNAD FROM AUST-AGDER ③

The Åmli *bunad* is considered the last link in the development of a national folk costume. The ensemble has, since the 1920s, been based on original single garments used in Åmli and neighbouring rural settlements between 1700 and the mid-1800s. A striking part of this *bunad* is the shoulder piece, in red (or green) damask. It has three pairs of silver eyes which are cross-laced over the chest with a silver chain.

Double collar stud fastenings for a blouse

Embroidered linen headscarf with a fringe

BRIDAL BUNAD FROM VOSS ④

The most eye-catching part of the bridal *bunad* from Voss is the splendid crown, or *Vosseladet* as it is known. It is covered in red fabric embroidered with beads. Silver coins and filigree silver ornaments inset with semi-precious stones hang from the brim. Apart from the crown and a special black jacket, the bridal costume is largely the same as the normal Voss *bunad* worn for festive occasions.

Voss's bridal crown dating from the early 19th century

Agnus Dei **pendant worn with bridal gown**

BUNADS FROM OPPDAL ⑤

There is one *bunad* that can be used in the whole of Trondelag, although many counties have their own version. The Oppdal *bunad* was reconstructed in 1963 from the fragments of old costumes. The multi-coloured woollen skirt is worn with a red, green or blue bodice. The man's *bunad* is based on an 18th-century garment. The breeches can be made of leather or black homespun.

Agnus Dei **pendant worn by the women**

Man's waistcoat made from linen and wool

BUNADS FROM NORDLAND AND TROMS ⑥

The Nordland *bunad*, created in 1928, was originally blue, but now also comes in green. It is based on a 200-year-old fabric from Vefsn. The bag or reticule is in the same colour and floral pattern as the skirt. The woman's *bunad* from Troms is inspired by costumes from Bjarkøy and Senja. The man's *bunad* is the same for Nordland and Troms.

A silver-clasped reticule for the woman

TRADITIONAL SAMI COSTUMES

The colourful costume, an important part of Sami cultural identity *(see p215)*

Sami costumes made from cloth can be traced back to the Middle Ages. They developed from earlier versions which were made from animal hide. Today, the three most distinctive outfits come from Kautokeino, Varanger and Karasjok.

The Kautokeino costume comprises a tunic top for the men, a pleated skirt for the women and a belt with silver buttons. Each item is richly decorated with bands of embroidery. The Varanger costume is also colourfully embellished, while that from Karasjok is remarkably simple and retains much of the cut of the ancient hide costume, the *pesk*. The women of Karasjok wear a beautiful fringed shawl.

NORWAY THROUGH THE YEAR

There are four clearly defined seasons in Norway, but as the saying goes: "Every season has its charm." Norwegians enjoy being one of the world's top skiing nations, and even town-dwellers will don their skis as soon as the first snow falls in November or December. The winter sports centres have something to offer everyone, both beginners and experienced skiers, and are extremely popular, particularly at

Summer flowers and snowclad mountains

Easter. The arrival of spring brings long light-filled days. Norway celebrates National Day on 17 May with children's parades and festivities. The arts and cultural scenes begin to stir after their winter slumber.

In summer Norwegians head for the islands and skerries. There are boat festivals, fairs and games all the way along the coast. Autumn is the season for theatre-going, concerts, opera, dance, film premieres and art exhibitions.

Bergen Festival concert in the magnificent Grieg Hall

SPRING

When the severe "King Winter" loosens his grip, the country bursts into life. The spring sun at the end of April heralds the last of the season's skiing trips in the mountains and encourages an urge to get out and about and experience life anew. The tourist season starts in earnest in May when the countryside is crisp and fresh, and the arts and cultural festivals are beginning to blossom. At this time of year activities such as dancing and musical events move outdoors. There are markets and shows to visit.

MARCH

Sun Party at Svalbard *(1st week of Mar).* The world's northernmost celebration of the return of the sun.
Holmenkollen Ski Festival *(2nd week Mar, see pp26–7).*
Alternative Fair, Bergen

(mid-Mar). An exploration of the "Age of Aquarius".
Oslo Festival of Church Music *(mid-Mar)* features a variety of concerts.
The Birkebeiner Race *(3rd week of Mar).* Ski marathon from Rena to Lillehammer *(see pp27, 131 and 137).*
Winter Festival, Røros *(all month).* Musical events in this old copper-mining town.

APRIL

Sami Easter celebrations and weddings *(end of Mar or early Apr).*
Vossajazz Hordaland *(early Apr).* International jazz festival, one of the first of the season.
Bergen Blues and Roots Festival (Ole Blues) *(end Apr–early May).* Voted the best Norwegian festival by its participants.
Day of Dance *(29 Apr).* Celebrated all over the country with performances and dance stunts in the streets and squares by amateurs and professionals.

MAY

May Jazz, Stavanger *(1st half of May).* A fast-growing festival offering big stars and exciting new talent.
17 May, *("Syttende Mai"),* Norway's National Day, is celebrated nationwide with children's parades and a host of festivities.
Bergen International Arts Festival *(end of May/early Jun)* offers ten days of music, drama and artistic events of international standing attracting large numbers of visitors.
Night Jazz Bergen *(end of May/early Jun).* Staged around the same time as the Bergen Festival, Night Jazz Bergen organizes more than 70 different concerts featuring both Norwegian and international artists.

Norway's National Day, 17 May, on Karl Johans Gate, Oslo

SUMMER

The long, light summer nights are not for sleeping. Summer is the peak season for festivals and outdoor productions ranging from musicals to historical plays and classical dramas using nature as a backdrop.

In many parts of the country traditions centre around types of food, such as the Oslo Seafood Festival in August. Often they are combined with varying degrees of physical challenges. Tourist offices can recommend events off the beaten track.

Salmon fishing in Ågårdselva, Østfold

JUNE

Salmon Fishing Season *(1 Jun–mid/end Aug)*. Dates may vary slightly.
Day of Music, Oslo *(1st Sat of Jun)*. Classical, jazz, pop and rock.
Norwegian Mountain Marathon *(1st week Jun)*. A remarkable marathon in the spectacular mountains of Jotunheimen.
Summer Concerts at Troldhaugen, Bergen *(Wed, Sat and Sun, mid-Jun to mid-Aug)*. The music of Edvard Grieg performed in his own home.
Stryn Summer Ski Festival Sogn og Fjordane *(mid-Jun)*. Skiing in shorts.
Nordland Festival, Sortland, Vesterålen *(mid-Jun)*. Deep-sea fishing.
North Sea Festival, Haugesund *(mid-Jun)*. European sports-fishing competition.
Norwegian Wood, Oslo *(mid-Jun)*. Rock music festival *(see p248)*.
Short Film Festival, Grimstad *(mid-Jun)*. Popular competition for short films.
St Hans Aften *(24 Jun)*. Midsummer is celebrated with bonfires and festivities.
Cultural Festival in Northern Norway Harstad *(around midsummer)*.

Risør Festival of Chamber Music, Risør *(last week of Jun)*. Top-class concerts in idyllic Sørlandet.
Extreme Sports Week, Voss *(last week of Jun)*. Mountain biking, mountain climbing, extreme skiing, plus music.
Vestfold Festival *(end of Jun/early Jul)*. Ten-day festival of music, dance and theatre.

JULY

Norsk Aften, Norsk Folke-museum, Oslo *(Tue, Wed, Fri and Sat from 1 Jul)*. The "Norwegian Evening" offers guided tours in the stave church and museum area; folk dancing and food.
Kongsberg Jazz Festival *(early Jul)*, with top musicians such as Joshua Redman.
Quart Festival, Kristiansand *(1st week of Jul)*. Rock concerts both in and outdoors featuring Norwegian and international acts.
Fjæreheia Grimstad *(from mid-Jul)*. Agder Theatre's outdoor performances of Ibsen dramas and musicals.
Molde International Jazz Festival *(last week of Jul)*, starring the world's best performers and first-class Norwegian artists.

Skiing in summer

Thousands of fans at the Molde International Jazz Festival in July

Telemark Festival, Bø *(last week of Jul)*. International folk music festival with something for all the family: song, dance, music, concerts, courses and seminars.

AUGUST

Wooden Boat Festival, Risør *(early Aug)*. Exhibition of coastal culture, old and new wooden boats; outdoor concerts.
Notodden International Blues Festival *(1st week of Aug)*. Concerts in clubs and outdoors. There is a "blues cruise" for those without a boat of their own.
Gålåvann Gudbrandsdalen *(4–14 Aug)*. The Ibsen drama *Peer Gynt* is performed outdoors in beautiful surroundings.
Nordic Hunting and Fishing Days Elverum *(1st half of Aug)*.
Stavanger Chamber Music Festival and **Oslo Chamber Music Festival** *(mid-Aug)* attract large numbers of visitors to the summer evening concerts.
Sildajazz, Haugesund *(mid-Aug)*. Colourful festival featuring 20 concert venues, children's and street parades, harbour market and pleasure craft.
Bjørnson Festival, Molde *(last week of Aug)*. International festival of literature. Bjørnson was one of Norway's greatest writers.
Norwegian Film Festival Haugesund *(end of Aug)*. More than 100 new films are shown during the eight-day festival. Buy a season ticket. Presentation of the Amanda Awards.

Bearberries colouring the mountains red in the autumn

AUTUMN

Walking in the forests and mountains, picking berries and gathering mushrooms are ideal pastimes in autumn. As the evenings begin to close in, Norwegians retreat indoors and enjoy the many cultural events that are staged in theatres large and small. Autumn brings plenty to refresh the mind: new books are published and major art exhibitions open at this time of year.

SEPTEMBER

The National Theatre (Nationaltheatret), Oslo *(1st half of Sep)*, alternates the start of the season each year with either the Ibsen Festival or the Contemporary Festival *(Samtidsfestival)* of new drama.
Ibsen Culture Festival, Skien *(1st half of Sep)*.
A celebration of the work of the Norwegian playwright

Chanterelle harvest

in the town where he grew up.
Young Jazz Ålesund *(end of Sep)*. Talented jazz musicians under the age of 30 perform in Norway's Art Nouveau town *(see p186)*.

OCTOBER

Ultima Contemporary Music Festival, Oslo *(1st half of Oct)*, presents the latest in music, dance and dramatic art in co-operation with theatres and museums, including Black Box Teater, Oslo Konserthus, Henie Onstad Kunstsenter, and Filmens Hus.
Fartein Valen Days, Haugesund *(end of Oct)*. The composer Fartein Valen (1887–1952) is showcased with a series of lectures and concerts in churches, galleries and in his childhood home.
Oslo Horse Show *(mid-Oct)*. A popular family event held in Oslo Spektrum.

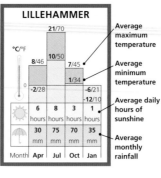

Climate

Western Norway has an Atlantic climate with warm winters and cool summers. The highest average temperatures are in Sørlandet and Vestlandet. Østlandet has an inland climate, with cold winters and warm summers. Vestlandet has the most rain; the north end of Gudbrandsdal and the depths of Finnmarksvidda have the least rain.

OSLO

Month	Apr	Jul	Oct	Jan
Average maximum temperature	9/48	22/72	12/54	9/48
	1/34		4/39	-2/28
Average minimum temperature				-7/19
Average daily hours of sunshine	6 hours	8 hours	3 hours	1 hours
Average monthly rainfall	41 mm	81 mm	84 mm	49 mm

LILLEHAMMER

Month	Apr	Jul	Oct	Jan
	8/46	21/70	10/50	7/45
	-2/28		1/34	-6/21
				-12/10
	6 hours	8 hours	3 hours	1 hours
	30 mm	75 mm	70 mm	35 mm

Average maximum temperature

Average minimum temperature

Average daily hours of sunshine

Average monthly rainfall

BERGEN

Month	Apr	Jul	Oct	Jan
	9/48	18/64	12/54	11/52
	3/37		6/43	4/39
				0/32
	5 hours	5 hours	2 hours	1 hours
	114 mm	148 mm	271 mm	190 mm

TRONDHEIM

Month	Apr	Jul	Oct	Jan
	8/52	18/64	10/50	9/48
	0/32		3/37	0/32
				-7/19
	5 hours	6 hours	2 hours	0.5 hours
	49 mm	94 mm	104 mm	63 mm

TROMSØ

Month	Apr	Jul	Oct	Jan
	3/37	15/59	9/48	5/41
	-2/28		1/34	-2/28
				-7/19
	5 hours	7 hours	1,5 hours	0 hours
	64 mm	77 mm	131 mm	95 mm

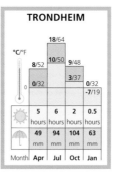

WINTER

The christmas season gets underway when the Christmas trees are lit, the first Christmas snow starts to fall and colourfully decorated gingerbread cookie houses start appearing. Restaurants are fully booked for their Christmas buffets, with the Norwegian speciality, *lutefisk* (dried fish treated with lye), on the menu.

New Year sees the start of the skiing season, and the prospect of fresh tracks lures many on to the slopes.

NOVEMBER

Rakfisk Festival, Valdres *(1st weekend in Nov)*. Fermented mountain trout is a delicacy, and visitors can choose from the best producers have to offer.
Museum of Children's Art, (Det Internasjonale Barnekunstmuseet), Oslo, has extended opening hours during the winter, on Tue, Wed, Thu and Sun morning. Paintings and drawings by children worldwide.
Lighting the Christmas Tree *(1st Sun of Advent)*. Trees are lit in towns and villages and there is music, speeches and group singing, as well as the traditional walk around the tree.

DECEMBER

Christmas Concerts *(all Dec)*. Well-known singers and entertainers give church concerts, often with local choirs and orchestras.

Christmas Markets *(Sun)*. Folk museums such as the Norsk Folkemuseum, Oslo, and Maihaugen, Lillehammer, arrange special folk dancing displays and concerts, the sales of crafts and Father Christmas workshops.
Gingerbread Houses, Galleriet, Bergen *(all Dec)*. The world's biggest gingerbread town according to the *Guinness Book of Records*. A remarkable show of 150 gingerbread houses, ships, aeroplanes and ski jumps skilfully made by children, young people and professionals.

Full moon over a wintery scene at Lillehammer

JANUARY

Ski-Kite, Møsvann, Telemark *(early Jan)*. Skiing with the aid of a kite. Lessons at the Rauland Ski Centre.
Festival of Northern Lights, Tromsø *(end of Jan)*. Visitors from around the world come to see the magnificent northern lights *(aurora borealis)*, which shimmer and dance across the sky on clear winter nights in northern Norway.

Giant snowman at the Snow Sculpture Festival, Vinje

Polar Jazz Svalbard *(end of Jan)*. The world's most northerly jazz and blues festival. Four to five days of concerts and events staged throughout the Svalbard town of Longyearbyen.

FEBRUARY

Snow Sculpture Festival, Vinje *(1st week of Feb)*. A sculpture park with a difference. Create your own masterwork in ice and snow and admire other people's eye-catching handiwork.
Opera Week, Kristiansund *(early Feb)*. Opera, ballet, art exhibitions and a number of other events are staged at Festiviteten.
Winter Arts Festival, Lillehammer *(mid-Feb)*. Concerts and ice and snow sculpture celebrating the season.
Røros Market *(3rd Tue of Feb)*. A big trade fair.

PUBLIC HOLIDAYS

New Year's Day (1 Jan)
Palm Sunday (Sunday before Easter)
Maundy Thursday
Good Friday
Easter Sunday
Easter Monday
Whit Sunday
Whit Monday
Labour Day (1 May)
National Day (17 May)
St Hans (24 Jun)
Christmas Day (25 Dec)
Boxing Day (26 Dec)

Traditional Christmas displays in a shopping centre

Sarcophagus in Roskilde Cathedral of Queen Margrete, ruler of Denmark, Sweden and Norway

THE KALMAR UNION

Håkon VI Magnusson married the Danish princess, Margrete. Their only child, Olav, became king of Denmark in 1375, and inherited the Norwegian throne on Håkon's death in 1380. This was the start of the 400-year-long Danish-Norwegian union.

When Olav died at the age of 17, Margrete became ruler of both countries, and of Sweden, too, in 1388. By adopting her nephew, Erik of Pomerania, as king of all three nations in 1397, she laid the foundation for the Kalmar Union, which was to last until 1523, when Gustav Vasa seceded from the Union and established a new dynasty in Sweden.

UNION WITH DENMARK

Margrete conducted a fair policy towards Norway. The country's position weakened in 1536 when Christian III declared that Norway would forever be a vassal state of Denmark.

Norway was unable to assert its authority in the union, because from the middle of 14th century the Black Death reduced the population by more than half. The Reformation forced Archbishop Olav Engelbrektsson, one of the few to campaign for Norwegian independence, to flee the country.

Norway was ruled by feudal overlords as a dependency of Denmark. Its middle class was weakened by the Hanseatic merchants from northern Germany who ruled trading life on the west coast.

CHRISTIAN IV

The union with Denmark was not without its high points. Norwegian industry gradually began to pick up. Fishing expanded; forestry and the export of timber became a new resource. As the Hanseatic League declined, Norwegian traders were able to step in. Mining became an important industry, especially under Christian IV (1577–1648), who took a great interest in Norwegian affairs. He visited the country on 30 occasions, founded the city of Christiania and streamlined the administration. The country was granted a new church ordination and its own military system.

Christian established Norwegian control of the north of the country. But his on-going conflict with Sweden resulted in Norway having to cede land in the east to Sweden. His son, Frederik III, introduced absolute rule in the "double monarchy" in 1660. This meant rule by officials appointed by

Bærums Verk, one of the first ironworks in Norway, dating from 1610

TIMELINE

1380 Håkon VI Magnusson, the last king of an independent Norway, dies

1400 Hanseatic League, based in Bergen, reaches the height of its power, controlling imports and exports

1536 Christian III of Denmark declares that Norway will forever be a vassal state of Denmark

| 1350 | 1400 | 1450 | 1500 | 1550 |

1349 Black Death reduces Norway's population by 50 per cent

Queen Margrete (r.1388–1412)

1397 Kalmar Union unites Norway, Denmark and Sweden under one king

1537 The Reformation: Archbishop Olav Engelbrektsson is driven out of Norway

1558 Hanseatic grip weakens

Painting of the poets' nationalist society, *Det Norske Selskab*, in Copenhagen, by Eilif Peterssen (1892)

the king instead of rule by aristocrats. Increasingly, officials came from the Norwegian middle class, which worked in Norway's favour.

In the early 18th century, under Frederik IV, the wars with Sweden continued. They produced a national hero for Norway, the naval commander Peter Wessel Tordenskiold, who, in a surprise attack, obliterated the Swedish fleet.

The Swedish warrior king, Karl XII, twice tried to conquer Norway, but was killed during a siege on Halden in 1718.

Demands grew for Norwegian independence. This was due in part to a revival in interest in the country's history, brought about by a patriotic society of poets and historians, *Det Norske Selskab*, in Copenhagen. Calls for a national university in Norway were finally conceded to in 1811. Nevertheless, it was mostly affairs outside the country that led to the parting of the "double monarchy" in 1814.

Naval hero Peter Wessel Tordenskiold

IN NAPOLEON'S SHADOW

The Danish-Norwegian king, Frederik VI, allied himself with Napoleon in 1807. As a result, Britain blockaded Norwegian harbours and halted all imports and exports. Isolation became total when, for a time, there was also a war with Sweden. Then followed the years of great need in 1808 and 1812. Crops failed, fishing yields were poor and there was much hunger.

In Sweden, the former French marshal, Jean Baptiste Bernadotte, became crown prince in 1810 under the name Karl Johan. He joined the coalition against Napoleon and was able to persuade his allies – Russia, Britain, Austria and Prussia – that he would be able to force Denmark to relinquish Norway to Sweden when Napoleon was defeated. When Napoleon was finally routed at Leipzig in 1813, Karl Johan marched toward Denmark, and at the Treaty of Kiel in January 1814, Norway was surrendered to Sweden.

| **1624** Oslo burns down. Christiania is established north of Akershus Castle | **1709** The Great Nordic War between Denmark-Norway and Sweden | **1718** The Swedish king, Karl XII, is killed at Frederiksten Fortress during his second attempt to conquer Norway | **1813** Karl Johan marches on Denmark | **1814** Norway is ceded to Sweden at the Peace of Kiel |

1600	1650	1700	1750	1800

'hristian IV 577–1648)

1660 Frederik III introduces absolute rule

1645 Under the Treaty of Bromsebro, Norwegian territories of Jemtland and Herjedalen are ceded to Sweden

1769 Norway's population totals 723,000 of whom 65,000 live in towns

1772 Patriotic society, *Det Norske Selskab*, is founded

1811 The University of Norway is founded in Oslo

A painting of *The National Assembly at Eidsvoll*, by O. Wergeland, 1885, hanging in the Storting in Oslo

THE NATIONAL ASSEMBLY AT EIDSVOLL

The Danish prince, Christian Frederik, was governor-general of Norway at the time of the Treaty of Kiel, which ceded Norway to Sweden. Both he and the Norwegian people opposed the agreement. An assembly of 21 of the most prominent men in Norway declared Christian Frederik to be the most suitable candidate for the throne of their country, but would not agree to his wish for an absolute monarchy. Instead, it was decided that the people should elect delegates to a national assembly. On Easter Sunday 1814, 112 representatives convened at Eidsvoll and on 17 May they adopted the Norwegian constitution. Christian Frederik was elected king of an independent, free Norway.

Meanwhile, Crown Prince Karl Johan of Sweden demanded that the Treaty of Kiel be implemented. There was a brief war. Karl Johan then accepted the Eidsvoll constitution and on 4 November 1814 the Storting (Norwegian Parliament) elected Sweden's elderly Karl XIII as king of Norway. He was followed in 1818 by Karl Johan himself.

UNION WITH SWEDEN

The *riksakt*, the convention that was ratified by the Norwegian and Swedish parliaments, ruled that the two countries should have a common king and would stand united in war. Apart from this, they were equal and independent of one another. But there were no provisions in the *riksakt* for a Norwegian foreign service or a national flag. The demand for a flag was not resolved until 1898. The tug-of-war over the foreign service was one of the reasons that led to the dissolution of the union. Another area of dispute was whether the king should be entitled to appoint the governor-general in Norway

By the time of his death in 1844, Karl Johan had become popular in Norway, despite attempting to suppress displays of national identity. *Torvslaget* (Battle in the Marketplace) on 17 May 1829 in Christiania (Oslo) was one such occasion. Norwegians were celebrating National Day when troops attacked. The poet Henrik Wergeland, who was in the crowd, received a blow from a sword. He was subsequently inspired to write with fervour in praise of a free Norway. *Torvslaget* had added new meaning to the 17 May festivities.

The Battle in the Marketplace, Christiania, 17 May 1829

TIMELINE

Henrik Wergeland

1814 Norway's constitution is adopted on 17 May by the National Assembly

1829 Battle in the Marketplace: troops attack crowds on National Day, 17 May. The nationalist poet, Henrik Wergeland, is wounded

1837 First performance at Christiania Theatre

1844 Karl Johan dies; succeeded by his son, Oscar I

1810	1820	1830	1840	1850

1816 Norges Bank established

1818 Karl Johan is crowned king of Norway in Nidaros Cathedral

1819 The first edition of *Morgenbladet*, Norway's first daily newspaper

1848 Marcus Thrane founds Norway's first workers' union

1854 The first railway line is opened for passenger trains from Christiania to Eidsvoll

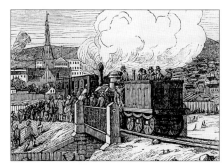

The Christiania–Eidsvoll railway line, completed in 1854

ECONOMIC GROWTH

An economic crisis in the first few years after 1814 was short-lived. Norges Bank was established in 1816, the country stabilised its currency and

was free of debt by 1850. This period marked a watershed in the Norwegian economy. Industry was in the throes of change and growing rapidly. Shipping was experiencing a golden age, particularly between 1850 and 1880, with the transition from sail to steam. Norway built its first railway in 1854; the telegraph arrived in 1850 and the telephone in 1880.

Textile worker at the Hjula weaving mill, 1887

An economic downturn in 1848–50 caused mass unemployment and prompted Marcus Thrane to establish the first workers' union. By 1865, Norway's population had doubled from 900,000 in 1800 to 1.7 million, and it continued to rise. Emigration to America began in 1825 and gradually increased in intensity – between 1879 and 1893 a quarter of a million people crossed the Atlantic.

A VOTE FOR FREEDOM

Political life toward the end of the period of union with Sweden was characterized by turbulence and the transition to democracy. Parliamentary rule was introduced in 1884, universal suffrage for men in 1898, and for women in 1913.

The long-standing conflict over demands for a separate foreign minister finally brought the union to its knees. In 1905, Norway's Michelsen government resigned because the king would not sanction the Storting's bill on the consular service. The king refused to accept the government's resignation on the grounds that: "A new government cannot now be formed." Michelsen used these words as a pretext to declare the union dissolved. As the king was outside the government and was unable to form a new one – which he was obliged to do under the constitution – he could no longer fulfil his role and was thus no longer the Norwegian king. Without a common king, the union ceased to exist. On 7 June, it was dissolved by the Storting, but Sweden demanded a referendum: 368,208 people voted in favour of secession; 184 against. The Swedish-Norwegian union ended peacefully.

Postcard marking the dissolution of the union with Sweden after a "yes" vote in the 1905 referendum

1860	1870	1880	1890	1900

1871 Opening of the telegraph line to Kirkenes in Northern Norway

1865 Norway's population exceeds 1.7 million people

1875 Norway's merchant navy becomes the third largest in the world

1879 Ibsen's play *A Doll's House* is published

1884 Parliamentary rule is introduced after a bitter struggle

1882 The height of emigration to North America

Christian Michelsen

1889 Compulsory schooling introduced

1898 Universal suffrage for men

1905 Under Prime Minister Christian Michelsen, the union with Sweden comes to a peaceful end

1899 The Norwegian Federation of Trade Unions (LO) is established

Prime Minister Christian Michelsen greeting Prince Carl and the infant Olav, 25 November 1905

A NEW ROYAL FAMILY

After 400 years of Danish and Swedish rule, the Norwegian royal family had died out and the nation turned to Prince Carl, second son of the heir to the Danish throne, to be its head of state. His wife was the British princess, Maud, and they had a two-year-old son, Olav. Prince Carl adopted the name Haakon VII and was crowned in Nidaros Cathedral.

For the first period following the dissolution of the union, domestic policy concentrated on social reforms. Roald Amundsen's successful expedition to the South Pole in 1911 created an enormous wave of national pride. With the writer Bjørnstjerne Bjørnson leading the way, Norway made its presence strongly felt in peacekeeping efforts. In 1901, the Storting had been given the honourable task of awarding the annual Alfred Nobel Peace Prize.

Norway remained neutral during World War I, but half of her merchant fleet was lost. Nevertheless, shipping and the export of iron ore provided good revenues and led to wild specu-

lation in shares and a boom period. Toward the end of the war, a shortage of provisions caused difficulties.

BETWEEN THE WARS

After the war, restrictions in many areas led to bankruptcies and industrial disputes. Farmers and fishermen who had invested heavily in new machinery and equipment in the boom-time were forced to sell up.

In 1930, as the Great Depression took hold in Norway, hardship increased. The banks failed and people lost their savings. Some 200,000 people were unemployed, and many industrial disputes resembled armed conflicts. Shipping fared better: the modern Norwegian merchant fleet had become the third largest in the world.

Between 1918 and 1935, Norway had nine different governments. Then Johan Nygaardsvold's Labour Party came to power and remained in office until 1945. Norway joined the League of Nations and participated in its activities under the guidance of the scientist and diplomat, Fridtjof Nansen.

The dispute between Denmark and Norway over the sovereignty of Greenland was brought before the International Court at The Hague in 1931, and Norway lost its claim.

Fridtjof Nansen, polar researcher

UNDER OCCUPATION

Norway declared itself neutral when World War II broke out in September 1939. Regardless, Germany invaded on 9 April 1940. Norwegian troops succeeded in sinking the German cruiser, *Blücher*, in Oslofjorden, and held back the German advance for 62 days before capitulating. On 7 June the king, the

TIMELINE

Haakon VII

1905 Haakon VII, Queen Maud and Crown Prince Olav take up residence in the palace in Oslo

1920 Norway joins the League of Nations

1945 Norway is free. King Håkon returns on 7 June

1947 Thor Heyerdahl crosses the Pacific in *Kon-Tiki*

1940 Germany occupies Norway

1910	1920	1930	1940	1950

1911 Roald Amundsen reaches the South Pole

1931 Norway loses the Greenland case after a ruling by the court in The Hague

1946 Trygve Lie becomes the first United Nations General Secretary

1905–07 Christian Michelsen is the first prime minister of an independent Norway

1949 Norway joins NATO

crown prince and the cabinet fled from Tromsø to continue the fight in exile in London.

Vidkun Quisling, with German backing, became prime minister of an occupied Norway, but he lacked popular support. There was mounting civil resistance. An underground military organisation *(Milorg)* was formed, eventually comprising 47,000 men, which was controlled by the government in exile. They passed intelligence to the Allies and conducted numerous covert operations against the occupying forces, the most renowned of which was at Rjukan, where resistance fighters destroyed a heavy water plant *(see pp156–7)*.

A massive oil platform under construction in Gandsfjorden, Stavanger

The Norwegian merchant navy played a major role in the war effort outside the country, but more than half the fleet was lost and 3,000 sailors perished. About 35,000 people were imprisoned during the occupation and 1,400 people, including 738 Jews, died in German concentration camps.

While retreating from Finnmark, the Germans forced the population to evacuate and scorched everything behind them. Germany capitulated on 7 May 1945; 8 May marked liberation day. A month later, King Haakon returned to Norway.

German troops marching along Karl Johans Gate in Oslo, 9 April 1940

MODERN NORWAY

Rebuilding the country after World War II took place faster than expected. During the first year of peace, output reached the pre-war level. Politically, Norway was more stable than during the interwar years. At the elections to the Storting in 1945, the Labour Party achieved a clear majority and, except for a short break, remained in power until 1963. Einar Gerhardsen, the "father of Norway", was prime minister. Norway joined NATO in 1949 and EFTA in 1960. Many social reforms were introduced and Norway was on the road to becoming a welfare state.

Following the Gerhardsen period, parliamentary power shifted between Labour and the non-socialist coalition parties. The longest-serving prime minister was Gro Harlem Brundtland. Since the 1970s the economy and welfare policies have been buoyed up by North Sea oil extraction and strong growth in the fishing industry. Two referenda on membership of the EU have ended in a "No", and Norway seems keen to keep its independent spirit.

	1970 Discovery of oil reserves in the North Sea, off the coast of Norway	1986 Gro Harlem Brundtland becomes Prime Minister	1993 Norway resumed limited Whaling		2000 Norway is elected as 2-year term member of the United Nations Security Council
957 Haakon VII dies and lav V succeeds as king					
1960	**1970**	**1980**	**1990**	**2000**	**2010**
1967 National insurance is introduced	1972 Norwegians vote "no" to membership of the EEC (EU)	1989 *Sametinget*, the first Sami parliament, opens in Karasjok	1994 Norway hosts the Winter Olympics in Lillehammer	2005 Jens Stoltenberg was elected Prime Minister	
1960 Norway becomes a member of EFTA		1991 Olav V dies. His son, Harald V, succeeds as king			

Oslo at a Glance

Oslo has changed its name several times in its history – from Oslo to Christiania and then to Kristiania. In 1925 the capital reverted to its original title, Oslo. The city enjoys an unsurpassed location. Within its boundaries, it is possible to swim in Oslofjorden in summer and ski on well-maintained ski trails in winter. The centre of Oslo is home to museums and galleries, a royal palace, parks and public institutions, all of which can be reached on foot. Its harbour is guarded by a 14th-century castle. There is a wide choice of shops, and in summer cafés spill out onto the pavements and waterfronts. Most sights are within walking distance from the centre, apart from those on Bygdøy.

LOCATOR MAP

Aker Brygge
Situated on the waterfront, this is a popular place to meet up for a drink, a meal or to shop. This former shipyard abounds with life. It is packed with shops and eating places (see p57).

CENTRAL OSLO WEST

BYGDØY
Pages 76–87

| 0 metres | 500 |
| 0 yards | 500 |

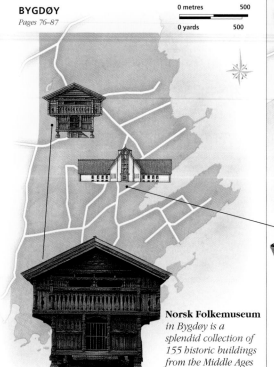

Norsk Folkemuseum
in Bygdøy is a splendid collection of 155 historic buildings from the Middle Ages onward (see pp82–3).

Vikingskipshuset
This museum houses three of the best-preserved Viking ships in the world, and is one of Norway's cultural jewels (see pp84–5).

◁ Jubilant crowds parade along Karl Johans Gate to Slottet (the Royal Palace) on National Day, 17 May

VISITORS' CHECKLIST

550,000. Gardermoen 45 km (28 miles) from the centre. Tourist Information Office: Fridtjof Nansens Plass 5, 24 14 77 00. 17 May on Karl Johan, Ultima Music Festival (first half Oct); Oslo Church Music Festival (first half Mar); Oslo Horse Show (mid-Oct).

Slottet

The Royal Palace is a Neo-Classical building on three floors. It was built as a royal residence in the reigns of King Karl XIV Johan and Oscar I, between 1825 and 1848 (see p51).

Karl Johans Gate *has been the city's main thoroughfare for more than 100 years. The lower part is pedestrianized; the upper section is used for parades (see p50).*

CENTRAL OSLO EAST

Stortinget

Constructed in yellow brick on a granite base, this is where Norway's National Assembly meets. It was completed and first used in 1866 (see p74).

Akershus Slott *Norway's best-preserved castle complex from the Middle Ages was begun in 1300 and occupies a spectacular harbour setting on Oslofjorden (see pp68–9).*

0 metres 500

0 yards 500

The upper part of Norway's foremost thoroughfare, Karl Johans Gate

Karl Johans Gate ❶

Map 3 D3. Ⓣ *Stortinget, Nationaltheatret.* 🚊 *11, 13, 17, 18, 19.* 🚌 *32, 34.*

Norway's best-known and busiest thoroughfare is Karl Johans Gate. It is named after the king of Norway and Sweden, Karl Johan (1818–44), and is known simply as Karl Johan by the people of Oslo. The street is flanked by stately, Neo-Classical buildings.

The upper section is the most imposing. Stortinget (the Norwegian parliament) is situated here and Slottet (the Royal Palace) takes pride of place at the western end of the street. Between these two buildings lie the university and Nationaltheatret, a park known as Studenterlunden, and a skating rink which is open to the public in winter (skates are available for hire). The lower part of Karl Johans Gate terminates at Central Station. Basarhallene (the market halls) at Kirkeristen can be found in this section.

Karl Johans Gate grew in importance after the Royal Palace, designed by the architect H D F Linstow, was completed in 1848. Linstow also planned Karl Johan.

In addition to the many public buildings, the street is lined with department stores, specialist shops and places to eat. Karl Johans Gate has been a popular meeting place since the 19th century. The citizens of Oslo used to stroll along Studenterlunden to see and be seen. Today, young people continue to meet on the "Strip". It is also the focal point for royal occasions and state visits. Undoubtedly the biggest day of the year on Karl Johan is Norway's National Day, 17 May, when thousands of children, accompanied by singers and musicians, parade toward the palace to be greeted by the royal family who come out on to the balcony.

In 2000 a system was installed to illuminate the façades along Karl Johans Gate and now lights switch on automatically each evening as darkness falls. The street teems with life until the early hours. Visitors are often surprised by the vibrancy of the nightlife in and around Karl Johans Gate, which is more on a par with some of the larger capitals of Europe.

Universitetet ❷

Karl Johans Gate 47. **Map** 3 D3. **Tel** 22 85 50 50. Ⓣ *Nationaltheatret.* 🚊 *11, 13, 17, 18, 19.* 🚌 *32, 34.*

The university dominates the northeast side of Karl Johans Gate. The Neo-Classical building was completed in 1852, 40 years after Frederik VI decreed that Norway could finally have its very own university. He gave it his name, the "Royal Frederik University in Oslo", by which it was known until 1939.

Over the years, most of the teaching, other than the Faculty of Law and some of the administration, has moved to Blindern on the outskirts of Oslo. The university complex is situated directly opposite the Nationaltheatret. It comprises three buildings which encircle University Square. To mark its centenary in 1911, the university built a new auditorium, the Aula, in an extension to the main building. The Aula is renowned for its murals by the Norwegian artist Edvard Munch, installed in 1916. The powerful background motif, *The Sun*, symbolizes light in the form of an explosive sunrise over the coastline. The main canvas on the right, *Alma Mater*, depicts a nursing mother representing the university, while that on the left, *History*, represents knowledge and wisdom. Edvard Munch regarded the paintings in the Aula as his major work.

Politicians and humanitarians from all over the world have, over the years, visited the Aula. It was used as the venue for the presentation of the Nobel Peace Prize until 1990 when the award ceremony was moved to Rådhuset (Oslo Town Hall).

On one day in mid-August every year, 3,000 students gather in University Square to register for a university place.

Oslo University's Aula with Edvard Munch's murals, 1916

Nasjonalgalleriet ❸

See pp52–3.

Historisk Museum ❹

See pp54–5.

Slottet (the Royal Palace) standing supreme on the hill at the top of Karl Johans Gate

Slottet ❺

Drammensveien 1. **Map** 2 C2.
Tel 22 04 87 00.
🚇 Nationaltheatret. 🚃 11, 13, 17,
18, 19. 🚌 32, 34. 🔵 guided tours
only; end Jun–mid-Aug: 6am–9pm
daily; tickets in advance from
post offices.
🎨 📷 ♿ 🚫 🏛

The Royal Palace (Det
Kongelige Slottet) occupies an
elevated position overlooking
the city centre and forms a
natural focal point on Karl
Johans Gate.

King Karl Johan decided to
build a royal residence in
Oslo on ascending to the
Swedish-Norwegian throne in
1818. He commissioned the
architect Lieutenant H D F
Linstow to design the project.

Work on the interior, by the
architects H E Schirmer and
J H Nebelong, began in 1836.
Peter Frederik Wergmann was
responsible for the Pompeii-
style wall friezes in the
Banqueting Hall. The Palace
Chapel and the Ballroom
were designed by Linstow;
the painter Johannes Flintoe
decorated the Bird Room.

The palace was not
completed until 1848, by
which time Karl Johan had
died. It was inaugurated by
Oscar I amid great festivities.

The grand buildings did not
become a permanent
residence until 1905 when
Norway finally became an
independent nation. King
Haakon and Queen Maud,
the newly crowned monarchs,
moved into what was then a
poorly maintained palace. It
has been gradually restored
and upgraded over time and
at the end of the 20th century
underwent a further
comprehensive restoration.

The palace is built of brick
and plaster. It has three
wings of three storeys each.
Slottsparken, the gardens
surrounding the buildings to
the south and east, are not
fenced off and are open to
the public. Dronningsparken,
to the west, is private property
and is not open to visitors.

The palace has a splendid
collection of fine art. In the
summer of 2000, the public
had the opportunity to view
the collection and some of the
interior, on guided tours. The
tours are now a regular
feature every year from the
end of June until mid-August.

A statue of Karl Johan
stands in front of the palace.

Nationaltheatret ❻

Johannes Dybwads plass 1. **Map** 3 D3.
Tel 22 00 14 00. 🚇 Nationaltheatret.
🚃 11, 13, 17, 18, 19. 🚌 32, 34.
Ticket Office 🔵 9.30am–6.30pm
Mon–Fri, 11am–5pm Sat. 🔵 public
hols. 📷 by arrangement. 🏛 🏛
open 1 hr before performances.

It was no coincidence that
a play by the Norwegian
dramatist Henrik Ibsen was
on the programme when the
National Theatre opened its
doors in 1899. The theatre's
first production was the
socially critical drama, *An
Enemy of the People.* Since
then, Ibsen's work has
become a central part of the
repertoire, and his powerful
plays have inspired many
generations of actors.

The Baroque-style building
was designed by Henrik Bull
and is regarded as the
country's most significant
expression of the renaissance
of brickwork in the 19th
century. Its Baroque-like
design is typical of theatre
architecture throughout
Europe toward the end of the
19th century. A fire caused
extensive damage to the
building in 1980 and the
subsequent restoration work
took five years to complete.

The ticket for a play also
gives access to one of
Norway's finest art collections.
Throughout the building are
paintings by Erik Werenskiold,
Karl Fjell, Christian Krohg,
P S Krøyer and busts by Gustav
Vigeland, Per Palle Storm and
other Norwegian artists. In
front of the theatre stand
sculptures of two of Norway's
most renowned writers –
Henrik Ibsen and Bjørnstjerne
Bjørnson – each on a pedestal.

The palace's Banqueting Hall with Wergmann's Pompeii-style friezes

Historisk Museum ➍

The Historisk Museum is part of the Museum of Cultural History, University of Oslo, which houses the Oldsaksamlingen (National Antiquities Collection), Etnografisk Museum (Ethnographic Museum) and Myntkabinettet (Collection of Coins and Medals). They document Norwegian and international history from the first settlements to the present day. Rare objects from Viking and medieval times are on show and medieval religious art is particularly well represented. There is also a rich collection from the Arctic cultures. The building was designed by Henrik Bull (1864–1953) and completed in 1902.

Inuit Mask
The mask from East Greenland represents a tupilak *– a figure which is animated through magic rituals and which brings ill fortune to its victim.*

★ Fish Skin Coat
This coat has been made out of fish skin by the Nanai people in sub-Arctic Siberia. The skins of large fish are dried and then beaten before being stitched together.

Lecture hall

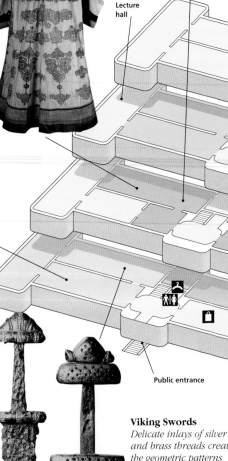

★ Portal from Ål Kirke
This intricately carved stave church doorway dating from 1150 is one of the few wooden objects from the early Middle Ages to be found in Europe. Some of the paint on the portal remains.

Public entrance

Viking Swords
Delicate inlays of silver and brass threads create the geometric patterns on these swords, which were discovered in Viking burial mounds.

STAR EXHIBITS

★ Fish Skin Coat

★ Portal from Ål Kirke

Chair from the Buli School of Masters in the Congo
This African carving of a woman carrying a chair dates from 1850. The woman's hairstyle and the scars from extensive tattoos indicate that she is the sister or the mother of a chieftain.

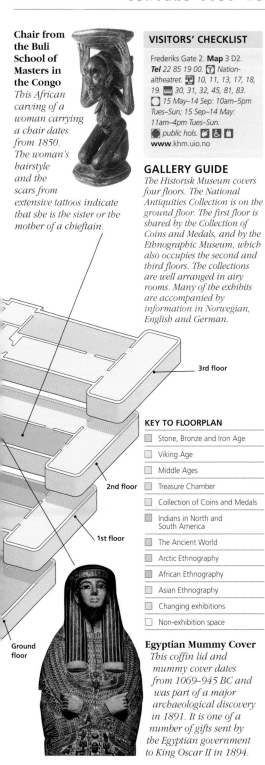

VISITORS' CHECKLIST

Frederiks Gate 2. **Map** 3 D2.
Tel 22 85 19 00. Nationaltheatret. 10, 11, 13, 17, 18, 19. 30, 31, 32, 45, 81, 83. 15 May–14 Sep: 10am–5pm Tues–Sun; 15 Sep–14 May: 11am–4pm Tues–Sun. public hols.
www.khm.uio.no

GALLERY GUIDE
The Historisk Museum covers four floors. The National Antiquities Collection is on the ground floor. The first floor is shared by the Collection of Coins and Medals, and by the Ethnographic Museum, which also occupies the second and third floors. The collections are well arranged in airy rooms. Many of the exhibits are accompanied by information in Norwegian, English and German.

3rd floor

2nd floor

1st floor

Ground floor

KEY TO FLOORPLAN

- Stone, Bronze and Iron Age
- Viking Age
- Middle Ages
- Treasure Chamber
- Collection of Coins and Medals
- Indians in North and South America
- The Ancient World
- Arctic Ethnography
- African Ethnography
- Asian Ethnography
- Changing exhibitions
- Non-exhibition space

Egyptian Mummy Cover
This coffin lid and mummy cover dates from 1069–945 BC and was part of a major archaeological discovery in 1891. It is one of a number of gifts sent by the Egyptian government to King Oscar II in 1894.

Theatercafeen **7**

Stortingsgaten 24–26. **Map** 3 D3.
Tel 22 82 40 50. Nationaltheatret. 13, 15, 19. 30, 31, 32, 45, 81, 83. 11am–11pm Mon–Sat, 3–10pm Sun.

In Oslo, friends often meet for a meal at the classy Theatercafeen, a restaurant conveniently situated just across the street from the Nationaltheatret.

Ever since it opened in 1901, it has been a focal point for Norway's most celebrated artists, authors and actors, including Knut Hamsun, Edvard Munch, Herman Wildenvey and Johanne Dybwad, many of whose portraits line the walls. While most of these names belong to a bygone era, Theatercafeen still attracts many well-known contemporary figures to its tables.

The restaurant has its own classical orchestra which plays from the balcony.

Det Norske Teatret **8**

Kristian IVs Gate 8. **Map** 3 D3.
Tel 22 47 38 00. Nationaltheatret. 30, 31, 32, 45, 81, 83. 13, 15, 19. **Box Office** 9am–8pm Mon–Fri, 9am–6pm Sat.

Norway's "second National Theatre", Det Norske Teatret, was opened already in 1913, but was forever on the move until finally in September 1985 it was able to welcome audiences to its own new, ultra-modern home.

The theatre has two stages, Hovedscenen with 757 seats and Biscenen with 200 seats. There are rehearsal rooms, beautifully decorated foyers and a bistro. Hovedscenen is fitted with advanced technical equipment and movable units, so stage layouts and sets can be changed quickly.

Det Norske Teatret is the main venue for works in the *nynorsk* language (*see p18*). The principal repertoire features Norwegian/Nordic drama, but both modern and classical plays are performed on a regular basis.

Sculptures by Turid Eng (1984) at the entrance to Oslo Konserthus

Oslo Konserthus ⑫

Munkedamsveien 14. **Map** 2 C3.
Tel 23 11 31 00. Ⓣ *Nationaltheatret.*
🚋 *13, 15, 19.* 🚌 *30, 31, 32, 45, 81,
83.* **Box office** ◯ *10am–5pm
Mon–Fri; 11am–2pm Sat; and 2 hrs
before performance.* ◐ *July.* ♿

Oslo's Concert Hall, situated
in the area of Vika, has
been a leading venue for
Norwegian cultural and
musical life since its opening
in 1977. The world's top
artists and orchestras regularly
perform here.
In the 1960s, the Swedish
architect, Gösta Åberg, won
the competition to design the
new building. The exterior is
clad in polished granite; inside
the floors and walls are of
white marble. The hall has
been specially designed to
stage orchestral works, with a
podium large enough to
accommodate 120 musicians.
It can be transformed into a
theatre for shows and musical
productions with seating for
an audience of 1,400.
The concert hall is the home
of Oslo-Filharmonien (the
Oslo Symphony Orchestra).
The orchestra plays a central
role in the musical life of the
city. It is also regarded as one
of the world's leading
symphony ensembles, and its
recordings have attracted
international acclaim.
More than 300 events
are held annually at the
Konserthus, with audiences
totalling more than 200,000
over the year.

Stenersenmuseet ⑬

Munkedamsveien 15. **Map** 2 C3.
Tel 23 49 36 00. Ⓣ *Nationaltheatret.*
🚋 *13, 15, 19.* 🚌 *30, 31, 32, 45, 81,
83.* ◯ *11am–7pm Tue & Thu;
11am–5pm Wed & Fri–Sun.* 📷 📹
2:30pm Sun. ♿ 🚫 📷

One of the most recent
museums to open in Oslo is
the Stenersenmuseet, named
after the author, art collector
and patron of the arts, Rolf
Stenersen. In 1936, he
donated his collection
to Oslo City Council. The
paintings remained in store
until 1994, when Stenersenmuseet was completed. It is
located in Konserthusterrassen
(beneath the Konserthus).
The Stenersen bequest is
one of three collections on
show in the museum. It
includes paintings and a large
number of graphics and
drawings by Edvard Munch,
who was a friend of

Stenersen. They span Munch's
output from his early work,
The Sick Room, to the later
Dance of Life. In addition to
Munch, Scandinavian art
is well-represented with
works by Kai Fjell, Jakob
Weidemann and Per Krohg.
The other two collections
feature paintings by Amaldus
Nielsen (1838–1932) and
Ludvig O Ravensberg
(1871–1958).
Nielsen was a landscape
painter who immortalized the
southern Norwegian coast in
his work. Ravensberg was
known for his naive
portrayals of Roman ruins of
old Oslo. He was strongly
influenced by Munch, who
was his relative.

Ibsenmuseet ⑭

Arbins Gate 1. **Map** 2 C3.
Tel 22 12 35 50. Ⓣ *Nationaltheatret.*
🚋 *13,15, 19.* 🚌 *30, 31, 32, 45, 81,
83.* ◯ *guided tours only.* 📷 📹
*noon, 1pm, 2pm Tue–Sun (Jul & Aug:
11am and 3pm).* ♿ 🚫 📷 📷

Henrik Ibsen, Norway's
revered playwright, produced
the major part of his work
while living in Munich
(1864–92).
After his return to Oslo, in
1895, Ibsen and his wife took
an apartment in Arbiens Gate,
on the first floor on the
corner facing Drammensveien.
This was where he wrote his
last plays, *John Gabriel
Borkman* (1896) and *When
We Dead Awaken* (1899). It
was in this home that he
suffered a stroke, which
prevented him from writing,

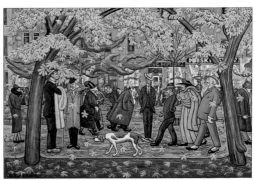

Høstens promenade, Ludvig O Ravensberg, Stenersenmuseet

For hotels and restaurants in this region see pp226–7 and pp242–3

The Baldishol Tapestry, one of the most prized exhibits in the Kunstindustrimuseet

and he subsequently died in 1906, aged 78 years.

Great attention has been paid to the restoration and redecoration of the couple's large apartment. Even the colour scheme resembles that of Ibsen's day and his study contains the original furniture.

Every day he would set off from here to walk to the Grand Café in Karl Johans Gate where he held court until ill-health confined him to the apartment.

The museum is open for guided tours and lectures.

Kunstindustri-museet ⑮

St Olavs Gate 1. **Map** 3 E2.
Tel 22 03 65 40. 🚇 Stortinget, Nationaltheatret. 🚌 60, and a short walk to 30, 31, 32, 45, 81, 83.
🕐 11am–3pm Tue–Fri (to 7pm Thu); noon–4pm Sat–Sun. ⬤ public hols.
🔲 🔲 🔲 🔲 🔲

The Museum of Applied Art (Kunstindustrimuseet) is one of the oldest museums in Europe. It was established in 1876, and contains a fine collection of Norwegian and foreign crafts, fashion and design products from the 17th century to the present day.

The museum holds Norway's biggest collection of tapestries from the 16th and 17th centuries, including the national treasure, the Baldishol Tapestry, dating from 1200. This is the only surviving Nordic tapestry that uses the Gobelin technique from the Middle Ages, and is one of the few remaining European tapestries to exhibit Roman characteristics. The tapestry was found when Baldishol Church in the county of Hedmark was demolished in 1879.

The museum also contains silver, glassware, ceramics and furniture. On show in the Royal Costume Gallery (Kongelig Norsk Dragtgalleri) are clothes from the Norwegian monarchy. In the Department of East Asian Art there is an imperial Ming vase dating from the 15th century.

Since 1904 the museum has shared an imposing building with the National College of Art and Design. Their joint library is open to the public.

Goblet by Torolf Prytz (1900)

HENRIK IBSEN

Described as the father of modern drama, Henrik Ibsen (1828–1906) is Norway's most famous writer. He left a remarkable legacy of plays that revolutionized modern theatre and are still performed worldwide. They included *Peer Gynt*, for which Edvard Grieg composed the music, *A Doll's House*, *Hedda Gabler*, *Ghosts*, *The Wild Duck* and *An Enemy of the People*. Ibsen was born in Skien (*see p148*) in southern Norway. He began writing while working as a chemist's assistant, but his first play, *Catilina*, was rejected. Undeterred, he took a job as a journalist in Bergen and later became director and playwright at Ole Bull's Theatre. From 1857–1863 he was director of the Norwegian Theatre in Oslo, but the theatre went bankrupt and he moved abroad. Over the next 30 years he wrote numerous dramas, concentrating on social issues and the pettiness of Norwegian society. They earned him literary fame and in 1892 he returned to Olso a national hero.

Portrait of Henrik Ibsen, dramatist

Akershus Slott ❶

See pp68–9.

Norges Hjemme-frontmuseum ❷

Akershus fortress area. **Map** 3 D4.
Tel *23 09 32 80.* 🔲 *Stortinget.*
🚋 *10, 12 and a short walk from
13, 15, 19.* 🚌 *60 and a short walk
from 30, 31, 32, 45, 81, 83.*
🕐 *1 Jun–31 Aug: 10am–5pm
Mon–Sat; 11am–5pm Sun; 1 Sep–
31 May: 10am–4pm Mon–Fri;
11am–4pm Sat–Sun.* 🔵 *public hols.*
🖼️ 🏛️

On 9 April 1940, German
forces occupied Norway.
While the Norwegians made
a valiant attempt at halting
their advance, the country
succumbed 62 days later.
For the next five years the
Norwegian Resistance
conducted a heroic campaign
against the occupying
German army, and their
exploits are well-documented
in Norway's Resistance
Museum. Taped speeches and
film clips recreate the World
War II years, and bring to life
the comprehensive collection
of documents, posters and
memorabilia from that time.

The museum is situated
in a 200-m (656-ft) long,
17th-century stone vault in
Bindingsverkshuset (Half-
Timbered House) at the top
of Akershus Slott. It was
opened on 8 May 1970,
which was the 25th
anniversary of the liberation.
Alongside the museum, there
is a memorial to the
Norwegians who were
shot here during the war.

Model of old Christiania in Høymagasinet

Høymagasinet ❸

Akershus fortress area. **Map** 3 D4.
Tel *22 33 31 47.* 🔲 *Stortinget.*
🚋 *10, 13 (Christiania Torv); 12,
13, 19 (Wessels Plass).* 🚌 *60
(Akershusstranda).* 🕐 *Jun–Aug:
noon–5pm Sat & Sun.* 🎫 ♿

A former hay barn at
Akershus Slott is the location
for Høymagasinet, a museum
devoted to the history of
Christiania from 1624 to
1840.

The year 1624 marked the
devastating fire that left most
of the old city of Oslo in
ashes. The Danish-Norwegian
king, Christian IV, decided to
rebuild the city further west
and named it Christiania.
During the first 100 years
reconstruction was slow, but
it gathered speed in the 18th
century. The history of the

city over 200 years is
illustrated with the help of
models and other displays, in
addition to a 25-minute long
multimedia programme.

The museum also offers
visitors short, guided walks
through the streets of
Kvadraturen *(see pp64–5),*
the original Christiania.

Norsk Arkitektur-museum ❹

Kongens Gate 2. **Map** 3 E4.
Tel *22 42 40 80.* 🔲 *Stortinget.* 🚋
10, 12, 13, 15, 19. 🚌 *60 and a short
walk from 30, 31, 32, 45, 81, 83.* 🕐
*10am–6pm Mon, Tue, Thu & Fri;
11am–6pm Wed; noon–4pm Sat &
Sun.* 🔵 *public hols.* ♿ 🍴 🏛️

Founded in 1975, the
Museum of Norwegian
Architecture features
drawings, photographs and
models covering 1,000 years
of the nation's building
history. On the 1st floor
there is a permanent
exhibition, *Houses of
History.* The museum also
arranges touring exhibitions
of present and past
architectural projects.

Norsk Arkitekturmuseum is
located in old Christiania, in a
building from the reign of
Christian IV. The oldest part
of the house dates from 1640.
It underwent extensive
renovation in 1993.

Norway's Resistance Museum depiction of the battles of April 1940

Teatermuseet ❺

Christiania Torv 1. **Map** 3 D4.
Tel 22 42 65 09. ⓣ Stortinget.
🚋 10, 12, 13, 15, 19. 🚌 60 and
a short walk from 30, 31, 32, 45,
81, 83. ⬭ 11am–3pm Wed;
noon–4pm Thu & Sun. ⬤ public
hols. 🈳 ✔ ♿ 🚫 🔓

Teatermuseet (the Theatre
Museum) is devoted to Oslo's
dramatic arts from the early
19th century onward. Theatre,
ballet, opera, musical revues
and the circus are represented
among the many paintings,
photographs, models, posters,
cartoons and costumes that
are on display.

A significant part of the
collection originates from the
Christiania Theatre, which
was built in 1837 and torn
down in 1899. It was for
many years the only theatre
in town and plays by the
Norwegian dramatists Henrik
Ibsen and Bjørnstjerne
Bjørnson were performed
here for the first time.

The Theatre Museum
occupies the first and second
floors of the city's oldest
town hall, Gamle Rådhus,
which dates from 1641.
There is a restaurant on the
ground floor.

**Wagnerian costume worn by the
opera singer Kirsten Flagstad**

Christiania Torv ❻

Map 3 D4. ⓣ Stortinget. 🚋 10, 12,
13, 15, 19.

The square is old, but the
name is rather new. It was
decided in 1958 that this part
of Oslo's original market
square *(torv)* should be called
Christiania, after the old name

Christiania Torv, featuring some of Oslo's best-preserved buildings

for Oslo. For many years the
square was plagued by heavy
traffic. It underwent extensive
renovation in the 1990s when
traffic was diverted through a
tunnel. Now free from
vehicles, Christiania Torv is
once more a pleasant place to
visit. In 1997, a fountain
created by the artist Wenche
Gulbransen was erected in
the square.

Around the square are
several historic buildings,
among them the city's first
town hall (now the Theatre
Museum) and the Garnison
Hospital, the oldest building
in the capital and home to the
Oslo Artists' Association.

Museet for
Samtidskunst ❼

See pp70–71.

Den Gamle
Logen ❽

Grev Wedels Plass 2. **Map** 3 D4.
Tel 22 33 44 70. ⓣ Jernbanetorget.
🚋 10, 12, 13, 15, 19. 🚌 30, 31,
32, 41, 45, 60, 81, 83.

If walls could talk those
of Den Gamle Logen (The
Old Lodge) would have a
fascinating story to tell about
the history of Oslo. The city
council held its meetings here
from the end of the 19th
century until 1947. The lodge
was also used as a court room
during the legal proceedings
against Vidkun Quisling *(see
p41)*, who was sentenced to

death for treason at the end of
World War II.

Constructed by Freemasons
in the 19th century, the design
of the Old Lodge is based on
drawings by Christian H
Malling and Jens S Seidelin.
It was opened in 1839.

The vast Neo-Classical
banqueting hall is the central
feature. Noted for its excellent
acoustics, it was for a long
time the city's foremost
concert hall. But immediately
after World War II, the lodge
was taken over by the Oslo
Port Labour Office and the
splendid banqueting hall
became a workers' canteen.

It reverted to its original use
as a concert venue in the
1980s when Oslo Summer
Opera moved in. The Old
Lodge has since undergone
extensive restoration and once
again its beautiful rooms are
being used for banquets and
musical events. In the
entrance there is a statue of
Edvard Grieg, created by Marit
Wiklund in 1993.

**Den Gamle Logen concert hall at
Grev Wedels Plass**

Museet for Samtidskunst ❼

The Museum of Contemporary Art is home to Norway's greatest collection of Norwegian and international modern art from the post-World War II period until today. Previously a department of the National Gallery, its opening in 1990 was heralded as a national event. It is now firmly established on the Norwegian arts scene and regularly hosts major international exhibitions. The permanent collection is so large that only part of it is on show at any one time. The museum may be new, but the building – the former head office of the Central Bank of Norway – is an example of Art Nouveau architecture from 1906. It is constructed in Norwegian granite and marble. The richly decorated Banking Hall provides an exciting contrast between old and new.

Winter Sun
Gunnar S Gundersen's Winter Sun *(1966) may be seen as an abstract impression of a landscape.*

★ Inner Room V
Per Inge Bjørlo's Inner Room V *(1990) is one of two permanent installations in the museum. It consists of metal plates and a sheet metal floor. The viewer is encouraged to step right into the installation.*

Stairs to 2nd floor

Lecture hall 2

Lecture hall 1

Main entrance

KEY

- ☐ Permanent exhibitions
- ☐ Temporary exhibitions
- ☐ Non-exhibition space
- ☐ Not open to the public

STAR EXHIBITS

- ★ *Inner Room V*
  by Per Inge Bjørlo

- ★ *The Rubbish Man*
  by Ilya Kabakov

Shaft
The museum's eye-catching landmark is Richard Serra's sculpture, Shaft *(1988). It stands at the entrance on Bankplassen.*

★ The Rubbish Man
Ilya Kabakov's installation (1983–95) is a "museum" of rubbish dedicated to the Man Who Never Threw Anything Away. Viewers can enter the room to experience the collector's mania and his passion for order.

VISITORS' CHECKLIST

4 Bankplassen. **Map** 3 D4.
Tel 21 98 20 00. Ⓣ Stortinget.
🚋 10, 12, 13, 15, 19. 🚌 60.
🕐 11am–5pm Tue, Wed, Fri;
11am–7pm Thu; noon–5pm Sat
& Sun. ● public hols. 📷 ♿
🍴 🛍 **www**.nasjonalmuseet.no

Tilted Form No. 3
Part of a series of six gouaches, Tilted Form No. 3 *(1987) is by the American Sol LeWitt, with variations on the same motif – the cube. This form of seriality is typical of the artist.*

Children's workshop

2nd floor

Skylight Hall

1st floor

Stairs to 1st floor

Ground floor

Banking Hall
The splendid Banking Hall (Banksalen) provides a challenging contrast to the contemporary art now adorning its halls.

GALLERY GUIDE
The museum has three floors. The ground floor has temporary exhibitions in addition to one of the museum's two permanent installations. There is also a bookshop and a café. The first floor is devoted to temporary exhibitions. The second floor features a permanent installation and a children's workshop.

Without Title
Per Maning is known for his photographic portraits of animals, mainly dogs, seals and monkeys. This portrait shows a cow with its eyes closed (1990), against a typical Norwegian landscape.

**Battle scene tableau on display
at Forsvarsmuseet**

Forsvarsmuseet ⑨

Akershus Slott, Building 62.
Map 3 D5. **Tel** 23 09 35 82. 🚉 10,
12, 13, 15, 19. 🚌 60. ⚪ Jun–Aug:
10am–6pm Mon–Fri, 11am–4pm
Sat & Sun; Sep–May: 10am–3pm
Mon–Fri, 11am–4pm Sat & Sun.
⚫ public hols. 🎫 🚻 ♿ ⌀ 🖼 🏠

The history of the Norwegian
armed forces, from Viking
times to the present day, is
represented in Forsvarsmuseet
(the Armed Forces Museum)
at Akershus Slott. Two large
brick buildings from the
1860s, once used as military
arsenals, provide an
appropriate historical setting.
  Of the military items on
display, there is a collection
from the time of the union
with Denmark in the 16th
century, and the subsequent
Nordic wars, through to the
struggle for independence
during the union with

Sweden. The exhibits are
arranged in time blocks, and
include a number of life-like
models and objects, such as a
German tank and a V-1 bomb
from World War II. There are
also temporary exhibitions.

Astrup Fearnley Museet ⑩

Dronningens Gate 4. **Map** 3 E4.
Tel 22 93 60 60. 🚇 Jernbanetorget.
🚉 10, 12, 13, 15, 19. 🚌 30, 31,
32, 45, 60, 81, 83. ⚪ 11am–5pm
Tue, Wed, Fri; 11am–7pm Thu;
noon–5pm Sat & Sun. ⚫ public hols.
🎫 1pm Sat & Sun. ♿ 🏠

The Astrup Fearnley Museum
shows both Norwegian and
international art from the
post-World War II period to
the present day.
  The majority of pictures on
display belong to the
museum's own collection.
There are works by Francis
Bacon, Lucian Freud and
R B Kitaj, key figures in the
School of London. Other
international names in the
collection include Anselm
Kiefer, Gerhard Richter, Cindy
Sherman and Damien Hirst.
Norwegian art is represented
with works by Knut Rose,
Bjørn Carlsen, Olav
Christopher Jenssen, Kjell
Torriset and Odd Nerdrum.
  Opened in 1993, the
building is characterized by

the use of modern materials
and design. The exhibition
halls are large and airy
with high ceilings allowing
plenty of space to show
contemporary art to its full
advantage. The two main
halls are called *Impulsen* (The
Impulse) and *Skulpturgården*
(The Sculpture Court).
  The museum was
established as a result of
funds and charitable trusts set
up by the Astrup and
Fearnley families who, since
the 1800s, have made their
mark on Norwegian business
life and society. Hans Rasmus
Astrup (1831–98) was a
politician and a successful
businessman who amassed a
considerable fortune. Thomas
Fearnley (1880–1961) was a
shipowner, with an interest
in the arts. He set up the
Thomas Fearnleys
Contribution and Gift Fund.
  In addition to the larger
shows, the museum also
mounts smaller exhibitions
of shorter duration.

**Børsen (the Stock Exchange)
featuring a Neo-Classical exterior**

Børsen ⑪

Tollbugata 2. **Map** 3 E4.
Tel 22 34 17 00.
🚇 Jernbanetorget. 🚉 10, 11, 13,
15, 19. 🚌 30, 31, 32, 45, 60, 81,
83. ⚪ by arrangement. 🎫 special
tours can be arranged.

One of the oldest
institutional buildings in
Oslo is Børsen (the Stock
Exchange). Long before the
construction of the royal
palace and the parliament
building, it was decided that
the trading of commodities
should take place on a site
of its own. As a result,
Børsen was opened in
1828, the first of Oslo's
grand buildings. Designed

Astrup Fearnley Museet showing art in a modern setting

The lavish interior of the Oslo Domkirke

by the architect Christian H Grosch, the Neo-Classical façade with its Doric columns contrasts strongly with the more modern buildings nearby. The two side wings and a southern wing were added in 1910.

Originally, there was an enclosed courtyard containing a statue of Mercury. The statue was moved outside when the courtyard was redesigned to house the new Stock Exchange hall in 1988.

The entrance hall is dominated by Gerhard Munthe's mural painting from 1912, *Handelen og Sjøfarten* (*Trade and Shipping*).

Børsen also has its own library, reading room, antique trade museum and a portrait gallery.

Oslo Reptilpark ⓬

Storgata 26. **Map** 3 F2.
Tel *41 02 15 22.* Ⓣ *Brugata.*
🕓 *10am–6pm Tue–Sun.*
🎦 🐾 ♿ 🅿

This small but friendly park in the centre of the city has become very popular for families with children in

recent years. More than 100 animals of many different species are exhibited here, including a boa constrictor, grass snakes, caiman, geckos, chameleons, varans and other lizards, tarantulas, black widows (the world's most venomous spider), piranhas and saltwater fish.

Tuesdays are particularly popular since visitors can witness "feeding time" at 5pm. Special group rates are available for both adults and children, with some discounts applying to as few as five people. Children under two are admitted free.

A caiman

Oslo Domkirke ⓭

Stortorget 1. **Map** 3 E3.
Tel *23 62 00 10.*
Ⓣ *Jernbanetorget, Stortinget.*
🚋 *10, 11, 17, 18.*
🚌 *13, 15, 19.*
🕓 *daily.* ✝ *11 am & 7:30pm Sun; noon Wed in Eng, Ger or Fre.* ♿

Oslo Domkirke (cathedral) is the principal church for the diocese of Oslo. The foundation stone was laid in 1694, and the church was built in several stages. The altarpiece and pulpit date from 1699; the interior was completed in the 1720s.

Since then there has been a series of reconstructions and renovations. In the mid-1850s the Baroque interior was remodelled in Neo-Gothic style. In the course of a subsequent restoration, 100 years later, the baptismal font, altarpiece and pulpit were changed back to the pre-1850 style. When the sacristy was renovated in 1963, rich decorations from the 18th century were discovered.

Among the adornments of the cathedral are stained glass windows by Emanuel Vigeland, a silver sculpture with a Lord's Supper motif by Arrigo Minerbi and bronze doors by Dagfin Werenskiold. The modern painted ceiling, depicting scenes from the Bible, was created by Hugo Louis Mohr between 1936 and 1950. In the course of this work, the original ceiling paintings were destroyed, an act which has since attracted much criticism.

The cathedral has 900 seats and was the venue for the wedding ceremony of Crown Prince Haakon and Mette-Marit in 2001.

In its tower hangs the great bell, weighing 1,600 kg (3,527 lb), and three smaller bells. The great bell has been recast six times.

Below the ground floor of the cathedral is a crypt.

Stortinget, home of the Norwegian parliament, centrally situated just off Karl Johans Gate

Stortinget ⑭

Karl Johans Gate 22. **Map** 3 D3.
Tel 23 31 30 50. ⓣ Stortinget.
🚋 13, 15, 19. 🚌 30, 31, 32, 41,
45, 81, 83. ◯ guided tours only.
📷 Sat: 10am Nor, Eng & Ger,
11:30am Nor & Ger, 1pm Nor, Eng & Ger; 1 Jul–20 Aug Mon–Fri: 10am Nor & Eng, 11:30am Nor & Ger, 1pm Nor, Eng & Ger. ♿

Norway's National Assembly has its seat in the grand Stortinget (Norwegian Parliament building). The building was designed by the Swedish architect, Emil Victor Langlet, after a long and bitter debate and a series of different proposals. The foundation stone was laid on 10 October 1861. Construction took five years and in March 1866 the assembly met for the first time in its own building.

Stortinget is built of yellow brick on a reddish granite base. The style is a blend of Norwegian and Italian building traditions. It has been expanded and partly reconstructed on several occasions. The new wing toward Akersgata was added in the 1950s.

The assembly chamber, which seats the 165 members of parliament, resembles an amphitheatre, with the speaker's chair positioned below Oscar Wergeland's painting of the 1814 Eidsvoll assembly, which ratified the Norwegian constitution (see

p38). The painting dates from 1885, and depicts the men who helped to shape Norway's constitution.

The building has been richly embellished by Norwegian artists, including the painter Else Hagen who decorated the stairwell. A tapestry, *Solens Gang*, by Karen Holtsmark, hangs in the central hall. The sculptures in the stair hall are by Nils Flakstad.

Oslo Nye Teater ⑮

Rosenkrantzgate 10. **Map** 3 D3.
Tel 22 34 86 00. ⓣ Stortinget.
🚋 13, 15, 19. 🚌 30, 31, 32, 45, 81, 83. **Box Office** ◯ 9am–4pm Mon, 9am–7:30pm Tue–Fri, 10am–6pm Sat.

There are three theatres in what is known as Oslo Nye Teater (the Oslo New Theatre): Hovedscenen (Main Theatre) in Rosenkrantzgate; Centralteateret in Akersgata;

Oslo Nye Teater, a modern and lively city centre theatre

and Dukketeateret (Puppet Theatre) in Frognerparken.

Hovedscenen was established in the 1920s with the aim of providing a stage for new Norwegian and foreign drama. However, the repertoire was for many years dominated by comedy with leading revue artists. There has also been a move toward creating a more urbane and modern theatre with a bolder, fresher approach and an emphasis on younger actors who are just beginning to establish themselves.

Regjeringskvartalet ⑯

Einar Gerhardsenspl 1. **Map** 3 E3.
Tel 22 24 90 90. ⓣ Stortinget.
🚋 10, 11, 17, 18. 🚌 33, 37, 46.

The large complex on Akersgata housing the various government departments is known as Regjeringskvartalet (the Government Quarter). It is dominated by a tall H-block in which the prime minister has a suite of offices on the top floors.

Regjeringskvartalet was developed in five stages during the years 1958–96. The architect for the four first stages was Erling Viksjø. Torstein Ramberg designed the fifth stage.

The complex has been the subject of great controversy. In

order to clear the ground, the historic, conservation-worthy Empirekvartalet (Empire Quarter) was torn down. This led to an intense debate about conservation in the 1950s. Today's politicians would probably not have authorized the demolition of such a distinctive area.

The 12-floor, concrete H-block was completed in 1958. A further two floors were added in 1990.

The building features decorative art by Kai Fjell, Tore Haaland, Inger Sitter, Odd Tandberg, Erling Viksjø, Carl Nesjar and Pablo Picasso. Nesjar and the Spanish master collaborated to transfer three drawings by Picasso on to the concrete façade on the Akersgata frontage.

Youngstorget with its market, opera house and trades union offices

Bust of E Gerhardsen, Prime Minister 1945–65, Regjeringskvartalet

Youngstorget ⓱

Map 3 E3. Ⓣ *Jernbanetorget.* 🚋 *10, 11, 12, 13, 15, 17.* 🚌 *30, 31, 32, 34, 38, 56.*

Many of the Labour movement's most important institutions have their headquarters around Youngstorget, among them the Norwegian Labour Party and the Norwegian Trades Union Federation, *Landsorganisationen.* Other political parties such as *Fremskrittspartiet* (Progress Party) and *Venstre* (Liberals), also have offices in the area.

Youngstorget was laid out in 1846, and was for many years a cattle market. The square is named after the merchant Jørgen Young, who originally owned the area. In 1990 it underwent a substantial renovation. A copy of

the original fountain from 1880 was installed and the market kiosks from 1876 were restored. There are shops, workshops and various places to eat and drink in the market.

Oslo Spektrum ⓲

Sonja Henies Plass 2. **Map** 3 F3. **Tel** 22 05 29 00. Ⓣ *Jernbanetorget.* 🚋 *10, 12, 13, 15, 18, 19.* 🚌 *30, 31, 32, 34, 38, 41, 45, 46.* **Box Office** ⭘ *9am–4pm Mon–Fri; 10am–3pm Sat.* 🚻 🎟 *by arrangement.*

The 10,800 capacity Oslo Spektrum is the main venue for large-scale sporting and cultural events and trade fairs. Designed by Lars Haukland, the complex was completed in 1991.

Major events such as the Norwegian Military Tattoo (September), the Oslo Horse Show, featuring dressage and show-jumping (October), and the Nobel Peace Prize concert (December) are held here. International pop stars regularly perform at the stadium. It is also the venue for national handball matches.

The façade is clad with a massive mosaic designed by

Rolf Nesch and crafted by Guttorm Guttormsgaard. Made up from 40,000 glazed bricks, it features an eye-catching mix of abstract shapes interspersed with human figures.

The Opera House ⓳

Kirsten Flagstads Plass 1. **Map** 3 E4. **Tel** 21 42 21 21. Ⓣ *Bjørvika.* 🚋 *34, 70, 504.* ⭘ *10am–11pm Mon–Fri; 11am–11pm Sat & Sun.* 🚻 🎟 *daily (Fri, Sat, Sun in English).*

Inaugurated in 2008, the Opera House is the home of the Norwegian National Opera and Ballet. Right on the waterfront at Bjørvika, much of the building is positioned in or under the sea. A defining feature of the design is its sloping roof, which is covered in white Italian marble and rises from the edge of the Oslofjord, ingeniously doubling as a public plaza. The centrepiece of the building is a 1,364-seat horseshoe-shaped auditorium, boasting high-quality natural acoustics. The interior is oak-panelled and minimalist in design.

Oslo Spektrum, the city's main venue for sport, culture and trade fairs

Dronningen, an architectural landmark on the Frognerkilen waterfront

Dronningen ❶

Huk Aveny 1. **Map** 1 C3. *Tel 22 43 75 75*. 🚌 *91 (Apr–Oct).* 🚌 *30 (a short distance away).* ⏰ *8am–4pm daily.*

Before and after World War II, Dronningen ("the Queen") was one of Oslo's most popular summer restaurants. The building, constructed in 1930, was one of the first to be designed in the Functionalist style in Norway. It is situated on Dronningskjæret in Frognerkilen. However, in 1983 it was converted to offices. The Royal Norwegian Yacht Club and the Norwegian Students' Rowing Club are based here.

Dronningen ("the Queen") was often associated with Kongen ("the King"), a restaurant and summer variety theatre on the opposite side of Frognerkilen. In 1986 it, too, was converted to offices.

Frognerkilen is a major sailing centre dotted with large yachting marinas.

Norsk Folkemuseum ❷

See pp82–3.

Vikingskipshuset ❸

See pp84–5.

Kon-Tiki Museet ❹

Bygdøynesveien 36. **Map** 1 C4. *Tel 23 08 67 67*. 🚌 *91 (Apr–Oct).* 🚌 *30.* ⏰ *Apr–May: 10:30am–5pm daily; Jun–Aug: 9:30am–5:45pm; Sep: 10:30am–5pm; Oct–Mar: 10:30am–4pm.* 🌐 *public hols.* 🈺 ♿ 📷

The world watched with interest when Thor Heyerdahl (1914–2002) and his five-man crew sailed across the Pacific in the fragile balsa-wood raft, *Kon-Tiki*, in 1947. Over the course of 101 days the raft covered 8,000 km (4,970 miles) from Peru to Polynesia. The voyage proved that it would have been possible for South Americans to have

Polynesian mask, Kon-Tiki Museet

reached Polynesia in bygone days on balsa rafts. The raft is the main attraction in the Kon-Tiki Museet. A number of objects connected with the voyage are also on show.

Text and montages in both Norwegian and English give a graphic account of how those on board must have felt to have been so close to marine life that it was possible to catch sharks with their bare hands. They describe how on one occasion they felt a massive whale shark pushing against the raft.

Heyerdahl embarked on a new expedition in 1970. He sailed a papyrus boat, *Ra II*, across the Atlantic from Morocco to Barbados to prove a theory that it was possible for West African explorers to have landed in the West Indies before Columbus. *Ra I* had broken up well into the voyage due to a design fault, but *Ra II* survived and is on display in the museum.

Seven years later, Heyerdahl steered the reed boat, *Tigris*, across the Indian Ocean to prove that the ancient civilizations of the Indus valley and Egypt had contact with each other.

The museum's exhibits include a large number of archaeological finds from Heyerdahl's expeditions to places such as Easter Island and Peru.

Its 8,000-volume library contains the world's largest collection of literature about Polynesia.

The balsa-wood raft, *Kon-Tiki*, in the Kon-Tiki Museet on Bygdøy

Norsk Sjøfarts-museum ❺

Bygdøynesveien 37. **Map** 1 C4. *Tel* 24 11 41 50. 🚌 91 (Apr–Oct). 🚌 30. ⬤ 15 May–31 Aug: 10am–6pm daily; Sep–15 May: 10.30am–4pm daily (10:30am–6pm Thu). ⬤ some public hols. 📷 ✔ ♿ 🍴 📷

The most southerly of the museums on the idyllic Bygdøy peninsula is Norsk Sjøfartsmuseum (the Norwegian Maritime Museum). It is located on the shore near the Frammuseet and Kon-Tiki Museet, and has its own quay and a marvellous view over Oslo's harbour and its approach from the fjord.

Norwegian maritime traditions, including the fishing industry, shipbuilding, shipping and marine archaeology, form the focal point of the collection. Norway's 1,500-year-old tradition of boat-building is a key part of its coastal culture.

The museum traces the development of shipping from the Middle Ages to present-day supertankers. The main theme linking the exhibits is man's use of the sea through the ages and how people have faced up to the challenges and dangers of this mighty element.

From the museum's main entrance, visitors enter the Central Hall containing a model of the Norwegian Navy's steam frigate, *Kong Sverre*, one of three of the largest and most powerful warships ever to be built in Nordic lands. Christian Krohg's painting, *Leiv Eiriksson Discovers America* (*see pp34–5*), hangs on one of the walls. The exhibition halls feature an abundance of model ships through the ages in addition to relics from various maritime activities.

In the Boat Hall traditional fishing craft and working vessels are on show, and there is a display on the diversity of coastal culture. The schooner, *Svanen*, is often moored at the quayside when it is not at sea as

Boat Hall of the Sjøfartsmuseum, Frammuseet and the polar vessel *Gjøa*

Figurehead in the Sjøfartsmuseum

a training ship for young people. Also standing outside the museum is the *Krigseilermonument*, which commemorates sailors killed in World War II (*see p77*).

The museum is the centre for a marine archaeological department, which protects any finds discovered along the Norwegian coast.

The well-stocked museum library contains a collection of drawings, marine literature, archives and photographs.

Frammuseet ❻

Bygdøynesveien 36. **Map** 1 C4. *Tel* 23 28 29 50. 🚌 91 (Apr–Oct). 🚌 30. ⬤ Oct–Apr: 10am–3:45pm daily; May–15 Jun: 10am–5:45pm daily; 16 Jun–Aug: 9am–6:45pm daily; Sep: 10am–4:45pm daily. ⬤ public hols. 📷 ✔ ♿ partial. 📷

No other sailing vessel has been further north or south in the world than the polar ship *Fram*. It was used for three Arctic expeditions by the explorers Fridtjof Nansen (1893–96), Otto Sverdrup (1898–1902) and Roald Amundsen (1910–12). On the third expedition, in 1911, Amundsen became the first person to raise a flag on the South Pole. The schooner was built by the Scottish-born

naval architect Colin Archer, and was specially constructed to prevent it from being crushed by pack ice. On its first commission with Nansen's expedition to the North Pole, it was frozen in at 78° 50'N. The vessel's rounded form allowed it to be pressed up on to the ice, where it remained undamaged until the ice thawed.

Fram also proved itself to be extremely seaworthy in the stormy Antarctic Ocean on Amundsen's historic expedition to the South Pole.

The museum opened in 1936 with the restored ship as its centrepiece. Expedition equipment, paintings, busts and photographs of the polar explorers are on show. The exhibitions have a represent-ative selection of animals from the Polar region, like polar bears, penguins and moscus ox. Outside the museum is Amundsen's first polar exploration vessel, *Gjøa*.

The deck of the polar exploration vessel *Fram* **at the Frammuseet**

Vikingskipshuset ❸

Detail from the Oseberg wagon

Three of the world's best-preserved Viking ships from the 9th century can be seen in Vikingskipshuset (the Viking Ship Museum), which forms part of the Museum of Cultural History, University of Oslo. Found in three large burial mounds on farmland, the ships are considered to be among Norway's greatest cultural treasures. The Oseberg and Gokstad vessels were discovered in Vestfold, and the Tune ship at Haugen in Tune, Østfold. They were used to transport the bodies of high-ranking chieftains on their last journey to the kingdom of the dead. Jewellery, weapons and implements were stolen by grave robbers but some pieces can still be seen here. The museum was designed by Arnstein Arneberg to create a light, airy setting for the ships.

Exterior view of the steep-pitched Vikingskipshuset

★ Oseberg Ship
In 1904 archaeologists opened the grave where the Oseberg ship was found along with the remains of two women and a large number of artifacts. About 90 per cent of the 22-m (72-ft) long ship is of original wood.

Entrance hall

Main entrance

KEY TO FLOORPLAN

- ☐ Oseberg Ship
- ☐ Gokstad Ship
- ☐ Tune Ship
- ☐ Oseberg Collection
- ☐ Non-exhibition space

★ Gokstad Ship
The excavation of the 24-m (79-ft) long Gokstad ship took place in 1880. The remains of a 60-year-old man, a sledge, three small boats, a gangplank and 64 shields were uncovered. The vessel has 16 pieces of planking on each side compared to the Oseberg's 12 pieces.

GALLERY GUIDE
The main attractions are arranged in the form of a cross. Nearest to the entrance hall stands the Oseberg ship and on the far side is the Oseberg Collection. The Gokstad ship stands alone in the left wing. The least well-preserved find, the Tune ship, is housed in the right wing. In the gallery above the entrance, reproductions of three wooden beds are displayed. To the left of the entrance is the museum shop.

STAR EXHIBITS

- ★ Gokstad Ship
- ★ Oseberg Ship
- ★ Oseberg Wagon

★ **Oseberg Wagon**
The richly carved Oseberg wagon is the only one known to exist from the Viking period in Norway. It was probably used by women of high status. Similar wagons have been found in Denmark and Germany.

VISITORS' CHECKLIST

Huk Aveny 35. **Map** 1 A3.
Tel 22 13 52 80.
🚌 91 (May– Sep). 🚌 30.
🕐 May–Sep: 9am–6pm daily;
Oct–Apr: 10am–4pm daily.
⬤ public hols. 📷 🎧 by prior
arrangement. ♿ 🏪
www.khm.uio.no

Animal Head
This animal-head post and four similar ones were found in the Oseberg ship. It is not known what they were used for. This one is in the shape of a predator's head with a gaping mouth, and is an example of the Viking wood-carvers' skills.

Burial Chamber
The Tune ship dates from around 900 and was found in a burial mound on the farm of Haugen in Tune, Østfold. It was made of oak and had been rowed with 10–12 oars. Above the ship's stern lay the remains of a burial chamber.

The Oseberg Collection features the remarkable equipment buried with the two women, including a wagon, sledges, iron-clad chests and caskets.

EXCAVATING THE SHIPS

Unearthing the 1,000-year-old Viking ships from the burial mounds proved a difficult task. The Oseberg ship was buried in blue clay and covered with stones beneath a 6-m (20-ft) high burial mound. The grave was almost hermetically sealed. Ground movement had partly compressed the ship and caused it to break up. The Gokstad ship was also buried in blue clay but the forces of nature had allowed it to lie in peace, and the ship and its contents were well preserved. Robbers had plundered some of the grave furnishings.

Excavation of the Oseberg ship in 1904

The Viking ship burial sites around Oslofjorden

Sjømannskirken, a church dedicated to the welfare of sailors

Sjømannskirken ❼

Admiral Børresens Vei 4. **Map** 1 B4.
Tel 22 43 82 90. 🚌 91 to Bygdøynes
(Apr–Oct). 🔵 noon–5pm Fri–Sun.
🚌 30. ✝ 11am Sun.

In 1954 Oslo Sjømannsmisjon
(the Seamen's Mission)
acquired a beautiful building
on Bygdøy as a centre to help
sailors and those working in
Oslo harbour. The house was
originally a private residence,
built by Arnstein Arneberg
(who designed the Viking
Ship Museum) in 1915. It was
consecrated as a church, and
a large assembly hall and a
sacristy were added in 1962.
Until then, the Seamen's
Mission had operated in very
basic conditions; preachers
used to conduct their sermons
standing on fishing crates.

In 1985, the church was
taken over by Den Indre
Sjømannsmisjon (Internal
Seamen's Mission). It contains
the seamen's memorial, which
was erected in 1966 to
commemorate Norwegian
sailors who died at sea.

Hukodden ❽

Map 1 A5. 🚌 91 to Bygdøynes
(Apr–Oct). 🚌 30. 🍴

Most of Bygdøy's south
side facing the fjord is public
land with tranquil walkways
along the shore and through
the woods. On the
southernmost tip of the
peninsula lies Hukodden
beach, teeming with bathers
on fine summer days. It is
easily accessible from the city
by boat or bus. Despite its
proximity to the city, the
water quality is good for
bathing. A beach restaurant
is open in season.

From the furthest point on
Huk there is a splendid view
over Oslofjord, from Dyna
lighthouse to Nesoddlandet in
the south and to the islands
in the west. The waterway
is busy with ships and
pleasure craft.

In the park area there are
two modern sculptures, *Large
Arch*, by Henry Moore, dating
from 1969, and *Ikaros*, 1965,
by Anne Sofie Døhlen. On a

spit of land to the north of
Huk there is a naturist beach,
and beyond is the popular
bathing spot of Paradisbukta
(Paradise Bay).

Bygdøy Kongsgård ❾

Map 1 A2. **Tel** 22 12 37 00.
🚌 91 to Dronningen, then by bus.
🚌 30. **Residence** 🔵 to the public.
Tracks 🔲 for walking. 🔲 of the
farm by prior arrangement.

King Olav V (1957–91)
used the royal estate
of Bygdøy Kongsgård as a
summer residence for many
years. He treasured the
tranquillity and idyllic
surroundings of the
14th-century royal farm.

King Håkon V Magnusson
had acquired the farm and
given it to Queen Eufemia in
1305. It became a monastic
estate in 1352, but was taken
over by the crown in 1532. At
the time of the Reformation
in 1536 it became a royal
ladegård (working estate).

King Karl Johan bought it
from the state in 1837.
Included in the deal was the
main building erected in the
1730s. It was in the garden
room here that King Christian
Frederik received his farewell
deputation on 10 October
1814. He had expected to
become king of Norway but
was forced to make way for
Karl Johan (*see p38*).

Oscar II took an interest in
the estate, and in 1881 he
established an open-air
museum of old Norwegian

The furthest point of Hukodden offering panoramic views over the inner Oslofjord

wooden houses in the grounds. This collection later became the foundation of the Norsk Folkemuseum (see pp82–3). King Oscar also built the Kongvillaene in Swiss Alps chalet style for employees of the court. Today only one of these villas remains, Villa Gjøa.

The main building, a stately wooden mansion painted in brilliant white, makes a lovely sight in summer when surrounded by green foliage.

Bygdøy Kongsgård covers a large area of northwestern Bygdøy. It comprises 200 hectares (500 acres) of forest and agricultural land. The area facing the sea is known as Kongeskogen (King's Wood). Here there are 9.5 km (6 miles) of public walking tracks. The grounds around the main house are part of the Norsk Folkemuseum.

The dining room in Oscarshall Slott with friezes by Adolf Tidemand

Bygdøy Kongsgård, the former summer residence of King Olav V

Oscarshall Slott ⑩

Oscarshallveien. **Map** 1 B2.
Tel 22 56 15 39. 🚌 30.
🚪 end May–mid-Sep: 10am–4pm
Thu, Fri & Sun. 🎫 📷 🚫

King Oscar I of Sweden and Norway (1799–1859) built a pleasure palace on a headland in Frognerkilen between 1847 and 1852, at the height of the era of National Romanticism. He named it Oscarshall and it became a favourite party venue for the kings of the Bernadotte dynasty. In 1863 the palace was sold to the state, since when it has been

at the disposal of the ruling monarch. It was never intended to be a residence, but rather a showcase for the architecture, handicrafts, applied art and fine art of the time, and for many years it was open to the public.

After the dissolution of the union in 1905 (see p39), Oscarshall was closed, and large parts of its artistic decoration were placed in the Norsk Folkemuseum. In 1929, plans were made to refurbish the palace as a residence for the crown prince, but they were later abandoned. Instead, the building was extensively restored and re-opened to the public.

Oscarshall is built in the style of an English castle. For inspiration, the architect, J H Nebelong, drew on Norman castle design and looked at the design of oriental white buildings with terraces and fountains. A Classical influence is evident in the proportions of the palace and in the strictly geometric shape of the rooms.

The drawing room is the largest room in Oscarshall with elegant windows and glazed doors opening on to the park. The entrance hall was inspired by a chapel from the Middle Ages with a circular stained-glass window

on one of the end walls. The dining room is noted for its decorations by Adolph Tidemand (1814–76), a popular artist famous for his portrayals of everyday life in Norway (see pp8–9). The king invited him to decorate the dining room with a series of 10 paintings inlaid in friezes around the upper walls. The pictures depict peasant life from childhood to old age.

The king's living room contains Gothic-style carved and moulded decorations and paintings based on the old Norwegian sagas.

Oscarshall Slott, Oscar I's 19th-century pleasure palace

Vigelandsparken ❶

**The Little
Angry Boy**

Oslo's largest park is named after the sculptor, Gustav Vigeland, whose 212 sculptures depicting humanity in all its forms are artfully positioned along the central axis. The focal point is the soaring Monolith on a stepped plinth surrounded by groups of figures. Vigeland started work on the park in 1924. By 1950, seven years after his death, most of the pieces were in place. The sculptures were modelled in full size in clay by Vigeland himself, but the carving in stone and casting in bronze were carried out by others. The interplay between the sculptures, the green areas and the architecture is a breathtaking sight.

Sundial (Soluret), stands on a granite plinth decorated with the signs of the zodiac.

Wheel of Life
The Wheel of Life (Livshjulet), *which sums up the park's dramatic theme, was modelled in 1934. The wheel is a symbol of eternity and consists of a garland of men, women and children holding onto each other in an eternal cycle.*

★ Monolith
The 17-m (56-ft) tall Monolith is the highest point in the park. It comprises 121 human figures, supporting and holding onto each other. On the plinth at the base of the column there are 36 groups of granite figures depicting the cycles of life and relationships.

Vigelandsmuseet *(see p92),* just outside the park, houses the artist's studio and an exhibition of his earlier works.

0 metres	100
0 yards	100

STAR FEATURES

★ Bridge

★ Fountain

★ Monolith

Triangle
The group of figures known as Triangle was one of the last pieces to be placed in Vigelandsparken. It was erected in 1993.

The Clan
The last large group of figures in the Vigeland complex, the Clan, was finally put in place in 1988 as a gift from IBM.

Bronze statuette, *Pike og øgle* (Girl and the Lizard), 1938

VISITORS' CHECKLIST

Kirkeveien. **Map** 2 A1.
Tel *23 49 37 00.* Ⓣ *Majorstuen.*
🚋 *12.* 🚌 *20.*
Park ◯ *daily (24 hrs).* 🍴 🖥
Vigelandsmuseet ◯ *Jun–Aug:*
10am–5pm Tue–Sun; Sep–May:
noon–4pm Tue–Sun.
Kafé Vigeland ◯ *10am–6pm*
daily. 🛍 🛈
www.vigeland.museum.no

Frogner ponds

★ Fountain
The fountain shows six giants carrying an enormous vessel on their shoulders. Around the edge of the pool are 20 groups of figures. The surrounding fountain square is in mosaic.

Kafé Vigeland and Visitors' Centre

Oslo Bymuseum
(see p92)

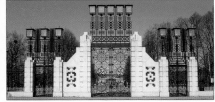

Main Entrance
The monumental entrance consists of five wrought-iron main gates and two smaller pedestrian gates leading through to the sculptures.

★ Bridge
The granite bridge is lined with 58 bronze sculptures, modelled in the years 1925–33, and depicting the various stages of life. The lizard groups on each corner symbolize mankind's fight against evil.

Oslo Bymuseum ❷

Frognerveien 67. *Tel* 23 28 41 70.
🚊 12. 🚌 20. ⏰ noon–4pm
Tue–Sun (to 7pm Tue). ● occasional
public hols and 1–15 Jan.
🖼️ 🚫 ♿ ✉️ 📷 📷

Housed in the Frogner
Hovedgård, a handsome,
well-preserved 18th-century
manor house, is Oslo
Bymuseum, a museum
devoted to the city's 1,000-
year history. The town's
growth, as well as its
commercial and cultural life,
comes to life through models,
room interiors, pictures,
sculptures, photographs
and displays. There is
particular emphasis on
the history of Oslo from
the Middle Ages to the
present day.

On the first floor, rooms
dating from 1750 are on
view in summer. Among
the attractions are Bernt
Anker's ballroom from the
1790s and landscape paintings
of Oslo, then Christiania, in
the 19th century.

With its origin in the
Middle Ages, the former
farm is in traditional style,
with three buildings laid
out around a square yard
behind the museum. Its
garden and old pastures
together form Frognerparken,
which also encompasses
Vigeland Park (see pp90–91).

Vigelandsmuseet, showcasing the work of the sculptor, Gustav Vigeland

Vigelandsmuseet ❸

Nobelsgate 32. *Tel* 23 49 37 00.
🚊 12. 🚌 20. ⏰ Sep–May: noon–
4pm Tue–Sun; Jun–Aug: 10am–5pm
Tue–Sun. ● some public hols. 🖼️
♿ 📷

A major part of Gustav
Vigeland's (1869–1943)
artistic output can be seen
in Vigelandsmuseet, just by
Vigelandsparken *(see pp90–91)*.

The collection contains
2,700 sculptures in plaster,
bronze, granite and marble,
12,000 drawings and around
400 woodcuts and carvings.
The original models for the
Vigeland Park sculptures as
well as casts for busts and
other monuments are on
display. Old photographs
show the making of the
sculpture park. The museum
is the result of a contract

drawn up in 1921 between
the artist and Oslo City
Council. Vigeland donated
to the city all his existing and
future works. In return the
council built him a studio,
which was later to be
converted into a museum
to exhibit his work.

Built in the 1920s, the
studio-turned-museum is
considered to be one of the
finest examples of Norwegian
Neo-Classicism. Vigeland
himself chose the interior
colour scheme.

Moving through the rooms,
it is possible to follow the
artist's development from
his 1890s' expressive and
thin-figure style to the heavier
expression of the years
between the two world wars.
The artist's living quarters are
also on view.

After Vigeland's death in
1943, his ashes were placed
in the tower at his request.

Gamlebyen ❹

2 km (1 mile) E of town centre.
🚊 18, 19. 🚌 34, 70.

In the Middle Ages, the
town of Oslo was centred on
Gamlebyen (the Old Town).
From the 12th century until
the great fire of 1624, nearly
all development in this area
lay between Ekebergåsen,
Bjørvika, Grønland and
Galgeberg. Many of the
medieval ruins in Gamlebyen
have been preserved,
including those of Mariakirken
(Maria Church), Kongsgården
(the Royal Manor) and
Clemenskirken (Clemens
Church). A medieval park has

A middle-class home of around 1900 in Oslo Bymuseum

For hotels and restaurants in this region see pp228–9 and pp244–5

been established next to the ruins of St Hallvard Cathedral. There are other reminders of the Middle Ages, including Oslo Ladegård og Bispegården (Oslo Manor and the Bishops' Residence).

For many years after World War II Gamlebyen suffered from heavy traffic. Strict regulations have since tackled the problem and Gamlebyen is experiencing new prosperity. The future opera house and a new town development are taking shape in Bjørvika. Houses and commercial buildings are being restored. Meanwhile, excavations have revealed the remains of timber houses and townhouses and an array of decorative items and utensils.

Munch-museet containing Edvard Munch's extensive artistic output

Gamlebyen's medieval park among the cathedral ruins

Munch-museet ❺

Tøyengata 53. *Tel* 23 49 35 21.
🚇 Tøyen/Munchmuseet. 🚌 20, 60.
🕐 Jun–Aug: 10am–6pm daily;
Sep–May: 10am–4pm Tue–Fri,
11am–5pm Sat & Sun.
⬤ 1 Jan, 1 May, 17 May, 24 & 25
Dec. 🖼 🗂 ♿ 🎫 📷 📱
www.munch.museum.no

The largest collection of work by Edvard Munch (1863–1944) is housed in Oslo's Munch-museet. Prior to his death, Edvard Munch bequeathed all the paintings in his possession to the City of Oslo. A century after his birth, the Munch-museet opened. Designed by Gunnar Fougner and Einar Myklebust, the museum is situated next to Tøyenparken on Oslo's east side, where the artist grew up. It was completely renovated and enlarged in 1994, on the 50th anniversary of Munch's death.

The collection is extensive, comprising 1,100 paintings, 4,500 drawings and 17,000 prints. It contains the main works from every period of the artist's productive life, including versions of *The Scream*, the worrying *Anxiety* (1894), the serene but melancholic *Young Woman on the Shore* (1896) and the sensuously claustrophobic *Kiss* (1897).

Some of Munch's major works may be on loan to museums elsewhere and not all pieces are displayed at the same time. But with 1,888 sq m (20,322 sq ft) of exhibition space and such a rich collection to draw on, the museum is never without material to provide a detailed account of the artist's life and work. Special exhibitions presenting new perspectives on his art are shown regularly.

Other examples of Munch's work can be seen in the Nasjonalgalleriet *(see pp52–3)*, Henie Onstad Kunstsenter *(see p120)* and Bergen's Rasmus Meyers Samlinger *(see p173)*.

EDVARD MUNCH

Norway's most renowned visual artist and one of the forerunners of Expressionism, Edvard Munch (1863–1944) made his debut at the Autumn Exhibition in Oslo when he was just 20 years old. He painted a number of masterpieces shortly after his debut, including *The Sick Child*, connected to a personal experience – his sister's death when she was 14 years old. After studies in Norway he moved to Paris in 1889, and later to Berlin, where he further developed his highly individual style with themes of love and death in the *Frieze of Life* series.

Spiritual experiences and angst characterize his work as is evident in his best-known painting, *The Scream* (1894), in which a desperate figure can be seen screaming on a bridge. The agitated style of his works reveals a troubled life: in 1908 he suffered a mental breakdown and a year later he returned to Norway. By then he was accepted as a major artist and was commissioned to do works for public buildings, including the Aula of Oslo University *(see p50)*.

Munch's self-portrait, *The Night Wanderer*

Floral splendour in the Botanisk Hage at Tøyen in Oslo

Botanisk Hage and Museum 6

Sars Gate 1. **Tel** 22 85 17 00.
🚇 Tøyen/Munch-museet.
🚌 20, 31, 32, 60. **Museum** ◯
11am–4pm Tue–Sun. **Botanisk Hage**
◯ Apr–Sep: 7am–8pm Mon–Fri,
10am–8pm Sat & Sun; Oct–Mar:
7am–5pm Mon–Fri, 10am–5pm Sat &
Sun. ● some public hols. 📷 🎫
♿ 🖊 🖥 🚻

Right across from Munch-museet is the Botanisk Hage, Norway's largest botanical garden. It is a popular excursion for Oslo's residents, who come both to admire the thousands of Norwegian and foreign plants and to escape from the hustle and bustle of the city.

One of the highlights is the Alpine Garden, with a waterfall and 1,450 species of mountain flora from Norway and abroad. In the Systematic Garden plants are grouped according to family and genus. The Medicinal and Herbal Garden contains medicinal plants, spices and cash crops. For those in wheelchairs or with impaired vision, the Aromatic Garden is a special attraction. Here, fragrant plants grow in raised beds and are accompanied by texts in Braille. In the Victoria House and Palm House are plants from tropical and temperate regions, including rare orchids, carnivorous pitcher plants, cacti, cocoa trees, fig trees and palms.

The Botanisk Hage is part of the Natural History Museum and since 1814 has formed the basis for research and education in botany at the University of Oslo.

In the middle of the Botanical Garden is a manor house, Tøyen Hovedgård, dating from 1780. The old greenhouses and three museum buildings form an attractive planted enclosure.

An extensive herbarium containing 1.7 million examples of herbs provides an important resource for the documentation and research of Norwegian flora.

Geologisk Museum 7

Sars Gate 1. **Tel** 22 85 17 00.
🚇 Tøyen/Munch-museet.
🚌 20, 31, 32, 60. ◯ 11am–4pm
Tue–Sun. ● some public hols.
📷 🎫 ♿ 🖥 🚻

A circular showcase of gemstones is the first eye-catching exhibit on entering the Geologisk Museum. The gems are mainly Norwegian in origin. The ground floor of the museum is devoted to a presentation of the geological processes at work in the Earth, including the formation of volcanoes, mountain ranges and rocks.

Norway as an oil-producing nation is the subject of a separate exhibition.

In an intriguing display about Oslofeltet (the Oslo Field), remarkable fossil-bearing rocks are on show alongside other geological items that would normally lie hidden deep below the crust of the earth or in the murky depths of the North Sea. Exhibits include fossils such as weird-looking trilobites, brachiopods, cuttlefish and various microscopic creatures.

Zoologisk Museum 8

Sars Gate 1. **Tel** 22 85 17 00.
🚇 Tøyen/Munchmuséet.
🚌 20, 31, 32, 60. ◯ 11am–4pm
Tue–Sun. ● some public hols.
📷 🎫 ♿ 🚻

The Norwegian Hall of the Zoologisk Museum features displays of stuffed native animals in recreations of their various habitats, including fish and marine and freshwater creatures, mammals and birds. Ptarmigan and reindeer can be observed against a mountain backdrop; cranes and black grouse are on show, and the pre-mating antics of the wood grouse are demonstrated. There are beaver dams and a display of the bird colonies that nest on the sea-cliffs.

In the Svalbard Hall exhibits feature Arctic animals, such as

Arctic animals on display at the Zoologisk Museum

polar bears and seals. The Animal Geography Hall presents large and small creatures in different world zones, such as penguins in Antarctica, and lions, hippopotamuses and crocodiles in the tropical regions. Also, there are several butterfly montages.

In the Systematic Hall there are detailed displays of Norway's animal life, from single-celled amoebas to the largest mammals. A "sound bar" provides recordings of animal noises from the wild.

Collections in the Norsk Teknisk Museum appealing to all ages

Grünerløkka, a renovated and old popular working class district

Grünerløkka **❾**

1 km (half a mile) N of the centre.
🚌 30, 58. 🚋 11, 12, 13.

The former working class district of Grünerløkka has undergone something of a renaissance in recent years. It is made up largely of apartment blocks dating from the end of the 19th century, which were under threat of demolition. But repeated proposals to clear the area and build afresh have finally been shelved and instead the old housing stock is being restored. Small and inadequate apartments have been combined, and units are becoming larger and fewer, but the neighbourhood still retains the character of old Oslo. As a result, people from all walks of life have been attracted to Grünerløkka and the area has become particularly popular among young people.

With the influx of this vibrant new community, a large number of cosmopolitan shops, cafés and restaurants thrive here, including the popular Sult (*see p244*).

Det Internasjonale Barnekunst-museet **❿**

Lille Frøens Vei 4. *Tel* 22 46 85 73.
🚇 Frøen. 🚌 46. 🕐 9:30am–2pm Tue, Wed & Thu, 11am–4pm Sun.
🌐 public hols. 📷 🎫 📵 🏛

Children's art from 150 countries has been assembled in Barnekunst-museet (the International Museum of Children's Art). Exhibits include paintings, sculptures, ceramics, collages and textiles by children from around the world.

The museum was set up in 1968 in collaboration with the SOS Children's Villages, an international organization for children in need.

Although the museum is designed to give space specifically to children's opinions and things that are dear to them, the works have been selected on the basis of quality, just as they would be in an adults' museum.

Visiting children can express themselves actively in a variety of ways, in the Music and Dance Room, the Doll Room and the Painting and Drawing Studio. Videos and films on children's art are shown on various weekdays and workshops held.

Barnekunstmuseet, a lively forum for children's art

Norsk Teknisk Museum **⓫**

Kjelsåsveien 143. *Tel* 22 79 60 00. 🚆 11, 12 to Kjelsås. 🚌 54. 🚉 to Kjelsås. 🕐 20 Jun–20 Aug: 10am–6pm daily; 21 Aug–19 Jun: 10am–4pm Tue–Fri, 10am–5pm Sat & Sun. 🌐 some public hols. 📷 🎫 ♿ 🏛 🏛

Technology past and present is the subject of Norsk Teknisk Museum (the Norwegian Museum of Science and Technology), founded in 1914 in Kjelsås. Exhibits include Norway's first steam engine, its first car, imported in 1895, and its first aeroplane, in addition to early sewing machines, vacuum cleaners and other everyday objects.

The ground floor is dedicated to industry. The first floor covers transport and communications, telecom technology and information technology. Here it is possible to follow the development of steam power and the transition to mass production. Telecommunication is traced from the first warnings sent via beacons to the development of the telegraph and telephones, mobile phones and the internet.

An exhibition illustrates oil and gas exploration in the North Sea, and shows how the raw material is pumped to the surface, transported and refined. In an unusual display titled *The Forest as a Resource*, the importance of cellulose in revolutionizing the production of paper 150 years ago is also highlighted.

There are educational exhibits and a science centre, Teknoteket, with hands-on activities. A variety of family events take place at weekends.

Emanuel Vigeland Museum, featuring the artist's work and mausoleum

Emanuel Vigeland Museum ⑫

Grimelundsveien 8, 5 km (3 miles) N of centre. **Tel** 22 14 57 88. Ⓣ *Slemdal*. 🚌 46. ◯ *noon–4pm Sun.* 📷

On the western side of Oslo lies one of the most unusual museums in Norway. It is dedicated to the artist Emanuel Vigeland, younger brother of Gustav, the sculptor who created Vigelandsparken *(see pp90–91).*

Emanuel Vigeland (1875–1948) pioneered fresco painting in Norway. He also perfected the art of medieval stained glass techniques.

The museum building was originally Vigeland's studio; on his death it became his mausoleum and was opened to the public in 1959. On show is his lifework, *Vita*, a series of fresco paintings from 1927–47, in addition to portraits, drawings and sculptures. The frescoes have to be viewed in somewhat subdued lighting, because in the 1940s the subjects in *Vita* were considered too daring for public taste and it was thought that strong lighting would make them even more provocative. Today, few people would regard Vigeland's work as indecent.

Another oddity is the unusually low-ceilinged entrance area. This has been attributed to the artist's desire for humility in the face of the art one is coming to view.

Examples of Vigeland's stained glass can be seen in the windows of Oslo Domkirke *(see p73).*

Holmenkollen ⑬

6 km (4 miles) N of centre. **Tel** 22 92 32 00. Ⓣ *Holmenkollen.* 🚋 🚌 **Skimuseet & Ski Jump** ◯ *Jan–Apr & Oct–Dec: 10am–4pm daily; May & Sep: 10am–5pm daily; Jun–Aug: 9am–8pm daily.* 📷 *by arrangement.* **www**.skiforeningen.no

Ski-jumping is almost always guaranteed to attract the crowds in Norway, and the impressive ski jump at Holmenkollen, which was renovated in 2009, is no exception. The venue for the annual Holmenkollen Races and ski-jumping events is Norway's biggest tourist attraction, drawing more than 1 million visitors a year. The races have been held here since 1892. Crown Prince Olav participated in the jumping competitions in both 1923 and 1924. The ski jump, which has been remodelled 15 times, was for many years regarded as the most important arena for Nordic skiing. The world championships have been held here on three occasions, as were many of the skiing events for the 1952 Winter Olympics. The complex has also become the main arena for the Biathlon, involving cross-country skiing and marksmanship.

The public can visit both the ski jump and the jump tower all year round. The tower, in particular, offers a splendid view over Oslo and the inner Oslofjord, with an outdoor viewing platform as well as panoramic views from the snack bar below.

The Skimuseet, at the base of the ski jump, opened in 1923. It focuses on more than 4,000 years of skiing history *(see pp26–7).* Displays illustrate various types of skis from different eras and regions of Norway, and follow the development of each of the skiing disciplines. The Olympics in Oslo in 1952 and Lillehammer in 1994 are also covered. In addition, Norway's prominent role in polar history receives special attention and the now antique-looking equipment used by Nansen and Amundsen can be admired. An auditorium showing historical ski films opened in 2010.

The large area outside the museum has a waterfall and spectacular views.

The striking profile of the former Holmenkollen ski jump

Frognerseteren on a winter's day, offering sweeping views over Oslo

Frognerseteren ⑭

7 km (4 miles) N of centre.
Restaurant *Tel* 22 92 40 40.
🚋 *Frognerseteren.* 🟦 🖥

About half an hour's walk from Holmenkollen hill is Frognerseteren, a favourite excursion spot. Originally it was a pasture, which was first inhabited in the 1790s.

A traditional wooden lodge, built by the municipality at Frognerseteren at the end of the 19th century, houses a restaurant. From its terrace there is a spectacular view over Oslo, the fjord and surrounding areas. Below the building, a stone monument commemorates the 1814 Constitutional Assembly.

The road northward from Holmenkollen to Frognerseteren was opened in 1890 in the presence of Oscar II and the German Emperor Wilhelm II. It was named Keiser Wilhelms Vei. After World War II it was renamed Holmenkollveien.

Frognerseteren is the last station on the Holmenkollen Tunnelbane line. It is a popular starting point for walks in the Nordmarka woods throughout the year, giving access to the network of footpaths and ski trails.

Just 15 minutes from the city centre, the Frognerseteren Restaurant is frequented by both locals and tourists before or after a hike in the surrounding woods. Here guests can sample traditional Norwegian food (including reindeer) and enjoy a spectacular panoramic view of the Oslo Fjord, 435 m (1,427 ft) above sea level.

The restaurant is housed in one of Oslo's most unusual buildings. Designed by the architect Holm Munthe (1848–98) and completed in 1892, the structure is built in the traditional Scandinavian "dragon style", so called because of the carvings of dragon heads located at the peak of the gables. Kafé Seterstua, on the same site, is also worth a visit, offering delicacies from self-service counters.

Prime minister Peder Anker (1749–1824) and his family

Bogstad Herregård ⑮

Sørkedalen 826, 8 km (5 miles) NW of centre. *Tel* 22 06 52 00. 🚌 41.
🟩 *mid-May–end Sep, only for guided tours.* 🟦 🟦 *1pm, 2pm Tue–Sat; 12.30pm, 1.30pm, 2.30pm, 3.30pm Sun.* 🟢 🟦 🟦 *(café and shop open noon–4pm Tue–Sun year-round).*

On a promontory on the eastern side of Bogstad Lake in Søkerdalen lies Bogstad Herregård, a farming estate which dates from the Middle Ages.

Bogstad originally belonged to the Cistercian Monastery on Hovedøya, an island situated in the innermost part of Oslofjorden. It then passed to the crown before being sold to the alderman, Morten Lauritzen.

The present manor house was erected in the late 18th century by Peder Anker (1749–1824) who later became prime minister. Most of the contents and the large art collection date from that time. The estate then passed to Baron Herman Wedel Jarlsberg. Oslo Municipality took over its forests and arable land in 1954 when the building, complete with contents, and the surrounding parkland became part of Norsk Folkemuseum.

The manor house is open to the public in the summer months, and in December it is the venue for various Christmas events.

In 1978 the wagonhouse and woodshed next to the driveway from Sørkedalsveien burned down and were later replaced by reproductions. Extensive restoration took place in 1999 when the barn was converted to provide banqueting facilities.

The park surrounding Bogstad Herregård was established around 1785 by the Norwegian garden designer Johan Grauer. For inspiration, Peder Anker had sent Grauer to England to study English landscape design. Grauer's park layout was one of the first Norwegian examples of the English landscape style.

Bogstad Herregård, a farming estate dating back to the Middle Ages

SHOPPING IN OSLO

While Norway is undoubtedly one of the most expensive places in Europe to shop, you can find some wonderful, high-quality items to take back with you. The high prices become a bit more palatable once you consider the 11–18.5 per cent discount offered by the country's tax-free-for-tourists scheme *(see p258)*. Moreover, if

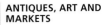

Norwegian souvenir sign

you shop smartly and have time you should be able to find a bargain or two. The most popular items to buy are souvenirs such as Viking- or troll-related items, traditional sweaters and cheese slicers, *rosemaling* ("rose paintings"), finely painted wooden plates, dolls in traditional *bunads* (costumes) and native Sámi (Lapp) items.

Designer boutiques in the Aker Brygge shopping mall

WHERE TO SHOP

Karl Johans Gate *(see p48)* is Oslo's main pedestrian thoroughfare, with a mix of major chains and smaller outlets. **Stortorvet** *(see p63)* and the market place at **Strøget** have more of the same, while just south, **Aker Brygge** *(see p57)* is good for designer shops. **Bogstadveien**, towards Majorstua, also has small designer boutiques. **Grønland** is good for inexpensive fabrics and fancy jewellery, while **Grünerløkka** *(see p95)* is the best area for Norwegian fashion designers.

SOUVENIRS

For Scandinavian souvenir items, head to **William Schmidt**, which sells a wide range of items including model ships, dolls, troll figurines, bags and moccasins. **Norway Shop**, near the city hall, is another good venue for Viking-themed items that include jewellery, drinking horns and Sámi goods.

WOOL SWEATERS

The Norwegian wool sweater personifies Scandinavian workmanship and attention to detail. Those made by Dahl and Nordstrikk are of high quality. **Oslo Sweater Shop** carries over 5,000 sweaters, as well as knitted jackets, caps and socks. Another good option for woven garments is **Unique Design**.

Traditional Scandinavian souvenirs on sale in the city

ANTIQUES, ART AND MARKETS

For antiques, try **Blomqvist Kunsthandel**, which has art, crystal and other fine items for sale and auction. **Far & Sonn Brukt Antikkmarked** has cheaper items, including old furniture.

For the best selection of Norwegian art, you can buy works straight off the walls at **Kunstnernes Hus**, a local exhibition space. **Abel Kunst** sells an impressive selection of contemporary painting and sculptures.

The city's weekend flea markets are another great place to seek out bargains for antiques, clothes, arts and crafts. **Vestkanttorget** (Sat 10am–5pm), near Vigeland Park is filled with bric-a-brac, while **Birkelunden** (Sun noon–6pm) in Grünerløkka is good for vintage clothing.

SHOPPING CENTRES AND DEPARTMENT STORES

Though tourist-related shopping in Oslo is best at small handicrafts stores, there are several shopping malls for more general items. **Byporten Shopping**, opposite Oslo Central Station, is the city's newest shopping centre and contains more than 70 shops that sell a number of well-known brands. **Oslo City** is one of the capital's largest department stores, with many specialty Nordic items. **Aker Brygge** is another popular shopping mall in the city, while **Paléet** has dozens of exclusive shops that sell clothing, art and cosmetics.

Examples of world-renowned Norwegian glassware

CLOTHING AND FASHION

Norwegian fashion designers to look out for include Kristian Aadnevik and Laura Armonaite. **MA Fashion** is one of the best places for modern designs, while **Norway Designs** stocks designer clothing and accessories. **Mona Strand** is one of Norway's hottest hat designers. Given the high price of new clothes in Norway, it makes sense to scour Oslo's used clothing boutiques. The Markveien branch of **Fretex** sells trendy second-hand clothes.

BOOKS AND MUSIC

The city's best bookshops are **Norli**, **Tanum Libris** and **Ark Bokhandel**, all with good selections of all the major European languages. **Bjørn Ringstrøms Antikvariat** is a huge used bookseller.

With regard to music shops, **Platekompaniet** is the best of the chain stores. For more eccentric tastes, **Big Dipper** is the city's largest indie music store, with much of its music on vinyl, while **Bare Jazz** sells a good selection of jazz CDs in a café setting.

GLASSWARE

Norway is well-known for its glassware; **Glasmagasinet** is the country's largest shop, and **Norway Designs** also carries an impressive inventory of glassware, ceramics and pottery.

JEWELLERY, GOLD AND SILVER

For antique jewellery and second-hand gold and silver items, **Esaias Solberg** is the city's oldest and best shop, selling earrings, necklaces, watches and houseware items. **David-Andersen** is also a good place for jewellery.

Karl Johans Gate shopping area in central Oslo

DIRECTORY

SOUVENIRS

Norway Shop
Fr. Nansens Plass 2
Tel 22 33 41 97

William Schmidt
Fretgof Namser Plass 9
Tel 22 42 02 88

WOOL SWEATERS

Oslo Sweater Shop
Biskop Gunnerus Gate 3
Tel 22 42 42 25

Unique Design
Rosenkrantz Gate 13
Tel 22 42 97 60

SHOPPING CENTRES AND DEPARTMENT STORES

Aker Brygge
Stranden 3B
Tel 22 83 26 80

Byporten Shopping
Jernbanetorget 6
Tel 23 36 21 60

Oslo City
Stenersgate 1
Tel 81 54 40 33

Paléet
Karl Johans Gate 37–43
Tel 22 03 38 88

ANTIQUES, ART AND MARKETS

Abel Kunst
Kristian's IV's Gate 15
Tel 22 20 25 02

Birkelunden
Birkelunden

Blomqvist Kunsthandel
Tordenskiolds
Tel 22 70 87 70

Far & Sonn Brukt Antikkmarked
3 Sanner Gate
Tel 22 35 05 36

Kunstnernes Hus
Wergelandsveien 17
Tel 22 85 34 10

Vestkanttorget
Amaldus Nilsens Plass

CLOTHING AND FASHION

Fretex
Markveien 51
Tel 22 35 59 16

MA Fashion
Hegdehaugsveien 27
Tel 20 60 72 90

Mona Strand
Noltekøkka Allè 10
Tel 22 69 74 55

Norway Designs
Stortingsgaten 28
Tel 23 11 45 10

BOOKS & MUSIC

Ark Bokhandel
Grensen 17
Tel 22 99 07 50

Bare Jazz
Grensen 8
Tel 22 33 20 80

Big Dipper
Torggata 36
Tel 22 20 14 41

Bjørn Ringstrøms Antikvariat
Ullesvålsveien 1
Tel 22 20 78 05

Norli
Universitetsgata 20–24
Tel 22 00 43 00

Platekompaniet
Bodstadveien 40
Tel 22 46 93 53

Tanum Libris
Karl Johans Gate 37–41
Tel 22 41 11 00

JEWELLERY, GOLD AND SILVER

David-Andersen
Karl Johan's Gate 20
Tel 24 14 88 00

Esaias Solberg
Kerkeristen
Tel 22 86 24 80

ENTERTAINMENT IN OSLO

Over the past few years, Oslo has been giving its Scandinavian brethren in Stockholm and Copenhagen a run for their money. It has reinvented itself as a hip, new getaway destination with loads of cultural and artistic goings-on, several well-attended festivals and a thriving café and nightlife scene to boot. In terms of nightlife, the city is home to over a hundred bars and clubs, many of them in the centre and several dozen of which keep their doors open until 4am. Be sure to pick up a copy of *What's On in Oslo*, available from most hotels and tourist information offices, and *Streetwise*, a free listings brochure covering bars and clubs in the city. Tickets to all theatre, ballet, opera, concert and festival events can be purchased at Billettsentralen or at any post office.

Sign for the
Oslo Nye Teater

THEATRE AND CULTURAL EVENTS

Oslo is, naturally, the perfect place to catch the works of Henrik Ibsen, Norway's greatest playwright. Ibsen productions are best seen in the **Nationaltheatret** – it was built in 1899 exclusively for performances of his plays – though other modern works are also put on. Tickets generally start at 150kr. The theatre organizes a special Ibsen festival every other year. In the same location, the **Amfiscene** has (cheaper) avant-garde performances. Ibsenmuseet (the Ibsen Museum, *see p58–9*) is a short walk from the Nationaltheatret, and offers a programme of talks presented by literary experts and theatre professionals.

Other theatre venues include **Det Norske Teatret** and **Oslo Nye Teater** and, for young new writing, **Den Åpne Teater**. One of the newest

venues is the **M/S Innvik**, a large ship moored in Bjørvika that organizes regular bespoke theatre shows. **Chat Noir** is the oldest revue theatre in Scandinavia and great for comedy, cabaret and vaudeville-type musical events. The chapel at the **Akershus Castle and Fortress** has theatre and concerts in summer; a Chamber Music festival is also held here in August.

Parkteatret is a smart cultural centre offering weekly music, films and theatre performances. One of the largest cultural events is the annual December gala evening at **Oslo Spektrum**, held in connection with the Nobel Peace Prize ceremony.

CLASSICAL MUSIC, OPERA AND BALLET

Oslo Konserthus is the home of the nation's largest symphony orchestra, the Oslo Philharmonic. Concerts

The Nationaltheatret, the city's principal stage-production venue

are generally held on Thursdays and Fridays in the spring and autumn, with tickets starting at around 200kr. **Chateau Neuf** and **Sentrum Scene** are popular entertainment theatres in Oslo, staging musicals, farces, comedies and cabarets. **Rockefeller Music Hall** also puts on a wide range of musical events.

Chamber music is increasing in popularity in Norway. In October, Oslo's **Ultima Contemporary Music Festival** features opera, ballet, classical and folk music performances at a variety of spots throughout the city. **Oslo Kirkemusikkfestival** (the Oslo Festival of Church Music) draws thousands of people to the capital's churches in March. In 2008, **Den Norske Opera** (the Norwegian Opera), opened in a new venue. The Opera features many of the world's

A church music ensemble at the Oslo Kirkemusikkfestival

A band plays at the Oslo Spektrum, the city's largest popular music venue

best-known works in its repertoire, and also presents three or four newly commissioned works every season. In total, they put on 20 different operas and operettas each year, as well as hosting the many modern dance performances by the **Nasjonalballetten** (the National Ballet), Norway's only classical ballet company. Both the opera and ballet seasons generally operate during the winter months, and tickets usually start at around 170kr, though you can occasionally get cheaper day-of tickets. An interesting alternative venue is the **Underwater Pub**, which is a unique way to see opera stars in the making – local opera students perform their latest librettos here on Tuesdays and Thursdays.

FOLK DANCING

Norway has a strong tradition of folk dancing. There are regular international and Norwegian traditional dance performances at **Dansens Hus** throughout the year. During the summer you can catch twice-weekly performances of folk dancing at the **Oslo Konserthus** *(see Classical Music, above)*. The **Norsk Folkemuseum** on Bygdøy has its own folk dancing group that put on shows in an open-air theatre several nights a week between July and August. Admission to the museum includes entry to dance performances. Both

Crown Prince Haakon and Princess Märtha Louise have participated keenly in folk dancing here.

CINEMA AND FILM

Most non-Scandinavian films are screened in their original language with Norwegian subtitles. **Kinematografer Oslo** is one of the city's largest cinemas, while **Film-teateret Teletorg** has a lovely old interior and **Saga Kino** screens its wide range of films across six screens; all of the above generally show the latest Hollywood blockbusters.

If your preference is for arthouse films, classic features and "alternative" movies just off the festival circuit, then **Filmens Hus** is the place to go.

Cinema tickets generally go for around 100kr, and are usually cheaper for matinee performances. You can call 82 05 00 01 or look at

www.oslokino.no to find out what features are playing at any of the city's cinemas.

ROCK, BLUES, COUNTRY AND IRISH

Most live music in Oslo happens during the weekend, though sometimes there are shows on Wednesday and Thursday nights. Big-name international bands mainly perform at **Oslo Spektrum**, as well as at the country's biggest rock festival, Norwegian Wood, held outside of Oslo in the early summer. Øyafestivalen, a rock festival held in Middelalderparken in downtown Oslo in mid-August, features international groups as well as popular Scandinavian bands.

For live rock music in the city centre, your best bet is **Last Train**, a popular venue; bands feature every night except Sunday. Another good bet is **Café Mono**, a dimly-lit place that's good for rock and punk music most nights from Sunday to Thursday. Nearby, **Blitz** and **Elm Street Rock Café** have live rock several evenings a week.

Elsewhere, **Garage Oslo** is a good spot to catch up-and-coming Norwegian rock 'n' roll bands, **Gloria Flames** is a great rooftop bar focusing on rockabilly, while **Muddy Waters** almost exclusively features blues and R&B. **Sound of Mu** is a British-run bar that has live music every night, much of it from Oslo's underground music scene.

Traditional dancing at the Norsk Folkemuseum

JAZZ

Scandinavians are well known for their love of jazz music and Norway has provided noted musicians such as Jan Garbarek, Terje Rypdal, Nils Petter Molvær and Sidsel Endresen. Oslo has a large number of jazz cafés and clubs, most of which usually charge a cover of 60–70kr when there is a live group performing. One of the best jazz venues in Oslo is **Blå**, a mellow joint that regularly features both established and up-and-coming musicians. Other good jazz bars include **Herr Nilsens Pub**, with live music from Thursday to Saturday, and **Café Con Bar**, where trios and quartets play late on Sundays. **Smuget** has jazz groups that perform late at weekends and most weekday nights, while **Bar Boca**, a tiny 1950s-style bar, occasionally puts on live jazz on Thursdays. In August, the Oslo Jazz Festival hosts the biggest names in world jazz.

Smuget's different stages host jazz music, rock bands and dance djs

BARS AND CAFES

Most bars and clubs in Oslo are open until 3am, though some close at 1am during the week. The Akerselva river is the rough dividing line between the upscale bars and clubs in the west and the more alternative, student-type venues in the east. In general, the areas around Majorstuen, Vika and Frogner have the most fashionable bars; Karl Johan's Gate and Akerbrygga are

The popular waterside location of Akerbrygga's bars

mainstream; Grünerløkka has hip lounges; and Grønland is a student area.

In the centre, the **Skybar** is located atop the Radisson SAS Hotel, and is where Oslo's elite come for the great views. The bars around Aker Brygge include **Bar 1**, which serves several hundred types of cognacs and whiskeys.

Behind the train station **Stargate** and **Choice** are fun, grungy bars, though **Fru Hagen** is a bit classier. Nearby, **Oslomekaniskeverksted** is a bar popular with young professionals. For something more alternative, head to Grünerløkka and its after-hours bars. **Parkteatret** is one of the area's best-loved spots as it puts on regular concerts and theatre performances. **Tea Lounge** is an airy spot with plush seating and a huge cocktails list. Just down the road is **Kaos**, a lounge bar with a terrace in the back that has great dancing; **SüdØst**, with its basement nightclub; and **Aku-Aku**, a jovial tiki bar adorned with original slats from Thor Heyerdahl's ocean expedition (see p79).

CLUBS

Oslo's club scene has been revitalized in recent years, and many venues charge upwards of 100kr entry. At many of the more fashionable spots, there is often a dress code of dark clothing and dark shoes, so it's best to not show up in trainers and jeans. **Blå** (see Jazz, above), in Grünerløkka, is a large space that is one of Oslo's

most popular venues to listen and dance to a range of live and DJ music. **Smuget** (see Jazz, above) is one of the city's best music and dance clubs, with a large dance floor and DJs playing to a diverse crowd. In the centre, expect long queues at **Pi, The Villa** and **Saktor**, all good hotspots for techno and electronica; keep an eye out for discount student nights at each.

Popular with the chic crowd is **LivingRoom**, while the retro-styled **Robinet** has a hedonistic feel. More mainstream options include **Bryggeporten Bar & Nattklubb**; **Galleriet**, with three floors comprising a live jazz club, dance club and pop bar; and **Headline**, which plays more mellow music. A long-standing favourite for electronic music is **Sikamikanico**, which is still thriving since its opening in 1995.

Revellers strut their stuff in one of Oslo's nightclubs

DIRECTORY

THEATRES

Amfiscene
Johanne Dybwadsplass 1.
Tel 81 50 08 11.

Akershus Castle and Fortress
Akerhus Festning.
Tel 23 09 39 17.

Chat Noir
Klingenberggata 5.
Tel 22 83 22 02.

Den Åpne Teater
Tøyenbekken 34.
Tel 22 05 28 00.

Det Norske Teatret
Kristian IV Gate 8.
Tel 22 42 43 44.

Ibsenmuseet
Henrik Ibsens Gate 26.
Tel 22 12 35 50.

M/S Innvik
Langakaia.
Tel 22 41 95 00.

Nationaltheatret
Johanne Dybwadsplass 1.
Tel 81 50 08 11.

Oslo Nye Teater
Rosenkrantz Gate 10.
Tel 22 34 86 00.

Oslo Spektrum
Sonja Henies Plass 2.
Tel 22 05 29 00.

Parkteatret
Olaf Ryes Plass 11.
Tel 22 35 63 11.

Rockefeller Music Hall
Torggata 16.
Tel 22 20 32 32.

CLASSICAL MUSIC, OPERA & BALLET

Chateau Neuf
Slemdalsveien 7.
Tel 22 96 15 00.

Oslo Konserthus
Munkedamsveien 14.
Tel 23 11 31 00.

Den Norske Opera / Nasjonalballetten
Kirsten Flagstads Pass 1.
Tel 21 42 21 00.

Oslo Kirkemusikkfestival
Tollbugata 28.
Tel 22 41 81 13.

Sentrum Scene
Arbeidersamfunnets Plass 1.
Tel 22 98 24 00.

Ultima Contemporary Music Festival
Kongensgate 4.
Tel 22 42 99 99.

Underwater Pub
Dalsbergstien 4.
Tel 22 46 05 26.

FOLK DANCING

Dansens Hus
Kristian IV's Gate.
Tel 22 42 00 60.

Norsk Folkemuseum
Museumsveien 10.
Tel 22 12 37 00.

CINEMAS

Filmens Hus
Dronningens Gate 16.
Tel 22 47 45 00.

Filmteateret Teletorg
Stortingsgaten 16.
Tel 82 03 00 01.

Kinematografer Oslo
Olav V's Gate 4.
Tel 82 03 00 01.

Saga Kino
Stortingsgata 28.
Tel 82 03 00 00.

ROCK, BLUES, COUNTRY & IRISH

Blitz
Pilestredet 30C.
Tel 22 11 23 49.

Café Mono
Pløensgate 4.
Tel 22 41 41 66.

Elm Street Rock Café
Dronningens Gate 32.
Tel 22 42 14 27.

Garage Oslo
Grensen 9.
Tel 22 42 37 44.

Gloria Flames
Grønland 18.
Tel 22 17 16 00.

Last Train
Karl Johans Gate 45.
Tel 22 41 52 93.

Muddy Waters
Grensen 13.
Tel 22 40 33 70.

Sound of Mu
Markveien 58.

JAZZ

Bar Boca
Thorvald Meyers Gate 30.
Tel 22 04 10 80.

Blå
Brenneriveien 9C.
Tel 22 20 91 81.

Café Con Bar
Brugata 11.
Tel 22 05 02 00.

Herr Nilsens Pub
Cl Hambros plass 5.
Tel 22 33 54 05.

Smuget
Rosenkrantz Gate 22.
Tel 22 42 52 62.

BARS & CAFES

Aku-Aku
Thorvald Meyers Gate 32.

Bar 1
Holmens Gate 3.
Tel 22 83 00 02.

Choice
Grønlandsleiret 38.
Tel 22 12 23 00.

Fru Hagen
Thorvald Meyers Gate 40.
Tel 22 35 67 87.

Kaos
Thorvald Meyers Gate 56.
Tel 22 04 69 90.

Oslomekaniskeverksted
Tøynebekken 34.
Tel 22 05 28 14.

Parkteatret
Olav Ryes Plass 11.
Tel 22 35 63 00.

Skybar
Sonja Henie Plass 3.
Tel 22 05 80 00.

Stargate
Grønlandsleiveret 2.
Tel 22 12 23 00.

SüdØst
Trondheimsveien 5.
Tel 22 35 30 70.

Tea Lounge
Thorvald Meyers Gate 33B.
Tel 22 37 07 05.

CLUBS

Bryggeporten Bar & Nattklubb
Stranden 1.
Tel 22 87 72 00.

Galleriet
Kristian IV's Gate 12.
Tel 22 97 97 97.

Headline
Rosenkrantz Gate 16.
Tel 22 41 02 02.

LivingRoom
Olav V's Gate 1.
Tel 40 00 33 60.

Pi
Storgata 24.

Robinet
Mariboes Gate 7.

Saktor
Karl Johans Gate 6B.
Tel 22 41 00 14.

Sikamikanico
Stortorvet 10.
Tel 22 41 44 09.

The Villa
Møllergata 23.

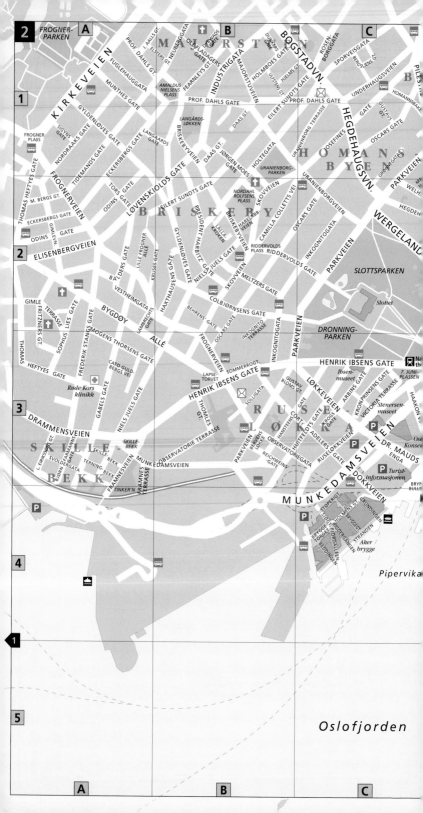

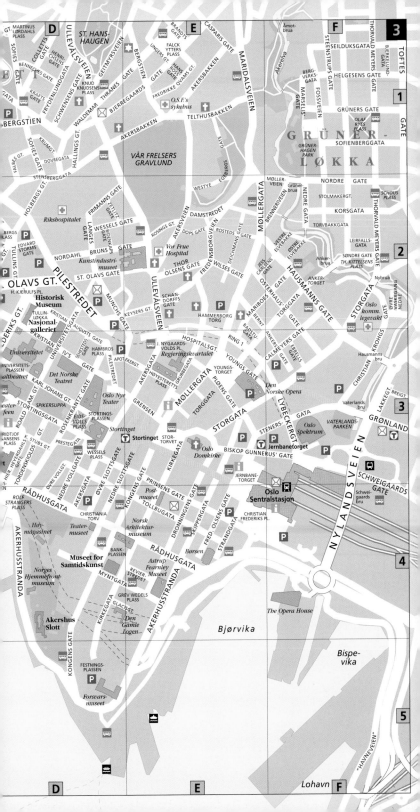

Street Finder Index

AROUND OSLOFJORDEN

he oldest settlements in the area surrounding Oslofjorden date from the Stone Age and Bronze Age, and it was here on the eastern and western shores that three of the best preserved Viking ships were unearthed. Although the land around the fjord close to Oslo is built-up, further south it is a haven of serene villages with quaint clapboard houses, quiet islands and boats galore.

The sight of Oslofjorden on a summer's day teeming with ferries, cruise boats, yachts and leisure craft is breathtaking. The 100-km (60-miles) long fjord extends deep inland from the Skagerrak to the port of Oslo. It narrows around Drøbak before opening out closer to the capital. The counties of Akershus and Østfold lie to the east, and Buskerud and Vestfold to the west.

More than one million people live around the shore in some of the oldest towns and villages in the country. Many of these settlements have a long history of trading and seafaring. The entire region bears evidence of its proximity to the capital. The infrastructure is well developed, road connections are good and Europe's longest road tunnel beneath the sea, 7.2 km (4 miles) long, links Frogn on the east with Hurum on the west. Many

people who work in Oslo commute from their homes around the fjord.

The Oslofjorden area offers a combination of an ancient cultural heritage alongside modern industry and commerce. Away from the industrial areas, the coast is peppered with islands large and small, inlets and coves, holiday resorts and marinas, and clusters of painted summer cabins. There are castles and Viking burial mounds to explore, and colourful timber-built villages to relax in with museums and art galleries. Boating, fishing, swimming and walking are among the many pursuits on offer.

Summers are usually warm in this region. Stavern *(see p125)* holds the record for 200 days of sunshine a year. The winters are seldom severe, and the amount of snow varies from place to place according to how high up or how far inland it is situated.

Badeparken at Drøbak, one of the most visited beaches on the eastern side of Oslofjorden

◁ Figurehead decorating one of the many timber houses in picturesque Drøbak

Halden ❶

County of Østfold. 🏙 28,000.
🚌 🚉 ℹ️ Torget 2, 69 19 09 80.
🎪 Food and Wooden Boat Festival
(4th weekend Jun).
www.visithalden.com

The town of Halden is the gateway to Norway for those arriving from Sweden to the southern regions. It is set back on Iddefjorden between a beautiful archipelago on one side and forests and lakes on the other. The town developed in the 16th and 17th centuries as an outpost on the border with Sweden. It has many well-preserved old buildings, and clusters of Neo-Classical houses.

Halden's crowning glory is **Frederiksten Festning**, an imposing fortress straddling the ridge above the town, complete with ramparts and powder houses and a warren of passageways. The first fortifications were built around 1643–5, and it was here, in 1718, that the Swedish king, Karl XII, was shot during his second attempt to attack the fortress.

The fortress comprises the citadel, beyond which lies Borgerskansen and three outlying forts facing south and east: Gyldenløve, Stortårnet and Overberget. The fortress museums contain extensive collections of war history and civil memorabilia. There is a pharmacy from the 1870s, and the old bakery and brewery in the inner fort.

The canal, Haldenkanalen, is part of Haldenvassdraget, which flows through a series

Historic Sarpsborg's busy commercial centre

of large lakes. Boats can navigate the 75-km (46-miles) stretch between Tistedal and Skulerud through three groups of locks. The 26.6-m (87-ft) high Brekke Locks, comprising four chambers, are the highest locks in northern Europe.

The M/S *Turisten* operates between Tistedal and Strømsfoss and Strømsfoss and Ørje in summer.

♠ Frederiksten Festning
1 km (half a mile) S of the centre.
Tel 69 19 09 80. **Fortress** ⬜ all year.
Museum ⬜ 18 May–31 Aug: daily;
Sep: Sun. 🎫 🗎 ♿ 🚻 ☐ ☐

Sarpsborg ❷

County of Østfold. 🏙 52,000.
🚌 🚉 ℹ️ Glengsgata, 69 15 65 35.
🎪 Gleng Music Festival (May/Jun),
Olav's Festival (end Aug).

King Olav the Holy founded Sarpsborg in 1016, making it Norway's third oldest town. In fact, its history can be traced back 7,000 years

through the discovery of burial mounds, primitive fortifications, stone monuments and rock carvings. At nearby Tune, the Viking ship, Tuneskipet, from around AD 900 was unearthed *(see p85)*.

The Glomma river and the waterfall, Sarpsfossen, formed the backbone of the commercial development of the town. The rivers were used for floating timber to the sawmills. The harbour became the country's second largest port for timber in the 19th century and the timber industry is still important to the town today.

Borgarsyssel Museum was opened in 1929 in the area where Olav the Holy had his castle. The ruins can be seen, as can those of a church, Nikolaskirken, from 1115. Medieval stonework from the region is exhibited in Steinhoggerhallen. In the museum's main building, the Østfoldgalleriet contains collections of folk art, arts and crafts and industrial products such as Rococo-style glazed earthenware from Herrebøe. Outside there is a monastic garden with herbs.

The open-air section features a collection of historic houses. Among them is a workmen's dwelling house, St Olavs Vold, from the 1840s. It is made up of 20 apartments each with one room and a kitchen.

🏛 Borgarsyssel Museum
Gamlebygaten 8. **Tel** 69 11 56 50.
⬜ Jun–Aug: daily; Sep–Apr:
Tue–Fri. ⬤ public hols. 🎫 🗎 ☐

Fredriksten Festning providing a dramatic backdrop to Halden

Fredrikstad ❸

See pp118–19.

Hankø ❹

County of Østfold. 🚌 *302 from Fredrikstad to Vikane.* 🚲 ⛴ ℹ *Turistinformasjonen, Fredrikstad, 69 30 46 00.*

The island of Hankø lies to the west of Fredrikstad toward the outer part of Oslofjorden. It became especially popular as a holiday resort in the 1950s and 1960s when King Olav had a summer residence, Bloksberg, here.

Although Hankø presents a bare rock face to the fjord, its sheltered eastern side is forested, providing a much favoured harbour and anchorage. The Norwegian Association of Yachting was founded here in 1882, since when the island has been a venue for national regattas, sailing races and world championship events.

Rowing has also had a long tradition on Hankø. The Fredrikstad Rowing Club was established here around 1870.

Galleri 15 occupying the manor house of Alby on Jeløy, near Moss

Moss ❺

County of Østfold. 👥 *28,000.* 🚉 🚌 ⛴ ℹ *Skogaten 52, 69 24 15 20.* 🎨 *Momentum Art Festival (end Aug–Oct).* **www**.visitmoss.no

An important industrial and trading centre for the County of Østfold, Moss is also known for its art galleries and streets lined with sculptures. Its harbour has long been a junction for boat traffic on Oslofjorden and today car ferries continually ply between Moss and Horten.

The Town and Industry Museum, **Moss by- og Industrimuseum**, charts Moss's industrial development.

Konventionsgården was built in 1778 and is the main building of Moss Jernverk (Moss Ironworks), which was constructed in the mid-18th century. It was here that the Moss Convention was signed in 1814 to ratify the union between Norway and Sweden rather than Denmark.

Moss is protected to the west by the island of Jeløy, once a peninsula connected to the mainland in the southeast. A canal, dug between Mossesundet and Værlebukta, cut Jeløy from the mainland, but did not deter a rash of house-building here in the 1960s. The manor house on the Alby Gods estate on Jeløy is the location for an art gallery, **Galleri F15**. The elegant Refsnes Gods is now a hotel *(see p230)*.

North of Moss is the idyllic harbour village of **Son**, a popular excursion spot. The buildings in the centre of Son recall a time in the 18th century when the timber trade, shipping and commerce, spinning and the production of spirits were thriving industries.

Son has charming little streets, an eco museum, a museum harbour, coastal cultural activities, exhibitions and many cosy places to eat.

🏛 **Moss by- og Industrimuseum**
Fossen 21–23. **Tel** 69 24 83 60.
⭕ *Tue–Fri & Sun.* ⚫ *public hols.*
♿♿

🏛 **Galleri F15**
Alby Gård 4 km (2 miles) W of Moss.
Tel 69 27 10 33. ⭕ *Tue–Sun.* ⚫ *some public hols.* 🏷♿♿🔲🔲

Hankø, a favourite haunt for yachting enthusiasts

Drøbak, south of Oslo, at Oslofjorden's narrowest point

Drøbak 6

County of Akershus. 🏠 *14,000.* 🚢
☀ *summer.* ℹ *Havnegaten 4, 64
93 50 87.* 🎭 *Oscarsborg plays (Jul).*

Half an hour's drive south of
Oslo on the eastern side of
Oslofjorden is the attractive
wooden village of Drøbak.
Originally it was a pilot
station and served as Oslo's
winterport when the fjord
closer to the capital was ice
bound. Today the village,
with its narrow 18th- and
19th-century streets, is a
popular place to live and a
favourite summer holiday spot.
From here, the 7.2-km (4.5-
mile) Oslofjord Tunnel, opened
in 2000, runs deep under the
fjord to its western shore.

Drøbak has Norway's
largest permanent year-round
Christmas exhibition with
Julehus (Christmas House)
and Julenissens Postkontor
(a post office, run by Father
Christmas's pixie-like helper).
The main square, Torget, and
the adjoining streets have
shops, art galleries and places
to eat. Badeparken, a park
area with a beach, is close by.

At the small harbour,
the sea-water aquarium,
Saltvannsakvariet, displays
local species of fish and
other marine life. Next to
it, **Drøbak Båtforenings
Maritime Samlinger** (the
Maritime Collection), focuses
on the area's coastal heritage.
Close to the centre, on
Seiersten, is **Follo Museum**

with a collection of 200–300-
year-old buildings.

On an island just west of
Drøbak lies **Oscarsborg
Festning**. The fortress is best
known for its role in the
sinking of the German
warship, *Blücher*, on 9 April
1940. Torpedoes fired from
here hit the vessel as it made
its way toward Oslo with the
first occupational forces on
board. This delayed the
occupation and gave the king
time to flee. In summer, plays
are staged at the fortress.

🏛 **Drøbak Båtforenings
Maritime Samlinger**
Kroketønna 4. **Tel** *64 93 50 87.*
◯ *Jun–Aug: daily.* 🎫

🏛 **Follo Museum**
Belsjøveien 17. **Tel** *64 93 99 90.* 🚌
504. ◯ *Jun–mid-Sep: Tue–Fri & Sun;
mid-Sep–May: Wed–Fri & Sun.* 🔵
some public hols. 🎫 🅿 ♿ 🚻 🛍 🍴

⚓ **Oscarsborg Festning**
Kaholmene. **Tel** *81 55 19 00.*
🚢 *from Sjøtorget to Drøbak.*
◯ *Jun–Aug: daily.* 🎫 🅿

Tusenfryd 7

County of Akershus. **Tel** *64 97 64 97.*
🚌 *special bus from Oslo Bussterminal
every half hour 10am–1pm.* ◯ *May–
Sep: daily.* 🎫 ♿ 🚻 🛍 🍴

Norway's largest amusement
park, Tusenfryd, is situated in
a rural location 20 km (12
miles) south of Oslo at the
intersection of the E6 and the
E18 motorways.

The park's main attraction is
Thundercoaster, the biggest
wooden roller-coaster in
Northern Europe. Opened in
2001, it thrills visitors with
drops of 32 m (105 ft).

There are numerous rides,
places to eat, shops and
entertainments in addition to
an area for water activities.
Nearly half a million guests
visit Tusenfryd every year.

**One of many rides at Tusenfryd
amusement park**

Henie Onstad
Kunstsenter 8

County of Akershus. **Tel** *67 80 48 80.*
🚌 *151, 152 from Oslo.* ◯
*11am–7pm Tue–Fri, 11am–5pm
Sat & Sun.* 🎫 🎦 ♿ 🅿 🚻 🛍 🍴
www.hok.no

The remarkable centre for
modern art, Henie Onstad
Kunstsenter, was a gift to the
nation from the three-times

Henie Onstad Kunstsenter, a fine collection of modern art

Olympic gold medal-winning skater, Sonja Henie (1928, 1932, 1936), and her husband, Niels Onstad. It houses the couple's art collection, including works by Matisse, Bonnard, Picasso and Miró, as well as Expressionist and abstract painters from the post-war period such as Estève and Soulages.

The trophy collection from Sonja Henie's exceptional sporting career is also on show. Alongside are the medals and cups she received for her outstanding performances in figure skating at the Olympic Games and in no fewer than 10 world championships.

The museum has a library, auditorium, a children's workshop, shop, café and an excellent restaurant.

Borre National Park with its many burial mounds from the Viking age

Model of a three-masted ship at Marinemuseet, Horten

Horten ⑨

County of Vestfold. 🏘 17,000. 🚉 to Skoppum 10 km (6 miles) W of town. ✈ 🚲 🛈 Tollbugata 1A, 33 03 17 08. **www**.visithorten.com

A bronze statue known as Hortenspiken (the Girl from Horten) welcomes visitors approaching the town from the north. The boat she is holding hints that this is a harbour town popular with pleasure boat owners. Horten developed around the 19th-century naval base of Karljohansvern, with its shipyard and harbour. In the well-preserved garrison buildings is **Marinemuseet**. Established in 1853, it is the oldest naval museum in the world. The museum contains an extensive collection of model ships, artifacts and exhibits relating to naval history. The world's first torpedo boat, *Rap*, 1872, is on display outside. A recent acquisition is the submarine, KNM *Utstein*, 1965, which is open to the public.

Next door is **Norsk Museum for Fotografi** (the Norwegian Museum of Photography). Cameras, photographs and other items are used to illustrate the development of the art.

Horten town centre, with its timber houses, retains much of its 19th-century character. In summer, the streets are decorated with flowers, and speed restrictions force cars to drive slowly. Outdoor cafés add to the charming atmosphere. But the town's main claim to fame is Storgaten, said to be Norway's longest shopping street.

Figurehead, Marinemuseet

🏛 **Marinemuseet**
Karljohansvern, 1 km (half a mile) E of the centre. **Tel** 33 03 33 97. ◯ May–Sep: daily; Oct–Apr: Sun. ● public hols. 🎫 ♿ 🛈

🏛 **Norsk Museum for Fotografi**
Karljohansvern, 1 km (half a mile) E of the centre. **Tel** 33 03 16 30. ◯ noon–5pm Tue–Sun. 🎫 📷 ♿ 🛈 🛈

Borre National Park ⑩

County of Vestfold. **Tel** 33 07 18 50. 🚌 01 from Horten. Park ◯ all year.
Midgard Historical Centre
◯ 11am–6pm daily. ● public hols; Sep–May: Mon. 🎫 📷 ♿ 🛈 🛈

The site of the most extensive collection of kings' graves in Scandinavia, Borre has seven large and 21 smaller burial mounds. Excavations at the end of the 1980s revealed that the oldest of the mounds dates from AD 600, i.e. before the Viking age, and it is likely that some of the mounds contain kings of the Ynglinge dynasty who had settled in Vestfold after fleeing from Sweden. The burial ground was used for another 300 years. A remarkable selection of craftwork has been unearthed. Given the name Borrestilen, the pieces feature intricate animal and knot ornaments, which were often used to decorate harnesses. The finds also confirm that the mounds might have contained ships similar to the Gokstad and Oseberg ships discovered around Oslofjorden (*see pp84–5*).

Borre was Norway's first national park. The grassy mounds are set among woodlands in a well-tended area at the water's edge. Each season offers outdoor events with a historic theme, such as Viking Age Markets. The Historical Centre has displays of finds from the area.

A Trip from Tønsberg to Verdens Ende ⓫

The shortest route between Tønsberg and the
southernmost tip of Tjøme, otherwise known as
World's End, is just 30 km (19 miles), but plenty of
time is needed to explore this stunning archipelago,
especially on the eastern side. The tour passes
through a string of attractive holiday resorts. There
are pretty coves, narrow sounds, old skipper's
houses and quaint boathouses. Bridges connect
the larger islands and the sea is never far away
for a refreshing swim.

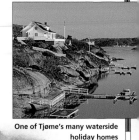

**One of Tjøme's many waterside
holiday homes**

Tønsberg ①
Founded in 871, Tønsberg
was a prosperous trading
centre in the Middle Ages.
The 19th-century tower,
Slottsfjelltarnet, was
built on the ruins of
an ancient castle.

Nøtterøy ②
Between Tønsberg
and Tjøme lies the
archipelago of
Nøtterøy comprising
175 islands. Nøtterøy
has a number of
ancient monuments,
including a
12th-century church.

Tjøme ③
The popular holiday area of
Tjøme comprises 478 islands.
The main island has many
attractive old houses.

KEY

▪ Tour route

⁼ Other routes

TIPS FOR DRIVERS

Starting point: Tønsberg is the
starting point for driving to the
islands of Nøtterøy and Tjøme.
Length: about 20 km (12 miles).
Places to eat: there are many
places to eat en route, including
a restaurant at Verdens Ende.

Verdens Ende ④
The lighthouse at Verdens
Ende, standing on the
southernmost tip of
Tjøme, is distinguished by
its pivoting fire basket.

Map labels: SANDEFJORD, HORTEN, OSLOFJORDEN, 312, 311, 510, 428, 308, 505, 309, 410, Snipe-torp, 409, Kjøpmanns-skjær, 415, 309, Arøysund, 390, 392, 391, Grimestad, 308, 390, 385, Tjøme, Ormelett, Hvasser, 308, 388

0 kilometres 3
0 miles 2

Sandefjord's whaling monument by Knut Steen, 1969

Sandefjord ⑫

County of Vestfold. 🏠 43,000.
⊠ 🚉 🚌 🚢 ℹ️ Thor Dahls Gate 1,
33 46 05 90. 🎭 Midsummer Boat
Procession (23 Jun), Summer Show
on Rika (Jul), Classical Music on a
Summer Night (1st and 2nd week Jul),
Christmas Market (last week Nov).

The present town of
Sandefjord is relatively new,
but archaeological finds from
the Bronze and Viking Ages,
such as the Viking ship
unearthed at Gokstadhaugen
in 1880 *(see pp84–5)*, point to
a long history of trading and
seafaring. The harbour on the
fjord was known around 1200.
In 1800, Sandfjord was burned
to the ground and rebuilt.

Until the early 20th century,
the spa, **Kurbadet** (1837),
was renowned for its health-
giving mud bath. It has been
restored and is now a
protected building, although
the mud bath is no more.

Whaling was a dominant
industry at Sandfjord for many
years until it was halted in
1968. **Hvalfangstmuseet** (the
Whaling Museum) shows the
development of the industry
from the primitive methods
of catching whales to the
introduction of factory ships.
There is a special section on
Arctic and Antarctic animal life.

The whaling monument on
Strandpromenaden was
designed by Knut Steen.

🎪 **Kurbadet**
Thor Dahls Gate. **Tel** 33 46 58 57.
🕐 for cultural events and guided
tours only. 📷 by prior arrangement.

🏛 **Hvalfangstmuseet**
Museumsgate 39. **Tel** 33 48 46 50.
🕐 daily. ● some public hols.
📷 🎥 🛗 🚻 📷

Larvik ⑬

County of Vestfold. 🏠 42,000.
⊠ 🚉 🚌 🚢 ℹ️ Storgata 48,
33 13 91 00. 🎭 Herregårdsspille
plays (mid-Jul), Jazz concerts (Fri in
summer). **www**.visitlarvik.no

Larvik came into its own in
the 17th century, when Ulrik
Frederik Gyldenløve was
appointed count of Larvik
and the county of Laurvigen.
In 1671 the town achieved
market town status.

The count's residence,
Herregården, was built in
1677 and is one of Norway's
finest secular Baroque
buildings. In 1835 the estate
was acquired by the Treschow
family who have played a
prominent role in Larvik's
economic life since then,
mostly in the forestry industry
alongside the Fritzøes. The
Larvik Museum, in a manor
house south of the town,
charts their business dealings
from 1600 onwards.

Larvik Sjøfartsmuseum
(Maritime Museum) focuses
on the nautical history of
Larvik, particularly the age of
sailing ships. Models by the
famous boat-builder, Colin
Archer, are on display and
there is an exhibition on Thor
Heyerdahl. Larvik is also

known for being the location
of Norway's only mineral
water spring.

🎪 **Herregården**
Herregårdssletta 6. **Tel** 33 13 06 58.
🕐 end Jun–mid-Aug: Tue–Sun;
mid-Aug–Sep & May–end Jun: Sun.
● public hols. 📷 📷

🏛 **Larvik Museum**
Nedre Fritzøe Gate 2. **Tel** 98 23 12
90. 🕐 end Jun–mid Aug: Tue–Sun;
mid-Aug–end Jun: Sun ● public
hols. 📷 📷 🛗 📷 📷

🏛 **Larvik Sjøfartsmuseum**
Kirkestredet 5. **Tel** 98 23 12 90.
🕐 end Jun–mid-Aug: Tue–Sun;
mid-Aug–Sep & May–end Jun: Sun.
● public hols. 📷 📷 🛗

Stavern ⑭

County of Vestfold. 🏠 2,000. 🚉 to
Larvik. 🚌 ℹ️ summer: Skippergaten
6, 33 19 73 00; winter: Larvik, 33 13
91 00. 🎭 Stavern Festival (Jun/Jul).
www.visitlarvik.no

A quaint mixture of old and
new, Stavern is a charming
place beloved by holiday-
makers. In summer the
population more than
doubles, due partly to the
town's record of more than
200 days of sunshine a year.

From the mid-1750s until
1864, Stavern was Norway's
main naval base with a
shipyard, Fredriksvern.
A gunpowder tower and
commandant's house remain
on Citadelløya (Citadel Island),
today a refuge for artists. The
town is made up of wooden
buildings, most of them
brightly painted in what is
known as "Stavern yellow".
Minnehallen, a monument
with a plaque containing
the names of seamen killed
during World Wars I and II,
is a fitting memorial to those
who lost their lives.

Herregården, Larvik, an example of Norwegian Baroque

Kongsvinger ❶

County of Hedmark. 🚶 *17,500.*
🚊 🚌 ℹ️ *Jernbaneplassen 5, 62
82 34 00.* 🎪 *Kongsvinger Market
(1st week May & last week Sep).*

The fortress town of
Kongsvinger, situated on the
Glomma River, was estab-
lished during the Hannibal
Feud in 1644 when a
fortification was built here
which grew to become a
solid fortress. Øvrebyen (the
Upper Town) was situated
near the castle ramparts.

With the arrival of the railway in the 1860s, Kongsvinger
became a market town. New
building was concentrated
around the train station. Later,
the quarter between the
station and Øvrebyen developed into the town centre,
and a bridge and town hall
were built. In 1965 the town
was designated as a "Development Centre" which led
to industrial expansion.

Kongsvinger Festning
(Fortress) is an irregular
star-shaped castle with 16
batteries, fine old buildings
and a museum of the armed
forces. From the castle
ramparts there is a splendid
view over the town and
river toward Sweden.

The forests between
Glomma and the Swedish
border were settled by
Finnish immigrants in the
17th century. **Finnetunet**, a
museum of Finnish culture at
Svullrya, in Grue Finnskog, is
made up of 13 buildings, the
oldest dating from the end of
the 18th century. It gives a
picture of farming culture and
the daily life of the people of

Houses at the Glomdalsmuseet, Elverum, recalling a bygone era

Finnskogene (Finn Forest). A
hiking track, Finnskogleden,
heads north through the
forests from Finnetunet.

🏰 **Kongsvinger Festning**
1 km (half a mile) N of town centre.
Tel 99 09 65 11. **Castle area** ☐
daily. **Museum** ☐ *Jun–Aug: daily.*

🏰 **Finnetunet**
40 km (25 miles) NE of Kongsvinger.
Tel 62 94 56 90. ☐ *Jun–Aug: daily.*
🅿️ ✔️ 🚻

Elverum ❷

County of Hedmark. 🚶 *19,500.* 🚊
🚌 ℹ️ *Storgata 24, 62 40 90 45.*
🎪 *Grundsetmart'n (Mar), Elverum
Football Tournament (Jun), Culture
Festival (Aug), Nordic Hunting and
Fishing Days (Aug).*

On 9 April 1940, the day
of the German invasion, the
Norwegian Parliament
approved the Elverum
Mandate, giving the fleeing
Norwegian government
considerable powers for the
remainder of World War II. The
following day King Haakon

rejected Germany's demand for
a new Norwegian government.
On 11 April, Elverum was
bombed; 54 people died. At
the high school, a monument
by Ørnulf Bast commemorates
the king's stand.

The city quickly rose from
the ashes after the war to
become an administrative,
commercial, educational and
military centre.

The quarter on the eastern
side of the Glomma River is
known as Leiret, and evolved
from the buildings below the
old fortification, Christiansfjell.
Grundsetmart'n, a winter
market that between 1740 and
1900 was the most important in
Scandinavia, is still held here.

Glomdalsmuseet, Norway's
third-largest open-air museum,
is a comprehensive collection
of 88 buildings from the
mountain villages and rural
lowland communities and
contains some 30,000 exhibits.

Connected by a bridge
across the Glomma is
Norsk Skogbruksmuseum
(the Norwegian Forestry
Museum), founded in 1954.
This is the only museum in
the country specializing in
forestry, hunting and fishing.
The open-air section features
different types of buildings,
from lumberjack cottages to
fishing huts and boathouses.

🏛️ **Glomdalsmuseet**
Museumsveien 15. *Tel 62 41 91 00.*
☐ *Jun–Aug: daily; Sep–May: Sun
only.* 🅿️ ✔️ ♿ 🛒 🚻

🏛️ **Norsk Skogsbruksmuseum**
Solørveien 151. *Tel 62 40 90 00.*
☐ *daily.* ● *some public hols.*
🅿️ ✔️ ♿ 🍴 🛒 🚻

Kongsvinger Festning and the panoramic view toward Sweden

Trysil ❸

County of Hedmark. 🏠 7,000.
🚌 🚆 Storveien 3, 62 45 10 00.
🎿 Trysil Ski Season Finale (end Apr),
Swingin' Trysil Blues, Jazz and Rock
Festival (end Jun), Sund Market (Sep).
www.trysil.com

In the past, the road through
the forest from Elverum to
Trysil was known as "the
seven-mile forest". The trip
used to be very slow for
drivers with heavy loads, but
today the roads are good and
the journey quick. Trysil is a
typical woodland valley with
spruce and pine forests and
marshland topped by
mountainous terrain.

The valley follows
the Trysil River from
the lake of Femunden
to the Swedish
border. Femunden
is Norway's third-
largest lake,
stretching 60 km
(37 miles) north.
Ferries operate
in summer. The
administrative centre
is at Innbygda.

**Snowboarder on
Trysilfjellet**

The mountain of **Trysilfjellet**
(1,137 m/3,730 ft) is the site
for Norway's biggest alpine
skiing centre. Sports fishing is
good in the Trysilelva and
"little" Ljøra.

In the eastern wilderness is
**Femundsmarka National
Park**, where the Svukuriset
tourist lodge is located,
and **Gutulia National Park**
with its 300–400-year-old
primeval forests.

Østerdalen and Rendalen ❹

County of Hedmark. 🏠 28,000. 🚆
🚌 ℹ️ Alvdal Tourist Information,
Aukrustsentret 2560, 62 48 89 99.

The two valleys of Østerdalen
and Rendalen run parallel in a
south-north direction. The
RV3 road through Østerdalen
follows the Glomma,
Norway's longest river, past
several places of interest.
Rena, the next town north of
Elverum, had a ferry crossing
already in the Middle Ages, as
well as accommodation for
pilgrims on their way to the
cathedral of Nidarosdomen
(see p199). Today, Rena is a
skiing centre and the starting
point for the Birkebeiner race
(see p136). A further 55 km
(34 miles) upriver,
Koppang has a folk
museum with
buildings from
the region. North
of Atna, the road
runs through virtually
uninhabited forest,
passing **Jutulhogget**, a
precipitously deep gorge.

Further north, in the small
town of **Alvdal**, the Husantu-
net is a folk museum with
17 houses from around 1600,
while **Aukrustsenteret** has
paintings and drawings
featuring colourful characters
from the books of author and
illustrator Kjell Aukrust. Alvdal
is the starting point for
family-friendly mountain
walks and also of Norway's

**Jutulhogget, a gorge more than
100m (328 ft) deep**

second-highest *turistvei* (tourist road), which runs to the
top of the 1,666-m (5,466-ft)
high **Tronfjellet** mountain.

At Tynset, the RV30 leads
northeast to the old mining
centre of **Tolga** and the village
of **Os**, close to the county
boundary with Trøndelag.

Rendalen valley can be
reached by taking the RV30
south from Tynset through
Tylldalen, where the harvest-
related feast day of **Olsok** (St
Olav's Day) is celebrated on
29 July. Alternatively, a road
from Hanestad, south of
Alvdal, leads to the valley
across the mountain passes,
ending at the church of **Øvre
Rendal** at Bergset, which
dates from 1759. Its vicarage
has a museum dedicated to
Jacob B Bull, who wrote
about daily life in the region.
From here, there is a mountain
road to the fishing village of
Fiskevollen on Sølensjøen
lake, and the 1,755-m (5,758-ft)
high mountain of Rendalsølen.

The RV30 runs from Bergset
south along the valley toward
Otnes by **Lomnessjøen** lake, a
particularly beautiful part of
Rendalen. Rushing south from
the lake, the Åkrestrømmen is
renowned for its abundance
of Common white fish
(*Coregonus lavaretus*). From
here the RV217 leads to two
other famous fishing spots –
Galten and **Isterfossen** – 45 km
(28 miles) to the northeast.

Åkrestrømmen ends in Stors-
jøen ("Big Lake") from where
the river Rena runs south to
join the Glomma at Rena.

🏛️ **Aukrustsenteret**
Alvdal centre. **Tel** 62 48 78 77.
⏰ May–mid-Oct: daily, mid-Oct–Apr:
by arrangement.

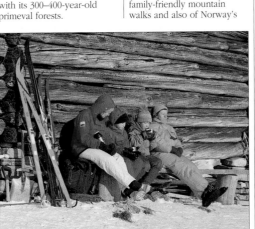

An old farm wall providing a sheltered resting place for skiers

Mjøsa

Counties of Hedmark & Oppland.
ℹ️ *Hamar, 62 51 75 00; Lillehammer, 61 28 98 00.*

Norway's largest lake, Mjøsa, is 117 km (72 miles) long and lies at the heart of an agricultural area. Many of the farms in Hedemarken, Helgøya and Totenlandet have been settlements since Viking times. They are bordered by forests and mountains, including Skreiafjellene (700 m/2,296 ft). Three towns, Lillehammer *(see pp136–37)*, Hamar and Gjøvik are spread around the lakeshore.

Before the arrival of cars and trains, Mjøsa was an important communications centre, even in winter when horses and sledges would cross the frozen lake. The completion of the railway to Eidsvoll in 1854 led to the arrival of a paddle steamer, *Skibladner*, known as "The White Swan of Mjøsa". Built in Sweden, it was transported to Mjøsa in pieces and reassembled. Today Norway's oldest ship ferries people between the Mjøsa towns.

Helgøya, "the holy island", situated in the widest part of the lake, was the site of medieval mansions for bishops and the aristocracy, and a seat for the king. Among the farming estates are Hovinsholm and Baldishol, where the Baldishol Tapestry (1200) was found *(see page 59)*. Further north, between Brumunddal and Moelv, lies Rudshøgda, the childhood home of the writer and singer, Alf Prøysen.

Hamar's ruined 16th-century cathedral encased in a glass dome

Hamar 6

County of Hedmark. 👥 28,000. 🚉 🚌 ℹ️ *summer: Akersvikaveien 1, 62 51 75 03.* 🎪 *Hamar Market (Aug/Sep).*

Hamar is the largest town on Lake Mjøsa. It was a Norse market town from 1049 until 1567 when a fire destroyed the cathedral. In 1849 Hamar achieved town status.

The remains of the cathedral, **Domkirkeruinerna**, are protected by a glass dome. Built in 1100, the cathedral was noted for its triple nave, but after the fire and subsequent pillaging, only crumbling columns and arches give an idea of its original appearance.

Hedmarksmuseet is a folk museum comprising more than 50 traditional buildings and a monastery herb garden. Just 2 km (1 mile) away is the **Norsk Utvandrermuseum**, (Norwegian Emigrant Museum), with a section devoted to those who emigrated to North America. The Railway Museum, **Jernbanemuseet**, features a narrow-gauge

railway (the *Tertitbanen*), engines and railway carriages.

Looking like an upturned boat, **Hamar Olympic Hall** was built as a skating rink for the 1994 Winter Olympics. Akersvika, to the south of the town, hosts a bird sanctuary.

🏛 Domkirkeruinerna
Strandveien 100. **Tel** *62 54 27 00.*
⏰ *mid-May–Aug: daily; Sep–mid-May: by arrangement.* 📷 🚻 ♿ 🛍 📷

🏛 Hedmarksmuseet
Strandveien 100. **Tel** *62 54 27 00.*
⏰ *mid-May–Aug: daily; Sep–mid-May: by appointment.* 📷 📷 🛍 📷

🏛 Jernbanemuseet
Strandveien 163. **Tel** *62 51 31 60.*
⏰ *daily.* ● *public hols; Sep–May: Mon.* 📷 🛍 📷

🏛 Norsk Utvandrermuseum
Åkershagan. **Tel** *62 57 48 50.* ⏰ *Jun–Aug: daily; Sep–May: Tue–Thu.* ● *some pub hols.* 📷 📷 ♿ 🛍 📷

Lillehammer 7

See pp136–37.

Aulestad, the home of Bjørnstjerne Bjørnson in Østre Gausdal

Aulestad 8

County of Oppland. 👥 400. 🚌 ℹ️ *Lillehammer, 61 28 98 00.* 🎪 *Aulestad Festival (May).*

The writer Bjørnstjerne Bjørnson (1832–1910) bought the farm of Aulestad, in Østre Gausdal, 18 km (11 miles) northwest of Lillehammer, in 1874. The following year, he moved here with his wife, Karoline.

As well as writing stories, poems and plays, Bjørnson was an outstanding orator and a key politician. He was awarded the Nobel Prize for literature in 1903.

The author's home, known as **Dikterhjemmet på**

The paddle steamer, *Skibladner*, plying Lake Mjøsa since 1856

The countryside near Ringebu looking toward Lågen river

Aulestad, remains as it was when he lived here. It contains a varied selection of Bjørnson memorabilia and the couple's fine collections of sculptures and paintings, photographs and manuscripts. The property was bought by the state in 1922.

🏛 Dikterhjemmet på Aulestad
Follebu, 18 km (11 miles) NW of Lillehammer. *Tel 61 22 41 10.* ◯ *mid-May–Sep: daily.* 🎫 🎥 📷 🏪

Ringebu **9**

County of Oppland. 🚶 *4,600.* 🚆 🚌 ℹ *Ringebu Skysstasjon (Train Station), 61 28 47 00.* 🎿 *Alpine World Cup (1st week Mar).*

Situated on the river Gudbrandsdalslågen, the village of Ringebu is known for its stave church. The **Ringebu Stavkirke** dates from the 13th century. It was extended between 1630 and 1631 by the builder Werner Olsen, who rebuilt several stave churches in the Gudbrandsdalen valley. The doorway with dragon motifs is from the original stave church, while the altarpiece and pulpit are Baroque.

Environs
The long valley of **Gudbrandsdalen**, running from north of Lillehammer up past Dovrefjell (*see p138*), cuts through a beautiful landscape, with many roads providing access into the mountains. It is at its widest in the district of

Fron, where it has been compared to Germany's Mosel valley. The octagonal church of Sør-Fron, in Louis XVI style, dates from the 18th century. The area is also known for its distinctive brown goat cheese.

🔒 Ringebu Stavkirke
1 km (half a mile) S of town centre. *Tel 61 28 43 50.* ◯ *May–Aug: daily; Sep–Apr: by prior arrangement.* 🎫 *May–Aug.* 📷

Vinstra **10**

County of Oppland. 🚶 *6,000.* 🚆 🚌 ℹ *Vinstra Skysstasjon (Train Station), 61 28 98 04.* 🎿 *Titano Festival (Jul), Peer Gynt-Festival (Aug).*

At Vinstra, the **Peer Gynt-samlingen** contains considerable material on both the historical and the literary figure of Peer Gynt.

The 65-km (40-mile) long Peer Gyntveien (Peer Gynt Road) is a mountain toll road running west of the Gudbrandsdalen valley from Tretten to Vinstra. Offering splendid views, it passes a number of hotels and mountain lodges, among them Skeikampen, Gausdal, Gålå, Wadahl and Fefor. The highest point on the road is at 1,053 m (3,455 ft). At Gålå there is the open-air theatre, Gålåvatnet Friluftsteater, which stages a musical interpretation of Ibsen's original *Peer Gynt* every year in early August.

🏛 Peer Gynt-samlingen
Vinstra, town centre south. *Tel 61 29 20 04.* ◯ *end Jun–mid-Aug: daily.* 🎥 📷

PEER GYNT

Henrik Ibsen's dramatic poem, *Peer Gynt*, was written in 1867 and is regarded as the most important of all Norwegian literary works. Ibsen had hiked in the area north of Vinstra in 1862 and the farm, Hågå, where his supposed model, the hunter and habitual liar Peder Lauritsen, lived in the 17th century is situated next to the Peer Gynt Road on the northeastern side of the valley – an attraction in itself. Ibsen's play starts with Peer telling his mother, Åse, about the buck ride along Gjendineggen. Åse berates him for running around in the mountains rather than courting the heiress at the farm of Hægstad. So Peer goes there, but instead meets Solveig, who says she will wait for the adventurer "both winter and spring" and who becomes his redeemer.

The "Peer Gynt" farm at Hågå, northeast of Vinstra

Lillehammer ❼

The skier in the city's coat of arms signifies that Lillehammer has long been a popular winter sports centre. In 1994 it came to worldwide attention as the venue for the XVII Winter Olympic Games, but its skiing traditions go back to 1206 when the royal infant, Håkon Håkonsson, was carried to safety across the mountains by skiers *(see pp26–7)*. The annual Birkebeiner Race is run on skis from Rena in Østerdalen to Lillehammer in memory of the rescue. Tourists and painters alike have also been attracted to Lillehammer by the beautiful scenery and the quality of the light. The city's other claim to fame, the Maihaugen outdoor museum, is the legacy of Anders Sandvig, a dentist with a passion for antiques and old buildings, who settled here in 1885.

Historic vehicle in the Norsk Kjøretøyhistorisk Museum

The museum of Maihaugen depicting life in the rural communities

🏛 Maihaugen
Maihaugveien 1. *Tel* 61 28 89 00. ☐ 1 Jun–30 Sep: daily; 1 Oct–16 May: Tue–Sun. ◐ public hols. 🏛🎫👥🚻🛒🛍

In 1887 Anders Sandvig established one of the biggest museums of farming culture in Norway, De Sandvigske Samlinger in Maihaugen.

Sandvig was a dentist who, during his travels in Gudbrandsdalen, started collecting both objects and houses. What began as a hobby grew to include 175 houses reflecting the building techniques and everyday lives of local people. The museum, which includes a farming estate, a mountain farm, a crofter's holding and a summer pasture hamlet, aims to show a living environment with animals and people going about their normal activities. One of Norway's oldest stave churches, Garmokirken, can be seen here.

Maihaugen also houses the Post Museum (Postmuseet), with its collection of objects connected to the history of the post office over the centuries.

🏛 Lillehammer Kunstmuseum
Stortorget 2. *Tel* 61 05 44 60. ☐ Jul–Aug: daily; Sep–Jun: Tue–Sun. ◐ some public hols. 🏛🎫👥🛒🛍

It was the 19th-century artist, Fredrik Collett, who first became fascinated by the light and motifs at Lillehammer. Erik Werenskiold, Frits Thaulow and Henrik Sørensen were among the many artists to follow in his footsteps.

Their work forms the basis of the superb collection of Norwegian painting, sculpture and graphic design on show at the museum, which also includes a selection of pieces by Munch, Christian Krohg and Adolf Tidemand.

The building itself is strikingly modern and also features a stone and water garden of stark beauty.

🏛 Norsk Kjøretøyhistorisk Museum
Lilletorget 1. *Tel* 61 25 61 65. ☐ daily. 🏛🛍

The Norsk Kjøretøyhistorisk Museum (Museum of Historic Vehicles) has around 100 vehicles, including cars, motorcycles, horse-drawn carriages and old pedal cycles such as the velocipede (the so-called "Veltepetter").

For train enthusiasts, there is an electric locomotive from 1909, and a superb large model railway.

🏛 Bjerkebæk
Nordseterveien 23. *Tel* 61 25 22 57. ☐ Jun–Sep: daily. ◐ public hols. 🏛🎫🛒🛍

Lillehammer's most notable resident was the author and Nobel Prize-winner, Sigrid Undset, who settled here in 1921. She lived with her books in splendid isolation in this house with its magnificent garden protected by a hedge. The house itself had been moved from Gudbrandsdalen and re-erected at Bjerkebæk.

Undset's great work about the medieval heroine, Kristin Lavransdatter, was published at the time she moved to Lillehammer. Her historical oeuvre about Olav Audunssøn in Hestviken was to follow.

🏛 Norges Olympiske Museum
Håkonshall, Olympiaparken. *Tel* 61 25 21 00. ☐ Jun–Aug: daily; Sep–May: Tue–Sun. ◐ some public hols. 🏛🎫👥🛍

Norges Olympiske Museum (the Olympic Museum) offers an opportunity to experience the atmosphere of the 1994 Winter Olympic Games, when 1,737 participants from 67 countries came to Lillehammer.

Innovative techniques are used to convey the history of the Olympics, going back to the Greek summer and winter games of 776 BC, and to glimpse the societies in which the games took place.

Pierre de Coubertin's re-creation of the games in Athens in 1886 is shown, as are the first Winter Olympics, held in Chamonix in 1924.

◁ View of Rondane with the peaks of Høgronden, 2,114 m (6,936 ft), and Digerronden, 2,020 m (6,627 ft)

Olympiaparken

1 km (half a mile) E of town centre. *Tel* 61 05 42 00. ◯ *daily year-round.*
The investment for the 1994 Winter Olympics provided Lillehammer with magnificent amenities, including Lysgårdsbakkene Ski Jumping Arena. In winter it is possible to take the chairlift to the top for a fantastic view. Håkons Hall, the ice-hockey arena, has facilities for other sports such as handball and golf. It also has a 20-m (66-ft)

Olympiaparken ski jump complex, 1994 Winter Olympics

climbing wall. Birkebeineren Skistadion is the starting point for a floodlit skiing track and cross-country trails.

Lilleputthammer

14 km (9 miles) N of town centre. *Tel* 61 05 62 60. ◯ *Jun–Aug: daily.*
The pedestrian part of Storgata in Lillehammer is known as "Gå-gata", the model for the miniature town of Lilleputthammer. It is an enjoyable place for children.

Hunderfossen Adventure Park

Fåberg, 13 km N (8 miles) N of town centre. *Tel* 61 27 72 22. ◯ *mid-May–Aug: daily.*
The world's largest troll and a glittering fairytale palace themed on old Norwegian tales welcome the visitor to Hunderfossen. There are some 40 rides and attractions for both children and adults, including a swimming pool and car circuit.

Nearby, the **Hafjell Alpine Centre**, with 25 km (16 miles) of graded slopes, is the largest

VISITORS' CHECKLIST

County of Oppland.
♦ 26,000. ▥ ▥
ℹ Jernbanetorget 2, 61 28 98 00. ◉ Winter Festival (Feb), Birkebeiner Race (Mar), Blues Festival (Apr), Literature Festival (May), Lillehammer Festival (Jun), Dølajazz (Sep).

Water ride at Hunderfossen Adventure Park

skiing complex in the area. There is a 710-m (2,330-ft) long artificially frozen bobsleigh run with 16 bends, or if ice is in short supply, there is a "wheeled bob" instead.

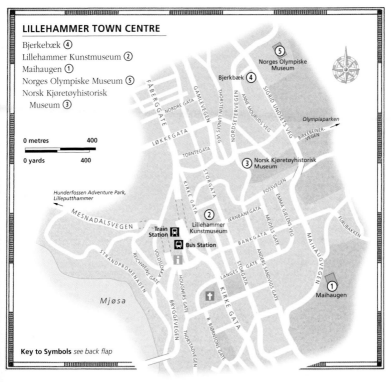

LILLEHAMMER TOWN CENTRE

Bjerkebæk ④
Lillehammer Kunstmuseum ②
Maihaugen ①
Norges Olympiske Museum ⑤
Norsk Kjøretøyhistorisk Museum ③

0 metres   400
0 yards   400

Hunderfossen Adventure Park, Lilleputthammer

Norges Olympiske Museum ⑤
Bjerkbæk ④
Olympiaparken
Norsk Kjøretøyhistorisk Museum ③
Lillehammer Kunstmuseum ②
Train Station
Bus Station
Maihaugen ①
Mjøsa

Key to Symbols *see back flap*

Rondane National Park, a much loved recreational area at all times of the year

Otta ⓫

County of Oppland. 🏘 *4,000.*
🚉 🚌 ℹ️ *Ola Dahl's Gate 1, 61 23
66 50.* 🎭 *Dance Festival (mid-Jul),
Kristin Festival (1st week Jul), Sjoa
Kajak Festival (3rd week Jul), Otta
Market (1st week Oct).*

Since the arrival of the
railway in 1896, Otta has
been a tourist hub, because of
its proximity to the national
parks of Rondane, Dovre and
Jotunheimen. Otta lies at the
junction of the Otta and Lågen
rivers. It is the regional centre
for North Gudbrandsdalen
and a main terminus for buses
to and from the adjoining
valleys and mountain areas.
Historically, Otta is known for
the Battle of Kringen in 1612,
when an army of local farmers
destroyed a Scottish army of
mercenaries on their way to
fight in the Kalmar War.

At Selsverket there is a
summer toll road to Mysuseter
and Rondane.

Rondane National Park ⓬

County of Oppland. ℹ️ *Otta Tourist
Information, 61 23 66 50.*
www.visitrondane.com

Established in 1962,
Rondane was Norway's
first national park. It has a
well-developed network of
routes with several tourist
lodges, including Rondvassbu
and Bjørnhollia.

The landscape is split by
deep gorges: Ilmanndalen

runs in an east/west direction;
Rondvatnet/Rondvassdalen
and Langglupdalen run south
to north. There are 10 peaks
in excess of 2,000 m (6,562 ft)
and even the lowest areas are
around 900 m (2,953 ft)
above sea level. Rondeslottet
("Ronde Castle") is the highest
mountain here, reaching
2,178 m (7,145 ft).

Rondane has both gentle,
rounded mountains and wild,
practically inaccessible parts
with deep, north-facing
glacial cirques. Among the
geological oddities from the
last Ice Age are strange
hollows of dead ice (a glacial
deposit left behind after the
glacier melted). Large
numbers of wild reindeer
populate the mountains.

The rural centre of **Folldal**
grew up around an 18th-
century community that
mined deposits of copper-rich
pyrite. The mines were later
moved to Hjerkinn at Dovre.

Original houses from Folldal
and Dovre have been
preserved in a rural museum.

The valley of Einunndalen,
extending north from Folldal,
is used as a summer pasture.

Dovrefjell ⓭

County of Oppland. ℹ️ *in Dombås,
61 24 14 44.*

The mountain plateau of
Dovrefjell marks the
conceptual divide between
Norway "north of the
mountains" and Norway
"south of the mountains". In
1814, Dovrefjell was used to
signify the unity of the nation
when the men at Eidsvoll *(see
p38)* sang *Enige og tro til
Dovre faller* ("In harmony and
faith till Dovre falls").

Kongeveien, the King's
Road from the south, crossed
the plateau. Mountain huts
built nearly 900 years ago

The mighty Snøhetta rising majestically over the Dovrefjell plateau

have saved the lives of many a traveller in these parts. The Dovrebane railway was completed in 1921.

Wild reindeer and musk oxen inhabit the region and rare species of birds, such as short-eared owl, cuckoo and hen harrier, live on the moorlands of Fokstumyrene.

Dovrefjell National Park was established in 1974. It surrounds Norway's fourth tallest mountain, the 2,286-m (7,500-ft) high Snøhetta ("Snow Cap"). Hjerkinn is the highest point on both the road and the railway. Here, Eysteins Kirke was consecrated in 1969 in memory of King Eystein (c.1100) who built the mountain huts. This is also the starting point of the infamously steep road, *Vårstigen*, to Kongsvoll in the county of Trøndelag *(see p186)*.

Lom Stavkirke constructed in the early Middle Ages

Lom ⑭

County of Oppland. 🏔 2,600. 🚌 to Otta. 🚌 ℹ️ Norsk Fjellmuseum, 61 21 29 90. 🎗 Fláklypa Veteran Car Rally (May). **www**.visitlom.com

The rural centre of Lom, on the banks of the Otta river, is a gateway to the valley of Bøverdalen, the Jotunheimen mountain range and Sognefjellet mountain. The stave church here, **Lom Stavkirke**, was built in 1000 and retains its original deep foundations. It acquired its cruciform shape around 1600. Details such as the dragon heads on the gables have much in common with the churches seen around Sognefjorden *(see pp180–1)*. **Norsk Fjellmuseum** (the Norwegian

Fossheim Steinsenter, with an 8-m (26-ft) tall model of a rock crystal

Mountain Museum), opened in 1994, is a good source of practical information on the mountain wilderness and it has videos showing mountain routes. This is in addition to its natural history exhibits. The Fossheim Hotel – a piece of cultural history in itself – houses **Fossheim Steinsenter** (the Fossheim Stone Centre) comprising a geological museum and a silversmith workshop.

East from Lom, at a crossing on the Otta river, is Vågå, which is also known for having a stave church (1130). Vågå is the burial site of the reindeer hunter Jo Gjende. Its other claim to fame is Jutulporten, a giant "door" in the mountainside that appears in Norwegian legend.

🏠 Lom Stavkirke
Lom. *Tel* 97 07 53 97. ⭕ mid-May–mid-Sep: daily. 🎗 📷 🏠

🏛 Norsk Fjellmuseum
Lom. *Tel* 61 21 16 00. ⭕ May–Sep: daily; Oct–Apr: Mon–Fri. 🎗 🎗 ♿ 📷 🏠

🏛 Fossheim Steinsenter
Lom. *Tel* 61 21 14 60. ⭕ daily. ● some public hols. 🎗 📷 🏠

Jotunheimen ⑮

See pp140–1.

Elveseter ⑯

Bøverdalen, 25 km (16 miles) SW of Lom. *Tel* 61 21 99 00. ⭕ 1 Jun– mid-Sep. **www**.elveseter.no

Lying in the shadow of Galdhøpiggen (2,469 m/ 8,100 ft), Norway's highest mountain, is the farming estate of Elveseter, which has accommodated visitors since 1880. More recently it has been rebuilt as a dedicated tourist hotel *(see p230)* in the architectural style of the valley. The oldest house, Midgard, dates from 1640. Nearby stands Sagasøylen, a 33-m (108-ft) tall monument decorated with motifs from Norwegian history, crowned by Harald Finehair on horseback.

From here, the scenic RV 55, Sognefjellsveien, continues to Skjolden in Sogn. The road was maintained by farmers from Lom and Sogn from around 1400 so that people from northern Gudbrandsdal could reach Bergen to trade their goods. According to a traffic survey from 1878, 16,525 people and 2,658 horses travelled across the mountain in that year.

The current road was built in 1938. Its highest point is 1,440 m (4,724 ft) above sea level. On the way to Skjolden on Sognefjorden it runs past the Sognefjell tourist hut, and Turtagrø hotel, a centre for climbers since 1888.

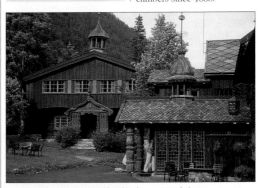

Elveseter, a farmhouse turned hotel in deepest Jotunheimen

Valdres and Fagernes ⑰

County of Oppland. 👥 2,000 (Fagernes). ✕ 🚌 ℹ️ Jernbaneveien 7, Fagernes, 61 35 94 10. 🎪 Valdres Festival (Jul), Folk Music Festival (Jul). www.visitvaldres.no

North Aurdal is the biggest community in Valdres, attracting a large number of visitors year-round. Around 150 years ago it was little more than a farming community, but that changed with the arrival of the railway in 1906. Then long-distance buses made their appearance and in 1987 Leirin airport was built, the highest airport in Norway at 820 m (2,690 ft). Despite the closure of the railway in 1988, the area is easily accessible.

The main valley through Valdres follows the river Begna to Aurdal and Fagernes, where the valley divides into Vestre and Østre Slidre. The mountain resort of **Beitostølen**, with its health and sports centre for disabled people, is at Øystre Slidre.

The Slidre valleys have several stave churches, including Hegge in Øystre Slidre and Lomen, Høre and Øye in Vestre Slidre. Long, narrow lakes and stretches of river characterize the region. **Valdres Folkemuseum** is situated on Fagernes, a peninsula in Strandafjorden. It has 100 buildings, some 20,000 artifacts, a separate high mountain section and a regional costume exhibition.

🏛 **Valdres Folkemuseum**
Tyinvegen 27. **Tel** 61 35 99 00. ⏱ Jun–Aug: daily; Sep–May: Mon–Fri. 🎟 🖼 ♿ 🍴 📷

Villandstua, Hallingdal Folkemuseum, featuring traditional rose-painting

Geilo ⑱

County of Buskerud. 👥 2,500. ✕ 🚌 🚌 ℹ️ Vesleslåttveien 13, 32 09 59 00. 🎪 End of skiing season (4th week Apr), Norwegian Food Festival (1st Sat Oct).

Thanks to its proximity to Hardangervidda (see pp158–9) and the mountain of Hallingskarvet (1,933 m/ 6,342 ft), Geilo has become one of Norway's most popular tourist destinations, conveniently located midway between Oslo and Bergen. There are opportunities for hiking, cycling and fishing, and a great selection of accommodation, from wooden cabins to elegant hotels, and many places to eat.

Geilo has also gained a reputation as a winter sports centre, with 33 alpine pistes, 17 ski lifts, three snowboard parks and 500 km (311 miles) of prepared tracks up in the mountains. The highest alpine piste is at 1,178 m (3,865 ft) with good snow conditions from November until May.

Hallingdal ⑲

County of Buskerud. 👥 4,200. ℹ️ Stasjonsgata 7, Nesbyen, 32 07 01 70.

The long narrow valley of Hallingdal, with mountains rising steeply on both sides, widens out beyond Gol to form an agricultural landscape.

Nesbyen, one of the populated areas along the way, is known for its extreme temperatures: the lowest recorded was –38° C, and the highest +35.6° C (a Norwegian record). The **Hallingdal Folkemuseum** in Nesbyen comprises 20 old houses, among them Staveloftet dating from around 1300, and the extravagantly rose-painted Villandstua.

Hallingdal's magnificent mountain regions, including Norefjell and Hallingskarvet, have made it popular with outdoor people. The valley of Hemsedal, on the road to Lærdal, has a ski centre, which is one of Scandinavia's finest.

🏛 **Hallingdal Folkemuseum**
Møllevegen 18, Nesbyen. **Tel** 32 07 14 85. ⏱ Apr–May & Sep–Oct: Sun; Jun–Aug: daily. ⏱ public hols. 🎟 🖼 🚫 📷 📷 📷

Numedal ⑳

County of Buskerud. 👥 7,500. 🚌 ℹ️ Stormogen in Uvdal, 32 74 39 00. www.visitnumedal.com

The landscape of Numedal is dominated by the 18-km (11-miles) long Norefjorden. Rødberg is the site of a huge power station powered by the

Østre Slidre, looking toward Beitostølen and Jotunheimen

Numedal river. It flows from its source high on Hardangervidda (*see pp158–9*) to a dam at Tunhovdfjorden. An animal park, **Langedrag Naturpark**, features species adapted to mountain life, such as polar foxes, wolves and Norwegian Fjord Horses.

From Rødberg the valley leads into Uvdal and the pass at **Vasstulan** (1,100 m/3,609 ft). Footpaths from here link into the network of mountain huts on Hardangervidda. The richly decorated **Uvdal Stavkirke** (stave church) dates from 1175.

On the eastern side of Norefjorden the road passes some weather-worn houses and a stave church (1600).

✈ Langedrag Naturpark
30 km (19 miles) NW of Nesbyen.
Tel 32 74 25 50. ◯ daily. ● some public hols. 🖼 🖫 ♿ 🖵 🖬

⛪ Uvdal Stavkirke
Kirkebygda, Uvdal. **Tel** 32 74 39 00.
◯ mid-Jun–Aug: daily. 🖼 🖫 🚫

The 12th-century Uvdal Stavkirke, on the site of an even older church

Kongsberg ㉑

County of Buskerud. 🏘 23,000.
🚉 🚌 🛈 Schwabes Gate 2, N3611, 32 29 90 50. 🎭 Kongsberg Market (4th week Feb), Kongsberg Jazz Festival (1st week Jul), Silver Festival (Aug). **www**.visitkongsberg.no

Silver mining was for 335 years the main focus of activity at Kongsberg until the Sølvverket (Silverworks) were closed in 1957. It was also the site of the royal mint.

The town was laid out by Christian IV in 1624, and developed rapidly. The large Baroque church, **Kongsberg Kirke**, was opened in 1761. Its

Ore-wagon at Bergverksmuseum (Mining Museum) in Kongsberg

lavish interior features wood carvings, *faux* marble work and an altar with biblical motifs. The organ (1760–65), by Gottfried Heinrich Gloger, is considered a masterpiece. The remarkable chandeliers were made at Nøstetangen Glassworks.

Kongsberg is the location for the Norwegian Mining Museum, **Norsk Bergverksmuseum**, which contains the Royal Mint Museum and the Sølvverket collections. The former technical school, **Bergseminaret**, is a splendid wooden building dating from 1783. To the west at Saggrenda it is possible to ride on a train deep into **Kongens Gruve** (King's Mine).

🏛 Norsk Bergverksmuseum
Hyttegata 3. **Tel** 32 72 32 00.
◯ daily. ● public hols. 🖼 🖫 by arrangement. ♿ 🖵 🖬

🏛 Kongens Gruve
8 km (5 miles) W of town centre.
Tel 32 72 32 00. ◯ 18 May–Aug: daily; Sep: Sun; other times by arrangement. 🖼 🖫 🍴 🖵 🖬

Drammen ㉒

County of Buskerud. 🏘 60,000.
🚉 🚌 🛈 Engene 1, 03008.
🎭 River Festival (Aug).
www.drammen.kommune.no

The river port of Drammen has Norway's largest harbour for the import of cars. Its location on the navigable Drammenselva has been the source of its prosperity. It was mentioned as early as the 13th century as a loading place and port for timber and when the Kongsberg silver mine opened, Drammen became the port for the Silverworks.

In the early days there were two towns, Bragernes and Strømsø, on either side of the river estuary. They were merged into one in 1811.

Drammens Museum, at the manor house of Marienlyst Herregård, has collections of city and farming culture.

The art gallery, **Drammens Kunstforening**, has Norwegian 19th- and 20th-century paintings and a large collection of Italian art from the 17th and 18th centuries.

The Drammenselva river is one of the best in the country for salmon fishing. For panoramic views, take the road via the Spiraltunellen to the summit of Bragernesåsen.

🏛 Drammens Museum
Konnerudgatan 7. **Tel** 32 20 09 30.
◯ Tue–Sun. 🖼 🖫 ♿ partly.
🚫 🖵 🖬

🏛 Drammens Kunstforening
Konnerudgatan 7. **Tel** 32 20 09 30.
◯ Tue–Sun. ● public hols.
🖼 🚫 🖵

The old manor house of Marienlyst, home to Drammens Museum

Tour along the Telemark Canal ❶

In 1861, during the heyday of waterways transport, Telemark's greatest river, Skienvassdraget, was transformed into the Skien-Nordsjø Canal. Thirty years later, the Nordsjø-Bandak Canal to Dalen was completed, creating the 105-km (65-mile) long Telemark Canal. Eight locks were built to lift boats 72 m (236 ft) above sea level. At the time it was hailed as the "eighth wonder of the world". In 1994, the canal received the Europa Nostra Gold Medal for restoration and conservation. Today, it has become one of the biggest attractions in the county.

Cabin-cruiser navigating the Telemark Canal

Dalen ⑤
Dalen lies at the end of the Telemark Canal on the magnificent Lake Bandak. The Dalen Hotel *(see p232)* resembles a fairytale castle.

Vrangfoss ④
The once 23-m (75-ft) high waterfall is now a power station, with the canal's largest lock system of six chambers. The lock gate is operated in almost the same way as it was 100 years ago.

Ulefoss ②
The lock system at Ulefoss take boats past an 11-m (36-ft) high waterfall. Ulefoss Manor is considered to be the foremost example of Neo-Classical architecture in Norway.

Akkerhaugen ③
The M/S *Telemarken* cruises from Akkerhaugen along the Telemark Canal to Lunde. In summer the canal is a hive of activity with canoes and pleasure craft jostling for space in the locks.

| 0 kilometres | 15 |
| 0 miles | 10 |

KEY

▪ Suggested car route

= Other roads

Skien ①
A statue of the dramatist Henrik Ibsen stands in Skien. His childhood home, Venstøp, is 5 km (3 miles) from the town centre and forms part of the Telemark Museum.

TIPS FOR THE TRIP

Boat trips: *Two boats, M/S Victoria and M/S Henrik Ibsen, operate connecting services between Skien and Dalen. M/S Telemarken goes between Akkerhaugen and Lunde (p267).*
Car journeys: *The peaceful 106 road meanders along the canal, past the lake, Flåvatnet.*

Kviteseid
Seljord
Fjågesund
Bø
Gvarv
Lunde
Pors-grunn

ARENDAL *LARVIK*

Kragerø ❷

County of Telemark. 🏠 11,000. 🚌 to Neslandsvatn. 🚢 ℹ Torvgata 1, 35 98 23 88. 🎿 Summer Ski Festival (4th week Jun), Easter Bathing (Easter Eve), Kragerø Festival (3rd week Jun). **www**.visitkragero.no

A popular holiday resort since the 1920s, Kragerø is surrounded by a magnificent archipelago of small islands divided by narrow, twisting waterways. The picturesque little town was the home of the artist Theodor Kittelsen (1857–1914), best known for his fine illustrations of Asbjørnsen & Moe's collection of Norwegian folk tales. Some of these can be seen in his house-museum.

The morainic island of **Jomfruland**, the outermost in the Kragerø archipelago, has a distinctive flora and bird life, an old brick lighthouse from 1839 and a newer one from 1939. It can be reached by local ferry from Kragerø.

Risør ❸

County of Aust-Agder. 🏠 7,000. 🚌 to Gjerstad, then bus. 🚢 ℹ Kragsgate 3, 37 15 22 70. 🎵 Festival of Chamber Music (4th week Jun), Arts and Crafts Market (2nd week Jul), Wooden Boat Festival (1st week Aug). **www**.infosor.no

Protected from the sea by just a few islets, Risør is known as the "White Town of Skagerrak". It is the row of dazzling white merchants' and ship owners' houses on Solsiden ("the sunny side") by the harbour, as well as the cottages nestling on Innsiden ("the inside") that have given the town its nickname. Despite several fires, the town has preserved much of its 19th-century layout.

Risør had its heyday toward the end of the sailing ship era, from around 1870. The traditions live on, as proved by the Wooden Boat Festival held here every August. Magnificent vessels fill the harbour and boat builders can be seen at their craft.

The wooden church at Risør, **Den Hellige Ånds Kirke**, was built in 1647 with Baroque details and a 17th- to 18th-century interior. The Stangholmen Fyr lighthouse, dating from 1885, has a summer restaurant and bar offering glorious views, as well as temporary exhibitions in its lamp room.

> 🏛 **Den Hellige Ånds Kirke**
> Prestegata 6. **Tel** 37 15 00 12. ⏰ Jul: daily; other times by arrangement. 🎫 by prior arrangement. ♿

Lyngør, the "Venice of the Norwegian coast" with its narrow waterways

Lyngør ❹

County of Aust-Agder. 🏠 130. 🚌 to Vegårshei, then bus. 🚢 to Gjeving, then taxi boat. 🚤 summer only. ℹ Wrold Wroldsens Gt 2 (Tvedestrand), 37 16 40 30. 🎵 Coastal Culture Week (mid-Jul), Tvedestrand Regatta (mid-Jul), Skjærgård's Music and Mission Festival (1st week Jul).

Winner of the "best preserved village in Europe" award in 1991, Lyngør is one of the idyllic islands in Skjaergård-sparken (Archipelago Park) which covers most of the coast of Aust-Agder county. Accessible only by boat taxi from Gjerving on the mainland, the island has no roads for motor vehicles and is a peaceful haven.

Lyngør has fine historic buildings near the old pilot and customs station. Narrow footpaths wind past painted houses with white picket fences and fragrant gardens. The forests that once covered the islands are long gone, but there is an abundance of flowers, initially brought here as seeds in the ballast of sailing ships.

In 1812, Lyngør was the scene of a bloody sea battle when the Danish-Norwegian frigate, *Najaden*, was sunk by the English vessel, *Dictator*. The population sought refuge in Krigerhola, a pothole near the sea. A cultural history museum is connected to the restaurant, *Den Blå Grotte*.

The islands share an early 13th-century church at Dybvåg on the mainland.

White-painted merchants' houses overlooking Risør harbour

Arendal town hall, 1813, Norway's second largest wooden building

Arendal ❺

County of Aust-Agder. 🏠 *39,000.*
☒ *Kristiansand.* 🚉 🚌 ℹ️ *Sam*
Eydes Plass, 37 00 55 44.
📷 *International Market (1st week*
Jul), Arendal Jazz and Blues Festival
(4th week Jul), APL Offshore Race
(1st week Aug).

Sørlandet's oldest town,
Arendal, dates back to 1723.
It was built originally on
seven islands. The buildings
on the peninsula of Tyholmen
next to the busy visitors'
moorings, Pollen, were saved
from fire around 1800. They
have since been carefully
preserved and were awarded
the Europa Nostra
conservation medal in 1992.

The town hall, **Rådhuset**,
is an architectural gem, built
in Neo-Classical style in the
early 19th century. At that
time, Arendal was the biggest
shipping town in the country,
with a merchant fleet larger
than that of Denmark.

Aust-Agder Museet has
archaeological and seafaring
exhibits. In the harbour of
Merdøy (half-an-hour by boat
from Langbrygga) the former
captain's home of Merdøgård
is open to the public.

From Tvedestrand, there are
boat trips on the M/S *Søgne* to
the islands beyond.

🚌 **Rådhuset**
Rådhusgaten 10. **Tel** *37 01 30 00.*
🕐 *for pre-booked tours only.*
📷 🎥 *by prior arrangement.* ♿

🏛 **Aust-Agder Museet**
Parkveien 16. **Tel** *37 07 35 00.*
🕐 *Mon–Fri & Sun.* ● *public*
holidays. 📷 🎥 ♿ 📱

Grimstad ❻

County of Aust-Agder. 🏠 *18,000.*
☒ *Kristiansand.* 🚉
ℹ️ *Storgata 1a, 37 25 01 68.*
📷 *Short Film Festival (mid–Jun), St*
Hans Festival (21–24 Jun).
www.grimstad.net

The old centre of Grimstad
dates from the days of sailing
ships, with narrow streets
winding between the hills.
Grimstad Bymuseum,
featuring arts and crafts and a
maritime section, is situated in
the town centre together with
the pharmacy from 1837
where Henrik Ibsen was an
apprentice and where he
wrote his first plays.

Northeast of the town is
Fjære Kirke, a church with a
memorial stone to Terje Vigen,
about whom Ibsen wrote. This
brave seaman came rowing
from Denmark to Grimstad
with two tons of barley in
the year of starvation, 1809.

Nørholm, on the south-
western outskirts, was the
home of Nobel-prize winning
novelist Knut Hamsun. The

Grimstad Bymuseum with a bust of
Henrik Ibsen in the foreground

coast toward Kristiansand is
renowned for its holiday
resorts and has often been
featured in paintings, poetry
and literature.

Lillesand is a charming
skerries town, with an elegant
town hall and white-washed
wooden houses. Sightseeing
boats depart from the town
for **Blindleia**, a 12-km
(7-mile) long series of inlets,
which are busy with small
craft in summer.

The beauty spots of **Justøy**
island and **Gamle Hellesund**
in Høvåg are close by. There
is a Bronze-Age settlement at
Høvåg. A coastal ferry calls at
one idyllic place after another,
including **Brekkstø**, an artists'
community on Justøy, a much
loved holiday spot.

🏛 **Grimstad Bymuseum**
Henrik Ibsens Gate 14.
Tel *37 04 04 90.* 🕐 *May–mid-Sep:*
daily; mid-Sep–Apr: by arrangement.
📷 🎥 *by arrangement.*

Kristiansand ❼

See pp152–3.

Mandal, characterized by narrow
streets and wooden houses

Mandal ❽

County of Vest-Agder. 🏠 *14,000.*
☒ *Kristiansand.* 🚉 *to Marnardal*
or Kristiansand, then bus. 🚌
ℹ️ *Bryggegata 10, 38 27 83 00.*
📷 *Shellfish Festival (2nd week Aug).*
www.visitregionmandal.com

Mandal owes its fortunes to
the timber trade in the 18th
century. But its boom years
were shortlived and with the
transition from sail to steam,
around 1900, one in four
inhabitants departed for

America. Yet, despite mass emigration, floods and fires, the town has retained more of its former characteristics than many others in Sørlandet. **Mandal Bymuseum**, located in an old merchant's house, has a large art collection, a ship gallery and a fishing museum. The town church dates from 1821 and is one of the bigger in the country.

The coastal road to Mandal passes near the harbour of Ny-Hellesund, where the writer Vilhelm Krag (1871–1933) lived. This was also where Amaldus Nielsen painted his famous picture *Morning at Ny-Hellesund* (1885, Nasjonalgalleriet, Oslo).

Norway's finest beach is nearby, the eggshell-white **Sjøsanden**. This is where the salmon river, Mandalselven, flows into the sea.

🏛 **Mandal Bymuseum**
Store Elvegata 5. **Tel** 38 27 31 25.
⭕ end Jun–mid-Aug: daily; mid-Aug–end Jun: Sun. ♿

Lindesnes ⑨

County of Vest-Agder, 35 km (22 miles) W of Mandal. ℹ Lindesnes Informasjonssenter, 38 26 19 02.
⭕ Foghorn Day (last Sun Jul).
Lighthouse Tel 38 25 54 20. ⭕
May–Sep: daily; Oct–Apr: Sat & Sun.
♿ 🚻 🏠 ⭕

The southernmost point on the mainland of Norway is the Lindesnes peninsula,

Traditional boat moored in Flekkefjord's Dutch Town

2,518 km (1,565 miles) from the North Cape in the far north. Here stands Lindesnes lighthouse, built in 1915 on the site of Norway's first lighthouse, which was lit in 1655.

The peninsula marks a distinctive change in the landscape between the small fjords and gently rounded islands to the east and the longer fjords to the west with more barren islets and wilder looking mountains.

The Skagerrak and North Sea meet at this point, some days with great force. This can be the roughest place on the south coast, but at other times the water can look quite benign and inviting.

Two small harbours on the southeastern side of the peninsula, **Lillehavn** and **Vågehavn**, enable sailors to shelter and weather the worst of the storms.

Flekkefjord ⑩

County of Vest-Agder. 🚶 8,500.
🚉 to station of Sira, 20 km (12 miles) N of town centre. 🏠 ℹ Elvegata 9, 38 32 69 95. ⭕ Salmon Festival (4th week Jul), Gyland Grand Prix (1st week Aug). **www**.visitsydvest.no

The port of Flekkefjord is the biggest fishing and fish farming town on the Skagerrak coast. The Dutch were early trading partners, hence Hollenderbyen (the Dutch Town), dating from 1700. The town museum, **Flekkefjord Bymuseum**, housed in a 1720s patrician building, recreates old shipping scenes.

At the mouth of the fjord is the island of **Hidra**, which can be reached by car ferry from the mainland. It is known for its scenic harbours – Kirkehan, Rasvåg and Eie – and vibrant island community, which has preserved much of its charm from its days as a sailing and fishing centre.

To the west of Flekkefjord is the fishing village of Åna-Sira, which marks the border between Sørlandet and Vestlandet. Nearby, the **Sira-Kvina Kraftselskap** arranges tours of its power station, one of seven on the Sira-Kvina waterway.

🏛 **Flekkefjord Bymuseum**
Dr Krafts Gate 15. **Tel** 38 32 26 59.
⭕ Jun–Aug: daily; other times by prior arrangement. ♿ 🏠 partly.

🏭 **Sira-Kvina Kraftselskap**
60 km (37 miles) N of Flekkefjord.
Tel 38 37 80 00. ⭕ end Jun–mid-Aug: daily (guided tours only). ♿ 🏠 ♿

Lindesnes lighthouse standing at the southernmost point of Norway

Kristiansand ❼

The capital of Sørlandet, Kristiansand, was founded by Christian IV in 1641. It immediately obtained market town status and certain trading privileges. The layout followed a strict grid pattern and, as a result, the town centre became known as Kvadraturen ("the quad"). Kristiansand expanded in 1922 and again in 1965. Now the fifth largest town in Norway, it is a delightful mixture of old and new. In addition to the town itself, the municipality incorporates the surrounding hills, forests and moors, small quiet lakes and farmland, as well as a stretch of coastline.

Restored house in the popular neighbourhood of Posebyen

⊞ Posebyen

NE part of town centre.
🛒 Jun–Aug: Sat.
In Kristiansand's early days as a fortress and garrison town, the soldiers lived in private houses in what has become the best preserved part of the old town. The name Posebyen stems from the French *reposer*, meaning to rest (French was the military language of the time).

The small, pretty houses in this area of town, complete with courtyards, stables and wagon sheds, wash-houses and outbuildings, have survived several fires and the threat of demolition. Nowadays Posebyen is a fashionable place to live, and the historic houses are maintained in good order by the inhabitants.

♣ Christiansholm Festning

Østre Strandgate. **Tel** 38 07 51 50.
⬤ Jun–Jul: daily; Sep–May: by prior arrangement. 📷 by arrangement. ♿
One of the main reasons why Christian IV wanted a town on the south coast was to strengthen the Danish-Norwegian union militarily in the frequent wars against neighbouring countries. In 1628 there was a blockhouse at the mouth of the fjord, and around 1640 a permanent fortification was established.

The solid Christiansholm Festning, on Østre Havn (the Eastern Harbour), was erected in the years after 1667. The town became a garrison, and the fortress was long regarded as the most important in the country after Akershus and Bergenhus. The fortress was the scene of a battle in 1807, when it was used to drive off the English warship, *Spencer*. Today, it is a public area.

🄰 Domkirken

Tel 38 10 69 00. ⬤ Jun–Aug: Mon–Fri and during services, Jul also Sat. 🛐 Sun. 📷 ♿
Kristiansand became a diocese in 1682 when the bishopric was moved here from Stavanger. The Neo-Gothic cathedral, Domkirken, is the fourth to be built on the site. It was completed in 1885, after a fire five years earlier, and can hold 2,000 people. The organ in the east gallery dates from 1967 and has 50 pipes. A painting on the altarpiece by Eilif Peterssen shows Jesus in Emmaus.

⊞ Gimle Gård

Gimleveien 23. **Tel** 38 10 26 80.
⬤ 20 Jun–20 Aug: daily; 21 Aug–19 Jun: Sun. ⬤ public hols. 📷 📷
The manor house of Gimle Gård was built for the wealthy shipowner Bernt Holm around 1800, in the Neo-Classical style popular at the time. It has a colonnaded loggia, and the interior contains many fine pieces of Empire-style furniture as well as additions from the end of the 19th century.

On the walls are 17th- and 18th-century paintings from Denmark, Germany, Italy and the Netherlands, most of which were part of Holm's private collection.

Turned into a museum in 1985, Gimle Gård provides an excellent glimpse of life of the Norwegian bourgeoisie during the Napoleonic era, from the stately salons to the basement kitchen.

Gimle Gård, a 19th-century manor house with a distinctive colonnade

For hotels and restaurants in this region see pp231–3 and pp249–50

🏛 Vest-Agder Fylkesmuseum

Vigeveien 22. **Tel** 38 10 26 80.
⏰ 20 Jun–20 Aug: daily; 21 Aug–
19 Jun: Sun. ⚫ some public hols.

Established in 1903, the open-
air Vest-Agder Fylkemuseum
features wooden buildings
from around the county,
arranged according to origin.
The Agdertunet and Setesdal-
stunet have farmyards,
storehouses on stilts and bath
houses, while Bygaden
consists of 19th-century town
houses, shops and workshops
from Kristiansand.

In the museum's main
building there is an exhibition
of traditional folk costumes
and examples of the typical
rustic decorations known as
rosemalt, featured on pottery,
tools, furniture and walls.

Not far from the museum,
Oddernes Kirke is one of the
oldest churches in the
country, dating from 1040.

Animals drawing the crowds at Kristiansand Dyrepark

🐾 Kristiansand Dyrepark

10 km (6 miles) E of town centre.
Tel 38 04 97 00. ⏰ daily. ⚫ some
public hols.

Wolves, lynx, elk, capercail-
lies and eagle owls are
among the Nordic species
that can be seen at the park.
From further afield, there are
giraffes, apes, alligators and
boa constrictors. Other
attractions include a
bobsleigh track, wave pool
and water chutes.

VISITORS' CHECKLIST

County of Vest-Agder. 🔲 75,000.
🔲 🔲 🔲 🔲 🔲 Rådhus Gate 6,
38 12 13 14. 🔲 International
Church Music Festival (mid-Jun),
Water Festival (2nd wk Jun),
Quart Music Festival (1st wk Jul),
Dark Season Festival (1st wk
Nov). www.sorlandet.com

🏛 Setesdalsbanen Museumsjernbane

Grovane Stasjon, Vennesla, 17 km
(11 miles) N of town centre.
Tel 38 15 64 82. ⏰ 16 Jun–1 Sep:
departures 11:30am and 2pm Sun; Jul:
departures also as at 11:30am, 2pm, 6pm
Tue–Fri (and 12 noon Thu).
Steam trains are running
once again on part of the
narrow-gauge Setesdalsbanen
line between Grovane and
Røyknes. The original railway
from Kristiansand opened in
1896. It was closed in 1962.
There are guided tours of the
engine shed and workshops.

KRISTIANSAND TOWN CENTRE

Christiansholm Festning ②
Domkirken ③
Gimle Gård ④
Posebyen ①

Gimle Gård ④

Kristiansand Dyrepark, Vest-Agder Fylkesmuseum

GIMLEVEIEN
FLATEN
ODERNESVEIEN
MARKUS THRANES GATE
ØSTRE VEIEN
TORRIDALSVEIEN
EGGVEIEN

Otra

TOMS VEI
VESTERVEIEN
TORDENSKJOLDS GATE
KRISTIAN IV GATE
H. WERGELANDS GATE
FESTNINGSGATA
RÅDHUS GATE
HOLBERG GATE
KRONPRINSENS GATE
ELVEGATA
VOLLGATA

Posebyen ①

Setesdalsbanen
Museumsjernbane

VESTRE STRANDGATE
SKIPPERGATEN
GYLDENLØVES GATE
KIRKE GATA
TOLLBODGATEN
DRONNINGENS GATE
KONGENS GATE
ØSTRE STRANDGATE

Train Station 🚆

Domkirken ③

Ferry Terminal ⛴   Bus Station 🚌

MARKENS GATE

Christiansholm Festning ②

0 metres   300
0 yards   300

Typical interior from one of the many old mountain farms in Rauland

Setesdal ⓫

County of Aust-Agder, Municipality of Valle. 🚗 1,500. 🚌
ℹ️ Valle Sentrum, 37 93 75 00.

The biggest of the Agder valleys is Setesdal. The steep Setesdalsheiene, 1,000-m (3,280-ft) high spurs of the Hardangervidda plateau, form towering walls on each side of the River Otra, which flows from the Byklebeiene hills.

Setesdal has maintained its distinctive rural culture, which manifests itself particularly in folk music, silversmithing, folk costumes and architecture. The museum, **Setesdalsmuseet**, in Valle, has a medieval open-hearth house and Rygnestadloftet, a small barn from around 1590. Not far from the museum, the fine Hylestad stave church once stood. Objects from the church (demolished in 1668) are sometimes displayed in the museum, although its portal with motifs from the *Volsunga* saga is now in the Historisk Museum in Oslo.

At **Setesdal Mineralpark** in Hornnes, rare minerals such as beryl, aquamarine and amazonite can be seen in large halls hollowed out inside the mountain.

🏛 **Setesdalsmuseet**
Rysstad on RV9. *Tel* 37 93 63 03.
🕐 20 Jun–1 Sep: daily; Sep–19 Jun: Mon–Fri. 🌐 public hols. 🖼
📷 by arrangement. 🔵 🔷 🎦 🎟

🏛 **Setesdal Mineralpark**
10 km (6 miles) S of Evje.
Tel 37 93 13 10. 🕐 May–Sep: daily. 🖼 🎦 🔵 🎟 🎦

Hardangervidda ⓬

See pp158–9.

Rauland ⓭

County of Telemark. 🚗 1,300. 🚌
ℹ️ Raulandshuset, 35 06 26 30.
🎭 Winter Folk Music Contest (Feb), Arts and Crafts Days (2nd week Jun).
www.rauland.org

The mountainous area around the beautiful lake of Totakvatnet is known for its well-preserved buildings and its culture. Many artists had strong ties with the lake-side village of Rauland, and their sculptures, paintings and drawings are on display at **Rauland Kunstmuseum**, including works by Dyre Vaa

(1903–80). Just east of here is an abundance of historic buildings, such as the old farmhouses near **Krossen**, and those at **Austbøgrenda**, one of which has wood-carvings from the 1820s. Other collections of wooden buildings, including an 1820s sawmill, are at Lognvik farm by lake Lognvikvatnet.

At the westernmost end of Totakvatnet, in Arabygdi, is the **Myllarheimen** cottage where the fiddler virtuoso Tarjei Agundson (1801–72) lived. In summer, folk music is sometimes performed.

🏛 **Rauland Kunstmuseum**
1 km (half a mile) W of Rauland centre.
Tel 35 07 32 66. 🕐 20 Jun–Sep: daily; other times by arrangement. 🔵 🎦

Rjukan ⓮

County of Telemark. 🚗 4,000.
🚌 ℹ️ Torget 2, 35 08 05 50.
🎭 Rjukan Rock Festival (end May), Women's Mountain Hike (1st week Sep). **www**.visitrjukan.com

Rjukan's international claim to fame was as the site of the hydrogen factory that was blown up in 1943 in a daring act of heroism by Norwegian Resistance fighters (*see box*). Before that, however, the small rural community played a key role in Norway's industrial development when a power

---

THE HEROES OF TELEMARK

On the night of 27–28 February 1943, at the height of World War II, there was a powerful explosion in the hydrogen factory at Rjukan. A by-product of the production here was heavy water, which the Allies knew was an important resource for the nuclear research being undertaken by Germany, and the possible production of nuclear bombs.

The sabotage had been meticulously prepared with the help of Allied paratroopers. Nine men from the Norwegian "Kompani Linge" descended from Hardangervidda through deep snow, crossed the precipitous gorge and laid the explosives which destroyed the plant. The heroic operation, code-named "Gunnerside", was one of the most effective acts of resistance during the war.

Kirk Douglas in the film *The Heroes of Telemark*, 1965

◁ **Sheep grazing on a sunny slope in Vest-Agder county**

station was built here in 1911. Fuelled by the 105-m (344-ft) high waterfall, Rjukanfossen, the power station, a hydrogen factory and a chemical plant helped the village expand into a model industrial community, with everything provided by the company, Norsk Hydro.

A new power station was built in 1971. The old one is now a museum, **Norsk Industriarbeidermuseum**, which tells the story both of the thrilling sabotage and of Norway's industrial past.

On the opposite side of the valley is the cable car, **Krossobanen**, erected by Norsk Hydro in 1928 to enable the residents of the shaded valley to glimpse the sun in winter. It rises to 886 m (2,907 ft) and is an excellent starting point for walking trips on Hardangervidda. Beside Rjukanfossen is the **Krokan Tourist Hut**, opened in 1868 when the untamed waterfall was a popular destination for tourists and painters. Today, because of the power station, the waterfall can be seen at full force only occasionally.

Gaustadtoppen, a peak 1,883 m (6,178 ft) high, can be reached via a well-marked path from the Stavro car park. The walk to the summit takes about two hours.

🏛 **Norsk Industriarbeidermuseum**
7 km (4 miles) W of town centre. **Tel** 35 09 90 00. ◯ Nov–Mar: Tue–Fri; Apr & Oct: Tue–Sat; May–Sep: daily. 🎟 🗗 🔥 ▢ 🗗

⚡ **Krossobanen**
1 km (half a mile) W of town centre. **Tel** 35 09 00 27 (bookings).
◯ daily. 🎟

The Rambergstugo house dating from 1784 at Heddal Bygdetun

Heddal ⓯

County of Telemark, Municipality of Notodden. 🚍 12,000 (Notodden). ▢ ▢ ℹ Teatergaten 3, 35 01 50 00. 🎟 Notodden Blues Festival (1st week Aug). **www**.notodden.kommune.no

The main attraction in the village of Heddal is **Heddal Stavkirke**, erected in 1242. With its three spires and 64 different roof surfaces, this "wooden cathedral" is the largest of the preserved medieval churches in Norway. It has three naves, a portico and an apse. Notable internal features include the richly carved bishop's chair, the altarpiece and the late 17th-century wall paintings.

Heddal Stavkirke is still the main church in the district. The vicarage barn beside the church houses various exhibitions and a restaurant.

Among the buildings on display at nearby **Heddal Bygdetun** is Rambergstugo, a house decorated in 1784 in the rustic style known as "rose painting", by the well-known painter, Olav Hansson.

The Norsk Hydro company was established in Notodden in 1905. The company museum,

Bedrifts-historisk Samling, shows its first years of operation, and looks at the lives of the railway navvies.

🔒 **Heddal Stavkirke**
Heddalsvegen 412. **Tel** 35 02 04 00. ◯ end May–beg Sep: daily; other times by arrangement. 🎟 🗗 ▢

🏛 **Heddal Bygdetun**
6 km (4 miles) W of Notodden. **Tel** 35 02 08 40. ◯ mid-Jun–mid-Aug: daily. 🎟 🗗 ▢

🏛 **Bedriftshistorisk Samling**
Notodden town centre. **Tel** 35 09 39 99. ◯ 15 Jun–18 Aug: daily; Jan–14 Jun & 19 Aug–31 Dec: by arrangement. 🎟 🗗 ▢ 🗗

Bø Sommarland, a paradise for water enthusiasts large and small

Bø Sommarland ⓰

County of Telemark. **Tel** 35 06 16 00. ▢ ◯ Jun–Aug: daily. 🎟 🔥 🍴 ▢ 🗗

Norway's biggest waterpark, Bø Sommarland, offers more than 100 activities of different kinds and appealing to different ages. There are paddling pools and safe water activities for youngsters. For older children, the range of attractions includes a water carousel, water slides, rafting and an artificial wave pool.

For those seeking bigger thrills, there are diving towers, a water rollercoaster, and the heart-stopping free-fall slide, Magasuget.

Dry land attractions include a fairground and several places to eat. The park lies just north of the small town of Bø.

Rjukan's Vemork power station, scene of a daring sabotage in 1943

Hardangervidda ⑫

Europe's largest high mountain plateau stands well above the tree line at 1,100–1,400 m (3,608–4,593 ft), punctuated with prominent peaks such as Hårteigen and the glacier of Hardangerjøkulen. A national park covers part of the region. Many rivers have their sources in the mountain lakes, the best known being Numedalslågen and Telemarksvassdraget in the east, and Bjoreia with the waterfall Vøringsfossen *(see p169)* in the west. Ancient tracks and well-trodden paths bear witness to the passage of people across the mountains in times past. Hunters stalked reindeer and fishermen still come to catch trout. Today, though, it is the *hytte-to-hytte* (hut-to-hut) hikers who make up the majority of visitors to Hardangervidda.

Vøringsfossen
The River Bjoreia plunges vertically 145 m (476 ft) down from the plateau into the valley of Måbødalen.

Trout Fishing
Hardangervidda is one of Norway's best areas for trout fishing. Information about fishing licences can be obtained in advance from tourist offices and huts.

Hårteigen
The strange shape of Hårteigen rises from the plateau. The gneissic outcrop is the remains of an ancient mountain ridge.

KEY

▬▬	Major road
▭▭	Minor road
– –	National park boundaries
‒ ‒	Hiking route
🏠	Mountain hut

0 kilometres   20

0 miles   10

Glacier Buttercup
Hardangervidda is the habitat for a rich variety of flowers, including the hardy glacier buttercup, Ranunculus glacialis.

Hardangerjøkulen

The 6th largest glacier in Norway, Hardanger- jøkulen is also the most accessible. It attracts visitors all year round, not least in May when many combine a spot of spring skiing with a visit to Hardangerfjord where fruit trees are in blossom.

VISITORS' CHECKLIST

Counties of Telemark, Buskerud and Hordaland. *Hardangervidda Natursenter in Eidfjord, 53 66 59 00.* Apr–Oct: daily; other times by prior arrangement. **www**.hardangervidda.org

Mountain Huts

Some mountain huts are only a short distance from the road, such as this one near Ustetind, while others can only be reached after a few hours by footpath.

Hiking

The terrain on Hardangervidda is generally easy-going, providing good walking for hikers of all levels.

Wild Reindeer

Hardangervidda's population of around 17,000 wild reindeer is the biggest in Europe. Ancient animal burial sites and other hunting evidence indicate that reindeer have been living on the plateau for many thousands of years.

Geilo

Uvdal

Tuva

Heinsæter

Stigstuv

Rauhellern

Sandhaug

Mårbu

Lågaros

ARDANGERVIDDA NATIONAL PARK

Mogen

Stavanger ❶

Sardines and oil have been the mainstay of Stavanger's economic development. Before the cathedral was built around 1125, Stavanger was little more than a fishing village. It was not granted status as a market town until 1425. From the 19th century, an influx of herring in the waters offshore gave rise to the town's lucrative fishing and canning industry. Then, in the 1960s, oil was discovered off the coast, boosting the town's prosperity. Today, Stavanger is the fourth-largest city in Norway with 110,000 inhabitants. It is situated between the flat countryside of Jæren to the south and, to the north, Boknafjorden, the southernmost of the west coast fjords.

Gamle Stavanger, with its winding streets of immaculately preserved timber houses

🏛 Gamle Stavanger

Stavanger town centre. 📷 Jun–Aug, visit the tourist office to book.
To the west and southwest of Vågen harbour is Gamle ("Old") Stavanger, a residential and commercial quarter characterized by its wooden houses and narrow cobbled streets. Between Øvre Strandgate and Nedre Strandgate, there are complete terraces of well-preserved, 19th-century whitewashed timber houses with small front gardens and picket fences. Once the homes of seafarers and local workers, the 156 protected houses are lovingly cared for by their modern-day owners.

🏛 Norsk Hermetikkmuseum

Øvre Strandgate 88A. **Tel** 51 84 27 00. ☐ mid-Jun–mid-Aug: daily; mid-Aug–mid-Jun: Tue–Sun. ● public hols, Dec. 📷 📷 📷 📷
The canning museum, Norsk Hermetikkmuseum, is situated in picturesque Gamle Stavanger. Housed in an old cannery, it provides an overview of an industry that in its heyday was of greater importance to the town, relatively speaking, than the oil industry is today. In the 1920s there were 70 canneries in Stavanger. Visitors are offered a glimpse of the pioneering time around 1850 when innovations such as "tinned suppers" made their first appearance, followed by developments in technology and the launching of tinned sardines on the world market in the early 20th century.

🏛 Stavanger Sjøfartsmuseum

Nedre Strandgate 17–19. **Tel** 51 84 27 00. ☐ Sun. ● public hols. 📷 📷 📷 📷 📷
The sailing vessel *Anna of Sand* was launched in 1848 and is Norway's oldest sailing ship still in use. Between voyages, it can be seen here at the Sjøfartsmuseum (the Maritime Museum), which also owns the pleasure yacht *Wyvern*, built in 1897 by Colin Archer (who built the polar vessel *Fram* for the explorer Fridtjof Nansen). The museum, located in two converted warehouses next to the harbour, focuses on the maritime history of south-western Norway.

🏛 Valbergtårnet

Valberget 2. **Tel** 51 53 12 19. ☐ Mon–Sat: daily. ● public hols. 📷 📷 by arrangement. 📷
The fire lookout tower on the hill of Valberget, designed by C H Grosch, was ready in 1852. Stavanger has suffered many big fires over the years – one, in 1684, was so catastrophic that the possibility of abandoning the town altogether was considered. That didn't happen and today the tower provides a splendid view of the town, the harbour and Boknafjorden.

🏛 Norsk Oljemuseum

Kjerringholmen. **Tel** 51 93 93 00. ☐ daily. ● some public hols. 📷 📷 Sun. 📷 📷 📷 📷
Oil and gas production in the North Sea has created an economic boom in Stavanger, with the consequence that the town is the most cosmopolitan in the country. The ultra-modern Norsk Oljemuseum (Petroleum Museum), designed by architects Lunde and Løvseth, was opened in 1999. It offers a graphic account of life at work and play on a drilling platform with a top-to-bottom presentation of an oil rig.

Models of the equipment used are on display, including drilling bits, diving bells and a 28-person survival capsule. Tableaux illustrate how oil and gas were created, the history of the industry, and the technology used to extract and distribute the oil and gas.

The Norsk Oljemuseum, featuring the history of Norway's oil industry

Stavanger's historic Domkirken, dating from around 1100

🏛 Domkirken

Haakon VII's Gate 7. **Tel** 51 53 96 50.
◯ Jun–Aug: daily; Sep–May: Tue–Thu
& Sat. Sun: for services only. ♿

Reinald, the first bishop of Stavanger, was an Englishman from Winchester, where St Swithun had been a bishop in the 9th century. During the reign of King Sigurd Jorsalfar, Reinald was given the means to construct a cathedral. The imposing Romanesque nave was completed around 1100, and dedicated to St Swithun, who thus became the patron saint of Stavanger.

After a fire in 1272, the cathedral was rebuilt with a magnificent Gothic choir which it still has today. About the same time, the Gothic eastern façade and the Bishop's Chapel were added. The two pyramid-shaped towers on the eastern façade date from 1746. The Baroque pulpit with its biblical motifs, according to legend, created by the Scottish immigrant Anders (Andrew) Smith in 1658. The stained-glass paintings behind the altar are by Victor Sparre and were installed in 1957.

Along with Nidarosdomen in Trondheim (see p199), the Domkirke is a remarkable example of a medieval cathedral. Kongsgård School (the Cathedral School) is situated next to the cathedral. Originally it was the home of the bishop.

🏛 Stavanger Museum

Muségaten 16. **Tel** 51 84 27 00. ◯ mid-Jun–mid-Aug: daily; mid-Aug–mid-Jun: Tue–Sun.
◯ Dec, some public hols. 🎫
🅿♿🚫📷📖

Stavanger Museum was founded in 1877. It contains an extensive collection of prehistoric finds from the county of Rogaland, including items from Viste, where there was a Stone-Age settlement, and

two 3,000-year-old, 1.5-m (5-ft) long, bronze lurs. These wind instruments were discovered in Hafrsfjord, site of the Battle of Hafrsfjord in 890 that led to Norway becoming a unified land.

A maritime section includes two working 19th-century sailing ships. The museum also has zoological and ecclesiastical history collections. In 1936 it bought the patrician house, Ledaal. The 200-year-old building serves both as a museum and a royal residence. The house is thought to be the model for "Sandsgaard" in the novels of Alexander Kielland, who became burgomaster of Stavanger in 1891.

Bronze lur from Hafrsfjord

VISITORS' CHECKLIST

County of Rogaland. 👥 117,000.
✈ 12 km (7 miles) SW of the centre. 🚌 🚆 Jernbaneveien 3.
⛴ Østre Havn. 🛈 1 Rosenkilde-torget, 51 85 92 00. 🎭 May Jazz (May), Fishing Festival (early Jun), Glamat Food Festival (end July), Chamber Music Festival (Aug).
www.regionstavanger.com

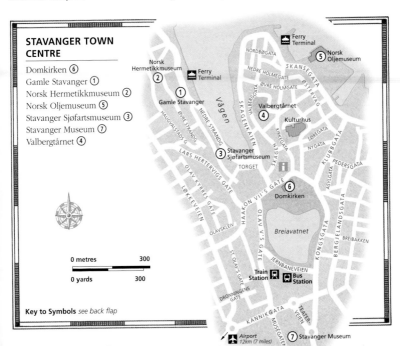

STAVANGER TOWN CENTRE

Domkirken ⑥
Gamle Stavanger ①
Norsk Hermetikkmuseum ②
Norsk Oljemuseum ⑤
Stavanger Sjøfartsmuseum ③
Stavanger Museum ⑦
Valbergtårnet ④

0 metres   300
0 yards   300

Key to Symbols see back flap

Wide horizons and a small place of worship on the Jæren plains

Egersund ❷

County of Rogaland. 🏔 14,000. 🚉
🚌 🚢 ℹ️ Jernbaneveien 18, 51 49
27 44. 🎭 Lighthouse Festival (early
May), Opening of Summer-Egersund
(early Jun), Egersund Festival (1st wk
Jul). **www**.reisemal-sydvest.no

When the sea is rough,
Egersund is the only good
natural harbour along the
Jæren coast to provide
shelter. It is Norway's largest
fishing harbour, but
picturesque old white
wooden houses still perch on
the steep rocks around the
wharves. The cruciform
church dates from 1620.

The cultural history museum,
Dalane Folkemuseum, is
located at Slettebø, once the
residence of a high-ranking
civil servant. Handicrafts, old
farming tools and industrial
equipment are on display.

Environs
At Eide, glazed earthenware –
once a major local industry –
is exhibited in a former
faience factory (part of the
Dalane Folkemuseum).
Northwest of Egersund is a
waterfall, **Fotlandsfossen**,
with salmon steps.

The agricultural and
industrial region of **Jæren** is
flat for Norway. There are
some sandy beaches, but no
islands to protect the shore.
The towering Eigerøy lighthouse presides over the coast.

🏛 **Dalane Folkemuseum**
2 km (1 mile) N of town centre.
Tel 51 46 14 10. 🕐 mid-Jun–mid-
Aug: daily; other times by prior
arrangement. 📷

Lysefjorden ❸

County of Rogaland. 🚌 🚢 car ferry
Stavanger–Lysebotn, 4 hrs. ℹ️ Turistinformasjonen, Stavanger, 51 85 92 00.

The breathtaking Lysefjorden
cuts through the mountains
like the blow of an axe. Only
in a few places is the
starkness of the mountain
sides interrupted by some
sparse greenery and a solitary
farm. About 12 km (7 miles)
from its mouth is
the spectacular
Prekestolen
(Pulpit Rock),
an overhanging
platform.
Dropping 597 m
(1,959 ft) to the fjord,
it is a popular site for base
jumping (parachuting from a
fixed object). For those less
adventurous, the view from
the top, reached by footpath,
is dizzying enough.

At the inner end of the fjord,
the **Lyseveien** road features 27

**Dramatic Prekestolen (Pulpit Rock)
towering over Lysefjorden**

hairpin bends with views of
Kjerag peak, 1,000 m (3,281 ft)
above the water. South of
Lysefjorden is Frafjorden and
the 92-m (302-ft) high
waterfall of **Månafossen**.

Suldal ❹

County of Rogaland. 🏔 4,000.
🚢 ℹ️ Turistinformasjonen, Sand,
52 79 05 60. 🎭 Ryfylke Festival
(Jun), St Olaf Celebration (4th week
Aug). **www**.suldal-turistkontor.no

The famous salmon river,
Suldalslågen, flows into
Sandsfjorden through the
town of Sand. Here, beside
a waterfall is **Laksestudioet**
(the Salmon Studio), where
a glass wall enables visitors
to watch the salmon and trout
as they negotiate the cascade
on their journey up river.
There is also an exhibition on
the history of salmon fishing.
The heritage of the English
"salmon lords" can be seen
throughout Suldal valley in
the grand manor houses that
they had constructed along
the river toward the
end of the 19th
century. At the
**Kolbeinstveit
Museum**, further up
the river, is a collec-
tion of old wooden

**Laksestudioet
in Suldal**

cottages, smoke houses, mills,
storage houses on stilts, and
the Guggedal loft and store-
house, dating from 1250.
From here, a road inland leads
to **Kvilldal Kraftstasjon**,
Norway's largest power station.

At the eastern end of the
river, steep mountains on
each side of the water form
the mighty **Suldalsporten**
(Suldal gateway), creating a
narrow sound before leading
into the lake, Suldalsvattnet,
from where the river springs.

🍴 **Laksestudioet**
Sand town centre. **Tel** 52 79 05 60.
🕐 15 Jun–31 Aug: daily; other
times by prior arrangement. 📷

🏛 **Kolbeinstveit Museum**
17 km (11 miles) E of Sand. **Tel** 52
79 29 50. 🕐 end Jun–
mid-Aug: Tue–Sun. 📷

🏛 **Kvilldal Kraftstasjon**
Soldalsosen. 🕐 by prior
arrangement. 📷 call Suldal
Tourist Office, 52 79 05 60. ♿

Utstein Kloster ❺

County of Rogaland. **Tel** 51 72 47
05. ◯ May–mid-Sep: Tue–Sun (Jul
also Mon). ● some public hols.

On the island of Mosterøy,
northwest of Stavanger, is the
12th-century monastery,
Utstein Kloster. It stands on
what was originally a royal
estate from the time of King
Harald Hårfagre. Around
1265, it was presented to the
Augustinians and remained
in their ownership until the
Reformation, when it became
the property of Norwegian
and Danish aristocrats.

The monastery, surrounded
by a large estate of 139 farms,
has been well preserved
despite fires and attacks. In
1935 the buildings were taken
over by the state and restored
as a national monument.

Haugesund, looking out across Karmsundet

Karmøy ❻

County of Rogaland. 🏚 39,400.
⊠ 🚌 🚢 👥 Turistinformasjonen,
Stratsråd Vinjes Gate 25, 52 01 08
20. Viking Festival (Jun), Skude
Festival (1st week Jul), Fisheries
Festival (4th week Jul).
www.visithaugalandet.no

The 30-km (19-mile) long
island of Karmøy lies like a
shield against the sea (the
Old Norse word *karmr* means
protection). On the inside is
the Karmsundet, a shipping
channel that was part of the
ancient *Nordvegen* (Northern
passage), from which the word
Norge (Norway) is derived. By
the bridge to the island, stone
megaliths known as the Five
Wayward Virgins guard the
sound. It is said that they were
raised over the five sons of a
monarch who fought the king
of Avaldsnes, where there was
a royal estate (870–1450). The
area's many burial mounds are
proof that Avaldsnes was an
important prehistoric centre.

Olavskirken (St Olav's
Church) was built at Avaldsnes
by King Håkon around 1250.
Next to the church leans the
Virgin Mary's Sewing Needle, a
7.5-m (25-ft) high stone pillar.
The nearby island of **Bukkøya**
hosts a reconstructed Viking
estate. Iron Age stone pillars
can be seen at Åkrahavn on
the western side of Karmøy.

On Karmøy's southern tip
lies the whitewashed town of
Skudeneshavn with a museum
at **Mælandsgården**. Karmøy's
main town is Kopervik.

🏛 Mælandsgården
Skudeneshavn. **Tel** 52 84 54 60. ◯
20 May–20 Aug: Mon–Fri & Sun;
other times by prior arrangement.

Haugesund ❼

County of Rogaland. 🏚 31,000. ⊠
Karmøy, 13 km (8 miles) S of town
centre. 🚌 🚢 Hurtigbåtterminalen.
👥 Strandgt 171, 52 01 08 30.
Sildajazz (Aug), Norwegian Film
Festival (Aug), Harbour Festival (Aug).

The three seagulls in the town's
coat of arms are a symbol of
Haugesund's seaside location,
and its fishing and shipping
industries, which have aided
the town's development. This
is a young town, but the area
has important historical
connections. To the north is
the burial mound of
Haraldshaugen, where King
Harald Hårfagre was buried
around 940. Norway's
National Monument (Norges
Riksmonument) was erected
on this site in 1872 to commemorate 1,000 years of a
united Norway.

Haugesund has museums, a
gallery and a town hall, which
is richly adorned with works
of art. It is a popular town
for congresses and festivals.

Out to sea in the west, and
with a good boat connection,
is the island of **Utsira**,
renowned for its rich bird life.

🏔 Haraldshaugen
3 km (2 miles) N of Haugesund
town centre.

🎇 Utsira
1 hr 20 min W of Haugesund by
boat. ✉ Municipality of Utsira, 52
75 01 00. 🏚 230. ⏱ timetable,
47 88 01 44 (Turistinformasjonen,
Haugesund).

Skudeneshavn, a pretty coastal settlement on Karmøy

Bergen ⑭

Granted town status by King Olav Kyrre in 1070, Bergen was at the time the largest town in the country and the capital of Norgesveldet, a region that included Iceland, Greenland and parts of Scotland. Even after Oslo became capital of Norway in 1299, Bergen continued to grow as a trading centre, especially for the export of dried fish during the era of the Hanseatic League trading company. Following a period of decline in the 15th century the town entered a new era of prosperity as a centre for shipping. In 2000 Bergen was named European City of Culture. Although it is a city it has all the charm and atmosphere of a small town.

Vågen harbour, with the Bryggen area on the right

Exploring Bryggen Area

The area north of Vågen harbour, between the Bryggen quay and Øvregaten, a street lined with Hanseatic buildings, has some of Bergen's most important sights. Old and new architecture provides an exciting backdrop to the hustle and bustle of the streets and the quays busy with ships loading and unloading their goods.

🏛 Norges Fiskerimuseum

Bontelabo 2. *Tel* 56 38 50 50.
☐ Jun–Aug: daily; Sep–May: Sun–Fri. 🔊 📷 🚻 ♿ 🍴 🛍
Situated on the waterfront, at the furthest end of Vågen harbour's north quayside, Norges Fiskerimuseum (the Norwegian Fishing Museum) provides a comprehensive insight into Norway's long-established fishing industry and its resources. Fishing boats and equipment through the ages are on show. Other displays cover various types of fishing such as herring and cod fishing, fish farming, whaling and sealing.

🏯 Håkonshallen and Rosenkrantztårnet

Bergenhus Festning. *Tel* 55 31 60 67.
Håkonshallen ☐ daily.
Rosenkrantztårnet ☐ 15 May–Aug: daily; Sep–14 May: Sun. ● public holidays. 🔊 🛍
Håkonshallen is a Gothic ceremonial hall built by King Håkon Håkonsson for the coronation and wedding in 1261 of his son, Magnus Lagabøter. It is thought to be the largest secular medieval building remaining in Norway. It was built of local stone with

Rosenkrantztårnet, a fortified residence built in 1560

architectural details in soapstone. Originally, the ceremonial hall was situated on the top floor. The middle storey comprised living and working areas and the cellar was used for provisions. In 1683 the hall was redesigned to store corn. The building was later restored and decorated with paintings by Gerhard Munthe, but in World War II it suffered extensive damage. The restoration work that followed created a grand venue for official functions.

The Rosenkrantz Tower is, along with Håkonshallen, part of the old fortifications of Bergenhus (Bergen Castle). The main building dates from the same period as Håkonshallen. The present tower was built in 1560 by the governor of Bergen Castle, Erik Rosenkrantz, as a defence post and residence.

🛐 Mariakirken

Dreggen. *Tel* 55 31 59 60. ☐ Jun–Aug: Mon–Fri; Sep–May: Tue–Fri. 🔊
Part of the chancel in Mariakirken (St Mary's Church) dates from the 11th century, around the time when Bergen was granted town status by King Olav Kyrre. As such it is the city's oldest surviving church.

In Hanseatic times the German merchants used it as their special church and richly embellished it. There is a splendid Baroque pulpit dating from 1677, decorated with painted constellations and Christian virtues such as Faith, Hope, Love, Chastity, Truth and Temperance.

🏛 Bryggens Museum

Dreggsalmenning 3. *Tel* 55 58 80 10.
☐ daily. ● some public holidays. 🔊 📷 by arrangement. ♿ 🚻 🛍
The excavations that were begun after a catastrophic fire on Bryggen in 1955 were the largest of their kind in northern Europe. Bryggens Museum is based on the archaeological findings and provides a picture of everyday life in a medieval town. It features a wealth of well-presented material, both graphic and written, including runic inscriptions from the 14th century.

The old wharf, Bryggen, with the Hanseatiske Museum on the right

VISITORS' CHECKLIST

County of Hordaland. 🏙 250,000.
✈ 20 km (12 miles) S of town. 🚇
🚢 Strømgaten 8. 🚢 Frieleneskaien
(Hurtigruten), Strandkaiterminalen
(regional). 🛈 Vågsallmenningen 1,
55 55 20 00. 🐟 Fish Market (Mon–
Sat; daily in summer). 🎭 Dragon
Boat Festival (May), International
Festival (May–Jun), Night Jazz (May–
Jun), Food Festival (Aug). **www**.
visitbergen.com

🏛 Bryggen

North side of Vågen harbour.
🕐 Jun–Aug, 55 55 20 00. ♿
The old timber warehouses
on the northern side of the
harbour were originally
known as Tyskebryggen (the
German Quay), because for
400 years, until 1754, they
were at the hub of Hanseatic
trade in Norway. Long before
the German Hansa traders,
this part of the town had
been a trading centre for fish
and fish products. On many
occasions over the centuries
the medieval gabled houses
facing the harbour have been
ravaged by fires. The last,
in 1955, left only 10 gables
standing. Today, Bryggen
is a centre for artists and a
popular restaurant area. It is
included in UNESCO's World
Heritage List.

🏛 Hanseatiske Museum

Finnegårdsgaten 1A. **Tel** 55 54 46
90. 🕐 daily. 🔵 1 Jan, 17 May, 24,
25 & 31 Dec. 🎟 🕐 summer.
Established in 1872, the
Hanseatisk Museum is located
in one of Bryggen's expansive
German merchant's houses
dating from the end of the
Hanseatic era. A number of
traders were housed here,
next to rooms for drying fish,
offices and storerooms. The
early 18th-century interiors
give a good impression of
how they lived and worked.

A separate section of the
museum features four assembly
rooms used for eating, entertainment, learning, and for
keeping warm in winter.

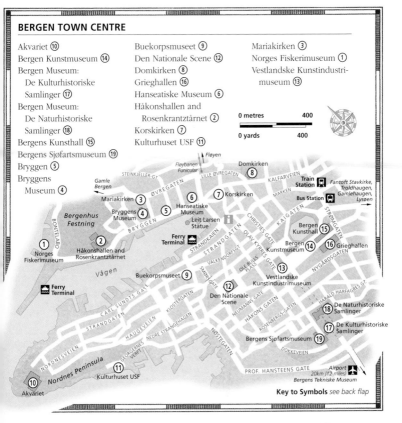

BERGEN TOWN CENTRE

Akvariet ⑩
Bergen Kunstmuseum ⑭
Bergen Museum:
  De Kulturhistoriske
  Samlinger ⑰
Bergen Museum:
  De Naturhistoriske
  Samlinger ⑱
Bergens Kunsthall ⑮
Bergens Sjøfartsmuseum ⑲
Bryggen ⑤
Bryggens
  Museum ④

Buekorpsmuseet ⑨
Den Nationale Scene ⑫
Domkirken ⑧
Grieghallen ⑯
Hanseatiske Museum ⑥
Håkonshallen and
  Rosenkrantztårnet ②
Korskirken ⑦
Kulturhuset USF ⑪

Mariakirken ③
Norges Fiskerimuseum ①
Vestlandske Kunstindustri-
  museum ⑬

0 metres   400

0 yards   400

Key to Symbols see back flap

Exploring Bergen Town Centre

Bergen has at its heart the peaceful haven of Lille Lungegårdsvann, a lake surrounded by parkland and trees and, in summer, a colourful show of rhododendrons. On its western side is Festplassen, the city's festival square with its music pavilion. Festplassen opens into the boulevard, Ole Bulls Plass, that leads to Den Nationale Scene (the National Theatre). A few blocks to the north of Festplassen is the famous Fisketorget (the Fish Market). Bergen's most important art galleries are situated on the south side of the lake.

The fish market taking place on Torget, Monday to Saturday

Buekorps boys parading in Bergen town centre

🛕 Korskirken
Korskirkealmenningen.
Tel 55 59 32 70. ◯ Mon–Sat. ⬆ noon Wed.
To the east of Torget and the innermost part of Vågen is Korskirken (the Church of the Cross). It was erected around 1100, originally as a three-aisled Romanesque long church. A south wing was added in 1615 and a north wing in 1623, thus creating its characteristic cruciform plan. A beautiful Renaissance portal with Christian IV's monogram graces the northern end.

🛕 Domkirken
Kong Oscars Gate 22. **Tel** 55 31 58 75. ◯ daily. Jun–Aug: 9.30am Sun in English.
Bergen's cathedral was originally a parish church, Olavskirken, dating from the latter half of the 12th century. When a Franciscan monastery was established in Bergen around 1250, the church was taken over by the monks. As with so many other buildings

in Bergen, Olavskirken was ravaged by fire. On one occasion it was restored by Geble Pederssøn, who in 1537 became Norway's first Lutheran bishop. He built a new tower and installed the clock above the western entrance. The multi-sided Gothic choir with its high windows has remained untouched. The church's large Rieger organ has 61 stops.

The poet Ludvig Holberg, considered the founder of modern Norwegian literature, was a pupil at the nearby Latin School from 1698 to 1702.

🎖 Buekorpsmuseet
Murhvelvingen. **Tel** 55 90 45 30. ◯ Sat & Sun. ● mid-Jul–mid-Aug.
The 400-year-old Muren (Wall Gate), originally the private home of a high-ranking official Erik Rosenkrantz, houses the Buekorpsmuseet. The Buekorps (literally "Bow Corps") are boys' brigades. They originated in the 1850s in Bergen, and have become

a very special part of the town's traditions.

At one time the various Buekorps were rivals, but today their drills and marches are more lighthearted. Their longbows, banners and historic photographs are on display in the museum.

🐟 Akvariet
Nordnesbakken 4. **Tel** 55 55 71 71. ◯ daily. ● 24, 25 Dec, 17 May.
The aquarium is one of Bergen's most popular attractions. It contains Europe's largest collection of sea and freshwater fish and invertebrates. Inside, there are nine large and 40 smaller tanks. In addition, there are two pools with sea birds, seals and penguins. One section is dedicated to the development of marine life.

Every day 3 million litres (666,000 gals) of seawater are pumped up from the depths of Byfjorden through 8,000 m (26,246 ft) of plastic pipes.

Young spectator at the seal pool in Akvariet (the Aquarium)

🏛 Kulturhuset USF
Georgernes Verft 12. **Tel** 55 30 74 10. ◯ daily.
The former United Sardines Factories (USF) have been renovated to house the USF Cultural Centre, a large contemporary arts complex featuring music, films, theatre,

Den Nationale Scene (the National Theatre), an imposing landmark in the heart of Bergen

dance, visual arts and handicrafts. It is rare in Norway to find such a varied artistic programme under one roof.

🎭 Den Nationale Scene

Engen 1. *Tel 55 54 97 00.*
Box office ◯ *Mon–Sat.* 🚻 ▣

The first Norwegian National Theatre has its roots in Det Norske Theater in Bergen, founded in 1850 by the violinist Ole Bull. Henrik Ibsen was a director here for six years from 1851, followed by Bjørnstjerne Bjørnson from 1857 to 1859.

Since 1909 the theatre has been housed in a splendid Art Nouveau building. The original theatre building, "the Theatre in Engen", was destroyed by bombs in 1944. Den Nationale Scene has played a significant role in Norwegian theatre history, both with its repertory and its plays.

🏛 Vestlandske Kunstindustri-museum

Nordahl Bruns Gate 9. *Tel 55 33 66 33.* ◯ *15 May–15 Sep: daily; 16 Sep–14 May: Tue–Sun.* ● *public hols.* 🖼 🚻 ⊘ ▣ 🚻 ▣

Also known as Permanentum, the West Norway Museum of Decorative Art features a collection of Norwegian and foreign treasures. It includes local goldsmith art and Buddhist/Chinese art from the Sung, Ning and Ching dynasties. Also on show is a violin made by Gaspar de Salo in 1562, which belonged to the musician Ole Bull *(see p177)*. Contemporary arts and crafts are exhibited too. Part of

the museum are the country mansion at Damsgård Hovedgård and the former Alvøen paper factory, situated 5 km (3 miles) and 20 km (12 miles) from Bergen respectively. The factory has been preserved complete with workers' cottages and the owner's mansion, now a museum.

🏛 Bergen Kunstmuseum

Rasmus Meyers Allé 3 & 7, Lars Hilles Gate 10. *Tel 55 56 80 00.* ◯ *mid-May–mid Sep: daily; mid-Sep–mid-May: Tue–Sun.* ● *public hols.* 🖼 🚻 ⊘ ▣ 🚻

The three main collections of Bergen Art Museum are based in two buildings by Lille Lungegårdsvann. Bergen Billedgalleri (the City Art Collection) was established in 1878 and expanded in 2000 with a new building in Lars Hilles Gate. It is known as Vestlandets Nasjonalgalleri

(Vestlandet's National Gallery) and has a fine collection of Norwegian and European visual art from the 19th and 20th centuries. Of great historical interest are J F L Dreier's paintings of old Bergen mainly from the 1830s.

In the same building is the Stenersen Collection. It has works by Munch, Picasso, Miró, Klee and Utrillo, among others, donated by Rolf Stenersen *(see p58).*

The focus of the Rasmus Meyer Collection is on Norwegian and Scandinavian works, 1760–1915, including Edvard Munch, J C Dahl, Adolf Tidemand, Harriet Backer and Christian Krohg. They were donated to Bergen by the art collector Rasmus Meyer, who died in 1916.

Note the decorative Rococo interiors with ceilings painted by Mathias Blumenthal.

Scene from Bergen's Inner Harbour, J C Dahl (1834), Bergen Kunstmuseum

⛪ Bergens Kunsthall

Rasmus Meyers Allé 5.
Tel 55 55 93 10. ◯ Tue–Sun.
◯ some public hols. 🎫 ♿ 📷

The Bergen Art Association was established in 1838. It holds nine or ten exhibitions of contemporary art every year at Bergens Kunstforening, of which the prestigious Festspillutstilling (May–August) is the most important. The building was designed by the architect Ole Landmark (1885–1970).

🎵 Grieghallen

Edvard Griegs Plass 1. **Tel** 55 21 61 50. **Box office** ◯ Mon–Sat and before events. ♿ 📷 🎫

Bergen's modern concert hall, Grieghallen, was opened in 1978. Designed by the Danish architect Knud Munk, it is the country's largest auditorium with 1,500 seats. A smaller hall accommodates 600 people. Grieghallen is also used for opera, ballet, theatrical productions and congresses. It is the central venue for events during the Bergen International Festival (Festspillene). The festival has been held every year in May and June since 1953, attracting artists from all over the world.

Bergen Filharmoniske Orkester (the Bergen Philharmonic Orchestra), also known as Harmonien, holds concerts every Thursday at Grieghallen from September to May. The orchestra was founded in 1765.

Whales skeletons in Bergen Museum's De Naturhistoriske Samlinger

⛪ Bergen Museum: De Naturhistoriske Samlinger

Muséplass 3. **Tel** 55 58 29 20.
◯ Tue–Sat. ● public hols.
📷 📹 ♿

Comprehensive botanic, geological and zoological collections as well as a botanical garden and plant house make up Bergen Museum's De Naturhistoriske Samlinger (the Natural History Collection). Both the natural history and the cultural history collections were founded by the president of the Norwegian Parliament, W F K Christie, in 1825. The natural history collection is housed in an imposing hillside building on Nygårdshøyden dating from 1866 and 1898. It was designed by J H Nebelong and H J Sparre.

The zoological section shows stuffed animals, birds and fish from all over the world, including an exhibition titled "Wild Life in Africa".

The geological section features an eye-catching mineral collection with fine samples from the Bergen region and further afield. The life of our early ancestors is exposed in "The Evolution of Man". Other exhibits focus on "Oil Geology" and "The Green Evolution – the Development of the Planet".

The botanical gardens, known as Muséhagen, are a mass of blooms in the

Grieghallen (1978), venue for the annual Bergen International Festival

For hotels and restaurants in this region see pp233–5 and pp250–3

summer months. In the greenhouses tropical plants can be seen all year round. Muséhagen was established in 1897 and over the years it has amassed 3,000 different species. The selection of plants is particularly large and varied. When the gardens outgrew their original site new gardens and an arboretum were created at Milde about 20 km (12 miles) south of the town centre.

The extensive research carried out by Bergen Museum's natural and cultural history departments paved the way for the establishment of Bergen University, which today has more than 17,000 students, seven faculties and 90 institutes.

The Stone Age Lofoten horse, in existence until around 1900

🏛 Bergen Museum: De Kulturhistoriske Samlinger

Håkon Sheteligs Plass 10.
Tel 55 58 31 40. ◯ *Tue–Sun.*
⬤ *public hols.* 🈂 ♿
Situated opposite the Natural History Museum, on the other side of Muséhagen, is the Cultural History Collection of

Romanesque bench from Rennebu church, De Kulturhistoriske Samlinger

Bergen Museum, De Kulturhistoriske Samlinger. The collection occupies a large building designed by Egill Reimers in 1927.

Innovative displays focus on Norwegian culture and folk art as well as some exhibits from foreign cultures. The unusual archaeological collection is based on finds from the counties of Hordaland, Sogn and Fjordane, and Sunnmøre in Western Norway. Exhibits are shown in themed displays such as "The Stone Age" and "The Viking Age". "Legacy from Europe" depicts the cultural exchange between Norway and the rest of Europe.

The colourful motifs of Norwegian folk art are explored in the "Roses and Heroes" exhibition, while beautiful local folk costumes (*see pp24–5*) are part of the "Rural Textiles" collection.

"Ibsen in Bergen" describes Henrik Ibsen's inspirational

work at Det Norske Theatre (the National Theatre) in Bergen from 1851–7.

Anthropological exhibitions include "Between Coral Reef and Rain Forest", "Indians, Inuit and Aleut: the Original Americans" and "Eternal Life: Egyptian Mummies".

The museum is noted for its collection of ecclesiastical art, including Russian icons.

🏛 Bergens Sjøfartsmuseum

Håkon Sheteligs Plass 15.
Tel 55 54 96 00. ◯ *Jun–Aug: daily;*
Sep–May: Mon–Fri, Sun. 🈂 ♿
The story of Norwegian shipping from early times can be explored in Bergens Sjøfartsmuseum (Maritime Museum), with special emphasis on Vestlandet. The ground floor covers the era up to 1900; the first floor focuses on the 20th century and the age of steam and motor craft, to the present day.

There is an extensive model collection of Viking ships and various working boats, including the deckhouse of the training ship *Statsraad Lemkuhl.* "Coastal and Fjord Boats" describes life aboard for the crew and passengers of the vessels working up and down the coast.

The Maritime Museum was founded in 1921. It is housed in a striking stone building, with an atrium in the centre, designed by Per Grieg and completed in 1962.

In summer children of all ages congregate in the atrium to play with remote-controlled model boats. On the "promenade deck" visitors are invited to relax in deckchairs and look out over one of Bergen's busiest harbours.

Bergens Sjøfartsmuseum, left, and De Kulturhistoriske Samlinger

Bergen Further Afield

When the old town of Bergen was combined for administrative purposes with a number of outlying districts in 1972, it increased in size tenfold. The "new" Bergen now includes fjords and mountains, lakes and plateaus, forests and fields, valleys and rivers, and a wealth of architectural treasures.

The funicular railway Fløybanen, with panoramic views of Bergen

🏛 Gamle Bergen

Elsesro, 5 km (3 miles) N of town centre. **Museum Tel** *55 39 43 00.* ⬜ *12 May–1 Sep: daily.* 🚫 ☑ 🚻 🛒
An open-air museum, Gamle Bergen was founded in 1949 on the old patrician site of Elsesro in Sandviken. The buildings, furniture, domestic utensils, clothes and everyday items on show provide a graphic illustration of life in Bergen in the 18th and 19th centuries. Workshop interiors and shops give an idea of the living conditions of the different social classes, such as sailors and high-ranking officials, artisans and labourers. Around the houses are streets and paths, squares and alleys designed to imitate the style of the times.

🎿 Fløyen

Vestrelidsalmenningen 23.
Kabelbanen Tel *55 33 68 00.*
⬜ *daily.* 🚻 🛒
The mountain of Fløyfjellet, commonly known as Fløyen, is named after the weathervane at its summit. This has stood here for centuries, showing wind strength and direction for the benefit of sailors entering and leaving the harbour below. It has been blown down, burnt down, even torn down, but each time it has been rebuilt.

A funicular, opened in 1918, carries passengers 320 m (1,050 ft) to the summit from the city centre near Fisketorget. At the top there are wonderful panoramic views and numerous paths for walking.

Fløyen is one of seven peaks around Bergen. Another is Ulrikken (642 m/2,106 ft), celebrated in Bergen's anthem by Johan Nordahl Brun.

Fantoft stave church, rebuilt after a serious fire in 1992

🔒 Fantoft Stavkirke

Fantoftveien 46, 5 km (3 miles) S of town centre. **Tel** *55 28 07 10.*
⬜ *mid-May–mid-Sep: daily.* 🚫
Fantoft Stavkirke (stave church) was originally built in Fortun in Sogn county around 1150. It was moved to Fantoft in 1882 where it was embellished with dragon finials and high-pitched roofs. In June 1992 the church was destroyed by fire, but was rebuilt within three years.

It was not uncommon for Norway's wooden stave churches to be relocated. Often they were transported by sea as it was more practical than using country roads. Vang Stavkirke in Valdres, for example, was sold to the king of Prussia. In 1842 it was driven across Filefjell mountain to Sogn from where it was shipped to Germany.

🏛 Gamlehaugen

Gamlehaugveien 10, 5 km (3 miles) S of town centre. **Tel** *55 92 51 20.*
⬜ *Jun–Aug: Mon–Fri.* ⬤ *when King is in residence.*
The King of Norway's official residence in Bergen is Gamlehaugen in Fjøsanger, just south of the city. It was built in 1901 by Professor Jens Zetlitz Kielland for the shipping magnate, Christian Michelsen, and is situated on a hill overlooking the land-locked fjord of Nordåsvannet.

Michelsen was Norway's first prime minister after the break up of the union with Sweden in 1905. On his death the property was purchased by the state. It features Swiss chalet-style woodcarvings and contains mostly Norwegian paintings from the late 1800s. English-style landscaped gardens surround the house.

Gamle Bergen, an open-air museum depicting life in old Bergen

For hotels and restaurants in this region see pp233–5 and pp250–3

🏛 Troldhaugen

Troldhaugveien 65, 8 km (5 miles)
S of town centre. *Tel 55 92 29 92.*
◯ Jan–Mar: Mon–Fri; Apr–Nov: daily.
◯ Dec. 🏛 ⚙ ⚙ ⚙ ⚙ ⬛ ⬛ ⬛

Troldhaugen, the former
home of the composer Edvard
Grieg and his wife Nina, is
beautifully situated on a
promontory on Nordåsvannet.
According to local legend, it
was a haunt for trolls, hence
the name Troldhaugen,
meaning "Hill of Trolls".

The couple lived here for
22 years from 1885 until
Grieg's death in 1907.
Designed by Schak Bull, the
interior walls are bare timber
in keeping with Norwegian
building traditions. The house
remains as it was in 1907,
complete with Grieg's
Steinway piano, a gift on the
occasion of the couple's silver
wedding anniversary in 1892,
and other mementos.

The small Composer's
Cabin, where several of Grieg's
influential compositions came
to fruition, was built in 1892.
There is also a museum
and a 200-seat concert hall,
Troldsalen, which is used for
musical recitals. Hidden in
a cave facing the l
ake are the
graves of Grieg
and his wife.

Interior of Lysøen, violinist Ole Bull's idiosyncratic summer residence

Edvard and Nina Grieg's home, Troldhaugen, in Fana

🏛 Lysøen

25 km (16 miles) S of town centre.
Tel 56 30 90 77. ◯ mid-May–Aug:
daily; Sep: Sun; groups by
arrangement. 🏛 ⚙ ⚙ ⬛ ⬛ ⬛
Ole Bull was one of the
greatest violin virtuosos of his
time, and in Norway he is
regarded as a national hero.
He was born in Bergen in
1810 and died at his summer
island retreat, Lysøen, in 1880.

The extraordinary house, his
"little Alhambra", was built in
1872 and extended in 1905.

Bull designed his summer
residence himself with the help
of the architect C F von der
Lippe. The house is inspired
by a diversity of classical and
medieval styles. Built in
Norwegian pine, it features a
tower with a Russian Orthodox
onion dome and a Moorish
door, and is exotically
decorated both inside and out.

Lysøen is a testament to its
capricious creator. In 1973
Bull's great-granddaughter,
Sylvia Bull Curtis, donated
the property to the Society
for the Preservation of
Norwegian Ancient
Monuments. The island
can be explored through its
many footpaths.

🏛 Bergens Tekniske Museum

Thormøhlens Gate 23.
Tel 55 96 11 60. ◯ Sun and, by
arrangement, Mon–Fri. 🏛 ⚙
The old Trikkehallen (tram
hall) in Møhlenpris houses
Bergens Tekniske Museum
(Technical Museum). Its
exhibitions on energy,
industry, communications and
science appeal to all ages.

There are displays of
technical appliances ranging
from vehicles and washing
machines to fire-fighting
equipment and military
materials. Here it is possible to
find vintage cars, motorcycles,
buses, a working smithy, a
printing-press and an early
steam-engine and carriages.
The museum also has model
boats and a model railway.

EDVARD GRIEG

Edvard Grieg (1843–1907) was Norway's
foremost composer, pianist and
conductor. He was born in Bergen in
1843. At the age of 15, on the advice of
the violinist Ole Bull, he enrolled at the
Leipzig Conservatory to study music.
Later, in Copenhagen, he came into
contact with influential composers of
the time, such as Niels Gade. Grieg's
aim was to create a Norwegian style of
music for which he sought inspiration
in folk music. Among his most well-
known works is the music for Ibsen's
Peer Gynt. In 1867 he married his
cousin, the soprano singer Nina Hagerup.

**Edvard Grieg
1843–1907**

Exploring Sognefjorden

The first tourists came to Sognefjorden more than 150 years ago. In those days travel was exclusively by cruise ship. Today, a number of ferries, the Hurtigruten cruises *(see p283)*, local buses and the E16 and 55 roads enable an ever-increasing number of visitors to enjoy the area.

Vassbygdvatnet, a picturesque lake in the Aurland valley

Balestrand
It is the scenery above all that makes Balestrand such a popular destination on Sognefjorden. Wide and fertile strips along the shore are set against a backdrop of mighty peaks and glaciers.

The view from Balholm in the centre of town takes in the entire fjord and it is this that has attracted tourists from all over the world, laying the foundations for the early development of hotels and communications. The chalet-style Kviknes Hotel *(see p233)*, built in 1877, has a hall with dragon carvings and a large art collection.

There are two Viking burial mounds at Balholm, dating from AD 800. One mound has a statue of Bele, a legendary king in Nordic mythology who was the father of Ingeborg, Fridtjof's beloved.

Sogndal
In the orchard-dotted area of Sogndal, the village of **Kaupanger** features a stave church dating from the 12th century. Nearby is the open-air Sogn Folkemuseum, with 32 historic buildings.

At the innermost tip of the fjord is the fast-flowing River **Årøyelva**, renowned for physically demanding salmon fishing (record catch: a fish weighing 34 kg/75 lb). The

path of the salmon is blocked by Helvetesfossen (Hell's waterfall), and the fishing spots below are wryly named "the platforms of despair".

Lærdal
The small centre of features a collection of beautiful timber buildings from the 18th and 19th centuries. On the banks of the river Lærdalselva, the **Norsk Villakssenter** (Norwegian Wild Salmon Centre) has an observatory for viewing the salmon. The only way to get from Lærdal to Aurland used to be either by a long detour via ferry, or the so-called Snøveien ("snow road") over the mountains. Open in summer only, it is lined by snow drifts even then. Since November 2000, however, a

24.5-km (15-mile) long tunnel cuts across deep under the mountain, linking the E16 near Lærdalsøyri with Aurlandsvangen and Flåm.

> **🏛 Norsk Villakssenter**
> Lærdal. **Tel** 57 66 67 71. ◔
> May–Sep: daily. ▨ ♿ ▯ ⏹

Aurland
The charming little town of **Aurlandsvangen** retains some of its original buildings, among them the guesthouse Åbelheim (1770). The 13th-century stone church contains stained-glass panels by Emanuel Vigeland. This is a good starting point for the hiking routes in the Aurland valley. Across the Aurland fjord, the 601 road leads to **Undredal**, the smallest stave church in the country.

Further west, on the E16, is **Gudvangen**, from where a ferry plies the dramatically narrow Nærøyfjord before continuing to Kaupanger on the other side of Sognefjord.

Flåmsbanen
One of the world's most breathtaking railway journeys is the Flåmsbanen. It is just over 20-km (12-miles) long, but has an impressive height difference of 864 m (2,835 ft) between Myrdal on the mountain plateau and Flåm by the shore of Aurlandsfjord.

The railway was opened in 1942. There are 20 tunnels on the line and nine stops, each with a different panorama, including the awe-inspiring waterfall of Kjosfossen. The 50-minute journey can be taken as part of the "Norway in a Nutshell" tour *(see p282)*.

Lærdalsøyri with its wharfside buildings bordering Sognefjorden

Borgund Stavkirke ⑯

Borgund Stavkirke at Lærdal is the only stave church to
have remained unchanged since the Middle Ages.
Dedicated to the apostle St Andrew, it dates from
around 1150 and is built entirely of wood. The interior
is very simple: there are no pews or decorations, and
the lighting is limited to a few small openings high up
on the walls. The exterior is richly decorated with
carvings, dragon-like animals in life and death
struggles, dragonheads and runic inscriptions. There is
a free-standing belfry with a medieval bell.
The pulpit dates from the 16th century.

VISITORS' CHECKLIST

County of Sogn and Fjordane,
30 km (19 miles) E of
Lærdalsøyri. 🚌 from Lærdal.
Tel *57 66 81 09.*
⏰ *May–Sep: 10am–5pm daily.*
🚫 *Oct–Apr.* ♿ 🅿 🚫 📷 📖
www.alr.no

Dragonheads
*The tower has a three-
tiered roof. The first
tier is decorated with
dragonheads on
the gables similar
to those on the
main roof.*

The windows
were originally
simply circular
openings in the
outer walls.

Nave
*Twelve posts (staves)
around the central part
of the nave support the
roof. Disappearing into
the semi-darkness of
the roof, they give an
increased sense of height.*

The roofs are
clad in pine
shingles.

Crosses
decorate
the gables
above the
doorways
and apse
tower.

Altar with
an altar-
piece dating
from 1654.

West Door
*The exterior of the
church is richly
adorned. The
decorations on the
Romanesque west door
show vine-like
ornamentation and
dragon battles.*

**Crosses of St
Andrew**
border the
central nave.

Roof Construction
*Seen from below, the roof is
composed of an intricate
framework using numerous
rafters and joists.*

Urnes Stavkirke occupying a lofty location above Lustrafjorden

Urnes Stavkirke ⑰

County of Sogn and Fjordane. 17 km (11 miles) NE of Sogndal. *Tel* 57 67 88 89. 🏠 🚌 *15 min walk from ferry.* ◯ *May–Sep: daily.* 📷 📹 ∅

The queen of Norway's stave churches, Urnes is also the oldest. It appears on UNESCO's list of World Heritage sites along with Røros, the Alta rock carvings and Bryggen in Bergen. Built around 1130–50, it contains beams from an 11th-century church that stood on the same site.

The most notable feature of the church is the north portal. This, too, dates from an earlier building and its carvings depict the conflict between good and evil in the form of animals engaged in battle with snakes. Such animal ornamentation is known as the "Urnes Style".

Two candlesticks on the altar in metal and enamel date from the 12th century and were made in Limoges in France.

Also situated in the district of Luster is Sogn's most beautiful stone church, Dale Kirke, built in 1250.

Jostedalsbreen ⑱

County of Sogn and Fjordane. 🚌 ℹ️ *Jostedalen Tourist Information, 57 68 32 50; Jostedalsbreen National Park Centre, Oppstryn, 57 87 72 00.* **www.**jostedal.com

The largest glacial area in continental Europe, Jostedalsbreen is 100 km (62 miles) long and 15 km (9 miles) wide. Together with Jostefonn, which used to

be joined to it, it covers 486 sq km (188 sq miles). Its highest point is Lodalskåpa (2,083 m/6,834 ft).

The ice cap sends fingers into the valleys below. In the 18th century a number of these glacial spurs extended so low they destroyed cultivated fields, but since then they have receded.

The starting points for glacier tours include Jostedalen (Nigardsbreen and Bergsethbreen glaciers), Stryn (Briksdalsbreen glacier) and Fjærland (Bøyabreen and Supphellebreen glaciers).

On the innermost reaches of the sparkling green Fjærlandsfjorden is **Norsk Bremuseum** (the Norwegian Glacier Museum), an award-winning "activity museum" devoted to snow, ice, glaciers, glacier hiking and climbing. A panoramic film presentation takes the viewer on a virtual glacier experience.

🏛 **Norsk Bremuseum**
Fjærland. *Tel* 57 69 32 88.
◯ *Apr–Oct: daily; other times by prior arrangement.* 📷 ♿ 🖥 🏪

Førde and Jølster ⑲

County of Sogn and Fjordane. 🏔 10,800. ✈ 🚌 🍴 *Langebruveien 20, 57 72 19 51.* 🎵 *International Folk Music Festival (1st week Jul).* **www.**sunnfjord.no

The town of Førde lies at the heart of the county of Sogn and Fjordane. It has a cultural centre, **Førdehuset**, housing an arts centre and gallery,

library, cinema and theatre. The **Sunnfjord Museum**, comprising 25 buildings from around 1850, is also in Førde.

East of the town, in Vassenden, there is another cultural heritage museum, **Jølstramuseet**, with houses from the 17th century. Nearby is the tranquil rural museum **Astruptunet**, where the painter Nikolai Astrup once lived (1880–1928).

This area is renowned for fishing. The Jølstra river has a salmon ladder dating from 1871. The river flows from Jølstravatnet lake, which teems with large trout. There is good fishing in Gularvassdraget.

🏛 **Sunnfjord Museum**
9 km (6 miles) E of Førde. *Tel* 57 72 12 20. ◯ *Jun–Aug: daily; Sep–May: Mon–Fri.* ⬤ *public hols.* 📷 📹 *by arrangement.* ♿ 🖥 🏪

🏛 **Jølstramuseet**
20 km (12 miles) E of Førde. *Tel* 57 72 71 85. ◯ *15 Jun–15 Aug: Sat & Sun; other times by arrangement.* 📷 📹 🏪

🏛 **Astruptunet**
26 km (16 miles) E of Førde. *Tel* 57 72 67 82. ◯ *late May–mid-Aug: daily; mid-Aug–Sep: Thu, Sat & Sun.* 📷 📹 ♿ ∅ 🖥 🏪

Nordfjord ⑳

County of Sogn and Fjordane. ✈ *Sandane.* 🚌 🚢 ℹ️ *Stryn Tourist Information, 57 87 40 40.* 🎿 *Summer Skiing Festival in Stryn (Jun); Fish Festival in Stryn (Jul).* **www.**nordfjord.no

The northernmost fjord in Sogn and Fjordane county is Nordfjord. Measuring 110 km

Astruptunet, home of the painter and graphic artist Nikolai Astrup

The hamlet of Ervik on Stad peninsula

(68 miles) in length, Nordfjord extends from Måløy in the west inland to Stryn near the border with eastern Norway.

The area around Stryn has been a sought-after destination since 1850 when the first English outdoor enthusiasts arrived. Opportunities abound for mountaineering, glacier hiking, skiing and fishing.

There are several glacier spurs from Jostedalsbreen. Briksdalsbreen can be reached by horse and carriage from Briksdal (tickets, Stryn tourist office); the one on Strynfjell is accessible by chairlift from Stryn Summer Ski Centre.

Loen, on Lovatnet lake, was devastated in 1905 when part of the mountain, Ramnefjellet, fell into the lake causing an enormous wave. It killed 63 people and destroyed houses.

From Stryn there are two roads around Nordfjorden. The northernmost (RV15) runs along Hornindalsvatnet, Europe's deepest lake, to **Nordfjordeid**, a centre for the breeding and rearing of Norwegian Fjord Horses. The southernmost (RV60, E39) passes through Innvik, Utvik and Byrkjelo to Sandane. The **Nordfjord Folkemuseum** in Sandane comprises 40 18th- and 19th-century houses.

🏛 Nordfjord Folkemuseum
Sandane. **Tel** 57 87 61 22. ☐ 1 May–30 Jun: Mon–Fri; 1 Jul–15 Aug: daily; 16 Aug–12 Sep: Mon–Fri; 13 Sep–30 Apr: by prior arrangement. ● public hols. 🖼
🛇 🖻 ☐ summer only.

Selje and Stad ㉑

County of Sogn and Fjordane.
🏃 3,100. 🚌 🚢 🛈 Selje Tourist Information, 57 85 66 06.

From Måløy on the outer reaches of Nordfjord it is not far to the Stad peninsula and **Vestkapp**, one of Norway's westernmost points. Here stands "Kjerringa", a 460-m (1,509-ft) high rock that plunges steeply into the water. From the top there are panoramic views out to sea. Below, in **Ervik**, a chapel commemorates the loss of the coastal passenger ferry, *St Svithun*, in World War II.

On the island of Selje are the ruins of a monastery built by Benedictine monks in the 12th century. The monastery is dedicated to St Sunniva, daughter of an Irish king, who fled east to escape betrothal to a heathen chieftain. Her party came ashore on Selje and sought refuge in a cave.

Geirangerfjorden ㉒

County of Møre and Romsdal.
🚌 🛈 Geiranger, 70 26 32 14.
www.geiranger.no

The inner part of Storfjorden divides to form two of Norway's best-known fjords: Tafjorden to the north and Geirangerfjorden to the south.

The 16-km (10-miles) long Geirangerfjorden is the quintessential fjord. A strip of dazzling green water snakes its way to the village of Geiranger, below precipitous mountains with farms perched on the slopes and cascading waterfalls.

The RV63, Grotli-Geiranger-Åndalsnes, is known as the Golden Route. Driving south from Geiranger, the road passes Flydalsjuvet, an overhanging cliff providing a picture-postcard view of the fjord and surrounding mountains. It continues to the mountain hut of Djupvasshytta, from where it is possible to reach the summit of Dalsnibba (1,476 m/4,843 ft).

North from Geiranger, a dramatic part of the Golden Route leads to Norddalsfjorden. This is known as Ørnveien (the Eagle's Road) and offers panoramic vistas. A ferry leads across the fjord to Valldal, where the next section, known as Trollstigveien (the Trolls' Path), leads to Åndalsnes (see p186) via some dizzying hair-pin bends and great views.

Tafjorden was hit by a tragedy in 1934 when an immense rock from Langham-maren crashed into the fjord, causing a huge wave which killed 40 people in Tafjord.

Geirangerfjorden, known as the pearl of the Norwegian fjords

Ålesund ㉓

Møre and Romsdal. 42,300. ✕
🚌 ⛴ ℹ️ *Keiser Wilhelms Gate 11,
70 15 76 00.* 🎭 *Dragon Boat Festival
(mid-Jun), Ålesund Theatre Festival
(2nd week Jul), Ålesund Boat Festival
(2nd week Jul), Norwegian Food
Festival (4th week Aug).*
www.visitalesund.com

The centre of Ålesund was
destroyed in a catastrophic
fire in 1904. Fellow
Europeans came quickly to
the rescue with help and
donations and in just three
years the town
was rebuilt
almost entirely
in the Art
Nouveau style.
For this reason,
Ålesund
occupies a very
special place in
the architectural
history of
Europe. It spans
several islands
linked by
bridges. Today,
it is an important fishing port,
but Ålesund did not receive
town status until 1848.

**Art Nouveau
detail, Ålesund**

The area of Borgund,
now part of Ålesund, was
a market town and centre
of the Sunnmøre region
from around 1200. From the
mountain lodge, **Fjellstua**,
there is a panoramic view
over the town.

Ålesund Museum has one
section devoted to the town
and another to the Arctic.

The Trolltindane, described in legends as a troll wedding procession

Sunnmøre Museum consists
of 40 historic houses and
boathouses and 30 different
types of fishing boats.

Southwest of Ålesund is
the island of **Runde**. It is
renowned for its nesting cliffs,
which provide a habitat for
around one million seabirds.
There are 100,000 puffins and
50,000 kittiwake pairs, and
the rare northern gannet can
also be seen here.

The Dutch East India vessel
Akerendam went down off
the island in 1725 with a
valuable cargo. Divers have
subsequently recovered a
large haul of gold and silver
coins from the wreck.

🏛 **Ålesund Museum**
Rønnebergs Gate 16. **Tel** *70 12 31
70.* ⬜ *daily.* ⬤ *some public hols.*
♿

🏛 **Sunnmøre Museum**
5 km (3 miles) E of town centre.
Tel *70 17 40 00.* ⬜ *mid-May–23
Jun: Mon–Fri & Sun; 24 Jun–Aug:
daily; Sep–mid-May: Mon, Tue, Fri,
Sun.* 🎫 ♿ *summer.* 📷 🏪

Runde
30 km (19 miles) SW of town
centre. 🚌 to Fosnavåg. ⛴
ℹ️ *70 01 37 90.*

Åndalsnes ㉔

County of Møre and Romsdal.
7,700. ✕ *Molde.* 🚌 🚂
🚂 *Jernbanegt 1, 71 22 16 22.*
🎭 *Norwegian Mountain Festival
(mid-Jul), Sinclair Festival (2nd week
Aug).* www.visitandalsnes.com

Where the Rauma river enters
Romsdalsfjorden lies the
resort of Åndalsnes, terminus
of the Raumabanen railway.
On the eastern side of the
valley is Romsdalshorn (1,554
m/5,098 ft). Opposite are the
ragged peaks of **Trolltindane**
(1,795 m/5,889 ft) with a
sheer vertical cliff to the
valley. This is a popular spot
for mountaineering.

Trollstigveien (the Troll's
Path) is a thrilling drive with
11 breathtaking hairpin bends
between Åndalsnes and
Valldalen to the south. Along
the road there are views of
the waterfalls, Stigfossen and
Tverrdalsfossen. Each summer a
ski race, *Trollstigrennet*, is held
on the Trollstigheimen pass.

Molde ㉕

County of Møre and Romsdal.
24,000. ✕ 🚌 *to Åndalsnes, then
bus.* 🚌 ⛴ ℹ️ *Storgata 31, 71 20
10 00.* 🎭 *Molde International Jazz
Festival (mid-Jul), Bjørnsson Festival
(mid-Aug).* www.visitmolde.com

Known as the "Town of
Roses" for its rose gardens
and lush vegetation, Molde is
an attractive fjord-side place.
The term "Molde Panorama"
is used to describe the

Bird's eye view of Ålesund from Fjellstua

scenery here: from Varden it is possible to see 87 snow-covered peaks on a clear day. In July Molde is the site of a lively jazz festival, attracting top musicians from abroad.

The outdoor museum of timber houses, **Romsdalsmuseet**, also contains a fascinating collection of national costumes.

Fiskerimuseet (the Fisheries Museum), on the island of Hjertøya near Molde, focuses on the cultural history of the coastal population.

While on the Molde peninsula, it is worth visiting both the fishing village of **Bud**, which faces the infamous stretch of sea known as Hustadvika, and the marble cave of **Trollkyrkja** (Troll Church), around 30 km (19 miles) to the north.

On Eresfjorden is a waterfall, **Mardalsfossen**, with the highest unbroken vertical drop in Northern Europe, 297 m (974 ft). It is at its most dramatic from 20 Jun–20 Aug.

Atlanterhavsveien (the Atlantic Road), from Averøy toward Kristiansund, is spectacular. It passes over islets and skerries and across 12 low bridges that have been built right out in the sea.

🏛 **Romsdalsmuseet**
Per Adams Vei 4. *Tel* 71 20 24 60.
⏷ Jun–mid-Aug: daily. 🖼 ▢ ▢ ▯

🏛 **Fiskerimuseet**
Hjertøy (boat from Molde in summer). *Tel* 71 20 24 60. ⏷ end-Jun–mid-Aug: daily. 🖼 ▢

Kristiansund ㉖

County of Møre and Romsdal. 🗺 17,000. ✈ ▢ ⛴ 🛈 Kongens Plass 1, 71 58 54 54. 🎭 Opera Festival (Feb), Children's Festival (Apr), Nordic Light Festival (Apr/May), Music Festival (Jun). www.visitkristiansund.com

From the cairn on the island of Kirkelandet there is a magnificent view over this and the two other islands that comprise Kristiansund.

The sheltered harbour, always busy with boats, gave rise to the coastal settlement of Lille-Fossen, or Fosna. In 1742 when it acquired town status it was renamed

The Atlantic Road, winding its way across islands and sounds

Kristiansund. Between 1830 and 1872 the town developed into the country's biggest exporter of *klippfisk* (salted, dried cod). Kristiansund was almost entirely destroyed by bombs in April 1940. The reconstruction created a new image for the town, with modern buildings such as the town hall and the church in many different colours.

Nordmøre Museum contains a special exhibition of archaeological finds from the Fosna culture, and a fisheries exhibition.

North of Kristiansund is the tiny island of **Grip**, inhabited only in summer. All that remains of this former fishing community is a 15th-century stave church in which the population took refuge from the fearsome storms. There is a boat connection in summer.

Long ago Kristiansund could only be reached by boat, but today there is an airport and road connections to the mainland. To the southeast the RV70 passes through a number of tunnels and over

bridges as the landscape becomes more mountainous. **Tingvoll Kirke**, also known as Nordmøre Cathedral, dates from around 1200 and has an exquisite altarpiece and runic inscriptions on the chancel wall.

At Tingvollfjorden the road passes Ålvundeid, where there is a side road to the magnificent **Innerdalen** valley with the Dalatårnet peak and the mountains of Trollheimen. At the end of the fjord is **Sunndalsøra**, where the famous salmon and sea trout river Driva has its mouth.

🏛 **Nordmøre Museum**
2 km (1 mile) N of town centre. *Tel* 71 58 70 00. ⏷ Mar–Nov: Tue–Fri & Sun; other times: Tue–Fri. 🖼 ▯ 🏷 partly. ▯ ▢ ▯

🐟 **Grip**
14 km (9 miles) N of Kristiansund. ▢ ⛴ from Kristiansund. 🛈 Turistinformasjonen, Kristiansund, 71 58 54 54.

🔒 **Tingvoll Kirke**
55 km (32 miles) SE of Kristiansund. *Tel* 71 53 03 03. ⏷ May–Sep: daily (concert 5pm Sat). 🖼

Kristiansund with its colourful houses and imposing church

Oppdal ①

County of Sør-Trøndelag. 🏛 6,300.
🚂 🚌 ℹ️ O. Skasliens Vei 15,
72 40 04 70. 🎿 Oppdal Free-ride
Challenge (Easter), Fell Market (Sep),
Vintersleppet (1st week Dec).
www.oppdal.com

Oppdal is a vibrant tourist centre all year round, but particularly in winter. Its excellent winter sports facilities include 200 km (124 miles) of ski slopes, a cable car and ski lifts, ski huts, cafés and restaurants. The skiing season starts with the Vintersleppet festival, while the off-piste Free-ride Challenge race attracts daring skiers around Easter.

The town occupies a beautiful mountain setting. It is an important junction on the Dovrebanen railway and has good road connections.

The open-air **Oppdal Bygdemuseum** has a fine collection of old houses of cultural interest. Outside the town, at **Vang**, there is a large Iron Age burial ground.

Oppdal is the starting point for the journey northward to Vårstigen (the Spring Path), the old pilgrims' route *(see p189)*, through Drivdalen valley and to Dovrefjell National Park *(see pp138–9)*.

From Festa bridge in the west, the toll road heads north to **Gjevilvasshytta**, an elegant tourist lodge incorporating Tingstua, the old courthouse from Meldal.

🏛 **Oppdal Bygdemuseum**
Museumsveien. **Tel** 72 42 15 50. ⭕
end Jun–mid-Aug: Tue–Sun. 📷 🚫 🏛

The 17th-century copper-mining town of Røros, preserved for posterity

Røros ②

County of Sør-Trøndelag. 🏛 5,500.
✈️ 🚂 🚌 ℹ️ Peder Hiorts Gate 2,
72 41 11 65. 🎿 Røros Market (3rd
week Feb), Winter Festival (mid-Mar),
Garpvukku Historical Play (2nd week
Aug). **www**.rorosinfo.com

Life in Røros revolved around the copper mine founded in 1644 on a bleak site 600 m (2,000 ft) above sea level. The mining town, complete with its turf-roofed timber cottages, church and company buildings, has survived, unscathed by fire, to become a UNESCO World Heritage site.

The town's most prominent landmark is the Baroque church of Bergstadens Ziir,

built in stone in 1780. Inside there is an imposing Baroque organ, pulpit and altar, and pews where the community were obliged to sit in strict hierarchical order.

Bergskrivergården, the mining company director's house, is situated on Bergmannsgata, the street that was home to those who had wealth and status. The mining museum, **Rørosmuseet**, housed in the reconstructed Smeltehytte (the old smelter), has models of the mines and smelting processes.

About 13 km (8 miles) east of Røros is the disused mine of **Olavsgruva**, featuring Bergmannshallen, a concert hall and theatre built inside the mountain. There are tours of the old mineshafts.

Røros has been immortalized in books by Johann Falkeberget (1879–1967), who lived locally. His story about a peasant girl who transported copper ore was made into a film, *An-Magritt*, starring Liv Ullmann.

🏛 **Rørosmuseet**
Sleggeveien. **Tel** 72 41 61 55.
⭕ daily. ⚫ some public hols.
📷 🚫 🏛 🏛

🎫 **Olavsgruva**
13 km (8 miles) E of town centre.
Tel 72 40 61 70. ⭕ tours only.
📷 ✓ Sat. 🚫 🏛

Oppdal, a region of farmland and mountains renowned for winter sports

Outer Trondheims-fjorden ❸

County of Sør-Trøndelag.
🄸 *Trøndelag Reiseliv, 73 84 24 40.*
www.trondelag.com

Approaching Trondheims-fjorden from the west, the shipping channel passes to the inside of Hitra, the largest island in southern Norway. The fjord itself begins at the promontory of Agdenes.

To the north of the fjord entrance lies the flat and fertile region of Ørlandet, site of the castle of **Austrått**. The estate was owned by the powerful Rømer family. Inger Ottesdatter Rømer, who died in 1555, is the main protagonist in Ibsen's play *Lady Inger of Østeråt*. The land then passed by marriage to the Bjelke family. The castle was built in Renaissance style between 1654 and 1656 by Chancellor Ove Bjelke, brother to Jørgen Bjelke, who in 1658 recaptured the county of Trondheim from Sweden.

Austrått appears rather stern and unwelcoming from the outside, with its soapstone doorway and coats of arms. Inside, it is quite the opposite. A brightly painted inner courtyard is embellished with carved pillars in the form of female figures – "the wise and foolish virgins".

West of Trondheim, an arm of the fjord leads to Orkanger near the Thamshavnsjenbanen (Thamshavn railway line). Here, electric locomotives and three-person carriages

from 1908 are on display. Pride of place at **Orkla Industrimuseum** (Orkla Industrial Museum) is given to the lavish train carriage used by the king. The museum also includes a mining museum and the old mines of Gammelgruva.

🏨 **Austrått**
Opphaug. **Tel** *72 52 18 04.* ⬜
Jun–mid-Aug: daily. 🖼 🔲 🔲 🔲

🏛 **Orkla Industrimuseum**
Løkken Verk (Løkken Mine).
Tel *72 49 91 00.* ⬜ *Jun–Aug: daily; Sep–May: Mon–Fri.* 🔴 *public hols.*
🖼 🔲 ♿ 🔲 🔲

Trondheim ❹

See pp196–99.

Inner Trondheims-fjorden ❺

County of Nord-Trøndelag.
🄸 *Trøndelag Reiseliv, 73 84 24 40.*
www.trondelag.com

On the inner Trondheimsfjor-den, the Byneset peninsula west of Trondheim is the site of Gråkallen, one of the city's main areas for sports and recreation. Off Fosen Quay in Trondheim, **Munkholm** island has served as a fortress, monastery and prison. It is now a popular bathing spot.

The fjord is at its widest east of Trondheim. Here, by Vaernes airport, the reputed salmon river of Størdalselva has its mouth. Inland, along the river is **Hegra Festning**. In 1940, General Holtermann

The island of Munkeholmen, in Trondheimsfjorden, once a prison

and his soldiers – 248 men and one woman – resisted a German attack here for 23 days. Further east at **Reinå**, Engelskstuggu (the English cabin) recalls the early English salmon-fishing pioneers.

On the small island of **Steinvikholm**, off the eastern shore of the fjord, is a castle built by Archbishop Olav Engelbrektsson in 1525. He fled here with the casket of Olav the Holy *(see p200)* during the Reformation. The peninsula of **Frosta** is an old *tingsted* (assembly site). It contains Bronze Age burial mounds and petroglyphs.

🏨 **Hegra Festning**
15 km (9 miles) E of Stjørdal. **Tel** *Stjørdal Tourist Office, 74 83 45 80.* ⬜ *mid-May–Sep: daily; other times by arrangement.* 🖼 🔲 🔲 🔲

Levanger ❻

County of Nord-Trøndelag. 🏘 *17,500.*
✈ *Værnes, 50 km (31 miles) SW.*
🚉 🚌 🄸 *Levanger, 74 05 25 00.*
🎪 *Levanger Market (early Aug).*
www.levanger.kommune.no

In inner Trondheimsfjorden is Levanger, site of Iron Age rock carvings, burial mounds and graves. South of here, near Ekne, is the **Falstad Fangeleir**, a former World War II concentration camp.

Out in the fjord is the island of Ytterøy, beyond which the Indreøy peninsula almost blocks the fjord before its end at Steinkjer *(see p200)*. Strauma on **Indreøy** is an idyllic timber-housed hamlet.

🏛 **Falstad Fangeleir**
20 km (12 miles) S of Levanger.
Tel *74 02 80 40.* ⬜ *Tue–Sun.* 🖼
🔲 ♿

The inner courtyard at Austrått with its "wise and foolish virgins"

Trondheim ❹

Ornament, Stiftsgården

According to the Saga writer, Snorre, in 997 King Olav Tryggvason decreed that there should be a town at the mouth of the Nidelva river. The town of Trondheim, then known as Nidaros, quickly became a centre for the Trøndelag region and, for a time, capital of Norway. After King Olav Haraldsson was canonized in 1031, pilgrims flocked to his shrine at the site of Nidaros cathedral. Fire and wars in the 17th century destroyed large parts of the medieval city. The modern town with its grid-like street layout was established after a catastrophic blaze in 1681.

View over Trondheim showing Nidaros cathedral in the background

Exploring Trondheim

Most of Trondheim's sights are within easy walking distance of each other. The town centre, known as Midtbyen, is almost totally surrounded by the fjord and the meandering Nidelva river. The main street, Munkegata, passes right through the heart of the town, from the cathedral of Nidarosdomen in the south to the famous fish market of Ravnkloa in the north.

After the fire in 1681, it was the military engineer Johan Caspar de Cicignon who was mainly responsible for the grid-like layout which exists even today. Yet in the narrow side streets it seems that property owners and chance also had a hand in the layout.

⛪ Erkebispegården

Kongsgårdsgaten 1B. *Tel* 73 53 91 60. ⬜ Jun–Aug: daily; Sep–May: Tue–Sun. ⬤ some public hols. 📷 ✓ ♿ partly. ✉ 🖼

Erkebispegården (the Archbishop's Palace) has been a political and spiritual centre of power in Norway since soon after the introduction of Christianity. Part of the north wing of the main house dates from the 12th and 13th centuries, and was built as a fortified bishop's palace. Other parts of the structure were commissioned between 1430 and 1530. After the Reformation, the Archbishop's Palace became the private residence of the feudal overlord. It later served as a military base. In the 19th century it housed the Norwegian crown jewels (now in Nidaros cathedral).

In the museum in the restored south wing there are original sculptures from the cathedral and finds from the palace, among them the archbishop's coin workshop.

There is also an armoury, Rustkammeret, with a large collection of firearms and a section about the Norwegian resistance movement in World War II.

🏛 Trondheim Kunstmuseum

Bispegaten 7. *Tel* 73 53 81 80. ⬜ Jun–Aug: daily; Sep–May: Tue–Sun. 📷 ♿ 🖼 ✉

Trondheim Kunstmuseum (Museum of Art) is located close to Nidaros cathedral and the Archbishop's Residence. It contains a fine collection of paintings dating back to its precursor, the Trondheim Art Society, founded in 1845.

The most important works in the gallery are Norwegian paintings from the beginning of the 19th century until today, ranging from the Düsseldorf School to the Modernists. There is also a collection of Danish paintings that would be hard to rival outside Denmark, and an international collection of graphic art.

🏛 Nordenfjeldske Kunstindustrimuseum

Munkegaten 5. *Tel* 73 80 89 50. ⬜ Jun–Aug: daily; Sep–May: Tue–Sun. ⬤ some public hols. 📷 ✓ ♿ ✉

The red-brick buildings of Katedralskolen (the Cathedral School) and Kunstindustri-museum (the Museum of Applied Art) sit opposite one another next to the cathedral. The museum's collections include furniture, silver and textiles. In a section titled *Three Women, Three Artists*, works by the tapestry artists Hannah Ryggen and Synnøve Anker, and the glass designer Benny Motzfeld, are on show.

🎭 Trøndelag Teater

Prinsens Gate 22. *Tel* 73 80 50 00. **Box Office** ⬜ Mon–Sat. ♿ ✉ during performances.

The splendid Trøndelag Teater complex was completed in 1997. It comprises five separate stages, with seating for between 50 and 500 people in each auditorium, and offers a broad repertoire.

Incorporated into the theatre is the main stage from the original theatre, constructed in 1816. Before this time, the theatre-loving citizens used to perform in their own homes. Another piece of the interior, rescued from the old building, is the Art Nouveau café.

Trøndelag Teater combining five stages in one building

🏛 Vitenskapsmuseet

Erling Skakkes Gate 47. **Tel** 73 59 21 45. ⬤ daily. 🎫 🔊 ⚒ Ø 🚻 🏛 📷

The collections of the Museum of Natural History and Archaeology are housed in three separate buildings, named after the founders of the Royal Society of Norwegian Science (1706).

The Gerhard Schøning building traces Norway's ecclesiastical history and exhibits church interiors and religious art. The Peter Frederik Suhms building focuses on the Middle Ages.

In the Johan Ernst Gunnerus branch there are the departments of zoology and mineralogy. Special displays cover such subjects as "From the Stone Age to the Vikings" and "The Culture of the Southern Sami".

⛪ Vår Frue Kirke

Kongens Gate 2. **Tel** 73 53 84 80. ⬤ Jun–Aug: Wed; other times: Sat.

The words "The holy Mary owns me" are inscribed in Old Norse on the walls of the Vår Frue Kirke (the Church of Our Lady). Built in the late 12th century, it was the only

Vår Frue Kirke, a 12th-century church near the town square

church in Trondheim to survive the Reformation. The church was originally known as Mariakirken (the Church of Mary). It has been extended on several occasions: the tower dates from 1739. The altarpiece came from Nidaros cathedral in 1837.

🏚 Bryggen

Øvre Elvehavn.

The warehouses and wharves at the mouth of the Nidelva river have been the focus of business and trading since early times. On a number of occasions the buildings were ravaged by fire.

Now restored, the colourful buildings line both sides of the river. On the city centre

side in Kjøpmannsgata they are in a terraced area from where it was possible to attack the enemy on the river with cannon fire. On the Bakklandet side, they are situated in the streets of Fjordgata and Sandgata. The oldest remaining wharf dates from around 1700.

Warehouses on the Nidelva river, restored after fire and decay

VISITORS' CHECKLIST

County of Sør-Trøndelag.
🏘 165,000. ✈ Vaernes, 50 km (31 miles) E of town centre. 🚆 Brattøra. 🚌 Brattøra. ⛴ Pier 2. ℹ Munkegata 19, 73 80 76 60. 🎉 Festival of St Olav (4th week Jul), Norfishing (2nd week Aug).
www.trondheim.com

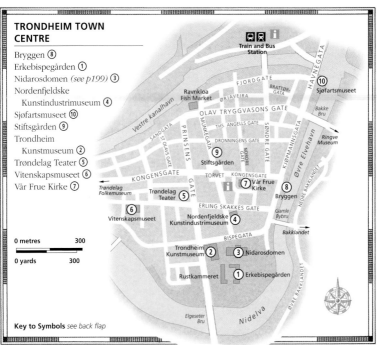

TRONDHEIM TOWN CENTRE

Bryggen ⑧
Erkebispegården ①
Nidarosdomen (see p199) ③
Nordenfjeldske
　Kunstindustrimuseum ④
Sjøfartsmuseet ⑩
Stiftsgården ⑨
Trondheim
　Kunstmuseum ②
Trøndelag Teater ⑤
Vitenskapsmuseet ⑥
Vår Frue Kirke ⑦

0 metres　　　300
0 yards　　　　300

Key to Symbols see back flap

The Queen's Room in Stiftsgården, Scandinavia's largest timber building

⛪ Stiftsgården

Munkegaten 23. *Tel 73 84 28 50.*
⬤ *Jun–Aug: daily for guided tours
only.* ⬤ *for royal visits.* 🖼️ 🅿️ 🚻

This royal residence of
Stiftsgården is one of the most
imposing old timber mansions
in Trondheim. It is an
important example of
Norwegian wooden
architecture, designed by
General G F von Krogh and
completed in 1778.
The style is Rococo,
with Baroque details.

The original owner
was Cecilie Christine
de Schøller, the
widow of the privy
councillor. Connected
to the royal court in
Copenhagen, she
was influenced by
foreign ideas and
was keen to build a
grand mansion in her attempt
to become the "first lady"
of Trondheim.

The building is 58-m
(190-ft) long and has 64
rooms. It was given the name
of "Stiftsgården" when it was
bought by the government in
1800 as a residence for the
chief officer of the diocese,
the *Stiftsamtmannen*. It
became a royal residence in
1906. The dining room, with
paintings of London and
Venice by J C C Michaelsen, is
especially worth a look.

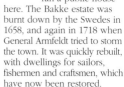

Balustrade detail,
Stiftsgården

🏛️ Trondheims Sjøfartsmuseum

Fjordgata 6A. *Tel 73 89 01 10.*
⬤ *Jun–Aug: 11am–6pm daily; Sep–
May: 11am–3pm Mon–Fri, noon–4pm
Sat & Sun.* 🖼️ 🚫 🚻

Trondheim Maritime Museum
is housed in a prison building
dating from 1725. It has a
comprehensive collection of
models of sailing ships,
figureheads and artifacts
relating to maritime life in
Trøndelag from the beginning
of the 16th century. The
exhibits include objects
rescued from the frigate
Perlen, which sank in 1781.

⛪ Bakklandet

1 km (half a mile) E of town centre.

East of the Nidelva river lies
Bakklandet, a
charming quarter
with narrow, wind-
ing streets dating
back to 1650. The
area originally bel-
onged to a nunnery.
From 1691 it was
owned by Jan
Wessel, the father of
the maritime hero
Tordenskiold, who
ran a public house
here. The Bakke estate was
burnt down by the Swedes in
1658, and again in 1718 when
General Armfeldt tried to storm
the town. It was quickly rebuilt,
with dwellings for sailors,
fishermen and craftsmen, which
have now been restored.

From the town centre,
Bakklandet can be reached
using the Old Town Bridge,
Gamle Bybro, which acquired
its carved gates in 1861. High
above Bakkland is the fortress
of Kristiansten, built by Johan
Caspar de Cicignon in 1682.

🏛️ Ringve Museum

Lade Allé 60, 4 km (2 miles) NE of
town centre. *Tel 73 87 02 80.*
⬤ *18 May–15 Sep: daily; other times:
Sun.* 🖼️ 🅿️ ♿ 🚫 📷 🚻 🖼️

Ringve is Norway's national
museum for music and
musical instruments. It was
opened in 1952, after Victoria
and Christian Anker Bachke

had designated in their will
their large country estate and
collection of musical
instruments to become a
museum. The instruments had
previously been owned by
Jan Wessel, father of the
maritime hero, Peter Wessel
Tordenskiold, after whom the
museum café, Tordenskiolds
Kro, is named.

The exhibition takes visitors
through the stages of musical
history, presenting its masters
and instruments to the
accompaniment of music
from each period.

The Botanical Gardens of
Ringve, surrounding the
mansion, are stocked with 2000
species of plants and trees.

🏛️ Trøndelag Folkemuseum

Sverresborg Allé, 4 km (2 miles)
S of town centre. *Tel 73 89 01 10.*
⬤ *daily.* ⬤ *public hols.* 🖼️ 🅿️
♿ *partly.* 🚫 🚻

Featuring more than 60
buildings from Trondheim
and around, Trøndelag
Folkemuseum gives a unique
insight into the building
traditions and daily life of the
region. The museum is
located next to the medieval
fortress of King Sverre, with a
splendid view over the town.

The 18th and 19th-century
Gammelbyen (Old Town) has
been recreated with a
dentist's surgery, a grocery
store and a shop selling old-
fashioned sweets. Look out
for Vikastua, a cottage from
Oppdal with an exceptional
rose-painted interior. The
stave church, originating from
Haltdalen, dates from 1170.

Trøndelag Folkemuseum focusing
on the traditions of the region

Trondheim: Nidarosdomen

Built on the site of Kristkirken, over the grave of
Olav the Holy *(see p200)*, the oldest part of Nidaros
cathedral dates from around 1320 in Norman, Romanesque and Gothic styles. The cathedral is the largest
construction in Norway from the Middle Ages, 102-m
(335-ft) long and 50-m (164-ft) wide. Several fires have
ravaged it over time and large parts lay in ruins when
restoration work began in 1869. A Gothic reconstruction
has now been completed. One of the chapels houses
the Norwegian crown jewels, including the
crowns of the king, queen and prince.

VISITORS' CHECKLIST

Bispegaten 5. *Tel* 73 53 91 60.
◯ *May–mid-Sep: 9am–3pm
(5:30pm Jun–Jul) Mon–Fri, 9am–
2pm Sat, 1–4pm Sun; mid-Sep–
Apr: noon–2:30pm Mon–Fri,
11:30am–2pm Sat, 1–3pm Sun.*
🎫 ♿ 📷 🍴 📷
www.nidarosdomen.no

**The main
tower** is
97.8 m
(321 ft)
high.

Rose Window
*Gabriel Kielland created
many of the cathedral's
beautiful Chartres-inspired
stained-glass works,
including the magnificent
rose window.*

Nave
*Inspired by the
architecture
of Lincoln
Cathedral and
Westminster
Abbey, the
nave is 21 m
(69 ft) high.*

**Northern
transept**
from the
12th century
in Roman-
esque style.

The altar table
is in patinated
bronze.

Silver Crucifix
*The cross, by W Ras-
mussen, was donated
by Norwegians in
the USA for the
cathedral's 900th
anniversary in 1930.*

West Front
*The middle row of
sculptures on the
ornate west wall shows,
from left to right, the
Norwegian saints
Archbishop Øystein, St
Hallvard, St Sunniva
and St Olav (Olav the
Holy), and the
heavenly virtue: Love.*

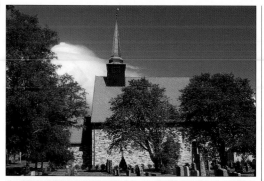

The church at Stiklestad, built 100 years after the fatal battle

Stiklestad ❼

County of Nord-Trøndelag, 4 km (2 miles) E of Verdal town centre. 🚌 to Verdal, then taxi. 🚌 during Olsok feast. www.stiklestad.no

Stiklestad is one of the most famous places in Norwegian history. It was here at a battle in 1030 that King Olav Haraldsson, later St Olav, died. The site is marked by the **Stiklestad Nasjonale Kultursenter** (National Cultural Centre). The St Olav Monument is, according to legend, situated exactly where the body of the king was hidden in a shed the night after the battle. His remains were later buried in Nidaros (now Trondheim) *(see p199)*.

Every year, around the time of the St Olav celebrations of Olsok (29 July), the play *Spelet om Heilag Olav (The Story of St Olav)*, by Olav Gullvåg and Paul Okkenhaug, is performed in the amphitheatre at Stiklestad, attracting an audience of 20,000. At the top of the amphitheatre is a statue by Dyre Vaa depicting Olav the Holy on his horse *(see below)*.

The altarpiece in **Stiklestad Kirke** is said to have been built above the stone against which Olav the Holy died. A church was built on the site shortly after the battle and replaced 100 years later by the present long church.

The tableaux in the church date from the 17th century and resemble a picture book from the Bible. The frescoes in the choir by Alf Rolfsen, showing scenes from the battle, were commissioned for the church's restoration for the St Olav Jubilee in 1928.

Verdal Museum, near the church, has a typical 19th-century farm from Verdal among its exhibits.

🏛 **Stiklestad Nasjonale Kultursenter**
4 km (2 miles) E of Verdal town centre. **Tel** 74 04 42 00. ⬭ daily. ⬤ some public hols. 🏷 ♿ 🍴 🏚

🏛 **Verdal Museum**
4 km (2 miles) E of Verdal town centre. **Tel** 74 04 42 00. ⬭ 10 Jun–10 Aug: daily. 🖥 ♿ 🏚

Bølareien, a 6,000-year-old rock carving of a reindeer

Steinkjer ❽

County of Nord-Trøndelag. 🚶 21,000. 🚌 🚂 🛈 Namdalsveien 11, 74 16 36 17. 🎪 Steinkjer Market (Aug). www.steinkjer-turist.com

Archaeological finds indicate that there has been human settlement in the Steinkjer area for 8,000 years. Burial mounds, stone circles and memorial stones have been discovered at Eggekvammen, Tingvoll and Egge, near the Byafossen waterfall. There are petroglyphs from the Stone Age and Bronze Age near Bardal, and there is also a large area of rock carvings near Hammer, 13 km (8 miles) west of Steinkjer town centre. Other finds indicate that there was an important trade and shipping centre at the head of Beitstadfjorden. Snorre writes in his sagas that Olav Tryggvason established a market town here in 997.

ST OLAV AND THE BATTLE OF STIKLESTAD

Olav Haraldsson was declared king of a united Norway at the assembly of Øretinget in 1016. He went on to convert the entire country to Christianity and in so doing made many enemies, particularly among farmers who feared that the king would become too powerful. Instead, they gave their support to King Canute of Denmark. In 1028, Canute sent 50 ships with an army to invade Norway. Olav was forced to flee. In 1030, Olav returned to re-conquer his realm. In the Verdalen valley he came face to face with his enemy at Stiklestad and died in the ensuing battle, on 29 July 1030. A year after his death, his undecayed body was exhumed and he was declared a saint. Olav was moved from one church to another until, in 1090, he was laid to rest in Kristkirken, on the site of the future Nidaros cathedral. His shrine became a place of pilgrimage. Many churches have been consecrated in his honour.

Statue of Olav the Holy at Stiklestad

Steinkjer church stands on the hill of Mærehaugen. Before the introduction of Christianity there was a temple to the Norse gods here. This is the third church on the site. The first, from 1150, burnt down, the second was destroyed during a bombing raid in 1940. The new church, designed by Olav Platou (1965), is richly decorated by artists Sivert Donali and Jakob Weidemann.

Steinkjer has good communications: the Nordlandsbanen train line and the E6 pass through the town, and the RV17 leads to the coastal areas of Flatanger and Osen. On the eastern side of Snåsavatnet lake is Bølareinen, a 6,000 year-old life-size rock carving of a reindeer.

Snåsa is the starting point for trips to Gressåmoen National Park, and to the Snåsaheiene hills, noted for their excellent fishing. In the town, **Samien Sitje** is a museum devoted to the southern Sami culture.

Salmon fishing, a popular activity on the Namsen river

🏛 **Samien Sitje**
58 km (36 miles) NE of Steinkjer.
Tel 74 13 80 00. ◯ *20 Jun–20 Aug: Tue–Fri, Sun; 21 Aug–19 Jun: by prior arrangement.* 🖼 📷 🔊 📷 📷

Namsos ❾

County of Nord-Trøndelag. 🏔 *12,500.*
✕ 🚉 🚢 🛈 *Dampskipskaia, 74 22 66 04.* 🛍 *Namsos Market (3rd week Aug).* **www**.namsosinfo.no

Namsos is situated at the innermost tip of the 35-km (22-miles) long Namsenfjorden, inside the islands of Otterøy and Jøa, featured in the novels of Olav Duun (1876–1939). The town was established in 1845 as a shipping port, particularly for timber. It was twice destroyed by fire, and was razed to the ground by bombs in World War II, but has since been rebuilt.

The Namsen river, the longest in the county of Trøndelag, enters the sea

here. It is one of Norway's best salmon rivers. Popular fishing areas are Sellæg, Grong and Overhalla. Fishing is done from boats known as *harling*, but it is also possible to fish from the bank. The Fiskumfossen waterfall north of Grong has the longest set of salmon steps in northern Europe, at 291 m (955 ft).

The **Namsskogan Familiepark** in Trones features Nordic animals in their natural environment. Further north, a side road leads to Røyrvik, the starting point for a boat connection to the Børgefjell National Park.

🐾 **Namsskogan Familiepark**
70 km (43 miles) N of Namsos.
🚌 *from Namsos. Tel* 74 33 37 00. ◯ *Jun–Aug: daily.* 🖼 📷 *by arrangement.* 🔊 📷 📷

Rørvik ❿

County of Nord-Trøndelag. 🏔 *4,000.*
🚢 🛈 *Vikna, 74 36 16 70.* 🛍 *Rørvik Festival (4th week Jul), Hurtigruten Day (1st week Jul).*

North of Namsos is the archipelago of Vikna, comprising nearly 6,000 islands. Rørvik is one of the main centres of population. At the **Nord-Trøndelags Kystmuseum** (Coastal Museum) 19th-century rowing boats used for fishing, typical of Trøndelag, are on display.

A large part of outer Vikna is a conservation area with an

abundance of nesting birds, as well as otters, porpoises and several species of seal.

To the north of Vikna, near the county boundary with Nordland, the mountain of Lekamøya rises from the sea. *Leka-møya* (the Leka Virgin) is the principal character in a Nordland folk tale. The main attractions on Leka are cave paintings in Solsemhulen and a burial mound, Herlagshaugen. The museum of cultural history, **Leka Bygdemuseum**, is located nearby.

🏛 **Nord-Trøndelags Kystmuseum**
Museumsgata 2. *Tel* 74 39 04 41.
◯ *daily.* 🖼 📷 📷 📷

🏛 **Leka Bygdemuseum**
1 km (half a mile) N of Leka.
Tel Leka, 74 38 70 11.
◯ *Jul: daily.* 🖼 📷

A European shag, part of the rich bird life on the Vikna islands

Exploring Northern Norway and Svalbard

The Lofoten Islands, Nordkapp (the North Cape) and Helgelandskysten in particular have attracted tourists over the years. But it is the magnificent scenery of all of Northern Norway and Svalbard (Spitsbergen), combined with the midnight sun in summer and the wide range of outdoor activities on offer, which make this part of Norway so appealing to travellers. People cross the Arctic Circle to fish in the sea and rivers, to join whale and seal safaris, to go bird watching and cave walking, to take trips into the mountains, or simply to enjoy a holiday in a fisherman's cabin on stilts. Far to the north lies Svalbard, with its distinctive Arctic landscape, flora, animal and bird life.

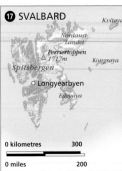

⑰ SVALBARD

Kvitøya
Nordaust-Landet
Perriertoppen
△ 1717m
Kongsøya
Spitsbergen
Longyearbyen
Edgeøya

0 kilometres   300
0 miles   200

The fishing hamlet of Hamnøy on Vestfjord in the Lofoten Islands

Sperm whale off the island of Andøya in Vesterålen

0 kilometres   100
0 miles   50

TROMSØ
Fag
SENJA ⑦
Finnsn
86
Andenes
Andøya
Risøyhamn
Andselv
Setermoen
VESTERÅLEN
Langøya
Sortland   Hinnøya
Harstad
E6
Lødingen
Bjerkvik
E10
⑤
E10
NARVIK ⑥
LOFOTEN
Austvågøya
Svolvær
Ballangen   Kiruna
Vestvågøya
Bognes
Leknes
Storriten
1503m
E10
Moskenesøy
Vestfjorden
Skutvik
Sørvågen
Nordfold
Værøy
Bonåsjøen
Røst
Kjerringøy
E6
BODØ ④
Saltstraumen
80   Fauske
17
Rognan
Sulitjelma
830
NORDLAND
Ørnes
Arjeplog
Arctic Circle
Snetinden
1594m
Hestemona
③ SALTFJELLET-SVARTISEN
NATIONAL PARK
Storforshei
HELGELANDSKYSTEN
17
② MO I RANA
Sandnessjøen
Korgen
E6
Okskolten
1916m
① ⓘ
Mosjøen
Rossvatnet
Vega
Hattfjelldal
Brønnøysund   Trofors
17   76
Leka   E6
Trondheim

SEE ALSO
• *Where to Stay* pp236–37
• *Where to Eat* pp254–55

For additional map symbols *see back flap*

GETTING AROUND

The most important route through the three counties is the E6, which extends some 1,600 km (994 miles) from southern Nordland to Kirkenes. Four roads go from the E6 to Sweden: from Trofors, Mo i Rana, Storjord and Narvik. Roads lead to Finland from Skibotn, Kautokeino, Karasjok and Neiden, and to Russia from Kirkenes via Storskog. The Nordlandsbanen railway line ends at Bodø. The Hurtigruten coastal express and a number of local boats serve the coast. There are eight main airports, including Svalbard.

KEY

— Major road

═ Minor road

— Railway line

▬ International border

▬ County border

▲ Summit

The Northern Lights dancing across the sky on a clear winter's night

Sami handicrafts being sold from a *lavvo* (traditional tent)

SIGHTS AT A GLANCE

The 1,065-m (3,494-ft) long Helgeland Bridge, north of Sandessjøen

Helgelandskysten ➊

County of Nordland. ✕ 🚌 🚢 ⛴
🛈 Helgelandsgaten 1,
Sandnessjøen, 75 04 25 80.
www.helgelandskysten.com

The shipping channel from
Leka northward along the
coast of Helgelandskysten
passes through a stunning
landscape of islands and
mountains. Whether seen
from aboard the Hurtigruten
(see p199), or from the RV17
as it winds along the coast,
this region never fails
to delight.

Helgelandskysten is also
known as the Realm of the
Nessekonge, the wealthy
merchants who held power
both economically and
politically over northern
Norway until the early 1900s.
They made their fortunes
trading with passing cargo
ships and fishing vessels.

On the island of **Torget**,
near Brønnøysund, is the
strange-looking mountain
Torghatten, which has a
160-m (525-ft) long passage
running right through it,
formed when the land was
lower than it is now.

On the northern side of
Vefsfjorden, on the island of
Alsten, is the Norse homestead of Tjøtta. The estate has
several ruined houses and
burial mounds from the Viking
Age. The island is dominated
by the majestic mountain range

De Syv Søstre (the Seven
Sisters), rising to 1,072 m
(3,517 ft). The 12th-century
stone church Alstadhaugkirke
was where writer Petter Dass
(1647–1707) was a clergyman.
In the rectory there is a
museum devoted to him.
Sandnessjøen is the biggest
settlement on the island.

Near the mouth of
Ranfjorden is the island of
Dønna, with the aristocratic
estate, Dønnes, and a stone
church from 1200. Among the
other islands, **Lovunden** is
known for its large colony of
puffins. **Hestemona**, situated
on the Arctic Circle, is
dominated by the 568-m
(1,863-ft) mountain of
Hestmannen, named after a
giant troll who, according to
an early saga, turned to stone.
Rødøy island marks the
furthest point north on the
Helgeland coast.

Mo i Rana ➋

County of Nordland. 🏘 25,000. ✕
🚌 🚉 🛈 O T Olsens Gate 3, 75 13
92 00. 🎭 Winter Light Festival (Jan),
Sjonstock Rock & Hemnes Jazz Festivals
(1st week Aug), Open Air Festival (4th
week Aug). www.arctic-circle.no

Little is known about the
origins of Mo i Rana, today
an industrial town, except that
it had a church and a Sami
market before 1860. The place
was bought by L A Meyer,
who started a guesthouse
and initiated trade with
Sweden. Today central Mo is
dominated by Meyergården, a
hotel and shopping complex.

The museum, Rana
Bygdemuseum, features the
collections of Hans A Meyer,
with sections on geology,
mining and rural culture.
Friluftsmuseet, an open-air
museum, about 9 km (6 miles)
from Mo town centre, is part
of Rana Bygdemuseum.

Environs

From Mo, the E6 runs
southward along Ranfjord,
eventually reaching **Mosjøen**
(75 km/46 miles southwest of
Mo) with its beautiful Vefsn
Museum, showing works by
contemporary Nordland
artists. The street Sjøgata is
lined with timber buildings
and warehouses dating from
the early 19th century.

About 20 km (12 miles)
north of Mo is **Grønligrotten**,
a limestone cave 107-m
(351-ft) deep with a gushing
stream which re-emerges in
nearby Setergrotten. Helmets
must be worn in the caves,
and a miner's lamp is needed
to explore Setergrotten.

The enchanting cave of Grønligrotten with an underground river

Saltfjellet-Svartisen National Park ❸

County of Nordland. 🏛️
ℹ️ *Mo i Rana Tourist Information, 75 13 92 00.* 📧

Gloriously untouched landscapes typify the national park of Saltfjellet and Svartisen. In the east, toward the Nordlandsbanen railway line, E6 and the Swedish border, the undulating terrain is punctuated by peaks rising to 1,700 m (5,577 ft). Further west there are wide mountain plateaus and forested valleys.

Between here and the coast, the Svartisen ice-cap, Norway's second largest glacier, is made up of two glaciers, Østisen and Vestisen. The glacier has several arms running down toward the surrounding valleys. The southeastern one, Østerdalsis-en, is strangely contoured. To reach it, take the 32-km (20-miles) long road from Mo, cross Svartisvannet by ferry (in season), and walk 3 km (2 miles) to the glacier toe.

Polarsirkelsenteret (the Arctic Circle Centre) is located in Saltfjellet, just by the Arctic Circle (84 km/52 miles north of Mo i Rana on the E6). It has a tourist information office, slide shows and a restaurant. Nearby there are three Sami sacrificial stones and a memorial to Yugoslav prisoners of war who were killed while working on the railway during World War II.

🏛️ **Polarsirkelsenteret**
84 km (52 miles) N of Mo i Rana. **Tel** 75 12 96 96. ⬜ May–15 Sep: daily. ⚫ 17 May. 📷 ♿ 🍴 📷

Marking the Arctic Circle at Polarsirkelsenteret on Saltfjellet

Norsk Luftfartsmuseum, a national aviation centre

Bodø ❹

County of Nordland. 🏔️ *42,000.* ✈️
🏛️ 🚌 ⛴️ ℹ️ *Sjøgata 3, 75 54 80 00.* 🎵 *Nordland Music Week (4th week Jul).* **www**.visitbodo.com

Nordland's capital, Bodø, occupies a wonderful setting with Saltfjorden and its islands and nesting cliffs to the west, the mountain ranges of Børvasstindene across the fjord to the south and the island of Landegode to the north. The midnight sun can be seen here from 1 June to 12 July.

Domkirken, Bodø's cathedral, is a modern, three-aisle basilica, designed by G Blakstad and H Munthe-Kaas, and consecrated in 1956. The stained-glass painting above the altar is by Aage Storstein.

Norsk Luftfartsmuseum (the Aviation Museum), illustrating Norwegian civil and military history, is one of Bodø's big attractions. Of particular interest are Catalina seaplanes, Mosquito fighter air-craft, the US spy plane U2 and Junkers 52.

Kjerringøy, 40 km (25 miles) north of Bodø, was Nordland's richest trading post in the 19th century. It is now part of Nordland's county museum and has 15 historic buildings complete with interiors. Nyfjøset (New Barn), which has a tourist information office and a café, is a replica of a barn that was demolished in 1892. The main museum building is located near the cathedral.

A past owner of Kjerringøy was Erasmus Zahl (1826–1900), who helped Knut Hamsun when he wanted to become a writer. In his books, Hamsun called the place Sirilund.

Saltstraumen is a natural phenomenon taking place 33 km (21 miles) southeast of Bodø. This is one of the world's strongest tidal currents. The water is forced at speeds of up to 20 knots through a 3-km (2-miles) long, 150-m (492-ft) wide strait. It changes direction every six hours. At Opplevelsessentret, a multimedia show explains the current. There is also an aquarium and a seal pool.

🏛️ **Norsk Luftfartsmuseum**
Olav V Gata. **Tel** 75 50 78 50.
⬜ daily. 📷 📷 ♿ 🍴 📷

WHALE WATCHING

Killer whales can be seen on organized safaris *(see p267)*, especially in Tysfjord – the deepest fjord in northern Norway – particularly between October and January when they arrive in the fjords to feast on herring. The killer whale is a toothed whale of the dolphin family. The female can be up to 7.5-m (25-ft) long, and a fully-grown male can measure up to 9 m (30 ft). The latter has a particularly powerful, triangular dorsal fin. The killer whale is fast, supple and greedy. It feeds on fish, but is also known to eat other sea animals such as whales and seals.

On the island of Andøya there are safaris to see seals and the enormous sperm whales.

A killer whale patrolling in Tysfjorden

Lofoten and Vesterålen ❺

Viewed from Vestfjorden, north of Bodø, the mighty mountains of the Lofoten Islands rise up like a wall in the sea. Lofoten comprises six large and many smaller islands. Corries, hollows and sharp peaks create an exciting backdrop to the fjords, moorlands and farms, small towns and fishing villages. The island of Moskenesøya is southernmost of the larger islands. Between Moskenesøya and the remote Skomvær Island lie 60 km (37 miles) of steep nesting cliffs, called *nyker*. Northeast of Lofoten is Vesterålen, which shares the island of Hinnøya with Lofoten, and also includes three other large islands: Langøya, Andøya and Hadseløya.

Kabelvåg
In the 19th century, Kabelvåg was the most important fishing village in Lofoten. The timber-frame church, known as Lofoten's "cathedral", seats 1,200.

Western Flakstadøya
has long, white, sandy beaches and in summer is a good place to swim – even this far north.

Nusfjord
The well-preserved fishing village of Nusfjord on Flakstadøya (see p210), has many picturesque 19th-century buildings illustrating the development of Lofotfisket (the Lofoten Fisheries).

Moskstraumen (the Moskenes Current) is an infamous maelstrom, portrayed in the literature of Jules Verne, Edgar Allan Poe, Peder Claussøn Friis and Petter Dass.

Vestvågøy Museum at Fygle, south of Leknes, tells the story of the life of local fishermen through the ages.

Norwegian Sea

Skomvær

Å
The E10 road ends at the southerly village of Å, site of two fishing museums, Lofoten Tørrfisk-museum and Norsk Fiskeværmuseum.

0 kilometres	50
0 miles	30

KEY

— Major road

— Minor road

⋯⋯ Road under construction (2007)

— Hurtigruten route *(see also p211)*

--- Other ferry

☒ Domestic airport

For hotels and restaurants in this region see pp236–7 and pp254–5

Andenes

Andenes, on the northern tip of Andøya in Vesterålen, has a large fishing quarter, a Polar Museum and the world's most northerly launching pad for rockets and scientific balloons.

VISITORS' CHECKLIST

Counties of Nordland and Troms.
🚶 56,000. ✈ *Leknes; Andenes; Svolvær.* 🚌 🚢 ℹ *Svolvær, 76 06 98 00.* 🎣 *Cod Fishing World Cup (Apr), Codstock Blues Festival (Whitsun), Lofoten International Chambers Music Festival (mid-July)*
www.lofoten.info

Trondenes

The 40.6 cm calibre Adolf Cannon, a relic from World War II, is one of the attractions at Trondenes (see p210).

GETTING AROUND

There are flights from Bodø to Svolvær and Leknes in Lofoten, and to Andenes in Vesterålen and to Røst. Helicopters operate to the island of Værøy. Hurtigruten coastal ships call at Stamsund and Svolvær. Road bridges and tunnels, buses, ferries and express boats connect the many islands.

Tjeldsundbrua

The 1,001-m (3,284-ft) long Tjelsund Bridge extends from the mainland across to Hinnøya, Norway's biggest and most populated island. The towers stand 76 m (249 ft) above the waterline.

Svolvær

Beneath the mountain of Svolværgeita (Svolvær goat) is Svolvær, the "capital" and transport hub of Lofoten (see p210).

Exploring Lofoten and Vesterålen

The coastline of the Lofoten and Vesterålen islands is dominated by sharp peaks such as Tinden and Reka on the island of Langøya, and Møysalen on Hinnøya. Small towns and fishing villages lie at the water's edge. Some of these settlements are deserted, like Nyksund, others, such as Myre, are thriving. At the northernmost tip of the Vesterålen island of Andøya is the port of Andenes. Svolvær is the most important town on Lofoten.

Jagged mountains forming a backdrop to the skerries in Lofoten

Svolvær

Regarded as the "capital" of Lofoten, Svolvær only received town status in 1996. Its location on Austvågsøya and good transport links make it an important gateway for tourism on the islands. The town's economy depends on Lofotfisket (the Lofoten Fisheries). In March and April every year the cod arrive in Vestfjorden to spawn and the fishing boats follow.

Other than fishermen and tourists, artists have long been attracted to Svolvær and a centre for North Norwegian artists has been established in the town, **Nordnorsk Kunstnersentrum**. Vågan town hall is worth a visit. It contains seven paintings by Gunnar Berg showing the battle of Trollfjord in 1880 when fishermen in small boats clashed with the rival new steamships.

The 569-m (1,867-ft) peak, **Svolværgeita** (the Svolvær goat), with its two horns, appears to rise from the town centre and presents a challenge for all climbers.

🏛 **Nordnorsk Kunstnersentrum**
Svolvær. **Tel** 76 06 67 70. ◯ mid-Jun–mid Aug: daily; mid-Aug–mid-Jun: Tue–Sun. ◉ public hols. 🖼 ▯

Vestvågøya

From the island of Austvågøya there is a road connection, via Gimsøy and two bridges, to Vestvågøya, where there is an airfield at Leknes and a Hurtigruten coastal express stop at Stamsund. **Stamsund**, like **Ballstad**, is one of the largest and most picturesque fishing villages in west Lofoten. Vestvågøya is also an important agricultural island, which has been farmed since the Stone Age.

Vestvågøy Museum at Fygle has a fine collection, including a fisherman's cabin dating from 1834. The island is rich in Stone and Iron Age monuments and Viking settlements. **Lofotr – Vikingmuseet på Borg** (Viking Museum at Borg), north of Leknes, features a reconstruction of a chieftain

The old trading post of Sund on Moskenesøya

homestead from AD 500–900. It is a lively museum, where Viking banquets and crafts demonstrations are arranged.

🏛 **Vestvågøy Museum**
2 km (1 mile) E of Leknes. **Tel** 76 08 00 43. ◯ Jun–mid-Aug: daily. 🖼 ▯ ▯

🏛 **Lofotr – Vikingmuseet på Borg**
Prestegårdsveien 59, Borg. **Tel** 76 08 49 00. ◯ mid-May–Aug: daily; Sep–mid-May: Fri. ◉ public hols. 🖼 ▯ ▯ ▯ ▯ ▯ ▯

Flakstadøya and Moskenesøya

The island of Flakstadøya is best known for the fishing village of **Nusfjord**. It was chosen in 1975 as part of the European Year of Nature Conservation to be a pilot project for the conservation of building traditions in Norway.

On Moskenesøya there is a string of fishing villages, including Reine, set in a wild mountainous landscape. The charming village of **Å** (see p202) lies at the southern end of the Lofoten road. **Sund** has a fishing museum and a smithy for artistic metalwork.

Between Moskenesøya and Værøy whirls the current of **Moskstraumen**, the world's biggest maelstrom. When the wind and the current are in the same direction, the roar can be heard 5 km (3 miles) away.

On **Værøy** and **Røst**, Lofoten's southernmost islands, vast numbers of sea birds nest in the strangely shaped cliffs of Trenykene. The fabled lighthouse of **Skomvær** stands alone at the outermost point.

Vesterålen Islands

Hinnøya is Vesterålen's (and Norway's) largest and most populated island. Its main town is **Harstad**, which developed around 1870 as a result of the abundance of herring. The Northern Norway culture festival, is held here each year, around the summer solstice.

On nearby Trondenes stands an early Gothic church. The northernmost island is Andøya, with the fishing community of **Andenes** (see p209).

Hurtigruten: "The World's Most Beautiful Voyage"

It was captain Richard With of the shipping company, Vesteraalske Dampskibsselskab, who initiated the coastal express amid much controversy. Few people believed that it would be possible to operate an express route all year round, least of all during the dark days of winter, since only poor maps existed of the treacherous Norwegian coast. However, a contract was signed between With and the government in May 1893. At

Channel beacon

the beginning there were weekly sailings and nine ports of call between Trondheim and Hammerfest in summer. In winter the boats stopped at Tromsø. The coastal express soon proved to be a lifeline for the communities along the route. Today, two shipping lines operate 12 ships, with daily south and northbound departures *(see p283)*. The cruise from Bergen to Kirkenes, calling at 34 ports, has been called "the world's most beautiful voyage".

HURTIGRUTEN PORTS OF CALL

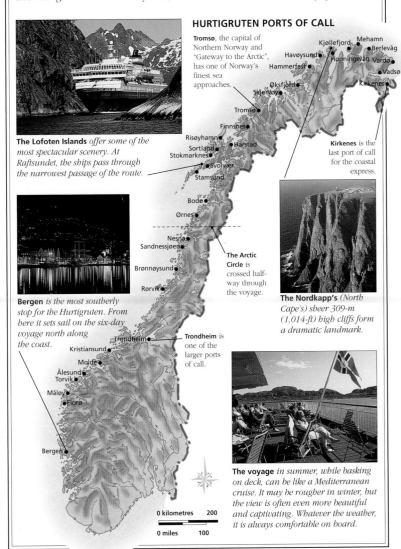

Tromsø, the capital of Northern Norway and "Gateway to the Arctic", has one of Norway's finest sea approaches.

The Lofoten Islands *offer some of the most spectacular scenery. At Raftsundet, the ships pass through the narrowest passage of the route.*

Bergen *is the most southerly stop for the Hurtigruten. From here it sets sail on the six-day voyage north along the coast.*

Kirkenes is the last port of call for the coastal express.

The Arctic Circle is crossed half-way through the voyage.

Trondheim is one of the larger ports of call.

The Nordkapp's *(North Cape's) sheer 309-m (1,014-ft) high cliffs form a dramatic landmark.*

The voyage *in summer, while basking on deck, can be like a Mediterranean cruise. It may be rougher in winter, but the view is often even more beautiful and captivating. Whatever the weather, it is always comfortable on board.*

Mehamn
Kjøllefjord
Berlevåg
Havøysund
Honningsvåg
Vardø
Hammerfest
Vadsø
Kirkenes
Øksfjord
Skjervøy
Tromsø
Finnsnes
Risøyhamn
Sortland
Harstad
Stokmarknes
Svolvær
Stamsund
Bodø
Ørnes
Nesna
Sandnessjøen
Brønnøysund
Rørvik
Trondheim
Kristiansund
Molde
Ålesund
Torvik
Måløy
Florø
Bergen

0 kilometres 200

0 miles 100

The busy port of Narvik close to the border with Sweden

Narvik ❻

County of Nordland. 🏔 18,600. ✈
🚉 🚌 ℹ Kongens Gate 26, 76 96
56 00. 🎿 Winter Festival (2nd week
Mar), Black Bear Rally (4th week Jun).
www.narvikinfo.no

Narvik developed as a
shipping port for iron ore
from Kiruna in Sweden. The
Ofotbanen train line to Kiruna
was completed in 1902, after
which Narvik was given town
status. Heavy bombardment
by the Germans in 1940
destroyed most of the town.

After World War II, Narvik
rose again to become Norway's
second largest shipping town.
Activities connected with iron
ore still form its economic
base. The Ofotbanen passes
below the mountains high
above Rombaksfjorden,
offering stunning views.

From Oscarsborg a cable
car, **Fjellheisen**, climbs up to
700 m (2,296 ft). In summer it
operates until 2 am (midnight
sun: 31 May–14 Jul).
Krigsminnesmuseet (the
War Memorial Museum), near
the main square, focuses on
the military campaigns fought
here in 1940. Allied as well as
German soldiers are buried
near Fredskapellet (the Peace
Chapel) in the cemetery.

From Narvik, the E6 runs
southward, crossing a number
of fjords either by ferry or
bridges, including the
impressive 525-m (1,722-ft)
long bridge spanning the
beautiful Skjomenfjorden. On
Hamarøy, around 100 km (60
miles) south of Narvik, is the
strangely shaped mountain of
Hamarøyskaftet and the
childhood home of Nobel

Prize-winning novelist Knut
Hamsun (1859–1952).

Environs
The scenic E10 road,
Bjørnfjellveien, starts at
Rombaksfjorden and ascends
to 520 m (1,706 ft) through
the wild mountains of Ofoten
to the Swedish border.

🏛 Krigsminnemuseet
Torvhallen. **Tel** 76 94 44 26.
⭕ daily. ⬤ public hols.
🎫 📷 by arrangement.

Senja ❼

County of Troms. 🏔 9,000. ✈ 🚌
ℹ Ringveien 2, Finnsnes, 77 85 07
30. 🎿 Finnsnes Festival (4th week
Jul), Ocean Fishing Festival (late Jun),
Tranøy Festival (2nd week Aug),
Husøy Festival (2nd week Aug).

Norway's second largest
island, Senja, can be reached
by road (E6) from Bardufoss,
across the bridge at Finnsnes.
The landscape is green and
welcoming on the mainland
side, becoming harsher toward
the sea coast. **Ånderdalen
Nasjonalpark** has an unspoilt

Family of swans in Ånderdalen
Nasjonalpark on Senja island

landscape inhabited by elk
and eagles.

Back on the mainland, in
the south of Troms county
large areas of wilderness,
including Øvre Dividal national
park, are home to bears.

From Skibotn, about 100 km
(60 miles) east of Senja, the
E8 passes near the point
where Finland, Sweden and
Norway meet, the Treriksrøysa.

🎿 Ånderdalen Nasjonalpark
35 km (22 miles) S of Finnsnes.
ℹ Sør-Senja Museum, 77 85 46 77.

Tromsø ❽

See pp216–7.

Detail of rock engraving from
Hjemmeluft, near Alta

Alta ❾

County of Finnmark. 🏔 18,000.
✈ 🚌 ℹ Sentrumsparken 4, 78 44
95 55. 🎿 Borealis Winter Festival
(Mar), Finnmark Race (Mar).

The original village of Alta, at
the mouth of the Alta river,
has grown and merged with
its neighbours to form the
most populated urban area in
Finnmark. It includes
Bossekop, a commercial
market place rich in tradition
where Sami and Kvæn people
(immigrants of Finnish origin)
and Norwegians traded goods.
Apart from the church in
Bossekop, the entire area was
razed to the ground during
the German retreat in 1944.

Today, Alta is a growing
industrial and educational
centre, and an important
transport junction on the E6
with its own airport.

The lower part of the Alta
Valley is covered in spruce
forests and fertile agricultural
land. The Gulf Stream and
sunny summer nights provide

Pikefossen, a waterfall on the Kautkeinoelva river in Finnmark

fertile conditions, even at 70°N. Altaelvar is one of the world's most attractive salmon rivers for fly-fishing. Every year salmon weighing more than 20 kg (44 lb) are caught.

In 1973, rock engravings between 2,000 and 6,000 years old were found near the village of Hjemmeluft. The engravings, now a UNESCO World Heritage Site, show wildlife and hunting scenes.

Alta Museum, winner of the Museum of the Year, 1993, is also located at Hjemmeluft. It features exhibits relating to the Alta River from the Stone Age Komsa culture (7000 BC –2000 BC) through to the latest hydroelectric project.

🏛 **Alta Museum**
Altaveien 19, Hjemmeluft.
Tel *78 45 63 30.* ⬭ *daily.* ⬤ *some public hols.* 📷 ✔ 🚻 🖥 🎫

Kautokeino ⑩

County of Finnmark. 👥 *3,000.*
🚌 ℹ *Siva Bygget, 78 48 65 00.*
🎿 *Easter Festival (Easter), Autumn Festival (Sep).*

The name "Kautokeino" is a Norwegianized form of the Sami word, *Guovdageaidnu*. Kautokeino is a mountain town surrounded by barren plateaus where reindeer husbandry is the most important economic activity.

The town has a large Sami community and has become a centre for education with a Sami High School. Reindeer

husbandry is one of the courses on the curriculum.

Kulturhuset (the Culture House), opened in 1980, houses the Sámi Instituhtta, a co-ordinating organization for Sami politics and culture. It has a theatre and a library and also mounts exhibitions.

Easter is a time of transition for the Sami, just before they set off with their reindeer for summer pastures on the coast. It is marked by colourful celebrations, with weddings, a *joik* (Sami chanting song) festival and reindeer racing, all attracting large numbers of visitors.

🎭 **Kulturhuset**
1 km (half a mile) N of town centre.
Tel *78 48 72 16.* ⬭ *Mon–Fri: daily (library) and for cinema or theatre performances.* ⬤ *some public hols.*

Karasjok ⑪

County of Finnmark. 👥 *3,000.* ✈
🚌 ℹ *Porsangerveien 1, 78 46 88 10.* 🎿 *Easter Festival (Easter).*

The Sami capital is Karasjok (Karásjohka in Sami). It is the seat of the Sami Parliament, **Sametinget**, opened in 1989. Its new building was inaugurated by King Harald in 2000. The architects, Christian Sundby and Stein Halvorsen, used elements from reindeer husbandry as a base for their design. A long hallway, Vandrehallen, reminiscent of the dividing fences used for the reindeer, winds through the building. The plenary hall is like a *lavvo* (pointed Sami summer tent) and decorated with a magnificent artwork in blue and gold by Hilde Skancke Pedersen.

Around 80 per cent of the population of Karasjok is of Sami origin. Their culture is the subject of **De Samiske Samlinger**, a museum featuring Sami handicrafts and way of life, clothing and building traditions.

The climate in these parts can be extreme. The record low temperature is –51.4° C (–60.5°F), and the highest temperature 32.4° C (90°F).

🏛 **Sametinget**
Kautokeinoveien 50. ***Tel*** *78 47 40 00.* ⬭ *Mon–Fri.* ✔ ♿
🏛 **De Samiske Samlinger**
Museumsgate 17. ***Tel*** *78 46 99 50.*
⬭ *daily.* ⬤ *public hols.* 📷 ✔ ♿ 🎫

The striking Sami Parliament building in Karasjok, opened in 2000

For hotels and restaurants in this region see pp236–7 and pp254–5

Tromsø ⓭

Roald Amundsen's statue in Tromsø

Known as the "Paris of the North", Tromsø is the largest town in the polar region of Scandinavia. It is located 300 km (186 miles) inside the Arctic Circle, on the same latitude as northern Alaska. Central Tromsø covers an island in the busy Tromsøy-sund. There was a farming estate here in early Viking times, and the first church was built around 1250.

During the Hanseatic period, trade and commerce boomed; Tromsø officially became a market town in 1794. From the 1820s it developed as a thriving port for sea traffic in the Arctic Ocean. Nansen and Amundsen started their polar expeditions from here. The world's northernmost university opened in Tromsø in 1972.

Tromsøy-sund with Ishavskatedralen and the peak of Tromsdalstind

🏛 Polaria

Hjalmar Johansens Gate 12.
Tel *77 75 01 00.* ☐ *daily.* ⬤ *some public hols.* 📷 ♿ 🖥 🛒

Polaria is a national centre for research and information relating to the polar regions, particularly the Arctic. It is also a great place to experience the Arctic landscape. In a fascinating panoramic film from Svalbard *(see pp220–1)*, the viewer becomes a wanderer in a polar landscape beneath the Northern Lights, sensing what it feels like to be in the Arctic wilderness.

An aquarium features Arctic species of fish. Other creatures include the red king crab, *paralithodes camtschaticus*, which can weigh up to 10 kg (22 lb). This Arctic species has migrated from Russia and is spreading steadily southward along the Norwegian coast. Another attraction is the glass-bottomed pool for seals, which can be viewed from below.

🏛 Tromsø Kunstforening

Muségata 2. ***Tel*** *77 65 58 27.*
☐ *Tue–Sun.* ⬤ *some public hols.* 📷 🚫 🖥 🛒

Established in 1877, Tromsø Kunstforening is the oldest art society in Northern Norway. It exhibits Norwegian and international contemporary art, and arranges around 20 exhibitions every year. The society is based in a 19th-century building, which once housed Tromsø Museum.

Façade of Tromsø Kunstforening, built in 1894

🏛 Nordnorsk Kunstmuseum

Sjøgata 1. ***Tel*** *77 64 70 20.*
☐ *Tue–Sun.* ⬤ *some public hols.* 📷 ♿ 🖥 🛒

The regional art museum for Northern Norway, Nordnorsk Kunstmuseum, was established in 1985 primarily to show painting and handicrafts from the northern regions, including sculpture and textile art. The museum also arranges temporary exhibitions of work both past and present.

🏛 Polarmuseet

Søndre Tollbugata 11.
Tel *77 60 66 30.*
☐ *daily.* 📷 ♿ 🛒

Polar hunting and research expeditions are the focal points of Polarmuseet. Displays feature Fridtjof Nansen's journey to the North Pole in his ship *Fram*, the life of Antarctic explorer Roald Amundsen and Salomon Andrée's attempted balloon flight to the North Pole (1897).

There are exhibitions devoted to the first hunters on Svalbard, the trappers of polar bears, polar foxes and seals, who wintered in the icy wasteland. Everyday articles, utensils and a wealth of other material left by hunters, whalers and sealers around Northern Norway form part of the collection.

The museum is located in the harbour area of old Tromsø, surrounded by sturdy warehouses, fishermen's bunkhouses and wooden buildings from the 1830s.

🔒 Ishavskatedralen

2 km (1 mile) E of town centre.
Tel *77 75 34 40.*
☐ *daily.* 📷 ♿

Consecrated in 1965, Ishavskatedralen (the Arctic Ocean Cathedral, also known as Tromsdalen Church) was designed by Jan Inge Hovig. It is built of concrete. The shape of its roof symbolizes the way in which the Northern Lights brighten up Tromsø's dark winter months.

A massive 23-m (75-ft) high, triangular stained-glass window by Victor Sparre (1972) fills the east wall. It

The striking east wall of Ishavskatedralen, composed entirely of stained glass

comprises 86 panels of jewel-like glass pieces on the theme of the Second Coming of Christ.

🏛 Nordlysplanetariet

3 km (2 miles) N of town centre. **Tel** 77 61 00 00 (Tourist Information). ⏰ call for opening times.

Situated on the university campus in Breivika, near Tromsø Botaniske Hage (Botanical Gardens), is Nordlysplanetariet (the Northern Lights Planetarium). It is known for screening the film *Arctic Light*, which provides a realistic experience both of the strange, blue aurora borealis (known as the Northern Lights) – often visible in the Arctic sky during the dark winter months – and of the incredible midnight sun, responsible for the light nights of summer.

The planetarium, which is being rebuilt, with the new building set to open in 2011, should not be confused with the Nordlysobservatoriet (Northern Lights Observatory), a research centre in Skibotn in Lyngen.

🏛 Tromsø Museum, Universitetsmuseet

Lars Thøringsvei 10. **Tel** 77 64 50 00. ⏰ daily. 🎦 ♿ 📷 🍴

Now part of the University Museum, Tromsø Museum is the regional museum for Northern Norway. Established in 1872, it holds considerable collections from the Stone Age, Viking era and early Middle Ages, including a reconstructed Viking longhouse. Of particular interest are the late medieval church carvings from the Hanseatic period and those in Baroque style.

From its early days the museum specialized in Arctic landscape and culture. Sami history has a prominent place and there are comprehensive displays devoted to aspects of Sami life.

The museum also has a lot to offer younger visitors with regular film shows and a life-size replica of a dinosaur.

VISITORS' CHECKLIST

County of Troms.
🏠 63,600. ✈ Prostneset.
🚢 Prostneset. ℹ Storgata 61–63, 77 61 00 00.
🎬 Tromsø International Film Festival (2nd week Jan), Northern Lights Festival (3rd week Jan), Midnight Sun Marathon (mid-Jun), Beer Festival (3rd week Aug).
www.destinasjontromso.no

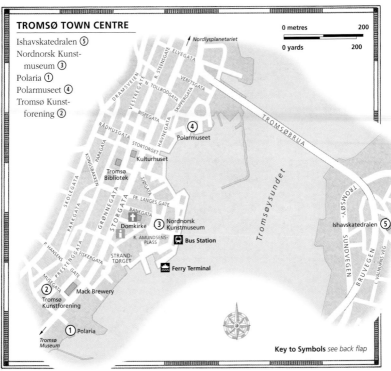

TROMSØ TOWN CENTRE

Ishavskatedralen ⑤
Nordnorsk Kunst-museum ③
Polaria ①
Polarmuseet ④
Tromsø Kunst-forening ②

0 metres 200
0 yards 200

Nordlysplanetariet

Polarmuseet ④
Kulturhuset
Tromsø Bibliotek
Nordnorsk Kunstmuseum ③
Domkirke
Bus Station
Ferry Terminal
Mack Brewery
Tromsø Kunstforening ②
Polaria ①
Tromsø Museum

TROMSØBRUA
Tromsøysundet

Ishavskatedralen ⑤

Key to Symbols see back flap

Verdens Barn (the Children of the World) sculptures at Nordkapp

Hammerfest ⑫

County of Finnmark. 🏠 *9,200.*
✈ 🚌 ⛴ 🛈 *Sjøgata 6, 78 41 21
85.* 🎭 *Hammerfest Days (3rd week
Jul), Polar Nights Festival (3rd week
Nov).* **www**.hammerfest-turist.no

The polar bear on this town's
coat of arms recalls the days
when Hammerfest was a
hunting and trapping centre. A
settlement by the 9th century,
Hammerfest was given
town status in 1789.
It is the world's most
northerly town at 70°
39' 48"N, as recorded
on Meridianstøtten (the
Meridian Pillar), which
marks the first international
measurement of the Earth
in the 19th century.

The town has endured
many catastrophes, inclu-
ding being destroyed by a
hurricane in 1856 and
being razed to the
ground in World War
II. Each time it has
been rebuilt in true **The Meridian Pillar**
pioneer spirit. In 1890 **at Hammerfest**
it was one of the first
towns in Europe to install
electric street lighting.

Hammerfest church is
unusual in that it has no altar.
Instead, the back wall is a
monumental abstract painting
in glowing colours. The Polar
Bear Club, **Isbjørnklubben**,
has a museum illustrating the
town's Arctic traditions.

🏛 **Isbjørnklubben**
Rådhusplassen 1. **Tel** 78 41 31 00.
⬚ *daily.* 🈁 🎦 🛗 🛈

Nordkapp ⑬

County of Finnmark. 🚌 *summer.*
🛈 *Northcape Tourist Information,
Honningsvåg, 78 47 70 30.*
www.northcape.no

It was the English sailor,
Richard Chancellor, who
named Nordkapp (the North
Cape) in 1533, during his
attempt to find the Northeast
Passage to China. Various
important people travelled
to view the North Cape,
including the French
king, Louis Philippe of
Orleans, in 1795, and
Oscar II in 1873. The
latter was responsible for
encouraging tourist ships
to include the North Cape
on their itineraries and
tourism grew rapidly. An
impressive new road –
part of it below the sound
of Magerøy – links the
cape to the mainland.
Every year, more
than 200,000 people
come to the cliff top.
Nordkapphallen (the
North Cape Hall),
inside the mountain, offers a
panoramic view of the coast.
A videograph showing
Finnmark's changing seasons
plays on a 225°-wide screen.
Visitors also have the chance
to become a member of the
Royal North Cape Club.

From the top of the North
Cape there is a signposted
path to the promontory of
Knivskjellodden, which is
Europe's most northerly point,
at 71°11'08"N. **Honningsvåg,**

35 km (22 miles) southeast of
the cape, is where Hurtigruten
(see p211) calls. It also has a
Nordkapp museum.

🏛 **Nordkapphallen**
35 km (22 miles) N of Honningsvåg.
Tel 78 47 68 60. ⬚ *daily.*
🈁 🛗 🛈 🎦 🛈

Vardø ⑭

County of Finnmark. 🚶 *2,400.* ✈
🚌 ⛴ 🛈 *Kaigata 12, 78 98 69 67.*
🎭 *Winter Festival (Apr), Winter Blues
(Nov), Pomor Festival (4th week Jul).*
www.varanger.com

Two events at the beginning
of the 14th century were to
enforce Vardø's position as a
bastion against incursions
from the east: Håkon V built a
fortress and Archbishop Jørund
consecrated the first church.
The fortress, **Vardøhus
Festning**, was rebuilt in the
18th century as a star-shaped
fortification with parapets of
earth and peat, eight cannons
and a mortar. There are tours
of the commanding officer's
residence, the old depots and
the barracks. Four kings have
written their names on a beam
from the original fortress.

Vardø is connected to the
mainland by a tunnel below
the sound of Bussesundet,
constructed in 1982. Fishing
and fish processing are the
basis of the local economy.

The fishing village of
Kiberg, to the south, was
known as "Little Moscow"
because of partisan activity
during World War II. To the
north, the deserted hamlet of
Hamningberg lies in a moon-
like landscape made up of
strange rock formations.

🏰 **Vardøhus Festning**
Festningsgata. **Tel** 78 98 85 02.
⬚ *daily.* 🈁 🎦 *by arrangement.* 🛗

**A sun salute, fired from Vardøhus
Festning on the sun's reappearance**

Vadsø, on the Barents Sea, owing its development to Finnish immigration

Vadsø ⓯

County of Finnmark. 🏘 6,200. ⊠
🚌 🚢 🛈 Kirkegata 15, 78 94 04 44.
🎵 Varanger Music Festival (mid-Aug)

Originally situated on the
island of Vadsøya, the town
of Vadsø was moved to the
mainland around 1600.
Remains of its 15th and 16th-
century buildings still exist
on the island. Also there is
an airship mooring mast on
Vadsøya, which was used by
Amundsen's expedition to the
North Pole in the airship
Norge in 1926, and to launch
Umberto Nobile's airship
Italia in 1928.

Over the centuries many
Finns have settled in Vadsø
and the buildings bear the
hallmark of Finnish workmanship. **Ruija Kvenmuseum**
devotes considerable space to
the Kvænene (as the Finnish
were known). It is located in
a Finnish-style farmhouse,
Tuomainengården.

Invandrermonumentet
(the Immigrant Monument),
by the Finnish sculptor Ensio
Seppänen, was unveiled in
1977 by King Olav in the
presence of the Swedish king
and Finnish president.

The so-called Pomor trade
with the Russians, by which
fish was exchanged for timber,
also contributed considerably
to the town's development in
the 19th and 20th centuries.

🏛 **Ruija Kvenmuseum**
Hvistendahlsgate 31. **Tel** 78 94 28
90. ☐ 20 Jun–20 Aug: daily; other
times: Mon–Fri. ● public holidays.
📷 📹 🖥 summer only. 🛈

Kirkenes ⓰

County of Finnmark. 🏘 3,500.
⊠ 🚌 🚢 🛈 Sør-Varanger Bibliotek,
78 97 17 78. 🎿 Barents Ski Race
(Mar), Salmon Fishing Festival (1st
week Jul). 🐟 4th Thu of the month.
www.destinationkirkenes.no

At the head of Bøkfjorden
is Kirkenes, the biggest urban
centre in eastern Finnmark
and the last port of call for
Hurtigruten. Iron ore has
been the cornerstone of the
community and when the
town was destroyed by the
retreating German army in
1944, its 2,000 inhabitants fled
to nearby mineshafts.

The mines closed in 1996,
but their legacy lives on.
Opencast pits at **Bjørnevatn**,
south of the town, have
created a vast artificial valley
with a floor 70 m (230 ft)
below sea level.

Kirkenes' proximity to the
border with Russia draws
tourists to the area. A popular
excursion is via Storskog (the
official crossing point) to the
Grense Jacobselv river on
the border, through forests
of crooked birch trees
overlooking the Barents Sea.

At the mouth of the river
there is a chapel built in 1869
as a spiritual watchtower
toward the East. It was named
after Oscar II who visited the
region in 1873. A road leads
from Elvenes to Skafferhullet
and the Greco-Russian chapel
on the Russian side.

The pine forests and
moorland of **Øvre Pasvik
Nasjonalpark** (National Park),
on the Pasvikelva river,
extend to the Treriksrøysa
monument, where Finland,
Russia and Norway meet.
The river has been heavily
developed for hydroelectricity.

THE MIDNIGHT SUN

The expression "The Land of the Midnight Sun" is often
used to describe Norway and northern Scandinavia. The
concept of the "midnight sun" means that the uppermost
arc of the sun stays above the horizon for 24 hours. This
occurs north of latitude 66.5°N
during a few summer months.
Correspondingly, there is a period
of darkness during the winter,
when the sun never rises above
the horizon during the day. As if to
compensate for this, the Northern
Lights may sometimes blaze across
the sky. The midnight sun and
dark days of winter are caused by
the tilt of the earth's axis, and the
earth's rotation around the sun. To
see the midnight sun in these parts
can be a magical experience.

Midnight sun shining
over the North Cape

TRAVELLERS' NEEDS

WHERE TO STAY

Norway has a good selection of hotels covering all corners of the country, with a wide choice in terms of price and quality. Nevertheless, staying in a hotel is not always the best way of getting the most out of your holiday. In Northern Norway, for instance, it has become popular to stay in a *rorbu*, a small cabin once used by fishermen. Mountain huts,

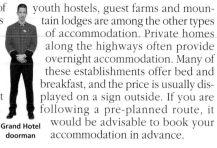

Grand Hotel doorman

youth hostels, guest farms and mountain lodges are among the other types of accommodation. Private homes along the highways often provide overnight accommodation. Many of these establishments offer bed and breakfast, and the price is usually displayed on a sign outside. If you are following a pre-planned route, it would be advisable to book your accommodation in advance.

The distinctive Radisson Blu Plaza hotel in Oslo (see p228)

CHOOSING A HOTEL

The choice of places for the visitor to stay in Norway is as diverse as the country's scenery.

There are large, fashionable hotels in the major towns and cities, modest lodges high in the mountains and bed-and-breakfast hotels along the main roads.

In between there is a wide selection of hotels and overnight accommodation in most price categories. The standard of cleanliness is very high in all Norwegian hotels, while room sizes, facilities and service might vary depending on price level.

The large, hotel groups are well represented in the towns and cities. In the outlying districts there are many comfortable *turisthoteller* (tourist hotels) and mountain hotels. The majority of these are situated in spectacular surroundings. In Vestlandet especially, many of the tourist hotels have been run by the

same family for generations and maintain a tradition of good service.

Mountain hotels and lodges can be found along many of the passes. They are a good starting point for sporting activities all through the year.

The best option in terms of price is youth hostels.

BOOKING A HOTEL

There is no central booking agency for hotels in Norway. Most of the hotel groups have their own booking centre.

In towns and larger villages the local tourist office can provide help when it comes to booking accommodation for visitors, even if it is outside their district.

Many of the hotels have their own websites and very often it is possible to make bookings on-line.

Rooms can also be booked over the telephone, enabling you to enquire about special rates or negotiate a favourable price reduction.

Elegant suite in the Radisson Blu Royal hotel, Bergen

HOTEL GROUPS

There are a number of large groups with hotels throughout Norway, mainly in the towns and cities. These hotels tend to focus on the business market, but in summer they often offer advantageous rates for tourists.

Best Western is a chain of 20 collaborating private hotels in the mid-price bracket. The hotels are small or medium-sized in a mix of town and country locations.

The Scandinavian group **Choice Hotels** has 66 hotels in Norway. They are divided into three categories: Comfort hotels, catering for business people and providing bed and breakfast; Quality hotels, for tourists and conferences; and Clarion, top-range town and city hotels. The Choice group operates the Nordic Hotel Pass, which gives reduced rates during the summer and at weekends.

The **First Hotels** group comprises business hotels in the upper price range. They are typically medium-sized hotels in towns and cities.

Radisson Blu has 19 hotels in Norway, including the Radisson Blu Plaza in Oslo which, with its 37 floors and 674 rooms, is northern Europe's largest hotel. The group also has a hotel in Svalbard. Radisson Blu has traditionally focused on the business sector, but more recently it has turned its attention to tourism.

Rica Hotels is a Norwegian-Swedish hotel chain with 60 hotels in Norway, ranging from the Rica Dyreparken

◁ **Theatrecafeen in Oslo, an example of the Art Nouveau (Jugend) style of decoration**

Kviknes Hotel *(see p233)* on the shore of Sognefjorden

family hotel in Kristiansand to the Grand Hotell in Oslo. Rica operates a summer holiday pass, which gives discounts on rooms and attractions.

Thonhotels is a Norwegian chain comprising 45 hotels catering for all price ranges.

Scandic is the leading hotel group in the Nordic region and has 18 hotels in Norway. It is part of Hilton Hotels. The group aims to be environmentally friendly: 97 per cent of the contents of all newly built hotels are of recycled materials.

PRICES AND PAYMENT

Hotels in Norway vary greatly in price. Those in the cities and towns are generally more expensive than those in the country.

The majority of hotels offer special rates in summer and at weekends. Many hotels operate discount schemes and hotel passes. One two-night stay is all it takes to justify the cost of a hotel pass.

All the usual credit cards are accepted. Larger hotels will also change money, but it is usually cheaper to do this at a bank *(see p276)*.

YOUTH AND FAMILY HOSTELS

There are 70–75 youth and family hostels in Norway. They are part of **Norske Vandrerhjem** (the Norwegian Hostelling Association).

Hostels are located all over Norway. They are designed to accommodate individuals as well as families. The largest hostel is Haraldsheim in

Oslo. Your budget will determine whether you share a dormitory with five or six other people or whether you go for a private room with your family.

Most hostels are of a good standard with favourable prices, and many are situated in attractive areas.

The association does not have a central booking office. Instead you are advised to visit its website to make a reservation. The website also gives details of where the various hostels are located.

DNT's hut on Kobberhaugen in the Oslomarka forest

DNT HUTS

Den Norske Turistforening (the Norwegian Mountain Touring Association, or **DNT**) has a network of mountain huts *(hytte)*, in beautiful hiking areas *(see p264)*.

Many huts are staffed and meals can be provided. They are reasonably comfortable with shower and toilet facilities. DNT also has self-service huts with necessities such as sheet sleeping bags and food supplies. Payment is based on the honour principle – you leave your

DIRECTORY

HOTEL GROUPS

Best Western
Tel 80 01 16 24 (free).
Fax 22 83 00 49.
www.bestwestern.no

Choice Hotels Scandinavia
Tel 22 33 42 00.
Fax 23 10 82 80.
www.choice.no

First Hotels
Tel 80 01 04 10 (free).
Fax +46 86 63 40 46 (Sweden).
www.firsthotels.se

Hilton Scandic Hotels
Tel 23 15 50 00.
Fax 23 15 50 01.
www.scandic-hotels.com

Radisson Blu
Tel 00 800 33 33 33 33 (free).
Fax +353 1706 0225 (Dublin).
www.radissonblu.com

Rica Hotels
Tel 66 85 45 60.
Fax 66 85 45 61.
www.rica.no

Thon Hotels
Tel 23 08 02 00.
Fax 23 08 02 90.
www.thonhotels.no

YOUTH HOSTELS

Norske Vandrerhjem
Torggata 1, 0181 Oslo.
Map 3 D3. *Tel* 23 13 93 00.
www.vandrerhjem.no

HUTS

Den Norske Turistforening (DNT)
Storgata 3, Oslo.
Map 2 E3. *Tel* 22 82 28 00.
www.turistforeningen.no

money in the box provided. There are also some unstaffed huts which do not provide any provisions.

Reservations can only be made for the staffed huts, and only for three or more nights, by telephoning the lodge directly. In other cases guests just turn up and are always given a place to sleep.

Choosing a Hotel

The hotels in this guide have been selected across a wide range of price categories for their facilities, location or character. The chart below lists hotels in Oslo, followed by a selection of places to stay in the rest of Norway. The map references can be found in the Street Finder for Oslo on pp104–7.

PRICE CATEGORIES (IN NORWEGIAN KRONE):
For a standard double room (not per person) per night, including tax, service and breakfast:

Ⓚ Under 1,000 NKr
ⓀⓀ 1,000–1,400 NKr
ⓀⓀⓀ 1,400–1,800 NKr
ⓀⓀⓀⓀ Over 1,800 NKr

OSLO

CENTRAL OSLO WEST Cochs Pensjonat   Ⓚ
Parkveien 25, 0350 Oslo **Tel** *23 33 24 00* **Fax** *23 33 24 10* **Rooms** *88*   **Map** *2 C2*

If you're looking for affordable city accommodation, this popular pension is a good choice. It is located right behind the Royal Palace and all 88 rooms are all non-smoking and most have private baths. Breakfast is not included but a well-priced breakfast buffet is served at a nearby café. Advance booking is recommended. **www.cochspensjonat.no**

CENTRAL OSLO WEST Ellingsens Pensjonat   Ⓚ
Holtegata 25, 0355 Oslo **Tel** *22 60 03 59* **Fax** *22 60 99 21* **Rooms** *18*   **Map** *2 B1*

Ellingsens Pensjonat is a cosy, budget-priced boarding house in a quiet residential area four blocks north of the Royal Palace. All 18 rooms are small and are equipped with a desk, chair and sink. Bathrooms and showers are located in the corridors. Exceptional value considering its central location. **www.ellingsenspensjonat.no**

CENTRAL OSLO WEST Frogner House Apartments   🛗 🅿   Ⓚ
Skovveien 8, 0257 Oslo **Tel** *93 01 00 09* **Fax** *23 13 30 39*   **Map** *2 B2*

The elegant Victorian Frogner House Apartments are located in one of the most exclusive areas of Oslo, within a short walk of the heart of the city. The airy apartments combine the comforts of serviced accommodation with the privacy and freedom of self-catering. Long- and short-term rents are available. **www.frognerhouse.no**

CENTRAL OSLO WEST Thon Hotel Munch   Ⓚ
Munchs Gate 5, 0165 Oslo **Tel** *23 21 96 00* **Fax** *23 21 96 01* **Rooms** *180*   **Map** *2 D2*

A short walk to Karl Johan, as well as easy walking distance to public transportation, the airport shuttle bus and a variety of shops, restaurants, museums and theatres, the Thon Hotel Munch claims to have the largest single beds in Oslo. Coffee is served in the breakfast room until 11pm. **www.thonhotels.com/munch**

CENTRAL OSLO WEST Best Western West Hotel   🛗 🍴   ⓀⓀ
Skovveien 15, 0257 Oslo **Tel** *22 54 21 60* **Fax** *22 54 21 65* **Rooms** *56*   **Map** *2 B2*

The West is situated in a fashionable, quiet, residential area behind the Royal Palace. All rooms are en-suite with queen- or king-size beds, wireless Internet connection and views of the tree-lined 19th-century street outside. Eight of the rooms have balconies. Family-run since 1968 with enthusiastic, helpful staff. **www.bestwestern.com**

CENTRAL OSLO WEST Clarion Collection Hotel Savoy   🛗 🅿 🍴   ⓀⓀ
Universitetsgaten 11, 0164 Oslo **Tel** *23 35 42 00* **Fax** *23 35 42 01* **Rooms** *93*   **Map** *2 D3*

Set in a traditional building in Oslo's theatre district, this hotel is near the city's main street, Karl Johan. All 93 rooms are individually furnished in Scandinavian style and are non-smoking. There is free wireless Internet access in the rooms and the lobby. A light evening meal is included in the room rate. **www.choicehotels.com**

CENTRAL OSLO WEST Radisson Blu Plaza Scandinavia Hotel   📺 🛗 🅿 🍴   ⓀⓀ
Holbergsgate 30, 0166 Oslo **Tel** *23 29 30 00* **Fax** *23 29 30 01* **Rooms** *673*   **Map** *3 D2*

This first-class, modern hotel has 673 rooms and suites, all air-conditioned with high-speed wireless Internet access. A good choice for families, with a children's playroom and child menu options in the hotel restaurant. Enjoy a drink and take in the stunning views at Summit 21, located on the 21st floor. **www.oslo.radissonblu.com**

CENTRAL OSLO WEST Saga Bed & Breakfast   🅿   ⓀⓀ
Eilert Sundts Gate 39, 0259 Oslo **Tel** *22 43 04 85* **Fax** *22 44 08 63* **Rooms** *37*   **Map** *2 B1*

One of the few places in Oslo with its own free parking, the Saga Bed & Breakfast is located in the city centre behind the castle in a quiet and safe area and within walking distance of many of Oslo's best-known attractions. Coffee, tea, waffles and fruit are served daily in the pleasant lounge. Closed for Easter and Christmas. **www.sagabb.no**

CENTRAL OSLO WEST Scandic Edderkoppen   📺 🛗 🍴   ⓀⓀ
St Olavs Gate 1, O165 Oslo **Tel** *23 15 56 00* **Fax** *23 15 56 11* **Rooms** *241*   **Map** *3 D3*

The Scandic Edderkoppen has its own theatre, sauna and fitness area. People-watch in the bar or eat in the theatrically themed Restaurant Justers, decorated with memorabilia from the career of famous Norwegian actor Leif Juster. Many of the rooms have balconies. **www.scandic-hotels.com/edderkoppen**

Key to Symbols *see back cover flap*

CENTRAL OSLO WEST Thon Hotel Stefan

Rosenkrantzgate 1, 0159 Oslo **Tel** *23 31 55 00* **Fax** *23 31 55 55* **Rooms** *150* **Map** *3 D3*

Modern comfort and warm hospitality mark out this city-centre hotel just around the corner from Oslo's principal shopping street and close to most major attractions such as the Royal Palace. The dining room serves home-made bread and fresh coffee, while the Juristen Café & Bar has a relaxed atmosphere. **www.thonhotels.no/stefan**

CENTRAL OSLO WEST Norlandia Karl Johan Hotell

Karl Johansgate 33, 0162 Oslo **Tel** *23 16 17 00* **Fax** *22 42 05 19* **Rooms** *114* **Map** *3 D3*

The Norlandia Karl Johan is a late 18th-century, five-storey hotel located on Oslo's main thoroughfare. All 114 rooms are decorated in neutral colours and have private bathrooms, minibars, televisions and wireless Internet access. Rooms overlook the garden at the rear of the hotel or the lively Karl Johan street. **http://norlandia.no/karljohan/**

CENTRAL OSLO WEST Rica Victoria Hotel

Rosenkrantzgate 13, 0121 Oslo **Tel** *24 14 70 00* **Fax** *24 14 70 01* **Rooms** *199* **Map** *3 D3*

This modern hotel in the centre of Oslo has a glass atrium and rooms that all feature wooden floors, modern decor and furnishings, and city or atrium views. All rooms also have coffee makers and flatscreen TVs. The hotel's Victoria Haven is a light and airy garden atrium restaurant that serves lunch buffets. **www.rica-hotels.com**

CENTRAL OSLO WEST Scandic KNA

Parkveien 68, 0202 Oslo **Tel** *23 15 57 00* **Fax** *23 15 57 11* **Rooms** *189* **Map** *2 B3*

A stone's throw from the Royal Palace and Akershus fortress, the Scandic KNA is very close to the airport train terminal. In the summer, you can eat on the terrace at 189 Rom & Kjøkken, the hotel's chic modern restaurant. Several superior rooms have private balconies with views over the Oslo fjord. **www.scandic-hotels.com/kna**

CENTRAL OSLO WEST Thon Hotel Cecil

Stortingsgata 8, 0161 Oslo **Tel** *23 31 48 00* **Fax** *23 31 48 50* **Rooms** *111* **Map** *3 D3*

This pleasant city-centre hotel is primarily geared towards business travellers. Conveniently located close to all the major attractions, its rooms are bright and comfortably furnished. A filling breakfast buffet is included, and basic evening meals are available during the week except during the summer months. **www.thonhotels.no/cecil**

CENTRAL OSLO WEST Thon Hotel Europa

St Olavs Gate 31, 0166 Oslo **Tel** *23 25 63 00* **Fax** *23 25 63 63* **Rooms** *167* **Map** *3 D3*

Located close to the Parliament, the Royal Palace and the National Gallery, the Europa's 167 large, well-equipped rooms were completely renovated in 2006. The guest rooms come in two modern styles, one in deep reds and the other in stylish browns. Café Europa serves breakfast, lunch and dinner. **www.thonhotels.no/europa**

CENTRAL OSLO WEST Thon Hotel Gyldenløve

Bogstadveien 20, 0355 Oslo **Tel** *23 33 23 00* **Fax** *23 33 23 03* **Rooms** *164* **Map** *2 C1*

The Gyldenløve is superbly located in Oslo's west quarter, on one of the city's best shopping avenues. Having undergone a major refurbishment programme it now has a modern, stylish, Scandinavian feel. There is a reasonable menu at the hotel's Portofino Café and Winebar. **www.thonhotels.no/gyldenlove**

CENTRAL OSLO WEST Thon Hotel Slottsparken

Wergelandsveien 5, 0166 Oslo **Tel** *23 25 66 00* **Fax** *23 25 66 50* **Rooms** *244* **Map** *2 C2*

A four-star apartment hotel that offers both hotel rooms and long-stay apartments. There are non-smoking and business rooms available, as well as rooms with disabled facilities. Breakfast and lunch buffets are served in an elegant dining room. The hotel bar is popular and has a touch of English charm. **www.thonhotels.no/slottsparken**

CENTRAL OSLO WEST Thon Hotel Vika Atrium

Munkedamsveien 45, 0250 Oslo **Tel** *22 83 33 00* **Fax** *22 83 09 57* **Rooms** *79* **Map** *2 C4*

Located next to Aker Brygge, Oslo's premier shopping, leisure and entertainment area, and within a five-minute walk of the Royal Palace, Karl Johans gate and the National Theatre, this ultra-modern towering glass-fronted hotel is popular with business-people and families alike. **www.thonhotels.no/vikaatrium**

CENTRAL OSLO WEST Hotel Bristol

Kristian IV's gate 7, 0164 Oslo **Tel** *22 82 60 00* **Fax** *22 82 60 01* **Rooms** *251* **Map** *3 D3*

The classy Bristol has been one of Oslo's top hotels since the 1920s and is a regular choice for visiting celebrities. Dripping in traditional elegance, the hotel's Library Bar and Wintergarden is a popular meeting point, and the Bristol Grill offers both international and Norwegian dishes. Luxury guaranteed. All rooms are non-smoking. **www.bristol.no**

CENTRAL OSLO WEST Hotel Continental

Stortingsgata 24/26, 0161 Oslo **Tel** *22 82 40 00* **Fax** *22 42 96 89* **Rooms** *154* **Map** *3 D3*

The Hotel Continental is regarded as one of the finest hotels in the world. It has been a family-run business for four generations and the building dates back more than a century. Located in the very heart of Oslo, it boasts two award-winning restaurants. **www.hotel-continental.no**

CENTRAL OSLO EAST Budget Hotel

Prinsens Gate 6, 0152 Oslo **Tel** *22 41 36 10* **Fax** *22 42 24 29* **Rooms** *53* **Map** *3 E4*

The Budget Hotel is located close to the central railway station and near the main street, Karl Johan. Small, basic but comfortable, the hotel has a welcoming atmosphere and rooms in two categories, budget and standard. Breakfast is not included but available at a reasonable price. Ideal for short stopovers and budget travellers. **www.budgethotel.no**

CENTRAL OSLO EAST Best Western Anker Hotel

Storgata 55, 0182 Oslo **Tel** *22 99 75 00* **Fax** *22 99 75 20* **Rooms** *161*   **Map** *3 2F*

The Anker is situated between Oslo's busy main street Karl Johan and Grunerlokka's young and trendy urban area. During the winter of 2006–07, many of its 161 rooms were tastefully refurbished. It has a pleasant restaurant, and in the summer there's an attractive backyard beer garden. **www.anker-hotel.no**

CENTRAL OSLO EAST Best Western Bondeheimen Hotel

Rosenkrantz Gate 8, 0159 Oslo **Tel** *23 21 41 00* **Fax** *23 21 41 01* **Rooms** *127*   **Map** *3 D3*

Located opposite the Parliament building and not far from the National Gallery, this classic seven-storey Norwegian building dates back to 1901. The Kaffistova restaurant serves traditional fare and the hotel's Heimen Husfield craft store stocks almost 4,000 gift items to help you remember your trip to Oslo. **www.bondeheimen.com**

CENTRAL OSLO EAST Comfort Hotel Boersparken

Tollbugaten 4, 0152 Oslo **Tel** *22 47 17 17* **Fax** *22 47 17 18* **Rooms** *198*   **Map** *3 E4*

The contemporary Boersparken is close to Oslo train station. All rooms have complimentary wireless Internet access and breakfast is served in the hotel's dining room. The lobby bar, with its distinctive red leather armchairs, serves drinks throughout the day. Has complimentary waffles and cakes from 3–7pm. **www.choicehotels.no**

CENTRAL OSLO EAST First Hotel Millennium

Tollbugaten 25, 0157 Oslo **Tel** *21 02 28 00* **Fax** *21 02 28 30* **Rooms** *112*   **Map** *3 E4*

A first-class modern hotel near to Karl Johan and the Akershus Fortress, the Millennium is close to restaurants, museums, and galleries. Rooms are spacious, with separate bedroom and living areas, and the top floor's ten rooms each have a terrace. The hotel's Primo Ciao Ciao restaurant serves authentic Italian food. **www.firsthotels.no/millennium**

CENTRAL OSLO EAST Rica Oslo Hotel

Nr.1 Europarådets Plass, 0154 Oslo **Tel** *23 10 42 00* **Fax** *23 10 42 10* **Rooms** *175*

Leather furniture and marble floors decorate this hotel's lobby, while art and sculpture from prominent Norwegian artists further adds to the artistic atmosphere. Rooms are individually decorated with paintings. Buffet meals and an à la carte menu are served at the Bjorgvigen Mat & Vinhus restaurant. **www.rica-hotels.com**

CENTRAL OSLO EAST Clarion Hotel Royal Christiania

Biskop Gunnerus' Gate 3, 0155 Oslo **Tel** *23 10 80 00* **Fax** *23 10 80 80* **Rooms** *508*   **Map** *3 E3*

Originally built for the 1952 Winter Olympic Games, the first-class Clarion Hotel Royal Christiania has an impressive marble and brass lobby. All 508 air-conditioned rooms are decorated in warm tones. The Atrium restaurant serves classic Norwegian dishes. **www.choicehotels.no/hotels/no036**

CENTRAL OSLO EAST Scandic Bjørvigen

Jernbanetorget 6, 0154 Oslo **Tel** *23 15 55 00* **Fax** *23 15 55 11* **Rooms** *239*   **Map** *3 E3*

Enjoy fjord views from this modern and well-equipped hotel located near Oslo's Central Station and the city's shopping and tourist attractions. Watch the buzz of Oslo's city life from the Restaurant Egon or enjoy a nightcap in the stylish lobby bar. Free for under 13s and half price for adolescents aged 13–17. **www.scandic-hotels.com/bjorvigen**

CENTRAL OSLO EAST Thon Hotel Opera

Christian Frederiks Plass 5, 0154 Oslo **Tel** *24 10 30 00* **Fax** *24 10 30 10* **Rooms** *434*   **Map** *3 E4*

Located on the platform at Oslo Central Station, this four-star hotel is a popular business venue. Most rooms offer views over either the fjord or the city. The second-floor Scala restaurant offers a tempting á la carte menu, after which you can burn off the calories in the fitness centre, with sauna and sun-bed facilities. **www.thonhotels.com/opera**

CENTRAL OSLO EAST Grand Hotel

Karl Johans Gate 31, 0159 Oslo **Tel** *23 21 20 00* **Fax** *23 21 21 00* **Rooms** *290*   **Map** *3 D3*

The Grand Hotel first opened its doors in 1874. Built in Louis XVI revival style, it is now a deluxe hotel with a hint of Nordic Art Nouveau. It has been extended and modernized over the years, and today is a superb mix of tradition and modern comfort. The hotel has a great choice of bars and restaurants. **www.grand.no**

CENTRAL OSLO EAST Radisson Blu Plaza Hotel Oslo

Sonja Henies Plass 3, 0134 Oslo **Tel** *22 05 80 00* **Fax** *22 05 80 10* **Rooms** *673*   **Map** *3 3F*

With 37 floors and breathtaking views of Oslo and the fjord, the Radisson Blu Plaza is Northern Europe's highest and Norway's largest hotel. It's also the first Radisson SAS hotel to receive the Nordic Eco Label, which means it meets the strictest environmental requirements on energy and water conservation. **www.oslo.radissonblu.com**

FURTHER AFIELD Bogstad Camp & Turistsenter

Ankerveien 117, 0766 Oslo **Tel** *22 51 08 00* **Fax** *22 51 08 50* **Rooms** *46 cabins/1000 camping units*

Set in beautiful natural surroundings 8 km (5 miles) from Oslo city centre, Norway's largest campsite covers about 40 acres bordering the Nordmarka wilderness area and Bogstad Lake. Low-cost camping and cabin options are available, some with their own showers and toilets. **www.bogstadcamping.no**

FURTHER AFIELD Gardermoen Airport Hotel

Sør-Gardermoen, 2060 Gardermoen **Tel** *63 94 08 00* **Fax** *63 94 08 01* **Rooms** *179*

Just four minutes from Oslo airport, this is an ideal choice if you need to catch a late-night or early-morning flight. Very reasonably priced with a friendly and informal style, the hotel has a free shuttle bus service to and from the airport. A restaurant with a fireplace and grill stays open late. **www.gardermoen-airporthotel.no**

Key to Price Guide *see p226* **Key to Symbols** *see back cover flap*

FURTHER AFIELD Oslo Vandrerhjem Haraldsheim   P   ⊗
Haraldsheimveien 4, 0409 Oslo **Tel** *22 22 29 65* **Fax** *22 22 10 25* **Rooms** *69*

This clean and affordable youth hostel is located 4 km (2½ miles) from downtown Oslo, in safe and attractive surroundings and with a splendid view of the city and the fjord. It's an ideal starting point for forest treks. Most rooms have four beds, and showers and toilets are located in the corridors. **www.haraldsheim.no**

FURTHER AFIELD Linne Hotel   🍴 🛏 P 🍴   ⊗⊗
Statsråd Mathiesensvei 12, 0598 Oslo **Tel** *23 17 00 00* **Fax** *23 17 00 01* **Rooms** *106*

Located in the heart of Groruddalen and just ten minutes north of the centre of Oslo, this 1960s hotel is a popular choice for meetings and conferences. The rooms are basic but comfortable and there's free covered parking. The à la carte Restaurant Statstraaden is popular with the business crowd. **www.linne.no**

FURTHER AFIELD Clarion Collection Hotel Gabelhus   🍴 🛏 P 🍴   ⊗⊗⊗
Gabelsgate 16, 0272 Oslo **Tel** *23 27 65 00* **Fax** *23 27 65 60* **Rooms** *114*   **Map** *2 A3*

The ivy-covered Gabelshus is located in an exclusive residential area with beautiful townhouses, embassies, high-class restaurants and cafés all within walking distance. Thoroughly renovated in 2004, it is now a stylish and charming boutique hotel that combines modern Scandinavian design with traditional architectural features. **www.gabelshus.no**

FURTHER AFIELD Radisson SAS Airport Hotel, Gardermoen   🍴 🛏 P 🍴   ⊗⊗⊗
Hotellvegen, 2061 Gardermoen **Tel** *63 93 30 00* **Fax** *63 93 30 30* **Rooms** *503*

This is the only hotel with business facilities at the Oslo Airport Gardermoen. Built using stone, metal, wood and glass to match its surroundings, this ultra-modern establishment is just a few minutes walk to the boarding gates. After a long flight you can unwind in the Take Off sports and wellness centre. **www.oslo.radissonsas.com**

FURTHER AFIELD Rica Helsfyr Hotel   🛏 P 🍴   ⊗⊗⊗
Strømsveien 108, 0663 Oslo **Tel** *23 06 78 78* **Fax** *23 06 78 80* **Rooms** *207*

Located on the outskirts of Oslo, approximately ten minutes by car from the city centre, this hotel is situated in pleasant surroundings away from the bustle of city life. An onsite restaurant and pub provide plenty of eating and drinking possibilities. The airport bus stops five minutes from the hotel. **www.rica.no/helsfyr**

FURTHER AFIELD Soria Moria Hotell and Conference Center   🍴 🛏 P 🍴   ⊗⊗⊗
Voksenkollveien 60, 0790 Oslo **Tel** *23 22 24 00* **Fax** *23 22 24 01* **Rooms** *156*

Perched 500 metres (160 ft) above sea level "on the roof of Oslo", this hotel has spectacular views over the city below and with the Holmenkollen ski jump just around the corner. The hotel can arrange a wide variety of activities in the region. Great for families and outdoor enthusiasts. **www.soriamoria.no**

FURTHER AFIELD Holmenkollen Park Hotel Rica   🍴 🛏 P 🍴   ⊗⊗⊗⊗
Kongeveien 26, 0787 Oslo **Tel** *22 92 20 00* **Fax** *22 14 61 92* **Rooms** *222*

This eye-catching luxury hotel was built in the Norwegian "dragon" style over 100 years ago and is situated high above the centre of Oslo, affording a unique view of the city and fjord. There are extensive fitness and spa facilities available, including a heated indoor pool and a gym. **www.holmenkollenparkhotel.no**

FURTHER AFIELD Lysebu   🍴 🛏 P 🍴   ⊗⊗⊗⊗
Lysebuveien 12, 0712 Oslo **Tel** *21 51 10 00* **Fax** *21 51 10 01* **Rooms** *62*

Situated in beautiful surroundings above the Oslo fjord on Holmenkollen Hill, this gorgeous "fairytale farm" is built in typical Norwegian style and has extensive facilities for meetings, conferences and special events. The restaurant serves world-class food, Nordic in nature with a French accent. **www.lysebu.com**

AROUND OSLOFJORDEN

FREDRIKSTAD Rica City Hotel   🛏 P 🍴   ⊗⊗
Nygaardsgaten 44/46, 1607 Fredrikstad **Tel** *69 38 56 00* **Fax** *69 38 56 01* **Rooms** *110*

The Rica City is the hub of Fredrikstad's dining and nightlife scene, with three restaurants, several bars and a nightclub. From the outside it looks a little dour, but the rooms have a classic English touch and all have wireless Internet access. If you like being where the action is, this hotel is a good choice. **www.ricahotels.com**

HALDEN Grand Hotell   🛏 P 🍴   ⊗⊗
Jernbanetorget 1, 1767 Halden **Tel** *69 18 72 00* **Fax** *69 18 72 59* **Rooms** *33*

This hotel was originally built in 1898 and its rustic charm is part of its appeal. The Grand is situated in the centre of Halden, only a short distance from train and bus connections and a variety of shops. A fully licensed bar offers traditional Norwegian food as well as an interesting international menu. **www.grandhotell.net**

HORTEN Norlandia Grand Ocean Hotell   P 🍴   ⊗⊗⊗
Jernbanegaten 1, 3187 Horten **Tel** *33 04 17 22* **Fax** *33 04 45 07* **Rooms** *100*

The three-star Grand Ocean lies in the heart of the charming naval town of Horten, with its green areas and beautiful location along the Oslo fjord. Built on the seafront, with excellent beaches just a few minutes' stroll away, the hotel's Ocean restaurant serves first-class Norwegian and international dishes. **www.norlandia.no/grandocean**

LARVIK Quality Hotel Grand Farris

Storgaten 38, 3251 Larvik **Tel** 33 18 78 00 **Fax** 33 18 70 45 **Rooms** 91

Centrally located in Larvik and within walking distance of the town square, the three-star Grand Farris is close to Fredriksvern Verft, one of Norway's most famous military constructions from the 1700s. The Grand Bar offers a sophisticated backdrop for cocktails. **www.choicehotels.no**

MOSS Hotel Refsnes Gods

Godset 5, 1518 Moss **Tel** 69 27 83 00 **Fax** 69 27 83 01 **Rooms** 61

The Refsnes Gods is located on the island of Jeløy near Moss, about an hour's drive from Oslo, and its elegant building dates all the way back to 1767. With lovely views over the Oslo fjord, the hotel is known for high-quality food and wine as well as a unique art collection. **www.refsnesgods.no**

SANDEFJORD Rica Park Hotel Sandefjord

Strandpromenaden 9, 3212 Sandefjord **Tel** 33 44 74 00 **Fax** 33 44 75 00 **Rooms** 231

Idyllically located next to the harbour close to the centre and the sea, this hotel caters for courses, conferences, business functions and holidays. Rooms are large with good views, many overlooking the fjord. The hotel's three restaurants – Kosmos, Parkstuen and Vinstuen – provide an array of menus for all tastes. **www.rica-hotels.com**

SANDVIKA Thon Hotel Oslofjord

Sandviksveien 184, 1337 Sandvika **Tel** 67 55 66 00 **Fax** 67 55 66 88 **Rooms** 246

This distinctive hotel is decorated in an exclusive Art Deco style with spacious rooms and large bathrooms. Next to the hotel are a beach, the Info-Rama and Sandvika Shopping centres as well as stations for trains, buses and the airport express. The hotel's Restaurant Aquarius serves elegant à la carte meals. **www.thonhotels.com/oslofjord**

STAVERN Hotel Wassilioff

Havnegata 1, 3290 Stavern **Tel** 33 11 36 00 **Fax** 33 11 36 01 **Rooms** 47

Described as a pearl in the middle of idyllic Stavern, Hotel Wassilioff is the first and only hotel in Norway with its own private fish market where fishing boats dock and deliver their fresh catches daily. Naturally, a meal in the hotel's seafood restaurant is a must! **www.wassilioff.no**

TJØME Engø Gård

Gamle Engøvei 25, 3145 Tjøme **Tel** 33 39 00 48 **Fax** 33 39 00 45 **Rooms** 24

Built in 1845 in the heart of a park on the Oslo fjord coastline, this stunning country-house hotel is a lavish retreat from the capital. The old farmhouse offers exceptional cuisine in a cottage setting and has an extensive wine list to drool over. Take a dip in the heated indoor swimming pool. **www.engo.no**

TØNSBERG Quality Hotel Klubben

Nedre Langgate 49, 3126 Tønsberg **Tel** 33 35 97 00 **Fax** 33 35 97 97 **Rooms** 145

Beautifully located in the centre of Norway's oldest city with a magnificent view of the harbour – and close to the market and the city's idyllic shopping streets – the Quality Hotel Klubben hosts an annual summer show performed at its own theatre. The Harlekin dance bar is a popular meeting point in town. **www.choicehotels.no**

EASTERN NORWAY

DRAMMEN Clarion Collection Hotel Tollboden

Tollbugaten 43, 3044 Drammen **Tel** 32 80 51 00 **Fax** 32 80 51 99 **Rooms** 127

Situated a five-minute walk from the railway and bus stations, the Tollboden has conference facilities and a business centre. Take advantage of the superb relaxation area with free bathrobes, sauna and sunbeds. Staff take pride in providing a personal service. **www.choicehotels.no**

DRAMMEN First Hotel Ambassadeur

Strømsø Torg 7, 3044 Drammen **Tel** 31 01 21 00 **Fax** 31 01 21 11 **Rooms** 230

Each of this hotel's rooms, some of which date back to the 1870s, has recently been individually decorated, and a new restaurant, bar and fitness centre are among the many amenities available. Disabled access and facilities are also provided. The Waldorf à la carte restaurant serves international fare. **www.firsthotels.com/ambassadeur**

DRAMMEN Rica Park Hotel Drammen

Gamle Kirkeplass 3, 3019 Drammen **Tel** 32 26 36 00 **Fax** 32 26 37 77 **Rooms** 100

Despite the rather square and dull exterior, the Rica Park is conveniently located directly opposite Drammen's popular theatre. If you're an angler, the nearby Drammenselva is one of the country's best sport fishing rivers. The hotel's two restaurants, Hannas Kjøkken and Urtehaven, serve a good standard of food. **www.rica-hotels.com**

ELVESETER Elveseter Turisthotell

Top of Norway, Elveseter, 2687 Bøverdalen **Tel** 61 21 99 00 **Fax** 61 21 99 01 **Rooms** 110

This traditional hotel complex is next to a river on a valley floor flanked by snow-capped mountains and has been welcoming guests since the 1880s. Today it comprises 19 rustic wooden buildings, complete with grass roofs. Facilities include a restaurant, bar, indoor pool and theatre. **www.ton.no**

Key to Price Guide see p226 **Key to Symbols** see back cover flap

ESPEDALEN Dalseter Høyfjellshotell

Espedalen, 2658 Espedalen **Tel** *61 29 99 10* **Fax** *61 29 99 41* **Rooms** *88*

This family-run hotel is located in beautiful surroundings with panoramic views of the Jotunheimen mountain range and is a meeting point for climbers in the summer and skiers in the winter. Facilities include an indoor swimming pool, exercise room, solarium and a large playroom for children. **www.dalseter.no**

GJØVIK Thon Hotel Gjovik

Strandgt. 15, 2815 Gjovik **Tel** *61 13 20 00* **Fax** *61 18 08 64* **Rooms** *83*

Fully renovated in 2006, this stylish and modern hotel boasts one of the best equipped spas in the country, making it a great place to relax. It is conveniently situated in the heart of Gjøvik with the town square, shopping and pedestrian streets all close by. **www.thonhotels.no/gjovik**

OPPADAL Kongsvold Fjeldstue

Dovrefjell, 7340 Oppadal **Tel** *72 40 43 40* **Fax** *72 40 43 41* **Rooms** *32*

One of the most prestigious hotels in Norway – the Queen of Denmark has her own room here – Kongsvold Fjeldstue blends tradition with modern comfort. The main building dates back to 1720 and all 32 ensuite rooms are exquisitely furnished, with no two rooms the same. **www.kongsvold.no**

HAMAR First Hotel Victoria

Strandgaten 21, 2317 Hamar **Tel** *62 02 55 00* **Fax** *62 53 32 23* **Rooms** *115*

Dating from 1869, the Victoria is Hamar's oldest hotel, although its rooms have all mod cons. Well-equipped conference facilities make this a good venue for business events. The onsite Christian Krohg restaurant is one of the best in Hamar and provides great views over Mjøsa, the largest lake in Norway. **www.firsthotels.com/victoria**

HAMAR Quality Hotel Astoria

Torggata 23, 2317 Hamar **Tel** *62 70 70 00* **Fax** *62 70 70 01* **Rooms** *78*

The renovated Quality Hotel Astoria is situated in the city centre by the main street, close to attractions such as the Glass Cathedral, the Viking Ship, Arena Skiblander and Lake Mjøsa. All rooms have standard modern amenities. **www.choicehotels.no**

HEMSEDAL Harahorn

Hemsedal, 3560 Hemsedal **Tel** *32 05 51 10* **Fax** *32 05 51 24* **Rooms** *35*

The Harahorn combines the comfort of a hotel with the atmosphere of a mountain cabin, with 19 buildings situated around a courtyard. Its wonderful restaurant serves traditional Norwegian and international dishes, complemented by an impressive wine list. The views are nothing short of breathtaking. **www.harahorn.no**

LILLEHAMMER Birkebeineren Hotel & Apartments

Birkebeinerveien 24, 2618 Lillehammer **Tel** *61 26 47 00* **Fax** *61 26 47 50* **Rooms** *48 rooms & 40 apartments*

Set among the greenery of Lillehammer's Olympic Park, this traditional-style, red wood building boasts modern facilities in its 48 hotel rooms and 40 apartments. There's no restaurant but guests can cook on the hotel's barbeque. There's also a volleyball court and a children's playground. **www.birkebeineren.no/english**

LILLEHAMMER Clarion Collection Hotel Hammer

Storgata 108b, 2615 Lillehammer **Tel** *61 26 73 73* **Fax** *61 26 37 30* **Rooms** *95*

This high-class hotel is located in the Storgata area in the centre of Lillehammer just minutes from the Maihaugen, Europe's largest open-air museum. Staff lay on free waffles in the afternoon and a snack buffet in the evening. Specially adapted rooms for the physically challenged are also available. **www.choicehotels.no**

LILLEHAMMER First Hotel Breiseth

Jernbanegata 1–5, 2609 Lillehammer **Tel** *61 24 77 77* **Fax** *61 26 95 05* **Rooms** *89*

One of the oldest hotels in Lillehammer, the Breiseth used to be an artists colony and is still decorated with original paintings from that era. The hotel has two restaurants, with breakfast served in Vigerust – and its views of the old railway station. **www.firsthotels.no/breiseth**

LILLEHAMMER Mølla Hotell

Elvegaten 12, 2609 Lillehammer **Tel** *61 05 70 80* **Fax** *61 05 70 81* **Rooms** *58*

The Mølla is the second-tallest building in Lillehammer, rising 11 storeys from its town-centre location. It houses one of Lillehammer's most prestigious restaurants, and also has a wonderful panoramic rooftop bar with views over a stream and waterfall. **www.mollahotell.no**

SØRLANDET AND TELEMARK

ARENDAL Clarion Hotel Tyholmen

Teaterplassen 2, 4836 Arendal **Tel** *37 02 68 00* **Fax** *37 02 68 01* **Rooms** *60*

This modern hotel is set in an idyllic, award-winning timber building on the wharf in the old town. Many of the rooms have great views of the water and boats below. Take your pick from three onsite restaurants, and try the local fish. Specially adapted rooms for the physically challenged are also available. **www.choicehotels.no**

ARENDAL Thon Hotel Arendal

Friergangen 1, 4836 Arendal **Tel** *37 05 21 50* **Fax** *37 05 21 51* **Rooms** *120*

Thon Hotel Arendal is located on Tyholmen in the centre of Arendal, close to the seafront and the maritime district of Pollen. Tyholmen is the old part of Arendal town, with a proud history as the most important port in Norway. Rooms are comfortable and well equipped. **www.thonhotels.no/arendal**

BØ Bø Hotel

Gullbringvegen 32, 3800 Bø **Tel** *35 06 08 00* **Fax** *35 06 08 01* **Rooms** *64*

Just two minutes walk from Bø town centre and close to the railway and bus stations, this family-friendly hotel is next to the Gullbring Cultural Centre, with its indoor swimming pool, cinema, gym and other attractions. The Bø becomes a "children's hotel" in the summer, with lots to keep young guests amused. **www.bohotell.no**

BØ Lifjellstua

Lifjellvegen 934, 3800 Bø **Tel** *35 95 33 80* **Fax** *35 95 33 67* **Rooms** *20*

The cosy and inviting Lifjellstua is located 750 m (2.460 ft) above sea-level in idyllic and beautiful natural surroundings on the top of Lifjell, and is a favourite tourist destination in both winter and summer. Following a radical refurbishment, it is now one of Norway's most comfortable mountain lodges. **www.lifjellstua.no**

DALEN Dalen Hotel

Dalen i Telemark, 3880 Dalen **Tel** *35 07 90 00* **Fax** *35 07 70 11* **Rooms** *42*

Known as the "fairytale hotel", the Dalen is built in an ornate, romantic style with dragon heads, turrets and spires. This restored building has retained its original character and is virtually identical today to the wooden castle that opened in 1894, when royalty and European nobility stayed here. An unforgettable location. **www.dalenhotel.no**

KRISTIANSAND Comfort Hotel Skagerak

Henrik Wergelandsgate 4, 4612 Kristiansand **Tel** *38 07 94 00* **Fax** *38 07 02 43* **Rooms** *67*

This quiet bed and breakfast hotel is located in the middle of the Kvadraturen quarter in the heart of Kristiansand. It has reasonable facilities, with breakfast served but no restaurant. There are, however, plenty of places to eat close by, and the main shopping area is also just around the corner. **www.choice.no**

KRISTIANSAND Radisson Blu Caledonien Hotel

Vestre Standgate 7, 4663 Kristiansand **Tel** *38 11 21 00* **Fax** *38 11 21 11* **Rooms** *205*

The largest hotel in southern Norway is situated in the heart of Kristiansand close to the sea. Staff can arrange boat rides, fishing trips, rafting and hiking around the region. Enjoy the relaxed atmosphere at the Brasseriet restaurant with its great views or have a pint at the Scottish-themed Telford's Pub. **www.radissonblu.com**

KRISTIANSAND Scandic Kristiansand

Markensgate 39, 4612 Kristiansand **Tel** *21 61 42 00* **Fax** *21 61 42 11* **Rooms** *112*

Just ten minutes walk from the train station and with the cathedral and beaches nearby, this hotel is an ideal base from which to explore picturesque Kristiansand. All rooms have good views of the town or out to sea. Health-conscious guests can work out at a nearby fitness centre. **www.scandic-hotels.com**

LANGESUND Quality Hotel & Resort Skjærgården

Stathelleveien 35, 3970 Langesund **Tel** *35 97 81 00* **Fax** *35 97 81 90* **Rooms** *161*

A perfect location on the beach, with one of the best ocean fishing spots in the Skagerrak just metres away, this hotel has tasteful, well-equipped rooms. The massive indoor and outdoor bathing complex houses jacuzzis, saunas, sunbeds and a water chute. Perfect for families. **www.choicehotels.no**

PORSGRUNN Hotel Vic

Skolegata 1, 3901 Porsgrunn **Tel** *35 56 98 00* **Fax** *35 56 98 01* **Rooms** *107*

The historic Vic is the only hotel in Porsgrunn and dates back to 1825 when a local noble rebuilt his elegant residence after a major fire. Parts of the original building are still evident, together with a newer section built in 1956. Quality food is available from a charming à la carte restaurant. **www.vichotel.no**

RAULAND Austbø Hotell

Rauland, 3864 Rauland **Tel** *35 07 34 25* **Fax** *35 07 31 06* **Rooms** *23*

This small mountain hotel has an informal atmosphere and offers single, double and family rooms – all with ensuite bathrooms. Beautifully situated above Lake Tansvatn, and close to nature trails and alpine skiing facilities, it is an ideal base for an outdoor holiday. **www.austbohotel.no**

SELJORD Uppigard Natadal

Natadal, 3841 Flatdal **Tel** *35 06 59 00* **Fax** *35 06 59 01* **Rooms** *19*

With its grass roofs, this charming collection of five traditional Norwegian log farm buildings from the 18th century makes for an unusual but memorable stay. The farm itself is believed to date back to the 11th century. A guided tour and a traditional lunch is available for groups by reservation. **www.natadal.no**

SKIEN Thon Hotel Hoyers

Kongensgate 6, 3724 Skien **Tel** *35 90 58 00* **Fax** *35 90 58 05* **Rooms** *100*

The unique Hoyers was built in 1853 and is Telemark's oldest hotel. Within easy walking distance of the Telemark Canal as well as a wide selection of shops and entertainment opportunities, the hotel's Madam Bloms restaurant offers a stylish and intimate dining experience and is possibly the best in town. **www.thonhotels.no/hoyers**

Key to Price Guide *see p226* **Key to Symbols** *see back cover flap*

SKIEN Clarion Collection Hotel Bryggeparken

Langbrygga 7, 3724 Skien **Tel** *35 91 21 00* **Fax** *35 91 21 01* **Rooms** *103*

Ideally located at the wharf by the entrance to the Telemark Canal. The hotel's warehouse architecture and designer furniture create a distinctive atmosphere. All rooms are comfortable and well equipped. On the top floor there's a whirlpool, sauna, Turkish steam bath, solarium and great views over Skien. **www.choicehotels.no**

VRADAL Vrådal Hotel og Hyttepark

Tiurgvegen 5, 3853 Vrådal **Tel** *35 06 93 00* **Fax** *35 06 93 01* **Rooms** *52, 36 cabins & 3 apartments*

A quiet, well-run family hotel built on the northern tip of Lake Nisser, the Hyttepark offers 52 rooms, 36 cabins and three apartments. Facilities include an indoor swimming pool, work-out room and children's playroom. The dining room overlooks Lake Nisser and serves a buffet dinner every evening. Live music in the summer. **www.vradal.no**

VRADAL Quality Straand Hotel & Resort

Vradalsvegen 1, 3853 Vrådal **Tel** *35 06 90 00* **Fax** *35 06 90 01* **Rooms** *125*

This family-friendly resort has almost every conceivable facility to keep the whole family amused, including a tennis court, billiards room, sun deck, childrens' playground and jogging track. A previous winner of the Hotel of the Year award, it has stunning panoramic views over Lake Nisser. **www.choicehotels.no**

VESTLANDET

BALESTRAND Kviknes Hotel

Kniknevegen 8, Balestrand **Tel** *57 69 42 00* **Fax** *57 69 42 01* **Rooms** *190*

Kvikne's has been welcoming guests since 1752 and the Kvikne family still owns the hotel today. This stunning hotel has one of the most breathtaking locations in all of Norway, built alongside the world's longest fjord, the Sognefjord, and with snow-capped mountains in the background. Bags of olde-worlde charm. **www.kviknes.no**

BERGEN Thon Hotel Bergen Brygge

Bradbenken 3, 5003 Bergen **Tel** *55 30 87 00* **Fax** *55 32 94 14* **Rooms** *229*

Centrally located by the historic Hanseatic Wharf and in walking distance to the shops, the Bergen Brygge is surrounded by the Rosenkrantz Tower, the Haakon's Hall and St. Mary's Church. The hotel claims to serve the best breakfast buffet in town. **www.thonhotels.com/bergenbrygge**

BERGEN Grand Terminus

Zander Kaaesgate 6, 5018 Bergen **Tel** *55 21 25 00* **Fax** *55 21 25 01* **Rooms** *131*

This elegant hotel was built in a classical style in 1928. Because of its age and design, the rooms vary a great deal in size and shape. The impressive dining room is one of the features of the hotel and is a popular venue at lunchtimes as well as evenings. There's also a bar which serves food. **www.ght.no**

BERGEN Steens Hotel

Parkveien 22, 5007 Bergen **Tel** *55 30 88 88* **Fax** *55 30 88 89* **Rooms** *21*

An elegant villa from 1890 that retains its traditional style, the peaceful Steens is situated in beautiful surroundings near Nygårds park. The grandiose dining room where breakfast is served still has the original oak-panelling and tapestry. Most rooms face the park. Good parking outside the hotel. **www.steenshotel.no**

BERGEN Clarion Hotel Admiral

C.Sundtsgate 9, 5004 Bergen **Tel** *55 23 64 00* **Fax** *55 23 64 64* **Rooms** *210*

Known as "the hotel with the sea on three sides," the top-class Clarion has stunning views of the wharf, the fish market and Mt. Fløien. Built at the turn of the century as a boat warehouse, it was turned into a waterside hotel in 1987. All 210 rooms have large windows, and 40 have harbour views. **www.clarionadmiral.no**

BERGEN First Hotel Marin

Rosenkrantzgaten 8, 5003 Bergen **Tel** *53 05 15 00* **Fax** *53 05 15 01* **Rooms** *152*

The Marin is a tasteful and elegant hotel on the famous Bryggen in Bergen. Its large, discerningly decorated and well-equipped rooms have a maritime theme, and all have dark wood floors. Several of the rooms offer views of the harbour and the fish market. The onsite restaurant serves delicious à la carte cuisine. **www.firsthotels.com/marin**

BERGEN Radisson Blu Hotel Norge

Nedre Ole Bulls Plass 4, 5807 Bergen **Tel** *55 57 30 00* **Fax** *55 57 30 01* **Rooms** *347*

One of Bergen's most prestigious hotels located in the heart of the city adjacent to the city park, the Norgel is rich in culture and is within walking distance of the city's attractions, historical sites and the shopping district. The onsite restaurant FISH is Bergen's only seafood bar. Its leisure facilities include a swimming pool. **www.radissonblu.com**

BERGEN Rica Neptun Hotell

Valkendorfsgate 8, 5807 Bergen **Tel** *55 30 68 00* **Fax** *55 30 68 50* **Rooms** *124*

Located in the centre of Bergen, the first-class Neptun contains 750 works of art and is synonymous with good food, wine and art. Visit the prize-winning gourmet restaurant Lucullus, renowned as one of the best in western Norway, or enjoy a glass of fine wine in Pascal Mat&Vin. **www.neptunhotel.no**

HAUGESUND Best Western Hotel Neptun   🅿   ⓚⓚⓚ

Haraldsgaten 207, 5521 Haugesund **Tel** *52 86 59 00* **Fax** *52 86 59 01* **Rooms** *43*

This small, basic but cosy hotel in the centre of Haugesund serves an appetising complimentary full breakfast each morning and rooms feature cable television, coffee maker, alarm clock and refrigerator. Free outdoor parking is also provided. There's no restaurant but the town's cafes and bars are nearby. **www.bestwestern.com**

HAUGESUND Rica Maritim Hotel   🅣🅗🅟🅗   ⓚⓚⓚ

Åsbygaten 3, 5528 Haugesund **Tel** *52 86 30 00* **Fax** *52 86 30 01* **Rooms** *311*

The refurbished Rica Maritim is a business hotel located in the Smeda strait in Haugesund. The hotel has a bar and nightclub, as well as four high-quality restaurants. It becomes family-friendly in the summer, with many activities provided for children. **www.rica-hotels.com**

KRISTIANSUND Comfort Hotel Fosna   🅗🅟   ⓚⓚⓚ

Hauggata 16, 6500 Kristiansund **Tel** *71 67 40 11* **Fax** *71 67 76 59* **Rooms** *50*

The Fosna has a pleasant waterfront location and incorporates an outdoor restaurant that opens during the summer months. With Kristiansund Airport only minutes away, it is a popular choice with the business crowd. **www.choicehotels.no**

KRISTIANSUND Rica Hotel Kristiansund   🅣🅗🅟🅗   ⓚⓚⓚ

Storgaten 41, 6508 Kristiansund **Tel** *71 57 12 00* **Fax** *71 57 12 01* **Rooms** *102*

This modern first-class business hotel is in a central location on Kristiansund's quay and is a short distance from the town's main shopping areas. The hotel's Sky Bar is located at the top of the building and has fantastic views over the water. The onsite JP Clausens Vin & Pianobar is one of the "in" places in town. **www.rica-hotels.com**

MOLDE Quality Hotel Alexandra   🅗🅟🅗   ⓚⓚⓚ

Storgaten 1–7, 6413 Molde **Tel** *71 20 37 50* **Fax** *71 20 37 87* **Rooms** *163*

Located in the centre of Molde by the harbour near the coastal steamer pier, the Alexandra has fantastic views of the fjord and the Romsdal Alps. It has well-furnished rooms, an in-house restaurant and bar and a fully equipped business centre. **www.choicehotels.no**

SKODJE Storfjord Hotel   🅟🅗   ⓚⓚⓚ

Øvre Glomset, 6260 Skodje **Tel** *70 27 49 22* **Fax** *70 27 49 23* **Rooms** *6*

Overlooking the breathtaking Storfjord and the Sunnmøre Alps, this captivating hotel is set in six acres of private grounds amidst thousands of acres of protected forest. An ideal retreat for those who enjoy active pursuits. Each of the six spacious rooms has a luxury bathroom suite and some have four-poster beds. **www.storfjordhotel.com**

STAVANGER Rogalandsheimen Inn   🅗🅟   ⓚ

Musegata 18, 4010 Stavanger **Tel** *51 52 01 88* **Rooms** *13*

The centrally located Rogalandsheimen is one of the oldest lodging houses in Stavanger. It is richly decorated with paintings and has a charming and informal atmosphere. A popular haunt of several famous Norwegian and foreign artists, it serves hearty breakfasts. **www.rogalandsheimen.no**

STAVANGER Quality Hotel Residence   🅗🅟🅗   ⓚⓚ

Ole Bulls Gate 5, 4306 Sandnes **Tel** *51 60 57 00* **Fax** *51 60 57 01* **Rooms** *157*

A modern, five-floor hotel situated in the centre of Sandnes, the Residence has contemporary decor in neutral tones. The hotel has its own nightclub with a DJ playing house music every weekend. For those looking for something quieter, the hotel shares space with a cinema and a shopping centre. **www.choicehotels.no**

STAVANGER Thon Hotel Maritim   🅗   ⓚⓚ

Kongsgaten 32, 4005 Stavanger **Tel** *51 85 05 00* **Fax** *51 85 05 01* **Rooms** *221*

With views over Lake Breiavannet, the Maritim is a medium-budget hotel close to several parks. The hotel is close to a private gym with preferential rates for guests, and the restaurant serves a breakfast buffet as well as dinner if requested in advance. Only open Monday to Thursday, and closed throughout July. **www.thonhotels.com/maritim**

STAVANGER Victoria Hotel   🅗🅟🅗   ⓚⓚ

Skansegaten 1, 4002 Stavanger **Tel** *51 86 70 00* **Fax** *51 86 70 10* **Rooms** *107*

The 100-year-old Victoria Hotel has preserved its elegant interior and has a reputation for traditional hospitality. It is just a short walk away from the main square, fish market and the old part of Stavanger. Onsite there is the Big Horn Steak House restaurant and the popular Holmen Bar. **www.victoria-hotel.no**

STAVANGER Clarion Hotel Stavenger   🅗🅗   ⓚⓚⓚ

Ny Olavskleiv 8, 4008 Stavanger **Tel** *51 50 25 00* **Fax** *51 50 25 01* **Rooms** *249*

The Clarion is a modern, 14-floor hotel situated in the centre of Stavanger, close to the cathedral. Rooms are decorated in a modern Scandinavian style with light wood furnishings. Visit the top floor wellness centre with jacuzzi and sauna, which looks out over Stavanger. **www.clarionstavanger.no**

STAVANGER First Hotel Alstor   🅣🅗🅟🅗   ⓚⓚⓚ

Tjensvollveien 31, 4021 Stavanger **Tel** *52 04 40 00* **Fax** *52 04 40 01* **Rooms** *81*

Housed in a modern Scandinavian building next to the Mosvannet park and lake, all the Astor's rooms include wireless Internet access, cable television and complimentary toiletries. The hotel's Restaurant Rossmann serves à la carte dishes featuring Scandinavian specialties and has an extensive wine list. **www.firsthotels.com/alstor**

Key to Price Guide *see p226* **Key to Symbols** *see back cover flap*

STAVANGER Radisson Blu Atlantic Hotel

Olav V's Gate 3, 4002 Stavanger **Tel** *51 76 10 00* **Fax** *51 76 10 01* **Rooms** *354*

Overlooking Lake Breiavatnet and next to the historic Old Stavanger area, this modern top-class hotel has 354 air-conditioned rooms spread over 13 floors. The hotel's Restaurant Ajax has a bright dining room serving breakfast, while the Antique Restaurant is a more formal eatery serving à la carte international cuisine. **www.radissonblu.com**

STAVANGER Rica Park Hotel Stavanger

Prestegårdsbakken 1, 4002 Stavanger **Tel** *51 50 05 00* **Fax** *51 50 04 00* **Rooms** *59*

The Rica Park is a first-class international hotel located in the heart of Stavanger within a few minutes' walk of the city centre. It was designed for business-people who need extra space to work, so all the rooms are large. It houses an informal, modern restaurant offering a range of local and international dishes. **www.rica-hotels.com**

ÅLESUND Clarion Collection Hotel Bryggen

Apotekergata 1–3, 6004 Ålesund **Tel** *70 12 64 00* **Fax** *70 12 11 80* **Rooms** *85*

The Bryggen was originally a warehouse, but today the hotel's interior tells the story of the clipfish industry, an important part of Ålesund's history. The ground floor has a well-equipped recreation area offering a great view across Brosundet. **www.choicehotels.no**

ÅLESUND Radisson Blu Hotel Ålesund

Sorenskriver Bullsgate 7, 6002 Ålesund **Tel** *70 16 00 00* **Fax** *70 16 00 01* **Rooms** *131*

By the quay in Ålesund you will find the modern and comfortable Radisson Blu Hotel Ålesund. Rooms have fantastic views of the Valderhaugfjord or the quay. The hotel has its own restaurant, Bulls Brygge, that offers tasty Norwegian and international dishes. **www.aalesund.radissonblu.com**

TRØNDELAG

HITRA Angelamfi Hitra

Grefsnesvågen, 7243 Kvenvær **Tel** *72 46 53 00* **Fax** *72 44 55 96* **Rooms** *29*

Angelamfi Hitra at Grefnesvågen is a luxurious holiday and conference complex located on beautiful Hitra island. It is close to the ocean and some of central Norway's best fishing grounds. Made up of 21 fishing lodges and eight self-catering apartments, it also has a spacious outdoor bathing complex. **www.angelamfi.com**

NAMSOS Børstad Hotel & Gjestgiveri

Carl Gulbransons Gate 19, 7800 Namsos **Tel** *74 21 80 90* **Fax** *74 21 80 91* **Rooms** *19*

Børstad has been a family-run hotel since 1946, and it retains its homely charm. The hotel has 14 rooms and two "exclusive" suites, and is located close to just about everything in Namsos. Breakfast is served each morning by the owners, who take a close personal interest in their guests. **www.borstadhotel.no**

OPPDAL Quality Hotel Oppdal

O.Skasliens vei 8, 7340 Oppdal **Tel** *72 40 07 00* **Fax** *72 40 07 01* **Rooms** *75*

Surrounded by Dovrefjell National Park and the Snohetta and Trollheimen mountains, this hotel in the Quality chain is located in the centre of Oppdal, Norway's largest alpine ski resort that also offers a variety of year-round activities. A good choice for thrill-seekers and outdoor enthusiasts. **www.oppdalbooking.no/ho**

SELBU Selbusjøen Hotell & Gjestegård

Mebonden, 7580 Selbu **Tel** *73 81 11 00* **Fax** *73 81 11 01* **Rooms** *58*

This historic building (once used as a sanatorium) is now a top-class resort beautifully situated on a peninsula of lake Selbusjøen. The lake is in the centre of Selbu, an hour's drive from Tronheim and only ten minutes from the nearest golf course. Plenty of outdoor activites are available in the stunning countryside. **www.selbusjoenhotell.no**

STEINKJER Tingvold Park Hotel

Gamle Kongeveg 47, 7725 Steinkjer **Tel** *74 14 11 00* **Fax** *74 14 11 01* **Rooms** *51*

This old hotel is set in beautiful grounds complete with stone formations from Viking times. The main 19th-century building is built out of timber and the interior and style reflect the era. All the buildings have been renovated and added to in recent years to provide high-quality accommodation. **www.tingvoldhotel.no**

STEINKJER Quality Hotel Grand

Kongensgate 37, 7709 Steinkjer **Tel** *74 16 47 00* **Fax** *74 16 62 87* **Rooms** *113*

A rather square and dull-looking hotel that makes up for its lack of visual appeal with good service and a homely atmosphere. Close to the city centre, it caters to both business guests and holiday travellers. Facilities include a pleasant restaurant, lobby bar and spacious areas used for exhibitions. **www.choice.no**

TRONDHEIM P-Hotel

Nordregate 24, 70101 Trondheim **Tel** *73 80 23 50* **Fax** *73 80 23 51* **Rooms** *49*

P-Hotel is located in beautiful surroundings in Trondheim, Nordregate, and offers high quality facilities at an attractive price. Free Internet access is available in the hotel and staff are available 24 hours a day. Breakfast is served in your room every day, along with a morning newspaper.

TRONDHEIM Thon Hotel Trondheim   ⊗

Kongensgate 15, 7013 Trondheim **Tel** *73 88 47 88* **Fax** *73 51 60 58* **Rooms** *115*

If you're looking for a basic budget hotel in the heart of Trondheim, then this fits the bill. Within easy reach of the main shopping area and the famous Nidaros cathedral, all rooms are medium-sized and decorated to a reasonable standard. The restaurant is only open for breakfast. **www.thonhotels.no/trondheim**

TRONDHEIM Clarion Collection Hotel Bakeriet   🍴 🛁 👤   ⊗⊗

Brattørgata 2, 7010 Trondheim **Tel** *73 99 10 00* **Fax** *73 99 10 01* **Rooms** *109*

Originally an 18th-century bakery located in Trondheim's historical heart, the Bakeriet offers easy access to the city's main attractions – including the Jewish Museum and the Royal Residence – and its numerous shops and restaurants. In the morning you can smell freshly baked bread from the hotel's café. **www.choicehotels.no**

TRONDHEIM Quality Hotel Augustin   🛁 👤   ⊗⊗⊗

Kongensgate 26, 7011 Trondheim **Tel** *73 54 70 00* **Fax** *73 54 70 01* **Rooms** *136*

Situated in downtown Trondheim at Prinsen corner, this reasonably priced hotel is proud of its warm welcome. Located close to the city's shops, restaurants and tourist attractions, it serves a tasty, value-for-money dinner deal on weekday evenings. **www.choicehotes.no/n0017**

TRONDHEIM Radisson Blu Royal Garden Hotel   🍴 🛁 👤 👤   ⊗⊗⊗

Kjøpmannsgate 73, 7410 Trondheim **Tel** *73 80 30 00* **Fax** *73 80 30 50* **Rooms** *298*

In the middle of historic Trondheim and on the banks of the river Nidelven, this is the largest hotel in town and has impressive indoor gardens, well-appointed rooms and a pool. The hotel is close to shopping, entertainment and transport. The hotel's Prins Olav Grill serves international cuisine in a cruise-liner setting. **www.radissonblu.com**

TRONDHEIM Rica Nidelven Hotel   🍴 🛁 👤   ⊗⊗⊗

Havnegate 1–3, 7400 Trondheim **Tel** *73 56 80 00* **Fax** *73 56 80 01* **Rooms** *221*

The Rica Nidelven Hotel is one of Trondheim's most modern and well-equipped business hotels and extends out into the waters of the Nidelven. An onsite art gallery has regular exhibitions. The hotel's Restaurant Nidelven specializes in sumptuous breakfast buffets and a Mediterranean-inspired à la carte menu. **www.rica-hotels.com**

TRONDHEIM Britannia Hotel   🍴 🛁 👤 👤   ⊗⊗⊗⊗

Dronningensgate 5, 7011 Trondheim **Tel** *73 80 08 00* **Fax** *73 80 08 01* **Rooms** *247*

The Britannia, which opened in 1897, was Trondheim's first luxury hotel and has been synonymous with the highest standards of service, comfort and cuisine ever since. Behind the elegant façade and stylish interior is a modern hotel offering the latest facilities, with six restaurants as well as a piano and cocktail bar. **www.britannia.no**

VEGA Vega Havhotell   🛁 👤 👤   ⊗⊗

Viksås, 8980 Vega **Tel** *75 03 64 00* **Fax** *75 03 64 01* **Rooms** *21*

Set in calm and quiet surroundings, Vega Havhotell is situated on the tip of Vega with good views towards the seas and outlying islands. There are 21 renovated rooms and one suite. The hotel's kitchen specializes in Norwegian fare using local ingredients. It also has a well-stocked wine cellar. **www.havhotellene.no**

NORTHERN NORWAY AND SVALBARD

BODØ Clarion Collection Hotel Grand   🛁 👤   ⊗⊗

Storgata 3, 8006 Bodø **Tel** *75 54 61 00* **Fax** *75 54 61 50* **Rooms** *97*

A reasonable bed and breakfast hotel situated in the heart of Bodo that is a good base for sightseeing trips of the ancient city. Within easy reach of the main railway station and other public transport options. If you want to unwind, visit the relaxation area, with its Finnish and Roman saunas. **www.choicehotels.no**

BODØ Radisson Blu Hotel Bodo   🍴 🛁 👤 👤   ⊗⊗⊗

Storgata. 2, 8039 Bodø **Tel** *75 51 90 00* **Fax** *75 51 90 01* **Rooms** *190*

Built in 1971, the Radisson Blu is a modern, 12-storey hotel situated in the harbour area of Bodø. The rooms have interiors themed in Scandinavian, Chinese, Japanese and British-style décor. There's bowling and billiards in the hotel basement, as well as a fitness centre with sauna and solarium. **www.bodo.radissonsblu.com**

HAMMERFEST Hotell Skytterhuset   🛁 👤 👤   ⊗

Skytterveien 24, 9601 Hammerfest **Tel** *78 42 20 10* **Fax** *78 42 20 11* **Rooms** *75*

If you're looking for peace and quiet and an informal, friendly atmosphere, then the Skytterhuset could be the place for you. The hotel is situated next to Hammerfest stadium and is surrounded by a large and mature garden with a pond. Free wireless Internet access and good meeting facilities are provided. **www.skytterhuset.no**

HAMMERFEST Rica Hotel Hammerfest   🛁 👤 👤   ⊗⊗⊗

Sørøygata 15, 9615 Hammerfest **Tel** *78 42 57 00* **Fax** *78 42 57 01* **Rooms** *86*

Centrally located in Hammerfest, this hotel enjoys magnificent views of the sea. Winter activities include snow mobile safaris to the North Cape Plateau. In the summer the cellar dining room opens onto the harbour front where daily specials based on the day's catch from the fjord are served. **www.rica-hotels.com**

Key to Price Guide *see p226* **Key to Symbols** *see back cover flap*

HARSTAD Grand Nordic Hotel

Strandgaten 9, 9485 Harstad **Tel** *77 00 30 00* **Fax** *77 00 30 01* **Rooms** *117*

The Grand Nordic is superbly located in the centre of Harstad only a short distance from the lively port area. Harstad's attractions include the world's northernmost 9-hole golf course and the Northern Norway Festival. The Grand Spiseri and Dansebar serves à la carte dishes, while Sjøbua is a friendly pub with a seafaring theme. **www.nordic.no**

HARSTAD Thon Hotel Harstad

Sjøgaten 11, 9400 Harstad **Tel** *77 00 08 00* **Fax** *77 00 08 08* **Rooms** *141*

With spectacular views over Vågsfjord, this Thon Hotel is uniquely located by the harbour, just a short walk to Harstad Concert Hall and the city centre. A ferry terminal with routes to the many neighbouring islands is nearby. **www.thonhotels.com/harstad**

KIRKENES Rica Arctic Hotel

Kongensgate 1–3, 9915 Kirkenes **Tel** *78 99 59 00* **Fax** *78 99 59 01* **Rooms** *82*

Surrounded by untouched landscape, the Arctic is located in the heart of Kirkenes, at the border of Finland and Russia, and is a melting pot of Norwegian, Finnish, Sami and Russian cultures. The hotel's Arctic Restaurant & Bar offers à la carte food and the disco is a local hot spot. **www.rica.no**

KVALØYA Lauklines Kystferie

Kattfjord, 9100 Kvaløya **Tel** *77 65 60 80* **Fax** *77 65 60 83* **Rooms** *6 cabins*

Lauklines is an old former trading post at Kattfjord on the island of Kvaløya. The six cabins are of a modern, high standard and have been restored according to tradition style. Fishing fanatics are well catered for here, with regular guided boat trips around the many islands. **www.lauklines.no**

LAKSELV Lakselv Hotel

Karasjokveien, 9711 Lakselv **Tel** *78 46 54 00* **Fax** *78 46 54 01* **Rooms** *44*

The Lakselv sits high above Porsangerfjord with horizon views of the wonderful surrounding countryside. The hotel's restaurant "Gjesten" and barbeque cabin "Naustet" serve meals based on local ingredients. A relaxation area has two saunas and a hot tub built into a traditional fishing boat. Closed at Christmas and Easter. **www.lakselvhotell.no**

LONGYEARBYEN Radisson Blu Polar Hotel Spitsbergen

Road 500, 9171 Longyearbyen **Tel** *79 02 34 50* **Fax** *79 02 34 51* **Rooms** *95*

The world's northernmost hotel is surrounded by nature. Located in one of the Europe's last true Arctic wilderness areas, the hotel has a brasserie and conference facilities. A wide range of summer and winter activities are available, including glacier walks and dogsled trips. **www.longyearbyen.radissonblu.com**

NARVIK Nordstjernen Hotell

Kungsgate 26, 8514 Narvik **Tel** *76 94 41 20* **Fax** *76 94 75 06* **Rooms** *25*

The Nordstjernen is a small, pleasant hotel on Narvik's main street. It was opened in 1970 and is still run by the same proprietor. Rooms are clean and simply decorated. It is located near the alpine skiing centre at Fagernesfjellet – voted one of the ten best skiing resorts in the world, and the best in Scandinavia. **www.nordstjernen.no**

NARVIK Quality Hotel Grand Royal

Kungsgate 64, 8514 Narvik **Tel** *76 97 70 00* **Fax** *76 97 70 07* **Rooms** *107*

The Quality Hotel Grand Royal is a unique conference hotel located in the centre of Narvik and a short distance from Mount Narvik, which offers spectacular skiing. Children 12 and under stay free if sharing a room with parents or grandparents and no extra bedding is required. All rooms are ensuite and have been refurbished. **www.choicehotels.no**

TROMSØ Grand Nordic Hotel

Storgaten 44, 9008 Tromsø **Tel** *77 75 37 77* **Fax** *77 75 37 78* **Rooms** *111*

The Grand Nordic Hotel is a comfortable, pleasant hotel located in the middle of the Storgata in Tromsø. This is where you will find the town's best shopping outlets, restaurants and cafés. Facilities include a restaurant, bar, conference facilities, solarium and fitness room. The airport bus stops right outside the hotel. **www.nordic.no**

TROMSØ Scandic Tromsø

Heiloveien 23, 9269 Tromsø **Tel** *77 75 50 00* **Fax** *77 75 50 11* **Rooms** *146*

Promoting itself as "the place for an Arctic adventure", the Scandic Tromsø is set amid stunning fjords and mountains. The hotel boasts a Nordic restaurant, bar-nightclub, a kids' playroom and a sauna. Just three minutes' drive from the airport, it offers business facilities and wireless Internet access. **www.scandic-hotels.com/tromso**

TROMSØ Rica Ishavshotel

Fr. Langesgate 2, 9008 Tromsø **Tel** *77 66 64 00* **Fax** *77 66 64 44* **Rooms** *180*

Known as the Paris of the North, Tromsø is an attractive city, and this hotel claims the title of the most distinctive-looking building in the region, with a metallic, "space-age" exterior. Perfectly located on the harbour, with panoramic water views, its top-floor Skipsbroen Bar is well worth a visit. **www.rica.no**

VADSØ Rica Hotel Vadsø

Oscarsgate 4, 9800 Vadsø **Tel** *78 95 52 50* **Fax** *78 95 10 02* **Rooms** *68*

A modern hotel centrally located in Vadsø, the capital of Finnmark, the Rica has clean rooms and friendly service. In recent years, king crabs have been fished in local waters and can be found headlining the restaurant menu. Try skiing or hiking in the spectacular surrounding countryside. **www.rica-hotels.com**

WHERE TO EAT

Norway's restaurant scene has become increasingly diverse over the last 15 years. There is something on offer for even the most discerning of palates, including exotic international cuisines. Norwegian specialities such as lamb and cabbage stew, marinated salmon *(gravlaks)*, dumplings *(kumle)* or reindeer medallions are not to be missed. The best selection is to be found in the towns. Look out for seafood dishes. There are daily deliveries of fresh

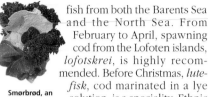

Smørbrød, an open sandwich

fish from both the Barents Sea and the North Sea. From February to April, spawning cod from the Lofoten islands, *lofotskrei*, is highly recommended. Before Christmas, *lutefisk*, cod marinated in a lye solution, is a speciality. Ethnic cafés and restaurants offer dishes from around the world and the food in less pretentious places is often good and not expensive. The price of alcohol, even beer, is high.

EATING OUT

The cities offer the greatest choice of places to eat. In Oslo, in particular, an entire spectrum of food is on offer, from truly Norwegian to the more exotic, with a wide variation in standards and prices. There are internationally renowned restaurants presided over by gold medal-winning chefs. Here, the menus will normally feature international cuisine, but will also offer Norwegian specialities with an emphasis on seafood. The best restaurants also have a good selection of game dishes, including reindeer, elk and wild fowl from the Norwegian forests and mountains.

In the mountain and tourist hotels it is standard practice to have dinner in the hotel restaurant, as this is often the only place to eat in the vicinity. The food is normally of a high standard. The same is true of the mountain huts.

Most towns have a selection of ethnic restaurants. Oslo has an especially wide choice of cuisines and the quality is generally of a consistently good standard.

In many of the towns and built-up areas you will also find traditional pubs and bars serving mainly beverages.

Restaurant sign, Bergen

A GREAT BUFFET LUNCH

The Norwegian buffet lunch constitutes a varied and very substantial meal. The idea is to help yourself from a buffet table groaning with meat and fish dishes. There is often a separate selection of hot dishes. Norway is the world's largest producer of salmon, and salmon dishes are often well represented. In mountain hotels and tourist lodges the lunch table is one of the highlights of the stay, offering an extravagant choice of delicacies. It is advisable to follow certain unwritten rules about the order in which to eat the food: start with fish and salads, go on to meat and hot dishes and finish with cheese and/or dessert. Feel free to ask the waiters for advice. Drinks are ordered separately at the table.

LOCAL EATING HABITS

Norwegian eating habits differ somewhat from those on the Continent, particularly with regard to lunch and dinner. Traditionally, Norwegians only very rarely eat a hot lunch at home. However, in the workplace, canteens are becoming increasingly popular and they serve hot food. If there is no canteen, people often take a packed lunch of wholemeal bread open sandwiches to work. Cafés and restaurants serve hot food at lunchtime.

Lunch is normally served between 11am and 2pm, while dinner is usually eaten around 5pm in the home. When eating out, dinner is usually delayed until 7–8pm. In the evening restaurants open around 5–6pm. It is

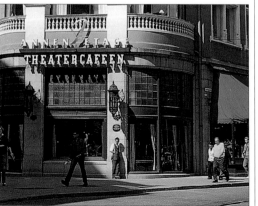

Theatercaféen, Oslo, traditionally an artists' haunt *(see p243)*

The fish market in Bergen, a popular place to buy snacks

rarely necessary to reserve a table for lunch, but a reservation is recommended for dinner, particularly on Wednesday, Friday and Saturday in popular places.

FAST FOOD

The most common fast food is a hot dog (*pølse*) with a roll or a potato pancake (*lompe*). This traditional dish is often served from kiosks, food wagons or serving hatches. It is topped with raw onion and various dressings. Some markets, such as the one in Bergen, have stalls selling ready-to-eat delicacies. Most urban areas have the usual selection of hamburger chains and kebab cafés.

Along the main roads in the more populated areas there are a large number of cafeteria-style places. The food is usually fairly simple and ready-to-eat, and is served so quickly that it almost counts as fast food.

PAYING AND TIPPING

Many eating places offer lunch at reasonable, set prices. In the towns it is possible to have a good meal for around 60–70 Nkr. Drinks add considerably to the price; even mineral water can cost as much as 20–30 Nkr. In a good restaurant, a three-course dinner with wine could cost 600–700 Nkr per person. A number of restaurants have regular, special offers, even for dinner. These are usually advertised on boards or posters outside. In such cases,

a good main course can be had for less than 100 Nkr. Most restaurants have menus displayed outside, but this is not mandatory.

Service charge is always included in the bill, but tipping the waiter is still the norm, especially if the service has been good – around 10 per cent is a guideline. Complain if the food does not live up to expectations. The restaurateurs themselves encourage guests to do so.

CHILDREN

Children are normally welcome in all cafés and restaurants. Most places have separate children's menus and special chairs for youngsters. If there is no special menu, one can usually be arranged by talking to the waiter. Children's menus will often consist of meatballs, sausages and chips or spaghetti.

It should be noted that it is not the norm to take children to dinner in restaurants. If you do, they will rarely be refused entry, but children are expected to be kept under control and should not leave the table and run around.

WHAT TO WEAR

There is no need to pack a lot of smart clothes just to wear in restaurants. Norwegians have a relatively informal dress code, and only a few restaurants require a tie to be worn. The rule is much the same in Norway as in other countries – the more expensive a restaurant the better one should dress.

ALCOHOL

Norway has a restrictive policy on alcohol and the duty levied is among the highest in Europe.

The minimum age for being served wine and beer is 18, and 21 for spirits. Eating places need a licence to serve alcohol, and some establishments often have a licence for beer and wine but not for spirits. Most big restaurants have full licences, and many of them offer a good selection of wine in all price ranges. In bars, people usually pay for their own drinks; buying a round is not the custom.

All wines and spirits are sold in special state monopoly outlets known as *Vinmonopolet*, which are often closed on and around public holidays and on Sundays, too. The state monopoly shops are only found in the larger towns and urban areas. In some smaller municipalities all serving of alcohol used to be prohibited.

SMOKING

Norway has very strict smoking laws, and new restrictions have been added in the last few years. Smoking is not permitted indoors in public places, unless there is a separate smoking room. This rule is rarely broken. The restriction also operates on train platforms, arrival and departure halls in airports, private offices and factory buildings. Smoking is not permitted in any restaurants, pubs or cafés, unless there is a separate, screened-off section for smokers.

Engebret Café, dating from 1857, Oslo's oldest restaurant (*see p243*)

The Flavours of Norway

Dominated by mountains, wilderness and the open sea, Norway has a vibrant cuisine rich in fresh seafood and wild game, offering scrumptious plates of smoked, pickled or fried fish, along with reindeer, elk, seal and whale meat. You'll also find many dishes based on potatoes – baked, boiled or mashed – while popular vegetables include cabbage, carrots, swede (*rutabaga*) and broccoli. For dessert, try the fruits and berries from the Hardanger region, most notably *multer* (a yellow berry similar to a cloudberry), *blåbær* (blueberries or blackberries), gooseberries, red- and blackcurrants.

Geitost and Jarlsberg cheeses

Fish drying in the pure air of the Lofoten Islands

SMØRBRØD

Once served as an appetizer, the classic Scandinavian open sandwich (*smørbrød*) is now a meal in itself, often served buffet-style. Prepared fish, meats and vegetables are neatly arranged on slices of freshly-baked grainy bread or flatbread and elegantly garnished. The most common ingredient, herring, comes in several dozen varieties, such as pickled, curried, fried and prepared in a spicy mustard or horseradish sauce. Salmon also features prominently – smoked, roasted, poached or cured in a salt, sugar and dill mixture. Accompanying the *smørbrød* may be salads, eggs, breads, terrines, marinated mushrooms, spare ribs and even oddities such as jellied eel and delicacies including smoked reindeer and caviar.

FISH & SEAFOOD

With 24,000km (15,000 miles) of coastline, 150,000 lakes and 50,000 islands, it is no surprise that fish and seafood predominate in Norwegian kitchens. Most popular are herring and salmon, both of which come grilled, cured or smoked (*røkelaks*), while herring, once a peasant staple but now quite pricey, is usually served pickled

Ham, onion and tomato

Smoked herring with raw egg yolk

Prawns, caviar and lemon

Plaice with asparagus and caviar

Rare roast beef with onion and horseradish

Cured herring

Aquavit

Selection of typical Norwegian *smørbrød*

NORWEGIAN DISHES AND SPECIALITIES

Norway's culinary traditions developed as a result of the country's isolated rural economy and its climate. Its people had to develop methods by which they could preserve the harvest through the long winter months. One result was a vast and inventive range of dried, smoked, salted and pickled meats (*spekemat*) and fish. Some of the country's seminal dishes are based on this produce, including *fenalår* (cured leg of mutton) and *pinnekjøtt* (steamed salted lamb ribs served with mashed swede or turnip). Other traditional favourites include *morr*, a smoked and cured sausage, and the delicate *smalahove*, smoked lamb's head, a Vestlandet speciality. Game dishes include breast of pheasant with mushroom sauce, and marinade of rabbit.

Dill fronds

Gravlax, *salmon preserved in a dill, sugar and salt mix, is served with a piquant dill and mustard sauce.*

Fishing boats moored in snowy Svolvaer

with mustard or onions. *Lutefisk* is a chewy fish marinated in lye. Other catch includes shrimp, haddock, mackerel, Arctic char and cod, which is often split and dried *(klippfisk)*. Fish soup is a very popular appetizer.

Norway is one of only two countries with a commercial whaling industry, resumed after decades of moratorium and boycott. With a small annual quota, whale *(hval)* meat is seen as a delicacy here and you'll hear little controversy over the ethics of eating it. Seal is also eaten, but normally only in Tromsø.

GAME

Elk, reindeer and woodland fowl have been staples of the Norwegian diet for centuries. Reindeer, still herded by Sámi semi-pastoralists, is often served thinly sliced in a thick cream sauce, although fillet of reindeer with lingonberries is also very popular. Game is often accompanied by chunky root vegetables and wild mushrooms, making hearty dishes fit for a cold climate.

Punnets of Norwegian gooseberries and redcurrants

CHEESES

Norway's most famous cheese export is Jarlsberg, a mild white cheese produced in rural dairies. However, many Norwegians prefer *geitost* (goat cheese), which is technically not cheese but caramelized goat's and cow's lactose. The most popular type is the sweet, brown *gudbrands dalsost*. A more acquired taste is *gammelost* ("old cheese"), an over-matured, highly pungent brown cheese – mere mention of it will make some Nordmen wince. Norwegian cheese is best served on Ryvita crisp-bread, another Scandinavian staple you'll find everywhere.

WHAT TO DRINK

Norway's most famous drink is Linie Akevitt (Aquavit), a potent brew of caraway and potatoes spiced with anise, fennel and coriander. Along with pilsner or red beer, Aquavit is the traditional accompaniment to many Norwegian dishes including mutton, cabbage, *smørbrød* and *lutefisk*. The Linie brand is aged in large oak sherry barrels, then shipped off in the hull of a Norwegian tanker on a round-the-world voyage to traverse the equator (the "linie"); the rocking effect produced by the waves is said to give it a finer taste. At Christmas, Norwegians enjoy *gløgg*, warmed red wine flavoured with cinnamon, raisins, ginger and cloves.

Lapskaus *is a traditional stew of various meats and vegetables, flavoured with bay and nutmeg.*

Reindyrstek, *roast reindeer fillet, is served with boiled potatoes, rich gravy and a lingonberry sauce.*

Tilslørte Bondepike *("veiled farm girl") is layers of apple purée with sweet cinnamon crumbs and whipped cream.*

Choosing a Restaurant

The restaurants in this guide have been selected across a wide range of price categories for their good value, exceptional food or interesting location. The entries are listed area by area and are alphabetical within each price category. Oslo map references can be found on the Street Finder, pp104–109.

PRICE CATEGORIES (IN NORWEGIAN KRONE):
Price categories are for a three-course meal for one person, half a bottle of house wine, and extras such as service charge and cover charge.

Ⓚ Under 400 NKr
ⓀⓀ 400–500 NKr
ⓀⓀⓀ 500–700 NKr
ⓀⓀⓀⓀ Over 700 NKr

OSLO

CENTRAL OSLO WEST Hambro's Café and Confectioner's   Ⓥ   Ⓚ
Kristian IVs Gate 7, 0164 Oslo **Tel** *22 82 60 26*   **Map** *3 D3*

At Hotel Bristol, one block from the Parliament, this sophisticated café has a classical, Italian design with light flowing in through large windows. The appealing interior creates a stunning contrast to the confectioner's colourful pastries. Snacks, sandwiches, filled ciabattas and delicious cakes are available, and the café is fully licensed.

CENTRAL OSLO WEST Vegeta Verthus   Ⓥ   Ⓚ
Munkedamsveien 3b, 0161 Oslo **Tel** *21 66 28 65*   **Map** *2 B3*

This simply-designed vegetarian restaurant is located in a side street near the Nationaltheatret. Whether you are vegetarian or not, the Vegeta Vertshus serves delicious food that could change the way you think about food forever. The enormous buffet is highly recommended, offering a large selection of salads, soups and desserts.

CENTRAL OSLO WEST Coco Vika   Ⓥ   ⓀⓀ
Dronning Mauds Gate 1–3, 0250 Oslo **Tel** *22 83 18 18*   **Map** *2 C3*

An excellent and very reasonably priced restaurant serving mainly Asian-inspired cuisine. Centrally located near Aker Brygge, it is a popular venue with locals, who often come here for lunch and to sit and chat with friends. Many types of dishes are available, from sandwiches and salads to sushi and tapas. A reasonable wine list is also offered.

CENTRAL OSLO WEST Dinner Bar & Restaurant   🖬 Ⓥ   ⓀⓀ
Stortingsgata 22, 0161 Oslo **Tel** *23 10 04 66*   **Map** *3 D3*

Despite its simple name, this exclusive restaurant has served gourmet Chinese Szechuan food in the heart of Oslo for over a decade and is regarded as one of the best Oriental kitchens in the capital. Peking duck is a speciality here, or try the Szechuan chilli pepper kam-kon-pot with pan-fried strips of beef and vegetables in a vinegar sauce.

CENTRAL OSLO WEST Egon Karl Johan   🖬🖬 Ⓥ   ⓀⓀ
Karl Johans Gate 37, 0162 Oslo **Tel** *22 41 77 90*   **Map** *3 D3*

Located in Karl Johans Gate in the Paleet shopping complex, Egon is a relaxed and family-friendly chain of restaurants popular in Norway. An international menu claims to have something for everyone, including salads, steaks, fish, Tex-Mex and pizzas. The menu has been translated into the major languages.

CENTRAL OSLO WEST D/S Louise Restaurant & Bar   🖬🖬Ⓥ   ⓀⓀⓀ
Stranden 3, 0250 Oslo **Tel** *22 83 00 60*   **Map** *2 C4*

Large and welcoming restaurant with an international à la carte menu that combines Norwegian and international cuisine guided by current culinary trends. Located on a number of floors in the centre of Aker Brygge, it has great views of the harbour and is decorated with more than 1,000 items of nautical bric-a-brac. Outside seating in the summer.

CENTRAL OSLO WEST Lofoten Fiskerestaurant   🖬 🖬 Ⓥ   ⓀⓀⓀ
Stranden 75, 0250 Oslo **Tel** *22 83 08 08*   **Map** *2 C4*

This fish and seafood restaurant located next to Oslo's quay is elegantly decorated in a maritime theme and offers some of the best views of the Oslo fjord. It serves high-quality dishes with a seasonal twist such as scallop, king crab and calamari, accompanied by a herb salad, smoked bell-pepper aioli and croutons.

CENTRAL OSLO WEST Lorry Restaurant   🖬🖬🖬   ⓀⓀⓀ
Parkveien 12, 0350 Oslo **Tel** *22 69 69 04*   **Map** *2 B3*

Serving artists, writers and city folk since 1887, the Lorry is an informal, timeless restaurant at the northern corner of Slottsparken with a good reputation for its enormous selection of beers – which at the last count was nearing 130 different brands. A wide variety of food is available, including meat, fish, vegetarian and children's dishes.

CENTRAL OSLO WEST ORO Restaurant og Bar   🖬🖬Ⓥ   ⓀⓀⓀ
Tordenskiolds Gate 6 A, 0160 Oslo **Tel** *23 01 02 40*   **Map** *3 D3*

ORO Restaurant and Bar is a modern eaterie and bar located in the centre of Oslo that combines classic gourmet cuisine with new influences to create exciting culinary experiences. Both their five- or seven-course menus are mouthwatering, and they are happy to recommend a bottle from their exclusive wine list to accompany dishes.

Key to Symbols *see back cover flap*

CENTRAL OSLO WEST Theatercafeen

Stortingsgata 24–26, 0161 Oslo **Tel** *22 82 40 50*

Map *3 D3*

Theatercafeen has a lively atmosphere and attracts customers from all walks of life, ranging from the rich and famous to tourists. On *The New York Times*' Top Ten list of the world's most famous cafés, there's live piano and violin music in the evenings and during the day on Saturdays. The menu is international and reservations are recommended.

CENTRAL OSLO WEST Restaurant Oscarsgate

Pilestredet 63, 0350 Oslo **Tel** *22 46 59 06*

Map *2 C1*

The wine list here is a wine-lover's dream, with many vintage bottles from the Burgundy and Bordeaux regions. There are also more reasonably priced options from other countries. The highly qualified chefs (many of whom have worked in the some of the most respected restaurants in Europe) have created an exquisite eight-course dinner menu.

CENTRAL OSLO EAST Kaffistova

Rosenkrantz' Gate 8, 0159 Oslo **Tel** *23 21 42 10*

Map *3 D3*

Part of the Hotell Bondeheimen and located a stone's throw from Karl Johans Gate, the Kaffistova offers a comprehensive choice of traditional Norwegian dishes. A popular place for Norwegian specialities such as *raspeballer* (potato dumplings), *boknafisk* (dried and salted cod) and *rømmegrøt* (sour cream porridge).

CENTRAL OSLO EAST A Touch of France

Øvre Slottsgate 16, 0157 Oslo **Tel** *23 10 01 65*

Map *3 D3*

As the name suggests, A Touch of France offers a selection of classic French food as well as other international dishes. The *bouillabaisse* and *Magret de Canard avec Figues Rôties* are highly recommended. Unpretentious and charming, it's wise to book tables in advance at this popular brasserie.

CENTRAL OSLO EAST Den Røde Mølle

Brugata 9, 0186 Oslo **Tel** *22 17 10 39*

Map *3 F3*

This restaurant was originally best-known for its pizzas – which it still specializes in today – but it has branched out and now offers a simple and honest à la carte menu that includes pasta, fish and meat dishes. There's a special children's menu for the under-12s and a spacious outside seating area.

CENTRAL OSLO EAST Kafe Celsius

Rådhusgata 19, 0158 Oslo **Tel** *22 42 45 39*

Map *3 D4*

Nestled in a courtyard dating back to 1626, Kafe Celsius is situated in Oslo's oldest building near to Christiania Torg. It comprises a number of galleries and a charming eating area in the courtyard. Pleasant and low-key, it offers plenty of Norwegian specialities on an informal à la carte menu.

CENTRAL OSLO EAST Mirawa Barbeque

Øvre Slottsgate 27, 0157 Oslo **Tel** *22 42 95 39*

Map *3 D3*

In this unique restaurant, you are seated inside a traditional Mongolian tent that's decorated with leathers and furs and traditional Mongolian tools. An extremely popular establishment, it is known for its generous portions and hospitable atmosphere. Chinese dishes are also available.

CENTRAL OSLO EAST Det Gamle Raadhus Restaurant

Nedre Slottsgate 1, 0157 Oslo **Tel** *22 42 01 07*

Map *3 E3*

Steeped in tradition, this popular restaurant close to Akershus Festning is housed in one of Oslo's oldest buildings (which was the first City Hall) dating from 1641. Today it is well known for its fish and game dishes. Their *lutefisk* platter, served just before Christmas, is one of the house specialities. There's outdoor service in the summer.

CENTRAL OSLO EAST Engebret Cafe

Bankplassen 1, 0151 Oslo **Tel** *22 82 25 25*

Map *3 D4*

Little seems to have changed inside this historic building that lies close to Norges Bank in Bankplassen. The menu emphasizes seafood entrées, and during the autumn there's usually a good selection of game dishes available. The mid-morning sandwich buffet is renown, and during the summer guests can eat in a beautiful outdoor dining area.

CENTRAL OSLO EAST Restaurant Mona Lisa

Grensen 10 (Entrance Øvre Slottsgate), 0159 Oslo **Tel** *22 42 89 14*

Map *3 E3*

Although Italian cuisine is the staple fare at this traditional first-floor restaurant located close to Egertorget, there are also Norwegian and French-inspired alternatives. The inviting interior is perfect for intimate dinners. The menu is a little limited in choice but is high in quality.

CENTRAL OSLO EAST Solsiden Restaurant

Søndre Akershus Kai 34, 0150 Oslo **Tel** *22 33 36 30*

Map *3 D5*

An old soap warehouse on the quayside below Akerhus Castle has been converted into this outstanding fish restaurant that fairly claims to serve some of the best seafood dishes in Oslo. There's a live lobster tank and oysters, salmon and other Norwegian seafood delicacies, all prepared with organic ingredients by master chefs.

CENTRAL OSLO EAST Stortorvets Gjestgiveri

Grensen 1, 0159 Oslo **Tel** *23 35 63 60*

Map *3 E3*

The exterior of this 300-year-old building has remained almost unchanged over the centuries, and the restaurant area, with its many charming rooms, has retained its historical feel. The food is traditionally Norwegian, and includes delights such as filet of zander served with fresh summer vegetables and yoghurt sauce and roasted reindeer.

CENTRAL OSLO EAST Grand Cafe

Karl Johans Gate 31, 0159 Oslo **Tel** *23 21 20 00*   **Map** *3 D3*

This famous café is where Henrik Ibsen had his daily meal. Located on the ground floor at the Grand Hotel, it is centrally positioned on Oslo's main street, Karl Johan. The bar-lounge offers an ideal place for pre-theatre drinks. Great outdoor area in summer.

CENTRAL OSLO EAST Statholdergaarden

Rådhusgaten 11, 0151 Oslo **Tel** *22 41 88 00*   **Map** *3 D4*

Statholdergaarden is a Norwegian gourmet restaurant where culinary world champion Bent Stiansen is in charge of the kitchen. He creates a new six-course menu every day based on the freshest ingredients inspired by European food traditions. Statholderens Krostue is the more informal restaurant in the cellar serving open sandwiches at lunchtime.

FURTHER AFIELD Kafe Asylet

Grønland 28, 0188 Oslo **Tel** *22 17 09 39*   **Map** *3 F3*

Low ceilings, uneven floors and crooked windows characterize this pleasant old timber building in the Grønland area, just northeast of Oslo central station (the entrance is through the backyard where you can eat out in the summer). The cooking is simple, traditional and tasty, and a good sign is that the locals like to eat here.

FURTHER AFIELD Najaden

Bygdøynesveien 37, 0286 Oslo **Tel** *22 43 81 80*   **Map** *1 B4*

Located in the Sjøfartsmuseum (the Maritime Museum), this is the place to enjoy a meal on Bygdøy. In the summer you can eat outside and take in the panoramic views over the fjord and city. The atmosphere is nautical and the Scandinavian menu offers both fish and meat dishes. A trip to the museum is a must.

FURTHER AFIELD Restaurant Egon Frogner

Bygdøy Allé 53, 0265 Oslo **Tel** *23 08 58 10*   **Map** *1 B1*

Another Egon restaurant located near central Oslo that offers breakfast and lunches, starters, steaks, fish dishes, pizza, wok dishes, moussaka, fajitas, hamburgers, salads and desserts. They also provide a good children's menu and a standard selection of wines, beers and spirits. The steak sandwich with Béarnaise sauce is recommended.

FURTHER AFIELD Sult

Thorvald Meyers Gate 26, 0555 Oslo **Tel** *22 87 04 67*   **Map** *3 F1*

Centrally located in fashionable Grünerløkka, the menu at Sult (the Norwegian word for hunger) is prepared by creative chefs using only the freshest ingredients. The restaurant defines its style of cooking fish and seafood as "neo-Norwegian". On summer days outdoor service starts at 2pm. Adjacent to the restaurant is the bar Tørst (thirst).

FURTHER AFIELD Big Horn Steak House Majorstua

Bogstadveien 64, 0366 Oslo **Tel** *22 69 03 00*   **Map** *2 C1*

Based on the American Wild West, this cellar restaurant specializes in steaks and meat dishes. It is located in lively Majorstua and decorated with hundreds of Americana objects to give it a "Wild West" feel. A VIP room is available for parties of up to 12 people. With large, US-style portions, you won't leave this place hungry.

FURTHER AFIELD Feinschmecker Spisested

Balchensgate 5, 0265 Oslo **Tel** *22 12 93 80*

This renowned restaurant is one of the best in Oslo, and has one star in the prestigious Michelin Guide. The food is fantastic and there is an impressive wine list. In addition to the à la carte menu (which features a three-course vegetarian menu), the restaurant offers a five-course menu every day based on the season's specialities.

FURTHER AFIELD Frognerseteren

Holmenkollveien 200, 0791 Oslo **Tel** *22 92 40 40*

Frognerseteren offers something for everyone with a café and the Finstua restaurant set in historical surroundings high up in the Holmenkollen hills. Eat here and you really are on top of Oslo, with magnificent views of the city and the Oslo fjord. The kitchen presents traditional Norwegian cooking using local ingredients in a seasonal menu.

FURTHER AFIELD Hos Thea

Gabels Gate 11, 0272 Oslo **Tel** *22 44 68 74*   **Map** *2 A3*

This stylish eatery with a homely atmosphere is located near Drammensveien and attracts a loyal clientele active in the media and arts. The century-old building, once a private home, is south of Oslo's commercial centre. Dishes include veal tenderloin with butter-poached spring cabbage and oven-baked Chilean sea bass.

FURTHER AFIELD Klosteret Restaurant

Fredensborgveien 13, 0177 Oslo **Tel** *23 35 49 00*   **Map** *3 E2*

Old brick arches, wrought iron, candles and Gregorian music create a romantic atmosphere in this cellar restaurant. The Klosteret (Convent) has its own *chambre separée* for special occasions and the wine list is highly regarded as one of the best around Oslo. The menu features continental and French fare.

FURTHER AFIELD Lanternen Restaurant

Huk Aveny 2, 0287 Oslo **Tel** *22 43 78 38*   **Map** *1 A4*

This jewel of a restaurant located in the inner Oslofjord on the Bygdøy peninsula is a scenic ten-minute boat ride from the City Hall or a five-minute walk from the Viking Ships and the Norwegian Folk Museum. It has a huge outdoor seating area, where summer diners are served grilled specialities such as Norwegian salmon hot off the broiler.

Key to Price Guide *see p242* **Key to Symbols** *see back cover flap*

FURTHER AFIELD Markveien Mat & Vinhus

Torvbakkgate 12, 0550 Oslo Tel 22 37 22 97

An attractive venue with art covering the yellow walls, this restaurant serves simple but stylish and delectable food with the emphasis on high-quality, locally sourced ingredients. The staff are always happy to translate the detailed menu, which includes a five-course meal every day. Excellent wine list and top-class service from the staff.

FURTHER AFIELD Bagatelle Restaurant

Bygdøy Allé 3, 0257 Oslo Tel 22 12 14 40   **Map** *1 B1*

Housed behind a discreet burgundy red façade on one of the most beautiful streets in Oslo is one of the most celebrated restaurants in Norway. A luxurious menu is masterfully complimented by an equally formidable wine list. French cuisine dominates but the main ingredients almost always come from the Norwegian countryside.

FURTHER AFIELD De Fem Stuer

Holmenkollen Park Hotel Rica, 0787 Oslo Tel 22 92 20 00

The dining rooms in this restaurant of the Holmenkollen Park Hotel Rica impart a warm, romantic country-style atmosphere with good views over large expanses of the city. Featuring international cuisine with a Norwegian slant, dishes are based on fresh, seasonal, local produce. The chefs often participate in international competitions.

FURTHER AFIELD Holmenkollen Restaurant

Holmenkollveien 119, 0787 Oslo Tel 22 13 92 00

This historic restaurant overlooking the city is partially built from logs and local stone and is perched near the summit of a hill outside Oslo. Nearby is the city's world-renowned ski jump, adding to the restaurant's mountain-chalet appeal. A Norwegian-inspired menu is offered, but be prepared for coach-loads of tourists arriving to take in the views.

FURTHER AFIELD Restaurant Le Canard

President Harbitz' Gate 4, 0259 Oslo Tel 22 54 34 00   **Map** *2 B2*

Located in the suburb of Frogner, west of the centre of Oslo, this intriguing mansion has welcomed everyone from the Queen of Norway to film stars all wanting to try the first-class food. The menu proudly details the origins of the produce used and includes a delicious cheese and dessert section, as well as a special gourmet section.

AROUND OSLOFJORDEN

ENGALSVIK Engelsviken Brygge Fiskerestaurant

Engelsvikenveien 6, 1628 Engalsvik Tel 69 35 18 40

This ideally located fish restaurant has great views of the fjord and the boats moored close to the outside seating area. There's a well-frequented pub with a lively after-work scene. Families are made to feel welcome with a special children's menu. Try the boiled Atlantic halibut served with fresh asparagus, hollandaise sauce and boiled potatoes.

FREDRIKSTAD Major-Stuen

Voldportgaten 73, 1632 Fredrikstad Tel 69 32 15 55

Folksy restaurant located in the old town of Gamle Fredrikstad with a wide choice of substantial and light dishes. The three-course lunchtime menu represents great value for money at just 70 NOK with coffee. There's a children's menu available and a popular pizza menu too. The pub serves all the usual beers, wines and spirits.

FREDRIKSTAD Balaklava Gjestgiveri

Kirkegaten 31, 1631 Fredrikstad Tel 69 32 30 40

The focus at this traditional, atmospheric restaurant is on gourmet cuisine with an international slant, based on fresh ingredients from the region. The inn comprises five well-preserved buildings situated in a fortress and also has coffee rooms and a hotel. It is well worth checking out the wine cellar. Outside seating during the summer.

FREDRIKSTAD Restaurant Fredrik

Nygaardsgaten 44–46, 1607 Fredrikstad Tel 69 38 56 00

Fredrik, the à la carte restaurant in the "Restauranthuset" building, is the dining room of Hotel City. The chef, Josef Siebenherz, and his team have created a seasonal menu based on traditional Norwegian cuisine. The fine-dining atmosphere attracts the business crowds and there is a bar to sit at to enjoy a pre-dinner drink.

FREDRIKSTAD Tobias

Nygaardsgate 44-46, 1607 Fredrikstad Tel 69 38 56 00

With its distinctive brick-wall environment, Tobias offers everything from delicious pizzas and light dishes to their house speciality called Kjeller Biff, which is a steak served on a hot rock that you cook yourself. If you're feeling thirsty, then try the "metre of beer" – five glasses on a metre-long plank. There is also a play corner for children.

HALDEN Bakgården Restaurant

Storgaten 22 B, 1776 Halden Tel 69 18 82 90

This is a well-priced, family-friendly restaurant that offers a varied children's menu as well as dishes à la carte. Steak is a firm favourite among the regulars but the fresh fish dishes, such as halibut with sour crème sauce and vegetables, are renowned and definitely worth a try.

HALDEN Hannestadgården   🏃 🛗 🍸 V   ⓚⓚ
Tollbugata 5, 1767 Halden **Tel** *69 19 77 81*

Located in the sleepy town of Halden, Hannestadgården is a nightclub, restaurant, dance club, pub and piano bar all rolled into one. If something happens in Halden, it often happens here. The somewhat limited restaurant menu, with three starters, five mains and two deserts, isn't revolutionary, but offers old favourites like hamburgers and surf 'n' turf.

HØVIKODDEN Bolgen & Moi   🏃 🛗 🍸 V   ⓚⓚⓚ
Sonja Heniesvei 31, 1363 Høvikodden **Tel** *67 52 10 20*

The interior of this modern brasserie has clean lines and, in keeping with the fact that the restaurant is located in the Henie-Onstad Kunstsenter, it also has an art exhibition that changes regularly. At lunch they offer snacks and a light three-course menu, while three- and five-course menus are available in the evening.

LARVIK Becks Brasserie & Bar   🏃 🛗 🍸 V   ⓚⓚⓚ
Fritzøe Brygge 1, 3264 Larvik **Tel** *33 12 14 71*

This restaurant's distinctive look was created by English restaurant architect Simon Barley and is ultra-stylish and trendy. The large glass wine-chiller cabinets hint at the good selection of bottles to accompany your meal. The menu has an international slant, with at least six fish and ten meat dishes available at all times. There's also a cool bar to sit at.

LARVIK Brasserie Vadskjæret   🏃 🛗 🍸   ⓚⓚⓚ
Havnegate 12, 3263 Larvik **Tel** *33 14 10 90*

On the north side of the harbour with fantastic views over the fjord, this brasserie's dishes focus on meat and fish, and often you'll find whale steak or fillet on the menu – a reminder of the area's whaling industry. If the weather's good you should sit outside and soak up the sun and views. They also provide a spot to park your boat!

LARVIK Trudvang Gjestegaard   🛗 🍸 V   ⓚⓚⓚ
Gårdsbakken 43, 3256 Larvik **Tel** *33 16 52 70*

This grand building dating back to 1881 was once an art gallery and musical hall. Today it is a welcoming hotel with a real sense of history and charm. The elegantly decorated restaurant serves traditional Norwegian food, including two varied cold buffets, as well as dinner dishes such as medallions of reindeer with a rich game sauce (in season).

SANDEFJORD Tesalongen Spiseri & Catering   🏃 V   ⓚ
Kongensgate 5, 3210 Sandefjord **Tel** *33 46 42 71*

This cosy café in the middle of Sandefjord above the "Byparken" specializes in traditional Norwegian food, both hot and cold. As well as a tempting array of open sandwiches there's a creative tapas menu that's great value for money. As the name suggests, there's also a good selection of tea (and coffee) to choose from.

SANDEFJORD Mathuset Solvold   🍷 🍸 V   ⓚⓚⓚⓚ
Thor Dahls Gate 9, 3210 Sandefjord **Tel** *33 46 27 41*

A renowned restaurant that makes a feature of its well-stocked wine cellar, Mathuset Solvold offers light meals as well as a gourmet French-inspired menu with additional flavours from Spain, Italy and Asia. Main courses include duck liver and braised pork-belly with salsa "verduzzo". For dessert try the rum and lime cream with coconut lime sherbet.

SARPSBORG Festiviteten   🏃 🛗 V   ⓚⓚⓚ
Sandesundveien 2, 1724 Sarpsborg **Tel** *90 75 23 00*

Festiviteten has been welcoming people through its grand doors for over 100 years. With its stunning period architecture, it is a popular location for large dinners and banquets, but also invites smaller parties to savour its delicious food, which the chefs take great care to present beautifully on the plate. Somewhat formal, but a stylish experience.

TØNSBERG Esmeralda   🏃 🛗 🍸 V   ⓚ
Nedre Langgate 26C, 3126 Tønsberg **Tel** *33 31 91 91*

This restaurant, pub, piano bar and pizzeria all rolled into one is a lively spot on the harbour jetty. With a distinctly Italian spin, it has a good selection of Italian and Spanish wines, as well as interesting choices from new world wine countries. Very family friendly, with a children's menu and vegetarian meals available.

TØNSBERG Fregatten Restaurant & Bar   🍸 V   ⓚ
Storgaten 17, 3126 Tønsberg **Tel** *33 31 47 76*

Fregatten offers an unusual menu combining Norwegian, Japanese and Chinese food, with an emphasis on fish and shellfish dishes. Located in congenial maritime surroundings in Storgaten, it is part of the Maritime Hotel and often changes its international menu to reflect the seasons. In summer there's outside dining in the Monastery Yard.

TØNSBERG Mamma Rosa   🏃 V   ⓚⓚ
Stoltenbergsgaten 46, 3110 Tønsberg **Tel** *33 31 91 01*

Mamma Rosa is a cosy Italian restaurant situated on the banks of a canal in Tønsberg. There is a huge variety of pizzas to choose from, as well as several pasta, fish and meat dishes. A children's menu is also available. The restaurant doesn't open until after 3pm, but stays open until late.

TØNSBERG Brygga Restaurant   🏃 🛗 🍸   ⓚⓚⓚ
Nedre Langgate 32, 3126 Tønsberg **Tel** *33 31 12 70*

Traditional Norwegian restaurant in a relatively newly built courtyard on the wharf. Serves a fairly simple but varied menu of meat, pasta, salads and fish and, somewhat bizarrely, a full English breakfast for lunch. Children under 14 can choose from their own menu, and there's plenty of outside seating in the summer.

Key to Price Guide *see p242* **Key to Symbols** *see back cover flap*

EASTERN NORWAY

BÆRUMS VERK Værtshuset Bærums Verk

Vertshusveien 10, 1352 Bærums Verk **Tel** *67 80 02 00*

There are few places in Norway like Værtshuset Bærums Verk, the oldest restaurant in Norway. The red-painted building lies in romantic surroundings at the start of the Lommedalen Valley. The 360-year old restaurant has several rooms, all slightly different in character, from where you can sit and admire this charming rustic building.

DRAMMEN Café Picasso

Nedre Storgate 16, 3015 Drammen **Tel** *32 89 07 08*

A café serving meat, fish, pasta and Mexican fare, and in the summer you can eat outside in the courtyard. It is a relaxed, informal and cosmopolitan place, with more than a touch of Paris about it. Guests often sit for hours with cups of coffee or glasses of wine and read their newspapers.

DRAMMEN Lauritz Restaurant & Bar

Bragernes Torg 2 A, 3017 Drammen **Tel** *32 83 77 22*

The place where friends meet in the heart of Drammen, this intimate pub with an Irish influence has one of the best selections of drinks in town, with everything from Belgian wheat beers to Irish stouts on tap. The food is varied and fairly standard pub fare. On Fridays and Saturdays a younger crowd takes over.

DRAMMEN Glass Brasserie & Bar

Nedre Strandgate 4, 3015 Drammen **Tel** *32 82 00 70*

Glass runs a very modern kitchen with its grounding in Norwegian cuisine but with influences from France, Italy and the Far East. As the name suggests, the restaurant has huge windows, which creates a feeling of light and space for diners. The views over the jetty and water outside are wonderful.

DRAMMEN Pigen

Bragernes Torg 9, 3017 Drammen **Tel** *32 83 45 50*

Pigen is centrally located on Bragernes Torg and has an unconventional atmosphere and a varied menu. There's a real mixture of old and new, with modern furniture set in a 100-year-old building. The menu includes three different types of home-made burgers and there's a great children's menu too.

DRAMMEN Åspaviljongen

Bragernesåsen, 3015 Drammen **Tel** *32 83 37 47*

Beautifully located with great views over the whole of the Drammensdalen (valley), this restaurant's à la carte menu is compact but interesting, with four to five options for each course. Dishes include chicken schnitzel with an Italian sauce and a lemon sorbet with vodka. Great views from the outside terrace. Live jazz every Sunday evening.

DRAMMEN Skutebrygga

Nedre Strandgate 2, 3015 Drammen **Tel** *32 83 33 30*

Skutebrygga has been inspired by ships, the sea and Drammen's rich maritime history. Inside the main restaurant you will find objects and pictures from different eras of the city. Lunch is served between 11am and 4pm, and after that the evening menu takes over, with meat and fish dishes such as Asian fish skewers and fried lamb fillet with mango.

DRAMMEN Sofus Vertshus Kro

Øvre Torggate 6, 3017 Drammen **Tel** *32 83 80 05*

Around 100 years ago the building this restaurant resides in was a well-known hotel. Now it is two restaurants combined into one: inside there's a more formal atmosphere with a roaring log fire in the winter, while in the summer guests move out to the Stallgaarden restaurant in the courtyard and eat under open skies.

GJØVIK Skibladner

Jernbanegate 2, 2802 Gjøvik **Tel** *61 14 40 80*

Skibladner is one of Norway's best-loved tourist attractions. This preserved and restored paddle steamer is over 150 years old but continues to run a timetabled service across Lake Mjøsa in the summer months. The onboard restaurant serves traditional fare, such as a salmon menu with cucumber salad, steamed potatoes and melted butter.

HAMAR The Irishman Folk Pub

Strandgt. 31, 2317 Hamar **Tel** *62 52 33 92*

No matter where you travel, sooner of later you'll come across an Irish pub. This one, in Hamar, promises a big welcome as well as large portions of honest pub grub, including steaks, egg and bacon sandwiches and waffles. It has one of the best selections of draft beers in town.

HAMAR Christian Krohg

Strandgaten 21, 2317 Hamar **Tel** *62 02 55 00*

Located in the First Hotel Victoria, Hamar's oldest and most reputable hotel, Christian Krohg is named after a famous Norwegian artist and has been voted the best restaurant in town for over ten years in a row. The views over Lake Mjøsa are not to be missed. Dishes include wild boar with mustard and thyme sauce.

HAMAR Stallgården Restauranthus

Torggata 82, 2317 Hamar **Tel** *62 54 31 00*

By far the largest dining and drinking location in Hamar, with a café, bar and nightclub sitting on top of the charming restaurant Bykjeller'n – a stone-vaulted cellar, which was originally conceived as a coal cellar and is now tastefully lit with candles and electric lights. The menu revolves around meat, with a wide choice of steaks.

LILLEHAMMER Blåmann Restaurant & Bar

Lilletorget 1, 2615 Lillehammer **Tel** *61 26 22 03*

This restaurant is, as the name suggests, decorated in shades of blue. Food ranges from Norwegian to Mexican and is served from the open kitchen. The outdoor seating area hangs over the Mesna river and is a great place to eat and watch the world go by.

LILLEHAMMER Egon Restaurant

Elvegata 12, 2609 Lillehammer **Tel** *61 05 70 90*

You'll find this Egon Restaurant in a milling house dating from 1863. The walls of this characterful building are over 1 m (3½ ft) thick, with massive beams, giant millstones and tools from the old mill days on display. In the summer you can sit out on the terrace overlooking the river and hear the water flowing by.

LILLEHAMMER Telemarkstunet

Kantveien 135, 2618 Lillehammer **Tel** *61 26 41 41*

All roads, it seems, lead to Telemarkstunet, with its endearing slogan, "Not so Trendy, but very Trevlig" (cosy in Norwegian). Guests arrive by chairlift from the bottom of Lysgårdsbakkene, by car, bus or on foot. Inside this traditional Telemark farmstead with its thick wooden walls you are served honest Norwegian fare from the region.

LILLEHAMMER Paa Bordet Restaurant

Bryggerigata 70, 2609 Lillehammer **Tel** *61 25 30 00*

A small restaurant in an old timber building one block below the main street, Paa Bordet offers a gourmet menu that has won praise from many critics, including one national newspaper that gave it full marks. Every week a new five-course meal is created, accompanied by a relatively small but interesting and varied wine selection. Open Fri & Sat only.

LILLEHAMMER Restaurant Tapas

Jernbanegata 1, 2609 Lillehammer **Tel** *61 24 77 32*

As the name suggests, this restaurant pays homage to the ever-popular Spanish tapas style of eating, with many small dishes to choose from. If you are in the mood for a coffee then a barista coffee-maker will happily whip you up a cappuccino, espresso or café au lait. A great place if you just want a light bite before going into town.

LILLEHAMMER Victoriastuen Restaurant

Storgate 84B, 2600 Lillehammer **Tel** *61 25 00 49*

Located in the Rica Victoria Hotel, this lobby-level restaurant offers some of Lillehammer's finest dining, using local produce whenever possible. Diners in the traditionally decorated restaurant can eat and people-watch at the same time out of the large windows. Specialities such as mountain trout and *frikadeller* (meatballs) are often on the menu.

SKOGSTAD Skogstad Hotell

3560 Hemsdal, Skogstad **Tel** *32 05 50 00*

At Skogstad they claim history and tradition are in the very walls. The hotel has been family owned since 1905 and comprises a restaurant and bistro, pub and bar, a new nightclub and a games room for younger guests. The creamy fish soup, with cod and lobster and finely chopped vegetables, is typical of the style of cuisine.

TRYSIL Restaurant Laaven 1790

Trysilfjell Turistsenter, 2420 Trysil **Tel** *62 45 26 00*

This popular place for lunch and après ski has a large, open fireplace and a rustic decor. The building dates back to 1790 and the log walls only enhance the atmosphere. The à la carte menu is steakhouse-inspired, with plenty of chicken, pork and beef dishes to choose from. At weekends it often gets very busy.

TRYSIL Trysil Gjestegårds

2420 Trysil **Tel** *62 45 08 50*

Trysil Gjestegårds is idyllically situated a short walk from Trysil town centre. As well as operating a 23-room hotel, the restaurant here affords panoramic views over the Trysil river and the surrounding mountains. It is a popular place with locals, who come here for the traditional Norwegian home-cooking. Fully licensed.

VINSTRA Per Gynt Gården

Per Gynt Seterveg, 2639 Vinstra **Tel** *61 29 54 00*

The Per Gynt Gården is possibly Norway's most luxurious mountain manor located in the breathtakingly beautiful valley of Gudbrandsdalen. The manor was the home and birthplace of the epic character Peer Gynt, which Ibsen immortalized in his famous play of the same name. With over 900 years of history, this is an amazing place to visit.

ØYER Number1

Øyertun, 2636 Øyer **Tel** *61 27 70 64*

This sleek, stylish restaurant, bar and café is located in the centre of Hafjell, a stone's throw from the Quality Hotel. It runs a modern kitchen with an international angle, including dishes such as chicken Thai with jasmine rice and wok vegetables, and fillet of beef medallion with blue cheese sauce, fried potatoes and seasonal vegetables.

Key to Price Guide *see p242* **Key to Symbols** *see back cover flap*

SØRLANDET AND TELEMARK

ARENDAL Madam Reiersen
Nedre Tyholmsvei 3, 4836 Arendal **Tel** *37 02 19 00*

A friendly restaurant with an adjoining bar and a great social scene on the quayside facing the Pollen yacht harbour, Madam Reiersen offers an international menu, including some low-carb alternatives for weight-conscious diners. There is live music every night of the week; Mondays is country and western night and Saturday afternoons there's jazz.

ARENDAL Ferdinand
Nedre Tyholmsvei 8, 4836 Arendal **Tel** *37 09 99 22*

This restaurant is set in a distinguished townhouse and is named after a local historian who campaigned for the building's preservation. Great job he did, too, as today it is a pleasant place to enjoy good food, with live music and a glass of wine from a varied wine list. In the summer there's a popular outdoor seating area in the back garden.

ARENDAL Tre Seil
Teaterplassen 2, 4836 Arendal **Tel** *37 07 68 00*

The picturesque views over the sea and the boats moored outside make this restaurant a pleasant venue to while away a few hours. As Clarion Hotel Tyholmen's flagship eatery, the menu is small but packed with quality dishes, comprising five starters, six mains and five desserts. At lunch a more simple selection of sandwiches is available.

GRIMSTAD Haven Brasserie
Storgata 4, 4876 Grimstad **Tel** *37 04 45 91*

This family-friendly brasserie only opened in 2001, but has already made a name for itself for serving tasty Norwegian-Italian food. Despite its idyllic waterfront location, with wonderful views of the harbour and the boats, it's the pasta and meat dishes that come most highly recommended. Great children's menu.

GRIMSTAD Apotekergården Restaurant & Bar
Skolegaten 3, 4876 Grimstad **Tel** *37 04 50 25*

If you come to Apotekergården then make sure you're hungry, as this stylish eatery (which was a chemists until the 1970s) is famous for its seven-course gourmet menu, which takes you on a culinary journey through an exciting, internationally inspired meal. If you can't manage it all, just go for the number of courses you can eat.

HAMRESANDEN Restaurant Lanternen
Hamresandveien 3, 4656 Hamresand **Tel** *38 14 42 80*

Set within the sprawling Hamresanden Resort, this summer destination has a charming restaurant where breakfast and simple lunch dishes are served. In the evening you can pick from a competent à la carte menu. Outside, the resort's terrace restaurant serves meals from the grill and has great sea views. Free children's buffet every Sunday.

HOVDEN Eminent Hovdestøylen Hotel
4755 Hovden i Setesdal **Tel** *37 93 95 52*

Eminent Hovdestøylen is a rustic hotel popular with people exploring the beautiful surrounding countryside. It is built alongside the clear waters of the River Otra and the restaurant serves delicious food from a lava stone grill. Both lunch and evening menus are offered, the latter comprising four starters, meat, fish and dessert dishes.

KRISTIANSAND Brasseriet Restaurant
Vestre Standgate 7, 4663 Kristiansand **Tel** *38 11 21 00*

Located on the ground floor in the Radisson Blu Caledonien Hotel in Kristiansand, the interior decoration in this restaurant is certainly memorable – a mix of maritime and movie themes. The service is good and the food is very reasonably priced. Although the menu is small, it offers some interesting fusion-inspired Norwegian dishes.

KRISTIANSAND Café Dronningen
Dronningensgate 5, 4610 Kristiansand **Tel** *38 17 40 00*

Café Dronningen, at Hotel Norge, is located in the heart of Kristiansand and is one of the most popular dining places in town. Breakfast, lunch, light dishes and dinner are served here, with the menu ranging from reasonable lighter meals to set three-course options. Their freshly baked bread has won an award for the best in Norway.

KRISTIANSAND Glipp
Rådhusgata 11, 4611 Kristiansand **Tel** *38 02 96 20*

Glipp is a small and pleasant restaurant with 60 seats that specializes in serving dishes from Spain, Italy and America such as tapas and bagels. In addition there's a dizzy array of other international meals to choose from, including pasta or pizzas, an American bagel, soups, wok or even tapas. Fully licensed.

KRISTIANSAND Restaurant Luihn
Rådhusgaten 15, 4611 Kristiansand **Tel** *38 10 66 50*

The Luihn is located by the peaceful Wergelandsparken in the centre of Kristiansand. It is named after the cobbler-master Hans J. Luihn, who was one of the founders of the town. There's a welcoming atmosphere and the high-class menu features French-inspired Norwegian dishes. The chef is famed for his *lutefisk*, and uses local produce.

KRISTIANSAND Sjøhuset Restaurant

*Østre Strandgate 12 A, 4610 Kristiansand **Tel** 38 02 62 60*

Located on the waterfront in a former salt warehouse dating back to 1892, the emphasis here is on fish and shellfish dishes. How does oven-baked monkfish, with Parma ham and a pesto of sun-dried tomato sound? There's outdoor eating capable of accommodating up to 300 guests during the summer months.

LANGESUND Wrightegaarden i Langesund

*Tordenskjoldsgate 2, 3790 Langesund **Tel** 35 97 39 00*

Artists such as Bob Dylan and Sweden's Ulf Lundell have graced the stage at this edgy concert venue that has outdoor performances every weekend during the summer. The onsite restaurant is the perfect place to come before a show, and many of the tickets include a meal from the à la carte menu here. Great outside seating on two levels.

PORSGRUNN Restaurant Osebro

*Storgata 176, 3915 Porsgrunn **Tel** 35 55 96 11*

This stylish and classical restaurant is set in a 250-year-old manor house and is wonderfully positioned beside a river. It is the perfect place to dine outside during summer months and has a tempting international menu that includes a variety of steaks and meat dishes supported by pasta, salad and fish meals.

RISØR Kast Loss

*Strandgate 23, 4950 Risør **Tel** 37 15 21 00*

Balanced on the edge of a jetty in a redeveloped furniture factory, this is one of the most fashionable seafood restaurants in town. The interior decoration is maritime-inspired and makes you feel like you're dining at sea. During the summer you can do just that on the adjacent floating restaurant Trossa.

RISØR Spisestedet Buene

*Solsiden 22, 4950 Risør **Tel** 37 15 21 00*

The original warehouse that sat on the site of the current restaurant stored everything from grain to salt until it was razed by fire in 1991. With loving care it was restored into this fantastic eatery that serves an elegant gourmet menu and a recommended five-course meal with wine. Great children's menu and outside seating when the sun shines.

SKIEN Jegermesteren Restaurant

*Nedre Hjellegate 1, 3724 Skien **Tel** 35 52 41 73*

This intimate restaurant with just 50 seats is equally well-known for its wine list as it is for its food. Rare bottles from notable vineyards are available, and although prices reflect the vintages, there are more reasonably priced alternatives. The chefs specialize in serving small, deliciously delicate portions to balance every wine perfectly.

SKIEN Boden Spiseri

*Langbrygga 5, 3724 Skien **Tel** 35 52 61 70*

This very popular restaurant is housed in the oldest building in town – a clapboard-sided building that was a harbour-front warehouse in the 1870s. There are two dining areas – at ground level there's Norwegian and international food served in romantic country-style surroundings, while in the cellar snacks and light meals are available.

SKIEN Brasseriet Madame Blom

*Kongensgate 6, 3724 Skien **Tel** 35 90 58 00*

Located within the Thon Hotel Høyers, chefs here combine Norwegian and international cuisines in a setting that borrows much from traditional English interiors. The menu is based on the seasons and the owners are particularly proud of their varied wine list. A bar and lounge await before or after your meal.

VRADAL Straand Sommerland

*Quality Straand Hotel & Resort, 3853 Vrådal **Tel** 35 06 90 00*

The Quality Straand Hotel and Resort in Vrådal is surrounded by forests and mountains and has endless views of Nisser Lake. Here you can eat at the new terrace and waterfront grill at Straand Sommerland. You can also try dishes such as cured meats served in the Stabburet Pub (Norway's smallest pub) or roasted leg-of-mutton in the Knights Hall.

VESTLANDET

BERGEN Mezzo

*Rosenkrantzgate 6, 5809 Bergen **Tel** 55 55 03 03*

With its traditional architecture and great location, the Finnegaarden Restaurant House is an imposing venue housing three of the best restaurants in Bergen. One of them is Mezzo, a Mediterranean-inspired concept that serves great food and wines. Try the truffle risotto with mushrooms and white asparagus, or the trout fillet with a green olive tapanade.

BERGEN Skibet Mex-Tex Restaurant

*Zachariasbryggen (Torget 2), 5014 Bergen **Tel** 55 55 96 55*

Mexican restaurant with a great view over the harbour in Bergen and out towards to the island of Askøy. Care is taken to present the food nicely. The most popular dish here seems to be the fajitas, and you decide if the filling is beef, chicken, spicy vegetables or scampi – or why not a mix of all three?

Key to Price Guide *see p242* **Key to Symbols** *see back cover flap*

BERGEN Bryggeloftet & Stuene Restaurant

Bryggen 11, 5003 Bergen **Tel** *55 30 20 70*

Enjoy a meal in the fascinating atmosphere of the old wharf known as Bryggen. Bryggeloftet & Stuene is a popular choice of restaurant for all occasions, from light lunches to grand dinners, and dishes include traditional Norwegian fish and game specialities. Choose from Stuene on the ground floor or go for the views in Bryggeloftet one floor up.

BERGEN Bryggen Tracteursted

Bryggestredet 2, 5003 Bergen **Tel** *55 31 40 46*

Rebuilt after a fire in 1701, this building has been an eating house ever since. The restaurant has the feeling of a well-preserved Hansa merchant's house and the serving staff dress in period costumes. The food also borrows from the Hanseatic times, with dishes such as steamed cod in white wine sauce, garnished with lobster and asparagus.

BERGEN Dickens

Kong Olav Vs Plass 4, 5012 Bergen **Tel** *55 36 31 30*

One of Bergen's most recognizable dining spots is a popular meeting place for people of all ages. In the same pink-coloured building is a welcoming bar called Kontoret ("office") with huge armchairs. The restaurant has an international menu – its Dickens burger with lettuce, tomato, onion, pickles and spring onion dressing is a favourite.

BERGEN Fløien Folkerestaurant

Fløifjellet 2, 5014 Bergen **Tel** *55 32 18 75*

At the top of the famous Funicular in Bergen, high above sea level, you will find Fløien Folkerestaurant. Opened in 1925, it has been completely restored and, with its distinctive architecture, prominent location and breathtaking views, is a tourist attraction in itself. On the large outdoor terrace you can gaze over Bergen while enjoying your meal.

BERGEN Holbergstuen

Torgallmenningen 6, 5014 Bergen **Tel** *55 55 20 55*

One of the oldest and best-known restaurants in the city centre. The interior is embellished with quotes from the Bergen poet, Holberg, and there's plenty of folk art adorning the walls. Not surprisingly, an arty crowd hangs outs here, and the atmosphere is cool and creative. The delicious lunch menu favours fish dishes – try the assorted herrings.

BERGEN Livingstone & André Italian Restaurant

Kong Oscarsgate 12, 5017 Bergen **Tel** *55 56 03 12*

Whether you're a local or a globetrotter this is a great place to come. The restaurant is centrally located near the fish market and has a charming herb garden in the courtyard. It's a perfect spot for relaxed lunches and evenings out, with a menu that takes you around the culinary globe from Europe, the US and the Far East.

BERGEN Smauet Mat & Vinhus

Vaskerelvsmaeut 1, 5014 Bergen **Tel** *55 21 07 10*

The building where this snug restaurant is situated dates back to 1870 and resembles a log cabin. There's a French-inspired à la carte menu as well as three-, five- and seven-course meals to be tempted by. Lots of energy emanates from the open-to-view kitchen. The crispy fried redfish with creamed savoy cabbage, chickpeas and chorizo is delicious.

BERGEN Wesselstuen

Øvre Ole Bulls plass 6, 5012 Bergen **Tel** *55 55 49 49*

Wesselstuen is one of Bergen's most traditional and classical restaurants. Actors, politicians, journalists and tourists have been eating here since 1957. The à la carte lunch and dinner menu is a fusion of unpretentious Norwegian and international food. Try the fillet of reindeer served with pickled red onion, potatoes and celery root purée.

BERGEN Fiskekrogen Fisk & Vilt Restaurant

Torget 2 (Fish Market), 5014 Bergen **Tel** *55 55 96 55*

Fiskekrogen is an award-winning seafood restaurant and one of the best places in Norway to experience gourmet food. Fresh fish are bought in daily from the fish market just next door. Everything is plucked from the fjords and served in traditional Norwegian style. Try the pan-fried mountain trout with caper butter and a fresh salad.

HAUGESUND Bestastua Mat Prat & Vinhus

Strandgata 132, 5527 Haugesund **Tel** *52 86 55 88*

This large restaurant situated in an old building in the centre of town is a combined restaurant, piano bar and nightclub. The restaurant feels typically Norwegian, with paintings of fjords and mountains covering the walls. Traditional Norwegian fare is served here, and after dinner you're invited to sip a cognac in the stylish cognac bar.

KRISTIANSUND Onkel & Vennene Hans

Kaibakken 1, 6509 Kristiansund **Tel** *71 67 58 10*

Onkel's coffee bar concept has its roots in Italy and France, but has also been heavily influenced by the American coffee-bar culture. The atmosphere is chilled out and laid back, with a trendy crowd sipping wonderfully prepared coffees, red wines and cognacs. The food isn't revolutionary – wraps, bagels and salads – but it doesn't need to be.

KRISTIANSUND Smia Fiskerestaurant

Fosnagata 30 B, 6509 Kristiansund **Tel** *71 67 11 70*

A blacksmith's workshop dating from 1787 is now home to this wonderful little fish restaurant with bags of charm and character as well as real historical merit. The high-sloped roof, heavy beams and brick-lined fireplace (in which roaring log fires are lit during the winter) make this a great place to eat. Outdoor seating in the summer.

MOLDE Molde Fjordstuer

Julsundveien 6, 6412 Molde **Tel** *71 20 10 60*

Molde Fjordstuer is a traditional and very popular seafood restaurant, particularly in the summer, so booking a table in advance is recommended. The décor is very nautical and the menu reflects the building's close proximity to the sea, although there are a few meat dishes available. From your table you can watch the boats coming back to harbour.

STAVANGER Holmen Bar – Victoria Hotel

Skansegaten 1, 4006 Stavanger **Tel** *51 86 70 00*

The leading salsa club in Stavanger attracts salseros from across the country to this lively bar that is a part of the Victoria Hotel. Although the menu is limited to chicken wings, onion rings and soups, it isn't the food that people come here for. There's a well-stocked bar and DJs play varied music ranging from Cuban to mambo.

STAVANGER Harry Pepper

Øvre Holmegate 15, 4006 Stavanger **Tel** *51 89 39 59*

Harry Pepper was Norway's first Mexican restaurant, and is still said to be the best. If you like your food hot and spicy then they say the Tex-Mex meals you are served here are the most authentic outside of Mexico. The cartoon-inspired menus are fun to read and include dishes such as blackened lamb with mustard sauce.

STAVANGER Pushkin Bar Og Restaurant

Ny Olavskleiv 16, 4008 Stavanger **Tel** *41 61 72 41*

When it first opened in 2006, this was the first and only Russian restaurant in Norway. In a country so vast, Russian cuisine is influenced by a wide range of styles, which is reflected in the menu here. Try *blini* (pancakes), *draniki* (potato pancakes), *pelmeni* (dumplings) or *borsch* – a beetroot vegetable and meat soup.

STAVANGER Bevaremegvel Bar & Restaurant

Skagen 12, 4006 Stavanger **Tel** *51 84 38 60*

The Bevaremegvel offers exquisite food and beverages in a continental environment with nice views out to the city streets. Besides the varied à la carte menu (available at lunch and dinner) the Bevaremegvel Bar serves more simple meals in addition to a wide selection of whisky, grappa, calvados and brandy, as well as classic cocktails.

STAVANGER N.B. Sørensens Dampskibsexpedition

Skagen 26, 4006 Stavanger **Tel** *51 84 38 20*

Designed with a distinct nautical flavour, the ground floor of this restaurant offers an international menu based on fresh Norwegian ingredients. Located in a wing in the new Culture House in Stavanger at the end of the Gands Fjord, with outstanding views over the water, it's an ideal location to dine outside during the summer.

STAVANGER Sjøhuset Skagen

Skagenkaien 16, 4006 Stavanger **Tel** *51 89 51 80*

The old restored bunkhouse on the wharf next to the harbour incorporates a number of inviting restaurants with a distinctly maritime atmosphere. There are rooms and niches on eight different floors that are filled with nautical bric-a-brac that create an interesting setting in which to enjoy a menu comprising Norwegian and international dishes.

STAVANGER Timbuktu Bar & Restaurant

Nedre Strandgate 15, 4005 Stavanger **Tel** *51 84 37 40*

A rich mix of exotic tastes constitutes the menu at Timbuktu, a light and airy bar and restaurant. The owners have developed and encourage a way of eating called "sharing", where guests are served food that is easy to pass around in bowls and trays.

STAVANGER Bistrohuset

Madlaveien 18, 4008 Stavanger **Tel** *51 53 95 70*

Bistrohuset is a food-lovers dream, with a number of differently themed restaurants and bars all under one roof. Their City Bistro à la carte restaurant has been reinvented to a light, breezy concept filled with works from local artists. There's always a good four-course menu available.

STAVANGER Straen Fiskerestaurant

Nedre Strandgate 15, 4005 Stavanger **Tel** *51 84 37 00*

Amusingly touted as being "world famous throughout Norway", this really is one of the best seafood restaurants in Stavanger. The old-fashioned interior is straight out of the 1950s and the windows open out to give fantastic views of the harbour. There is a nightclub upstairs and another restaurant downstairs that's served by the same kitchen.

ÅLESUND Fjellstua

Aksla, 6002 Ålesund **Tel** *70 10 74 00*

If you're scared of heights you might want to think twice about coming to this high-altitude restaurant that's the oldest dining place in Ålesund. Built into the side of a mountain overlooking the town, Fjellstua is worth a visit just for the 360-degree views alone. It offers a good variety of traditional Norwegian dishes in a relaxed atmosphere.

ÅLESUND Orient Bar & Restaurant

Kongensgate 30, 6002 Ålesund **Tel** *70 10 71 71*

This sushi-Asian restaurant is located in the heart of Ålesund and is the only sushi restaurant in western Norway. The interior is urban in style and the restaurant has its own coffee bar where you can surf the Internet. A broad spectrum of Asian styles is offered, including Cantonese, Szechuan, Japanese and Malaysian.

Key to Price Guide *see p242* **Key to Symbols** *see back cover flap*

ÅLESUND Hummer og Kanari

Kongensgate 19, 6002 Ålesund **Tel** *70 12 80 08*

With its high ceilings and huge arch windows looking onto the pedestrian street and views over the inner harbour, this cosmopolitan restaurant, bar and bistro is a good place to spend an hour or two while exploring Ålesund. The menu is European but leaning towards Italy, with dishes such as marinated chicken with tagliatellé and chilli sauce.

ÅLESUND Sjøbua Fiskerestaurant

Brunholmgate 1, 6004 Ålesund **Tel** *70 12 71 00*

This outstanding fish restaurant situated in a renovated warehouse once used for fish processing is by the Brosundet Canal in the heart of Ålesund. Artefacts and tools from the old warehouse decorate the restaurant, and reflect the maritime ambience. There are always a delicious assortment of fish and shellfish courses created from fresh produce.

ÅLESUND XL Diner

Skaregata 1, 6002 Ålesund **Tel** *70 12 42 53*

The exciting Creole kitchen is celebrated in this harbour-side restaurant that claims to have the best views in town. The high ceiling, hardwood floors and wall of windows create a clean, light atmosphere where you can enjoy Bacolao dishes or pick from a list of entertaining menu descriptions like "Deer you meet Rosemary" – you guessed it, it's reindeer!

TRØNDELAG

BESSAKER Robu-Kroa

7190 Bessaker **Tel** *72 53 68 80*

This no-frills restaurant is located on the seafront in the small coastal town of Bessaker, a location that's popular among fishing fanatics. Here, where the fjord meets the open sea, you can sit and choose from a simple menu that includes steaks and fresh fish while looking out to the jetty and the water below.

OPPADAL Cafe Ludvik

Inge Krokannsveien 21, 7340 Oppdal **Tel** *47 72 42 01 40*

One of Oppdal's most price-friendly restaurants is located in the Sagtunet shopping centre near the heart of the town. There are 120 seats indoors and a further 60 seats outside, with good wheelchair access. All occasions are catered for, from breakfast, lunch and light meals to a reasonable à la carte menu that includes pepper steak.

ORKANGER Bårdshaug Herregård

Orkedalsveien 102, 7300 Orkanger **Tel** *72 47 99 00*

Bårdshaug Herregård was built for consul-general Christian Thams at the turn of the 19th century. From this location he regularly entertained kings and princes; ask for a tour while you are here. An intriguing collection of menus are available whose names are inspired by Thams and his amazing life, including the King Oscar II and Diplomat's Menu.

RØROS Vertshuset Røros

Kjerkgata 34, 7374 Røros **Tel** *72 41 93 50*

The chefs here take their inspiration from the Mediterranean to compose delicious dishes using local ingredients, many sourced from the surrounding mountains. The building was previously both a shop and a bank before being turned into a hotel, restaurant and bar in the 1960s. There's an obvious pride taken in what the staff do here.

STEINKJER Brød og Sirkus

Kongensgate 40, 7713 Steinkjer **Tel** *74 16 21 00*

If you don't want to break the bank but don't want fast food then this is the place to come in Steinkjer. These specialist bakers and confectioners also offer a simple but tasty lunch menu and a more challenging evening menu of Norwegian dishes. Lighter meals include a noodle wok and feta ciabatta.

STEINKJER Mitt Hjem

Kongensgate 18, 7715 Steinkjer **Tel** *95 23 83 70*

Typical pub atmosphere, with a pub standard of food to match. There are often live bands playing here, when it can get very crowded. The bar is the central attraction, with a good selection of beers, wines and spirits. The bar menu is basic, with just one fish dish but several steak, pasta and pizza meals to choose from.

TRONDHEIM Restaurant Akropolis

Fjordgata 19, 7010 Trondheim **Tel** *73 51 67 51*

Akropolis is Trondheim's only Greek restaurant, which as well as serving a wide choice of classic Greek dishes also offers some international fare. Located in a cellar with walls painted with historic scenes from ancient Greece, families are particularly welcomed here and there's a good children's menu for younger diners. Fully licensed.

TRONDHEIM Tavern Vertshus

Sverresborg Allé 11, 7020 Trondheim **Tel** *73 87 80 70*

Traditional homely fare in an old inn that has remained virtually unchanged since its construction in 1739. The building's 16 different rooms are filled with antique furniture, giving a fascinating impression of Norwegian life over the past 250 years. Classic local dishes include home-made fishcakes served with boiled potatoes and chopped carrots.

TRONDHEIM Credo Restaurant & Bar

Ørjaveita 4A, 7010 Trondheim **Tel** *73 53 03 88*

This is a unique gourmet restaurant concept that is making a name for its unconventional approach to food. The building is split into three distinct areas: a restaurant, bar and cellar. There's no fixed menu, so ask the waiting staff for the fish or meat speciality of the day. The restaurant has its own wine cellar, which has more than 600 wines.

TRONDHEIM Fru Inger

Fosenkaia, 7010 Trondheim **Tel** *73 51 60 71*

A distinctive restaurant in a maritime environment at Fosenkaia near the Central Station in Trondheim. Known for its delicious fish dishes, but one meat course plus pizza and pasta are available. The interior has clean, modern Scandinavian design and there are great views out to the harbour. Dishes include *fiskesuppe*, the house speciality fish soup.

TRONDHEIM Havfruen Fiskerestaurant

Kjøpmannsgata 7, 7013 Trondheim **Tel** *73 87 40 70*

One of the foremost fish restaurants in Trondheim, Havfruen offers a distinctive atmosphere in an 18th-century wharf warehouse. The menu ranges from *bouillabaisse* to fish varieties from the Norwegian coastal waters, as well as meat dishes. Instead of a standard à la carte concept there's an eight-course menu that changes each month.

TRONDHEIM Vertshuset Grenaderen

Kongsgårdsgata 1, 7013 Trondheim **Tel** *73 51 66 80*

This 200-year-old building was originally a forge. It is located on historic ground between the Nidarosdomen Cathedral and the Nidelven river. There's a strong focus on medieval customs, with an evening show complete with jugglers, music and a five-course dinner for large parties. It boasts one of Trondheim's most attractive summer terraces.

TRONDHEIM Emilies Et Spisested

Erling Skakkes Gate 45, 7012 Trondheim **Tel** *73 92 96 41*

This small eatery a block away from the central square offers a fixed five-course menu with the option of selecting individual dishes. The cuisine is Italian-French inspired, and dishes are well-composed and attractively displayed. Service is friendly and professional. The Trøndelag Theatre is nearby, so this is a good choice for a pre-show meal.

NORTHERN NORWAY AND SVALBARD

BODØ Kafè Kafka

Sandgata 5B, 8006 Bodø **Tel** *93 40 60 03*

This "thinking man's" café – named after the Czech author Franz Kafka – has a distinct library quality to it, complete with bookshelves. It's common to see people sitting with their noses buried in books and sipping one of the many delicious freshly ground coffees available. The food is simple and includes baked potatoes, hamburgers and wok dishes.

BODØ Mon Ami

Storgata 12, 8001 Bodø **Tel** *75 52 24 80*

This cosy French-style café and restaurant is located on top of a glasshouse building in the centre of town. The glass walls and ceiling make you feel like you're sitting outdoors but you're still protected against the worst of the elements. Croissants, baguettes, soups, salads and light dishes are served, and there's a separate vegetarian menu.

BODØ Blix Restaurant

Sjøgate 25, 8004 Bodø **Tel** *75 54 70 99*

This informal and popular restaurant has seafood and steak among many specialities offered. The à la carte menu is small but beautifully prepared, with four starters, three fish and three meat courses, all paired with fresh local vegetables. The Norwegian breads here shouldn't be overlooked. Closed in July.

HAMMERFEST Kaikanten Bar & Spiseri

Sjøgate 19, 9600 Hammerfest **Tel** *78 41 04 70*

In this English-style "pizza pub", complete with leather armchairs, beamed ceiling and pool table, the emphasis is on socializing and enjoying a drink at the well-stocked bar. The background music is deliberately kept low so guests can hold a conversation. There are 16 pizzas to choose from, including a "make-your-own".

HAMMERFEST Odd's Mat og Vinhus

Strandgate 24, 9600 Hammerfest **Tel** *78 41 37 66*

This rustic restaurant celebrates the cuisine of northern Norway with an extensive menu that emphasizes fish and game. Located next to the town's largest pier, guests have stunning views overlooking the harbour. Inside, the owners have tried to capture the whole character of the region with textured woods and stone among the local materials used.

HARSTAD Clarion Hotel Arcticus

Havnegata 3, 9480 Harstad **Tel** *77 04 08 00*

The Arcticus is situated in the Harstad Kulturhus building on the pier near central Harstad, a short walk from the railway station. The hotel's Gallionen Restaurant specializes in cuisine from northern Norway and is part of the Arctic Menu group of restaurants dedicated to preserving local food traditions.

HARSTAD Restaurant Grand

Strandgaten 9, 9485 Harstad Tel 77 00 30 00

Part of the Grand Nordic Hotel, this is the place in Harstad to eat and dance the night away. The restaurant is decorated in modern colours and a slick interior, while the bar was given an 80s-inspired facelift in 2006. The menu is international and creative, offering good value for money. DJs play every Friday and Saturday night.

HARSTAD Restaurant De 4 Roser

Torvet 7a, 9485 Harstad Tel 77 01 27 50

French-Italian food is the theme at this stylish restaurant in the middle of Harstad town centre that also operates a café if you prefer a coffee and snack or lighter meal. The open kitchen adds a sense of theatre and energy to this small, cosy eatery with just 50 seats. The modern, continental menu offers five- and six-course meals.

KARASJOK Storgamman

Leavnnjageaidnu 1, 9730 Karasjok Tel 78 46 88 60

For a truly unique dining experience visit this traditional restaurant where guests are served authentic Lappish cuisine using recipes that date back hundreds of years. The building itself is made of thick timbers with a turf roof. Enjoy your meal while sitting on reindeer hides. Part of Rica Hotel Karasjok. Reservations essential. Open Jun–Aug.

MO I RANA Meyergården Hotell

Fridtjof Nansens Gate 28, 8622 Mo i Rana Tel 75 13 40 00

The kitchen in the Meyergården Hotell's Søilen Restaurant focuses on the use of local ingredients and produce. For instance, reindeer meat is supplied by the nearby Arktisk Rein og Vilt in Gruben and cheese comes from a farm in Utskarpen. Another of the Arctic Menu group of restaurants.

SVOLVAER Du Verden Restaurant

JE Paulsens Gate 12, 8300 Svolvaer Tel 76 07 70 99

A modern food philosophy from award-winning chef Roy Magne Berglund has turned this traditional fish restaurant overlooking the sea into a chic loft eatery. Despite the style, the atmosphere is informal and inviting. Berglund serves dishes such as pan-fried salmon filet served with cauliflower cream and sauce "beurre de noisette".

TROMSØ Kulturscenen & Studenthuset Driv

Søndre Tollbodgate 3 B, 9008 Tromsø Tel 77 60 07 76

This lively student headquarters situated in Tromsø's inner harbour in a charming 100-year old building is a great place to come to enjoy a relaxed, informal meal at prices that won't make even the hardest-up student blush. You don't need to be studying to come here to enjoy the simple snacks and light meals.

TROMSØ Le Mirage

Storgata 42, 9008 Tromsø Tel 77 68 21 50

Tromsø has more bars per capita than any other Norwegian city, making choosing where to spend your night out more difficult than usual. You could do worse that pick Le Mirage, which is a part of the acclaimed Peppermøllen mat & vinhus. Sink into one of the huge armchairs to enjoy a pre-dinner drink. The menu is varied and well-priced.

TROMSØ Aunegården

Sjøgata 29, 9008 Tromsø Tel 77 65 12 34

This restaurant comprises a number of rooms, including an "indoor" backyard. Each room has its own individual character and history – one of them was once a butcher's shop. It serves snacks and light meals and high-quality gourmet food. The cakes made in the restaurant's own bakery are much sought-after – the cheesecake is heavenly.

TROMSØ Peppermøllen Mat og Vinhus

Storgata 42, 9008 Tromsø Tel 77 68 62 60

The Peppermøllen Mat og Vinhus is one of Tromsø's oldest restaurants and known throughout Norway, combining good Norwegian ingredients with French cuisine. Norwegian raw ingredients form the basis of the menu, with fish as the speciality. Eat a meal in the same room that polar explorer Roald Amundsen occupied when he visited town.

TROMSØ Steakers

Fredrik Langes Gate 19, 9008 Tromsø Tel 77 61 33 30

Inspired by 1930s Chicago, Steakers is the place to come in Tromsø if you want to eat meat. This American steakhouse has an informal but stylish interior, and is well located at the quayside, from where you can watch the fishing boats come and go. Steaks come in various sizes, all the way up to a whopping 400 grams (14 oz).

TROMSØ Vertshuset Skarven

Strandtorget 1, 9008 Tromsø Tel 77 60 07 20

This local landmark in Tromsø is a favoured meeting place among locals and tourists alike. In this historic building by the harbour you'll find three dining spots: Vertshuset Skarven, which serves simple, light meals; the seafood restaurant Arctandria; and Skarvens Biffhus, which specializes in steaks and other meat dishes.

TROMSØ Emmas Drommekjokken

Kirkegate 8, 9253 Tromsø Tel 77 63 77 31

Anne Brit, known as "Emma," operates this dream kitchen and is the best-known culinary personality in the north of Norway. Although she uses mainly ingredients from the north – often fish from Arctic waters – she travels extensively in search of new flavours for her menu. The restaurant has been highly acclaimed and the wine list is exceptional.

SHOPPING IN NORWAY

Norway's larger towns have a wide selection of shopping centres and department stores. Generally, prices are high, but there are often good buys to be had when it comes to gold and silver items, watches, glass and leather articles. VAT on sales is particularly steep in Norway, but foreign visitors can reclaim a percentage of the total amount that they spend by taking advantage of the tax-free facility. Among the best buys are hand-knitted sweaters and cardigans in traditional patterns, known as *lusekofte*. Specialist craft shops in all the towns offer a good selection of beautiful hand-crafted articles made of wood, pewter, silver and linen. Sámi crafts and jewellery make exquisite gifts, while Norwegian food specialities and the famous aquavit always makes a good gift. Shopping in Oslo is covered on pp98–99.

Hand-knitted lusekofte

OPENING HOURS

Opening hours vary, but most shops are open between 9am and 5pm on weekdays. Shopping centres and department stores open at 9–10am and close between 6–9pm. In many towns it is becoming standard practice to stay open until 2–3pm on Saturday, while shopping centres and department stores open at 9am and close around 6pm. There are often late openings Thursday until 6 or 7pm, as well as the first Saturday of each month, known as *Super Lørdag* ("Super Saturday"). Shops are closed on Sunday, except in the run-up to Christmas when shopping centres and department stores open for business. Food stores generally remain open from 9am–10pm during the week and 9–6pm on Saturdays.

Newsstands often stay open until 9 or 10pm.

Many towns have a local petrol station that remains open until midnight, or even around the clock, which can be useful as most have small supermarkets selling everything from food, gifts, flowers and music to coffee, sweets and hot dogs.

HOW TO PAY

As a rule, department stores and shopping centres accept all internationally recognized credit cards, such as VISA, MasterCard, Diners, Eurocard and American Express. Travellers' cheques are on the decline as a form of payment and not all shops will accept them. If you are using travellers' cheques you must also have identification, such as a passport or driving licence. All shopping centres

Hand-crafted goods on sale in a Norwegian market

have cash machines (ATMs). Some Norwegian shopping centres may accept the Euro on purchases.

SALES TAX AND TAX-FREE SHOPPING

Sales tax (*moms*) levied on goods currently can be up to 24 per cent of the purchase price. Since Norway is not a member of the European Union, residents of EU and non-EU states, with the exception of visitors from Sweden, Denmark and Finland, can reclaim the sales tax paid on goods over a specified amount.

More than 3,000 shops in Norway offer tax-free shopping, allowing you to reclaim 11–18.5 per cent of the total price. Most tourist-oriented shops in the country fall under the tax-free umbrella, but there are no tax-free concessions in restaurants or for car hire.

Colourful shop-fronts in bustling Bergen

Stall-holders offering a selection of traditional Sámi crafts

For information on how to reclaim tax, pick up the brochure "How to Shop Tax Free in Norway", available at many shops.

SHIPPING ITEMS HOME

If you find you need to ship purchased items back home, visit a local post office. The *Verdenspakke* rates are generally quite good and offer efficient delivery, usually under two weeks to anywhere in the world.

RETURN POLICY

Most shops offer an excellent exchange of goods service. If there is anything wrong with the item you have bought you have the right to have it replaced or the money refunded. If you want to return something just because you regret having bought it, most retailers will take it back – even if they are not obliged to do so by law. The article must not have been used, and should preferably be in its original packaging. Most shops ask for the receipt and will give you a full refund, though some may insist that you buy something else instead.

DEPARTMENT STORES AND SHOPPING CENTRES

Norwegians love shopping. On Saturday, in particular, you could be forgiven for thinking that the country's entire population is on a nationwide shopping spree.

Streets, department stores and shopping centres all bustle with shoppers. Large shopping complexes, built in the 1990s on the periphery of towns, experienced such a rapid growth that local politicians sounded a warning as smaller retailers in town centres began to suffer economically. Nowadays the development of shopping centers is regulated by local authorities in an attempt to achieve an acceptable balance between small shops and larger malls.

Most such centres hold several dozen restaurants and shops which comprise exclusive designer shops as well as cheaper chain stores. The bigger centres include **Kløverhuset** in Bergen, **Trondheim Torg** and **Nerstranda Senter** in Tromsø.

Note that the sale of all wine and spirits in Norway takes place in specially designated state monopoly shops called Vinmonopolet.

MARKETS

April and May is a popular time for flea markets in Norway when jumble sales are held in practically every sports hall and school playground. They are organized to raise money for sports clubs and school brass bands, and are always advertised in the local paper.

DIRECTORY

SHOPPING CENTRES AND DEPARTMENT STORES

Kløverhuset
Strandgaten 15, Bergen.
Tel 55 31 37 90.

Nerstranda Senter
Nerstranda 9, Tromsø
Tel 77 65 37 00.

Trondheim Torg
Kongens Gate 11,
Trondheim.
Tel 73 80 77 40.

These get-togethers can be a very Norwegian experience, providing you with an opportunity to meet the locals in a positive and entertaining way (as well as providing great tasting homemade waffles and coffee). Often jumble sales will have a separate second-hand and antiques section where it is possible to find a bargain, though the most valuable antiques are usually auctioned.

Various market days are also arranged throughout Norway. One of the best-known is the market in Røros, held towards the end of February. This is a delightful experience, with everything from clothes to crafts and food on sale, but dress warmly as temperatures can fall to –20° C (–4° F).

Fresh fruit and vegetables on sale at a market in Bergen

What to Buy in Norway

Trolls from
Norwegian legends

If you are planning to take home a memento it is worth looking for something authentically Norwegian. The most popular souvenir is the traditional knitted cardigan, *lusekofte*. There is a wide selection of handcrafted articles such as pewter and glassware to choose from, and if you have a lot of room in your suitcase you could take home a reindeer hide. Sailing and outdoors enthusiasts will find high-quality sports clothes and equipment. Popular gifts for small children include Norwegian trolls, or cuddly toys such as snow-white polar bears and little furry seals.

Polar Bear
A soft little bear from the north is a lovely memento. You can also buy cuddly brown elk toys.

Slippers
Nothing beats felt slippers made from the matted wool of Norwegian sheep for warmth. The soles are leather. Such slippers are available in many mountain huts.

Knitwear
Knitting has a long tradition in Norway. All children, both boys and girls, learn to knit at school, though few acquire the skills required to knit a lusekofte. Good buys include hats, gloves and cardigans in traditional and modern designs, as well as ear warmers, mittens and scarves.

Silver and Pewter
Norway has many outstanding goldsmiths and silversmiths whose products can be found in shops such as Husfliden and Heimen in Oslo. Pewter products are particularly popular, especially authentic copies of old beer mugs, dishes and bowls. Queen Sonja sometimes chooses these to present to foreign dignitaries. Some shops offer an exciting range of modern jewellery.

Cheese Slicer
Invented in Norway, the practical cheese slicer comes in many shapes and forms, ranging from traditional to modern. The handle can be made of wood, metal or even reindeer horn.

Linen
Linen tablecloths, napkins and towels, often in traditional patterns, exude quality. Flax cultivation is on the increase in Norway.

Hand-Painted Wood and Porcelain
The painting of floral motifs on all kinds of objects from small boxes to large cupboards is known as "rosemaling" and follows a centuries-old tradition. Porcelain is available from glassware shops, which also stock tableware and ornaments.

Hand-decorated bowl

Porsgrunn porcelain

Glass Christmas Figures
Gnomes to decorate the Christmas table are available with either red or blue hats.

Sami Crafts

There are shops all over Norway selling excellent Sami products, but the best buys are probably to be had in Finnmark. Sami shoes (skaller) have a characteristic curled tip because they were worn for skiing. The Sami would slip the tip under a strap which was fastened to the skis. To keep moisture out of the shoes they packed them with dried grass.

Skaller – Sami shoes

Sami sheath knife

Sami silver spoon

Reindeer skin

Sami Jewellery

Beautifully crafted and of excellent quality, traditional bracelets are made of thin pewter thread, plaited in different patterns on a base of soft reindeer skin. Brooches come in ancient and contemporary designs.

Pewter thread bracelet

Silver brooch

Traditional brooch

NORWEGIAN SPECIALITIES

Norwegians cut *geitost*, their brown goats' cheese, into thin slices with a cheese slicer and use it as a sandwich topping. Norwegian smoked salmon is highly regarded by gourmets all over the world, and Norwegian milk chocolate is a perennial favourite.

Milk chocolate

Geitost cheese

Sailing Jacket

Helly Hansen is synonymous with quality, whether you want a thick winter fleece, a thin summer jacket or the proper gear for yachting. There is also a large selection of waterproof trousers for sport and leisure.

Smoked salmon

Aquavit in Miniature Bottles

Aquavit (see p241) can be bought as a set of miniatures, including the richly spiced oak-flavoured Gammel, the strong Taffel (for heavier meals) and the moderately spiced Linie Aquavit.

Life Jacket

In Norway the law requires everyone on board a boat to wear a life jacket. These light life jackets are soft and comfortable to wear and are popular among sailors.

Oppland Aquavit

Gammel Aquavit

Taffel Aquavit

Oslo Aquavit

Linie Aquavit

ENTERTAINMENT IN NORWAY

Norwegian cultural life is characterized by an excellent range of drama, musical, dance and artistic events, as well as a large number of festivals held throughout the year that feature performances by professional artists of national and international renown. While the larger theatres in the towns close during the summer (the new season begins towards the end of August), summer revues and

Regional folk dancers

historical plays, both indoor and outdoor, are staged throughout the country. A vibrant urban nightlife of bars and clubs is livened up by club musicians and stand-up comedians, and regional parks also offer a variety of popular, family-friendly attractions. Festivals are an important part of the nation's cultural life, ranging from rock, jazz and church music to food, theatre, folklore and film. Entertainment in Oslo is covered on pp100–103.

INFORMATION AND TICKETS

Innovasjon Norge (Innovation Norway) oversees the tourist information service and offers details on many cultural programmes, activities and festivals. There are also 260 authorized tourist information offices in Norway, many of which have detailed websites offering specific information. Hotels and travel agents can also be of help, though if you intend to go to a festival, theatre or concert, visit the venue's website, as most prepare their programme (and sell tickets) many months in advance. Most towns have their own local newspaper with up-to-date information about what's on.

Billettservice sells tickets (with added commission) to most large concert and performing arts events, though for some sold-out venues, it may

be possible to buy unclaimed tickets on the evening of the performance at the box office.

LARGE THEATRES & CULTURAL CENTRES

In addition to the permanent and mostly traditional theatres, many of the larger towns and cities in Norway outside of Oslo have multicultural performing arts centres offering a broad spectrum of events. Bergen's **Grieghallen**, Trondheim's **Olavshallen** and Stavanger's **Konserthus** are permanent homes for local symphony orchestras and varied programmes of classical music.

The larger cultural arts centres host numerous music performances by international stars, while other venues may feature smaller dance events, classical music recitals, musicals and rock concerts, as well as family entertainment.

A play at Bergen's Den Nationale Scene theatre

TRADITIONAL THEATRE

Henrik Ibsen's plays are the most frequently performed works in the world after those by William Shakespeare, making Ibsen the leading ambassador for Norwegian theatre. The country's best theatrical venues include Bergen's **Den Nationale Scene** and **Rogaland Teater** in Stavanger, both of which offer classic works, as well as more recent musicals, comedy and drama.

There are also many outdoor summer theatre performances such as at the **Porsgrunn Internasjonale Teaterfestival**, which has a large street theatre element, and **Figurteater Festivalen i Kristiansand**, a puppet festival that is a great place to take the kids.

Several towns have their own intimate comedy theatres, where the audience gets a chance to meet Norway's best entertainers.

The cast of a production at Trondheim's Trøndelag Teater

Members of the Carte Blanche company at Studio Bergen

CLASSICAL MUSIC, BALLET, DANCE & OPERA

In Bergen, the **Musikkselskabet Harmonien** symphony orchestra puts on regular concerts in the Grieghallen. Additionally, Trondheim, Tromsø, Stavanger and Kristiansand also have permanent orchestras and concert halls, providing year-round programmes of music.

Contemporary dance has a permanent home in Bergen at **Studio Bergen**, where the company, Carte Blanche, performs interesting new works by both Norwegian and foreign choreographers. First-rate international dance, opera and classical music concerts are on offer every year during Bergen's quality international festival, **Festspillene**.

JAZZ, ROCK & COUNTRY MUSIC

Jazz enthusiasts have plenty of festivals to look forward to in Norway. In May and June, towns in the west of the country stage numerous jazz events, while the international jazz festivals, **Sildajazz** in Haugesund and **Molde International Jazz Festival**, are world-renowned.

For rock fans, the **Quart Festival** in Kristiansand is a must, with indoor and out-door concerts all day and night. **Vestfold Festspillene** is a performing arts festival with around 50 performances of flamenco, blues and other music styles. Country music lovers should take a trip through the beautiful landscape of Telemark to **Seljord** in summer and the biggest country music festival in the Nordic region.

FOLK MUSIC & DANCING

Telemark is known for keeping alive traditions in Norwegian folk dancing and music, and July's **Telemark Festival** in Bø is the best event in the country to come and enjoy it. Other popular venues for seeing – and participating in – music and dancing are Ålesund's **Folkedansveka** in August and the **Førde International Folk Music Festival** in July, the latter of which features interesting groups from Asia, India, South America. Also popular is the **Jørn Hilme Festival**, held in late July in Fagernes, three hours north of Oslo.

Norway's two national orchestras are based in Bergen and Oslo

DIRECTORY

INFORMATION & TICKETS	Konserthus Bjergsted, Stavanger. **Tel** 51 53 70 00.	Musikkselskabet Harmonien Grieghallen, Bergen. **Tel** 55 21 61 00.	Sildajazz Knut Knutsens Gate 4, Haugesund. **Tel** 52 74 33 70.
Billettservice AS www.billettservice.no **Innovasjon Norge** www.innovasjonnorge.no	**Olavshallen** Kjøpmannsgata 44, Trondheim. **Tel** 73 99 40 00.	**Studio Bergen** Nøstegaten 119, Bergen. **Tel** 55 30 86 80.	**Vestfold** Stoltenbergsgata 38, Tønsberg. **Tel** 33 30 88 50.
THEATRE	**Porsgrunn Teaterfestival** Huken 3D, Porsgrunn. **Tel** 35 93 21 00.	**JAZZ, ROCK & COUNTRY MUSIC**	**FOLK MUSIC AND DANCING**
Den Nationale Scene Engen 1, Bergen. **Tel** 55 54 97 00.	**Rogaland Teater** Teaterveien 1, Stavanger. **Tel** 51 91 90 00.	**Molde International Jazz Festival** Molde, Møre and Romsdal. **Tel** 71 20 31 50.	**Folkedansveka** S Bulls Gate 4, Ålesund. **Tel** 70 10 06 50
Figurteater Festivalen Kongens Gate 2A, Kristiansand. **Tel** 38 07 70 50.	**CLASSICAL, BALLET, DANCE & OPERA**	**Quart Festival** Bygg 29, Odderøya, Kristiansand. **Tel** 38 14 69 69.	**Førde International Folk Music Festival** Angedalsvegen 5, Førde. **Tel** 57 72 19 40
Grieghallen Edvard Griegs Plass 1, Bergen. **Tel** 55 21 61 00.	**Festspillene** Vågsallmenningen 1, Bergen. **Tel** 55 21 06 30.	**Seljord Country Music Festival** Seljord, Telemark. **Tel** 35 05 51 64.	**Jørn Hilme Festival** Fagernes. **Tel** 61 36 46 71 **Telemark Festival** Gullbringveien 34, Bø. **Tel** 35 95 19 19.

SPORTS AND OUTDOOR ACTIVITIES

It is said that Norwegians are born with skis on their feet and rucksacks on their backs. They love the fresh air and engage in outdoor activities all year round, probably more so than any other European nation. But then conditions in every region are ideal for participating in the great outdoors, whether on foot or by boat. There are superb national parks and large tracts of untouched terrain. In many places, including the wild high

Signs in Jotunheimen

fells, hiking trails and ski tracks are marked out. In the south of Norway, boating enthusiasts will find numerous visitor harbours providing all the necessary amenities. Norway is also well geared for more demanding pursuits such as hang-gliding and white-water canoeing. Although it is a very long country, there is never far to go to the nearest hiking area or boating haven. Even in the largest towns, the outdoor life is always close at hand.

HIKING

Norway is a paradise for those who love to experience nature on foot, in summer and in winter. The expression, *søndagstur* (Sunday walk), prompts Norwegians to fasten their rucksacks and go out into the woods and fields. Usually they will make their way along narrow forest paths and signposted hiking trails. Many also spend their holidays walking from hut to hut at any time of year.

In the most popular high fell areas you never have far to go between the huts, which provide overnight accommodation (*see p225*). They are linked by a network of marked trails (and in winter, ski tracks). Most of these tourist huts and cabins are owned by **Den Norske Turistforening** (DNT; the

Norwegian Mountain Touring Club) and the 50 or so local branches of DNT situated around the country. There are some 400 huts and cabins in total. The huts vary in terms of standard and service, from the best-equipped, which are similar to a hotel, to the more spartan offering only basic facilities.

If you plan to hike from hut to hut it can pay to take out membership of DNT (445 Nkr in the Oslo area). An overnight stay in a one-to-three-bed hut costs 190 Nkr for members (95 Nkr for children) and 245 Nkr for non-members (125 Nkr for children). Breakfast costs 80 Nkr and supper 185 Nkr for members (prices apply to the Oslo area only). Lunch is normally a packed lunch and a drink from a Thermos provided by the hut.

The marked trails and ski tracks in the high mountains

Trout fishing in Sysendal in Hardangervidda National Park

are generally positioned where the view is the most spectacular yet where the terrain is not overly challenging. Always enquire at the hut you are leaving about the distance to the next hut and how demanding the walk is likely to be.

The snow lasts for a long time on the high mountain plateaus, and the best time to hike is from May to October. In August and September the mountains are bathed in a pageant of colour.

If you are hiking in the fells at other times of year, always obtain up-to-date information on the snow conditions. In the most popular areas, ski tracks are dug as soon as the first snows fall. They are usually accessible for people of average skiing ability.

DNT and most of the large bookshops stock a good selection of maps. Free maps are also available for planning routes and distances.

Trondsbu hut on the Hardangervidda plateau

Mountain hikers on Besseggen in Jotunheimen National Park

SAFETY

Nature can be beautiful and benign, but it can be challenging and dangerous if you overlook simple ground rules. It is important to read and follow the mountain guidelines known as *fjellvettsreglene*, which are a good reminder of how to act in variable conditions in the mountains, particularly in winter. The weather can change rapidly from sunshine to storms. The latest weather report is usually posted on the information board in hotels and huts.

Take clothes that will be suitable should the weather change for the worse *(see p275)*. Good maps are essential and remember to take a compass with you as well. Never go alone unless you are an experienced hiker.

EQUIPMENT

When out walking, it is important to have good equipment and an ample supply of food and drinks. At the same time, try to cut down on weight by selecting

what is most appropriate, but take account of likely changes in weather conditions. Sturdy shoes, preferably robust boots, are a necessity. Include a change of clothing, ideally woollen, as well as garments that will insulate you against wind and rain. Pack your gear in a plastic bag before placing it in your rucksack so that it will remain dry.

You should take a standard first-aid kit containing such items as plasters and cream for treating blisters and cuts, as well as mosquito repellent. Sunglasses and sun cream will be needed in the fells in summer as well as winter.

Sufficient energy-rich food and, in particular, adequate fluids are important for day trips. Very often you will come across streams along the way where you can fill your bottles. You can supplement your provisions at the tourist huts.

If you are camping, most of the gear, such as tent, cooking utensils and sleeping bag, needs to be purchased as there are no specialist rental companies for camping equipment in Norway.

TOURING THE NATIONAL PARKS

Norway has 23 national parks on the mainland and six on Svalbard, with a combined area of over 33,250 sq km (12,800 sq miles). The national parks have been designated as such because they contain unspoilt, unique or especially beautiful scenery, as well as being the natural habitat of flora and fauna. All activities liable to have an effect on the environment are banned. Information can be obtained from DNT branches, tourist information centres and visitor centres in the parks.

Hardangervidda is the largest national park, covering an area of 3,422 sq km (1,320 sq miles) *(see pp158–9)*. A large part of the park consists of a high mountain plateau. It is easily accessible from Eastern Norway as well as from Vestlandet by car, or by bus or train from Oslo or Bergen. The road and train connections between west and east access starting points for hikes of a moderate degree of difficulty.

A more demanding and spectacular national park is the mountain massive of Jotunheimen in central southern Norway *(see pp140–1)*. Jotunheimen has five peaks exceeding 2,300 m (7,546 ft), and has been an attractive tourist destination since the latter half of the 19th century. It is wild and majestic and can be explored using its network of hiking trails and ski tracks.

Rowing on one of the many lakes in Hardangervidda National Park

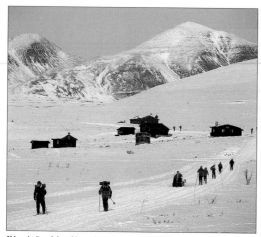

Skiers in Rondale taking advantage of the Easter holidays

SKIING

There are good reasons why Norwegian skiers have won more gold medals in the Winter Olympics and World Championships than anyone else. In many parts of the country conditions are ideal for both cross-country and downhill (Alpine) skiing. Distances between ski tows and lifts are never far. Even Oslo is only a short distance away from the ski runs.

The main centres for winter sports are in Eastern Norway. The resorts of Beitostølen, Oppdal, Geilo, Hemsedal, Lillehammer and Trysil are hives of activity all winter.

Cross-country skiing, known as *langren*, is Norway's national sport. The mountains here are less craggy than in Central Europe and are most suited to this form of skiing. The prepared ski tracks comprise two lanes. Always

Summer snowboarding and skiing at Stryn Summer Ski-Centre

remember to keep to the right to avoid on-coming skiers. The tracks are well marked and circumvent steep hills.

Many places also have illuminated trails for night-time skiing. These are normally 4–5 km (2–3 miles) long and circular. An evening run on a floodlit track is particularly atmospheric. Some skiers use headlamps to ski on unlit tracks.

There are facilities for downhill skiing all over Norway and the runs are graded in terms of difficulty. You can also try to master the Telemark technique – downhill skiing on cross-country skis. The larger ski centres have cross-country, downhill, Telemark and snowboarding equipment for hire. Do not be tempted to ski off-piste in unprepared areas, especially in unfamiliar terrain. It is possible to trigger an avalanche by off-piste skiing.

DNT provides information on cross-country conditions. **Skiforeningen** (Norwegian Ski Association) maintains the 2,600-km (1,616-miles) long network of ski-tracks in Oslo and its environs and provides daily updates on trail conditions on its website.

MOUNTAINEERING

With its mountainous terrain, Norway offers climbing for every ability from the less experienced to the serious mountaineer. Although the mountains are not as high as the Alps, they can be equally dramatic. The sharp peaks of Jotunheimen in the south of Norway are particularly appealing to climbers. Further north, popular climbing areas include Lofoten *(see p210)* and Lyngsalpene (Lyngen Alps) in Troms. Romsdalen's precipitous rock faces, which include Trollveggen (the Troll Wall), are among the most challenging.

The season for summer climbing is relatively short. Be prepared for harsh conditions, including snow and wind, at any time in the most exposed areas. Larger towns have training areas for climbers, such as at Kolsås, 15 km (9 miles) west of Oslo.

A number of books are available describing Norway's peaks and climbing routes. **Norges Klatreforbund** (the Norwegian Climbing Federation) has an informative website with details of mountaineering opportunities throughout the country.

A challenging climb high above a shimmering fjord

BOATING, RAFTING AND WHITE-WATER CANOEING

Norway has an enormously long coastline interspersed with fjords and islands, making it a boating paradise. Marinas hire out boats, including canoes, kayaks, yachts and motor boats. There are no special requirements to operate smaller craft, although you have to have basic seafaring skills.

The national centre for river sports is located in Heidal in

Gudbrandsdalen. For people without their own vessel (kayak or raft), guided tours can be arranged.

A number of rivers throughout Norway are great for white-water canoeing. **Norges Padleforbund** (the Norwegian Canoe Association) provides information on the best places to go.

FISHING

More than 50 per cent of Norwegians go fishing one or more times a year, a larger proportion than in any other country. But then the country has rich opportunities for both sea and freshwater fishing. The most common types of fish for sports anglers are cod and trout. There are 230 other salt-water species and 40 freshwater species.

Sports fishing is practised with a rod, hand reel and a single line with a hook. Along the coast, good catches can be made by fishing from the shore. If you have access to a boat it is possible to make excellent catches of cod, coley and mackerel. Norway also has a number of outstanding salmon rivers.

Be careful to observe the fishing regulations. Sea angling is free for recreational fishermen. Freshwater fishing is regulated; here, either state or private property rights need to be observed. Always check whether fishing is permitted in a particular watercourse. Rules and regulations vary from place to place. All anglers over 16 years must buy a fishing card, sold in shops, hotels, tourist offices and post offices. The

cards are valid for specific areas by the day or for longer periods. Fishing with live bait is forbidden.

Information is available from **Norges Jeger-og Fiskerforbund** (Norwegian Hunting and Fishing Association) or Fylkesmannens Miljøvernavdeling (County Environmental Departments).

WHALE SAFARIS

Every summer male sperm whales leave their families in the southern latitudes and migrate north to the coastal areas off Northern Norway. They visit the coast off the islands of Vesterålen to feed on fish and squid.

Whale-watching cruises operate from Andenes and Tysfjord, weather permitting. A whale safari lasts for six to eight hours.

The tours will almost certainly bring you close to these giants, which can measure up to 20 m (66 ft) long. Sometimes they will lounge on the surface of the water close to the boat while they take in air before descending to the depths of the ocean (*see p207*). You may be lucky and also spot humpback, minke, fin and killer whales in addition to dolphins.

Seal and seabird safaris are also available.

HUNTING

Game hunting takes place all over Norway. It is regarded as having great utilitarian value and hunters value the experience of being with nature. Animals hunted

DIRECTORY

USEFUL ORGANIZATIONS

Den Norske Turistforening DNT
Visitors' address: Storgata 7, Oslo.
Map 2 E3.
Tel 22 82 28 00.
www.turistforeningen.no

Norges Jeger-og Fiskerforbund
Tel 66 79 22 00.
www.njff.no

Norges Klatreforbund
Tel 21 02 98 30.
www.klatring.no

Norges Padleforbund
Tel 21 02 98 35.
www.padling.no

Skiforeningen
Tel 22 92 32 00.
www.skiforeningen.no

WHALE SAFARIS

Hvalsafari
Fyrvika, Andenes. *Tel* 76 11 56 00.
www.whalesafari.no

Tysfjord Turistsenter AS
Storfjord, Tysfjord.
Tel 75 77 53 70.
www.tysfjord-turistsenter.no

include elk, roe-deer, stags, small game, forest birds and grouse. Regardless of whether you hunt on private land or common land, you will need to pay for the right to hunt.

The hunting season is strictly regulated. Generally it runs from Aug–Dec, but local regulations may permit the hunting of some species until May. Note that a number of species are protected throughout the year.

Enthusiastic tourists on a whale safari in Tysfjorden, Nordland, spotting a killer whale

Specialist Holidays and Tours

A *hytter* walking cabin

Nestled into the Scandinavian peninsula with a 24,140 km- (15,000 mile-) long coastline and some of the most pristine landscape in the world, Norway is a fantastic country for taking advantage of the great outdoors. Its alpine mountains, lengthy fjords, harbour-side towns and sprawling plains and steppes are havens for exploring flora and wildlife among some of the most untouched, remote parts of Europe. There are numerous well-organized excursions available for every type of interest, and this will enable you to immerse yourself in Norway's stunning landscapes.

COASTAL STEAMER FJORD TOURS

The **Hurtigruten** is a famous coastal steamer ship that offers one of the most popular activities for visitors to Norway, as it is an excellent way to see parts of the country that are virtually inaccessible on foot or skis. The "classic journey" departs from Bergen and follows the coastline all the way up to Kirkenes along the country's picturesque fjords, stopping at dozens of ports to pick up and let off passengers.

The ship offers a variety of accommodation options, ranging from inexpensive seats to more luxurious suites and cabins, as well as amenities such as restaurants, bars and movie theatres. Other outfits, such as **Fjord Tours** and **Eventyrveien**, offer a variety of trips around the fjords of the southwest, including the famous Norway in a Nutshell tour, while groups such as **Prominent Hotels of the Fjords** and **Tide Sjø** offer more specialized fjord excursions.

REINDEER TOURS

Because reindeers are the stuff of childhood stories, it often comes as a surprise to realize that they actually exist in real life, herded year-round high up in the Arctic region. **Turgleder** runs an April tour that begins inland, in the heart of Arctic nomadic territory, and travels across windswept plateaus towards the coast, where reindeers graze and calve during summer. Participants take part in daily duties, eating, sleeping and travelling like local herdsmen, who share their vast knowledge of nature and outdoor life. In the evenings, the team decamps to an open fire in a Lávvu, a traditional Sámi tent.

Hurtigruten operates an excursion in February that combines a tour along the Norwegian coastline, with a visit to the annual reindeer racing championships in Tromsø and the Sámi National Day festivities in Lapland. It is an excellent means of learning

The Northern Lights, clearly visible in the Arctic Circle

about traditional Sámi culture. The Sámi Easter Festival, in April, offers another opportunity to observe reindeer racing.

NORTHERN LIGHTS TOURS

The Northern Lights, or Aurora Borealis, is a defining attribute of the Arctic firmament. Throughout the winter months, the night sky is regularly lit up by bright, streaming tapestries of green, blue and red that flicker across the heavens. Created by the collision of solar particle emissions with the earth's atmosphere, the strips of light may shine on for hours or last no more than a few seconds – what sort of experience you have is entirely up to the heavens to decide. Aurora are at their most spectacular on clear evenings in early autumn and late winter, when the sky is at its darkest, and your best bet for observing them is in the rural countryside, far away from cities, since urban flicker reduces the effect. For a variety of tours, contact **Natur i Nord** or **Fjord Travel**. The latter's fantastic Northern Lights Cruise Trip consists of a scenic train ride, four nights' cruise across the Arctic circle, the Northern Lights (depending on the weather) and dog sledding excursions.

Reindeer racing at the Sámi Easter celebrations in Lapland

Packs of dogs pulling sleds in the Norwegian countryside

FJORD, MOUNTAIN AND GLACIER HIKES

One of the best ways to experience Norway is to hike along a fjord up into mountain ranges and national parks. Along the way, you can stop off at *hytter* (cabins) that vary from large, staffed lodges to small, basic wooden huts. The hiking season is from early July to late September, and the best areas are the Rondane, Jotunheimen, Dovrefjell and Hardangervidda national parks. **Jostedalen Breførarlag** operates hikes on the nearby Jostedalsbreen glacier, while **Ice Troll** combines these hikes with glacier kayaking.

DOG-SLEDDING

A unique way to experience the Norwegian countryside is by driving a pack of sled dogs across several hundred kilometres of otherwise unforgiving steppe and mountain plateau. The best outfit for tours on solo or tandem, guide-assisted sleds is Norway's most renowned husky farm, **Engholm Husky**, located in the heart of Lapland. Novices are catered for. **Arctic Adventure Tours** and **Tromsø Villmarks-senter** offer similar tours that finish with a gourmet Arctic meal of reindeer stew served in a Sámi tent.

ARCTIC SAFARIS

It is an unforgettable experience to ski across Norway's most remote Arctic regions, and **Polar Charter** runs an exciting "skiing by boat" adventure. Participants travel to the far north by yacht and dock each day at various island and fjord-side ports, then head out to ski fresh, alpine mountain terrain.

The Dive Center operates sea rafting and diving trips along the Arctic coastline. Another invigorating trip is a winter snowmobile safari that traverses the Arctic island of Spitsbergen. These are organized by **Barents Safari** and **Svalbard Wildlife Service**.

Walkers hiking on one of Norway's many glaciers

DIRECTORY

COASTAL STEAMER FJORD TOURS

Eventyrveien
Gamlevegen 6, Gol.
Tel 32 02 99 26.
www.eventyrveien.no

Fjord Tours
Strømgate 4, Bergen.
Tel 81 56 82 22.
www.fjordtours.no

Hurtigruten
Havnegata 2, Narvik.
Tel 76 96 76 00.
www.hurtigruten.no

Prominent Hotels of the Fjords
Tel 57 87 58 00.
www.prominenthotels.com

Tide Sjø
Møllendalsveien 1a, Bergen.
Tel 55 55 20 00.
www.tide.no

REINDEER TOURS

Turgleder
Box 71, Rena.
Tel 91 16 73 03.
www.turgleder.com

NORTHERN LIGHTS

Fjord Travel
Østre Nesttunvei 4–6, Bergen.
Tel 55 13 13 10.
www.fjordtravel.no

Natur I Nord
Nansenveien 34, Tromsø.
Tel 77 66 73 66.
www.naturinord.no

FJORD, MOUNTAIN & GLACIER HIKES

Ice Troll
Breheimsenteret, Jostedal.
Tel 57 68 32 50.
www.icetroll.com

Jostedalen Breførarlag
Krundalen, Jostedal.
Tel 57 68 31 11
www.bfi.no

DOG-SLEDDING

Arctic Adventure Tours
Kvaløysletta, Tromsø.
Tel 77 66 66 75.
www.arcticadventuretours.no

Engholm Husky
Karasjok.
Tel 78 46 71 66.
www.engholm.no

Tromsø Villmarkssenter
9100 Kvaløysletta.
Tel 77 69 60 02.
www.villmarkssenter.no

ARCTIC SAFARIS

Barents Safari
Fjellveien 28, Kirkenes.
Tel 90 19 05 94.
www.barentssafari.no

The Dive Center
Stakkevollveien 72, Tromsø.
Tel 77 69 66 00.
www.dykkersentret.no

Polar Charter
Tromsø.
Tel 77 65 57 97.
www.polarcharter.no

Svalbard Wildlife Service
Næringsbygget Pb 164, Longyearbyen
Tel 79 02 56 60.
www.wildlife.no

PRACTICAL INFORMATION

Norway is a vast country. The distance from Oslo to the North Cape is the same as from Oslo to Rome. It is therefore advisable to spend a little time planning your trip.

Most reasonably-sized towns in Norway have a tourist information centre. The country can be explored by car, plane, ferry and train. The road system is well developed and train connections extend as far as Bodø, north

Tourist office sign

of the Arctic Circle. The coastline is indented with fjords, but a comprehensive ferry and tunnel network makes it easy to reach the islands and cross the fjords. The towns all have modern facilities for the traveller.

Many of the natural attractions such as national parks, skiing, hiking, fishing and mountaineering areas are situated off the beaten track, so good maps are a necessity.

Tourist information office in Bergen

TOURIST INFORMATION

Norway has a number of tourist information offices abroad. **Innovasjon Norge** (Innovation Norway) provides practical information on holidays on its website. It also lists the addresses and telephone numbers of the many local tourist offices.

Oslo has two main information centres – **Turistinformasjonen** near the Rådhus and Turistinformasjonen at Oslo Central Station. These offices have a joint website and you can obtain answers here to specific queries by e-mail. Brochures and travel tips may also be requested via e-mail or can be picked up from the tourist offices abroad or from local tourist offices in Norway. Every town has its own tourist office providing information on where to stay, where to eat and sightseeing in the area.

WHEN TO VISIT

The best time to visit Norway is in the summer between May and September. Eastern Norway along with the Oslo area has the most stable weather. Nevertheless, it is advisable to pack some lightweight waterproofs.

If you plan to experience the midnight sun, you will need to travel north of the Arctic Circle. At Bodø the sun is visible at midnight from 20 May–20 July, in Tromsø from 16 May–27 July, at the North Cape from 13 May–29 July. In the rest of the country at this time the nights are very short and light.

Besides having good summers, Norway is a winter wonderland with lots of opportunities for sport and outdoor pursuits. The severity of the winter between November and April varies from region to region. Cold and snow prevail for long periods in the north of the country, in the mountains and in the inland parts of southern Norway. The climate is often milder along the coast.

Norway has the most snow in January and February. This is a popular time to visit the hotels and tourist huts in the mountains, especially when combined with a skiing holiday.

PASSPORTS AND CUSTOMS REGULATIONS

All visitors, with the exception of those from the Nordic countries, require a valid passport. Citizens of some countries also require a visa. Contact the Norwegian Embassy or consulate in your home country for details.

Norway is one of the few European countries which is free of rabies, and every precaution is taken to maintain this status. You are advised against bringing a pet with you. If you do, it will have to be kept in quarantine for four months before being admitted.

Duty-free allowances on entering the country are 2 litres of beer, 1 litre of spirits, 1 litre wine and 200 cigarettes. The minimum age for bringing spirits into the country is 20; for wine and tobacco the age is 18. You are only permitted to bring medicines for personal use and you should have a letter from your doctor certifying your need for them.

OPENING HOURS AND ADMISSION FEES

In Norway you will need to pay an admission fee to visit most museums and art galleries. There is usually a discount for families, students, adolescents, pensioners and groups. Children are often admitted free of charge. In Oslo admission is free to Nasjonalgalleriet (*see pp52–3*) and to Frognerparken with Gustav Vigeland's sculpture

◁ **Cruise ship approaching the stunning Geirangerfjorden**

garden *(see pp90–91)*. The opening hours of museums vary; they usually open sometime between 9 and 11am and close between 4 and 7pm. From September to May the opening hours can be shorter. Most attractions open daily; some close on Monday.

Norway's protestant churches are normally closed outside services. Churches of special importance, such as cathedrals and stave churches, have longer hours to accommodate visitors, especially during the summer.

The Bergen Card

If you are planning to visit a number of sights in the capital, it is worth buying an *Oslo Kortet* (Oslo Pass) which, for a fixed price, gives admission to most museums and galleries and unlimited travel on public transport (except night buses and trams). Passholders are also entitled to discounts on other attractions. Available at tourist offices, most hotels, and Narvesen newsagents *(see p279)*, the pass can be bought as a single or family pass, for one or more days. A variation on the Oslo Pass is the Oslo Package, which includes hotels. Towns such as Bergen and Trondheim have similar arrangements.

DISABLED TRAVELLERS

It has become increasingly common for hotels to cater to the needs of disabled guests with improved access and specially adapted rooms.

NSB, the Norwegian State Railways, has special carriages to meet the needs of those with impaired mobility. The new Coastal Express ships are equipped to accommodate disabled passengers. **Norges Handikapforbund** (the Norwegian Association for the Disabled) can supply details.

ETIQUETTE

Norwegians are easy-going and informal. Following an initial introduction, people are generally on first-name terms, and this applies to men and women. When meeting someone for the first time it is customary to shake hands.

However, there are two special rules of etiquette. After a meal it is the practice to thank the host/hostess by saying *"takk"*.

In a slightly more formal context, at the beginning of the meal the host will propose a toast, *"skål"*. It is polite not to touch your drink before this toast is made.

After having spent a pleasant day or evening together with good friends, it is customary to ring the hosts a day or two later to thank them (*"takk for sist"*).

DRIVING, ALCOHOL AND TOBACCO

In Norway it is illegal to drive a car if your blood alcohol level is more than 0.2 per mil. For most people this is equivalent to less than a glass of wine. This rule virtually equates to a complete ban on drinking and driving.

Norway also has relatively strict laws regarding the use of tobacco in communal rooms. In restaurants and bars smokers are directed to separate screened-off areas. Smoking is prohibited in all public buildings.

The sale of all alcoholic drinks is subject to special restrictions. Beer with an alcoholic content on a par with pilsner (lager) can be purchased in grocery shops and supermarkets. Wines and spirits, however, are only sold in the specially designated, state-owned Vinmonopolet *(see p239)*.

The state-owned Vinmonopolet selling wines and spirits

DIRECTORY

TOURIST INFORMATION IN NORWAY

Innovasjon Norge
Akersgate 13, 0158 Oslo.
Postboks 448, Sentrum, 0104 Oslo.
Map 3 E3.
Tel 22 00 25 00.
Fax 22 00 25 01.
www.visitnorway.com
@ post@invanor.no

Oslo Turistinformasjon Rådhuset
Fridtjofnansens Plass 5, 0160 Oslo.
Map 3 D3.
Tel 81 53 05 55.
Fax 23 15 88 11.
www.visitoslo.com
@ info@visitoslo.com

Lillehammer Turistinformasjon
Jernbantorget 2, 2609 Lillehammer.
Tel 61 28 98 00.
Fax 61 28 98 01.
www.lillehammerturist.no

Kristiansand Turistinformasjon
Rådhusgata 6,
4611 Kristiansand.
Tel 38 12 13 14.
Fax 38 02 52 55.
www.sorlandet.com

Bergen Turistinformasjon
Vågsallmenningen 1, 5014 Bergen.
Tel 55 55 20 00.
Fax 55 55 20 01.
www.visitbergen.com

Trondheim Turistinformasjon
Munkegata 19, 7411 Trondheim.
Tel 73 80 76 60.
Fax 73 80 76 70.
www.visit-trondheim.com

Tromsø Turistinformasjon
Kirkegata 2, 9253 Tromsø.
Tel 77 61 00 00.
Fax 77 61 00 10.
www.destinasjontromso.no

DISABLED TRAVELLERS

Norges Handikapforbund
(information for disabled people)
Schweigaards Gate 12, 0185 Oslo.
Map 3 F3. ***Tel*** 24 10 24 00.
Fax 24 10 24 99.
www.nhf.no

Personal Security and Health

Police insignia

Norway is a safe tourist destination, even in the cities and towns, with one of the lowest crime rates in Europe. But just as anywhere else, it is always sensible to take basic safety precautions. In all built-up areas there are places which are more exposed to crime than others and Oslo is no exception. According to statistics, however, the few violent episodes that do occur usually involve the criminal fraternity and rarely affect tourists. Nevertheless, it is always advisable to lock your car and avoid leaving valuables visible to passers-by, regardless of where you are in the country.

Policeman   **Policewoman**

Police car

PERSONAL SECURITY

Pickpocketing can be a problem in Oslo. The capital is visited periodically by well-organized international gangs. They operate in crowded places, particularly in busy shops and airport terminals. Do not carry your wallet in your back pocket. Valuables should be kept close to your body so they are difficult to steal. In restaurants and cafés be careful not to hang your handbag over the back of a chair. Put it on the floor beside your chair and place a foot on the strap, or keep it on your lap.

Always keep your passport and tickets separate from your wallet, and keep your credit card and PIN number separate from each other.

Most hotels have safes that you can use to avoid carrying large amounts of money around. Even though theft from hotel rooms is unusual, avoid placing valuables where they are visible.

In Norway it is common practice to withdraw money from cashpoint machines (ATMs). Should you encounter technical problems when making a withdrawal, be on your guard for anyone standing behind you in the queue offering to "help" you. You should politely decline and look for another cashpoint or go into a bank.

POLICE AND SHERIFFS

Norway is divided into 27 police districts each with its own police chief *(politi-mester)*. Some police districts have a number of smaller sheriff offices *(lensmannskon-torer)*, which also have police jurisdiction. The Directorate of Police is the body responsible for police administration.

Norwegian police are generally unarmed. They are helpful and polite. Feel free to ask police officers on patrol for directions or advice. Remember that it is strictly against the law to drive when you have been drinking. Even

Standard sign displayed outside Norwegian police stations

a relatively moderate amount of alcohol in the blood can result in an unconditional prison sentence and a hefty fine. It can be expensive to infringe traffic regulations, especially speed limits.

LOST PROPERTY

Inform the police immediately if anything of value is lost or stolen. In order to make a claim with your insurance company you will need a document from the police to confirm that the item has been stolen.

It is possible that missing items will be found and handed in at a public lost property office. Bus stations, airport terminals and train stations usually have their own lost property offices.

If you lose your passport you are advised to contact your nearest embassy or consulate immediately.

MEDICAL TREATMENT

The Norwegian health service is well developed across the whole spectrum, from private doctors to large public hospitals. In towns there are both public and private out-of-hours clinics for emergencies known as *legevakt*. Waiting times for private rather than public medical treatment are generally shorter, but private is more expensive. Emergency medical treatment is free in

Norway for EU and EEA citizens. Treatment only covers urgent help, with the exception of renal dialysis and refilling visitors' own oxygen cylinders.

You are strongly advised to obtain a European Health Insurance (EHIC) card before you travel, as treatment of citizens from EU and EEA countries is conditional on you being able to produce this, along with a valid passport or other form of identification. Citizens of non-EU and non-EEA countries must meet the cost of medical treatment them-selves if they do not have travel insurance.

PHARMACIES

In Norway only pharmacies are permitted to sell medicines. Some remedies can be bought without a prescription, but most require a doctor's written instruction. If you are dependent on a prescription-only drug it is advisable to bring enough supplies to cover your entire stay. However, you are entitled to visit a doctor's surgery and request any medicines if necessary.

Pharmacies have similar opening hours to other shops. Larger cities have a 24-hour opening rota system – all pharmacies display a list.

Mountain rescue patrol equipped with stretchers and sleighs

FORCES OF NATURE

Norway is a vast country with wide variations in geographical and climatic conditions. Both at sea and in the mountains the wind and weather can change rapidly, and there is good reason to respect the forces of nature.

Unfortunately drowning accidents claim many lives. Those affected include tourists who have ventured out to sea in unseaworthy vessels or in bad weather. It is advisable to consult local people with a knowledge of the area and conditions before setting forth into unknown waters.

Pharmacy sign

·APOTEK·

The mountains are renowned for sudden bad turns in the weather. Sunny, still conditions can change in just a few hours to heavy mist, snow or howling wind. Again, follow the ground rules and take advice from

people familiar with the terrain and weather before setting off. Staff at your accommodation will be able to recommend signposted paths and how long it should take from one point to the next.

In summer mosquitoes are a problem in some areas and you will need to cover up. Mosquito sticks and sprays are available from pharmacies and grocery stores.

Although bears and wolves roam freely in certain areas, there is no need to be alarmed. They are timid and avoid contact with people. There have been no serious confrontations between humans and these animals in recent times.

DIRECTORY

EMERGENCY NUMBERS

Fire *Tel 110.*

Police *Tel 112.*

Ambulance *Tel 113.*

EMBASSIES

Canada
Wergelandsveien 7, Oslo.
Map 2 C2. *Tel 22 99 53 00.*

Ireland
Haakon VIIs Gate 1, Oslo.
Map 2 C3. *Tel 22 01 72 00.*

New Zealand Consulate
c/o Halfdan Ditlev-Simonsen
Ogcoas, Strandveien SO, Lysaker.
Tel 67 11 00 33.

United Kingdom
Thomas Heftyes Gate 8, Oslo.
Map 2 A2. *Tel 23 13 27 00.*

USA
Drammensveien 18, Oslo.
Map 2 C3. *Tel 21 30 85 40.*

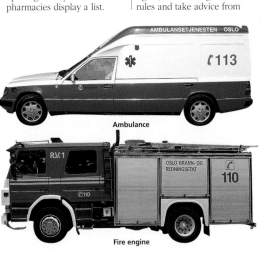

Ambulance

Fire engine

Banking and Local Currency

Travellers to Norway may bring in and take out any amount of cash. However, you must notify officials at the red zone of the airport if you have amounts exceeding 25,000 Nkr. The use of credit cards is widespread. It is easy to use your credit card to obtain local currency, although traveller's cheques are a safer option. There are exchange bureaux at all the international airports. Many hotels will also change money, but for the best exchange rates and lowest commission charges go to a bank. Note that Norway is not a member of the EU.

Foreign exchange bureau at Oslo Central Station

One of the commercial banks' automated teller machines

BANKS AND FOREIGN EXCHANGE BUREAUX

The majority of banks have foreign exchange bureaux and there is little variation in the exchange rates they offer. Most banks also have ATMs, known as Minibanks, which accept major bank and credit cards, such as MasterCard, Bank Accept and Visa, to withdraw Norwegian currency. These cash machines usually have multilingual instructions. The amount of commission charged for withdrawals depends on the type of card you have. Normally, you can withdraw up to 9,900 Nkr over four days with a maximum of seven withdrawals. Alternatively, you can withdraw cash at the counter using Visa. These withdrawals can take time because the bank must first obtain authorisation.

There are exchange bureaux on arrival at most airports, at the busiest border crossings and at the *flytog* terminal (for the express train between Oslo's Gardermoen airport and the city centre).

BANKING HOURS

Banks in Norway stay open from 9am to 3:30pm, although in summer they close a bit earlier, at 3pm.

All banks are closed on Saturday and Sunday, but some have extended opening hours on Thursday, usually to around 5 or 6pm.

On days before a public holiday, such as New Year's Day, most banks close earlier than the usual time of 3:30pm.

CREDIT CARDS

The use of credit cards is widespread in Norway. They are accepted in hotels, restaurants, service stations and most shops. MasterCard and Visa are the most widely used cards. Some places do

DIRECTORY

BANKS

DnB NOR
Stranden 21, 0250 Oslo.
Map 2 C4.
Tel 07 700.

Nordea
Akersgate 55, 0180 Oslo.
Map 3 E3.
Tel 06 001.

Postbanken
Post offices in most urban areas.

FOREIGN EXCHANGE BUREAUX

DnB NOR Oslo Lufthavn
Gardermoen Flyplass.
Tel 07 700.

Nordea Flytogterminalen
Sentralbanestasjonen, Oslo.
Tel 23 15 99 20.

American Express Card Services Unit
DnB NOR Bank ASA, 0021 Oslo.
Tel 66 98 43 71.

LOST CREDIT CARDS

American Express
Tel 80 06 81 00.

Diners Club
Tel 21 01 50 00.

MasterCard/ Eurocard
Tel 21 01 52 22.

Visa
Tel 815 00 500.

The head office of DnB NOR at Aker Brygge in Oslo

not accept American Express because of the high transaction fees charged to retailers.

It is possible to withdraw cash on a credit card in most banks. It is also possible to get cash back when making purchases in most shops.

TRAVELLER'S CHEQUES

Traveller's cheques can be purchased from your local bank at home. They are accepted almost everywhere. Remember to sign your traveller's cheques. If you do not they can be misused if they are lost or stolen, and you will be liable for the loss.

Traveller's cheques are steadily losing ground to credit cards. In terms of security, however, traveller's cheques are generally more secure than cards.

TELEGRAPHIC TRANSFERS

Norwegian banks are helpful when it comes to receiving money transferred telegraphically from abroad. But this type of transaction can be slow and costly. The sender's bank abroad forwards money to its banking partner in Norway, which transfers it to a bank for the receiver to collect. Quicker transfers can be made via MoneyGram to American Express in Oslo.

CURRENCY

Norway's currency is the Norwegian *krone* (kr, Nkr or NOK). One *krone* equals 100 øre. The smallest coin is 50 øre, the largest is

20 *kroner*. Notes are issued in denominations from 50 Nkr to 1,000 Nkr.

Using the 1,000 Nkr note should not be a problem, but it is most practical to carry notes no larger than 500 Nkr.

In view of the fact that Norway is not a member of the European Monetary Union, the Euro is not legal tender, except in certain places such as at airports and tax-free shops. However, it is up to individual retailers how they stand with regard to the Euro. Time will tell if it becomes accepted in an increasing number of outlets.

50 kr

100 Nkr

Bank Notes
Norwegian notes are issued in five denominations – 1,000, 500, 200, 100 and 50 kroner. *They each carry a portrait of a well-known cultural figure.*

200 Nkr

500 Nkr

1000 Nkr

Coins
Norwegian coins are issued in denominations of 20, 10, 5 and 1 kroner, *and in 50* øre. *On the front is a traditional Norwegian design. The new 1 Nkr and 5 Nkr coins have a hole in the centre.*

50 øre

1 Nkr

5 Nkr

10 Nkr

20 Nkr

Communications

Post Office logo

Telecommunications services in Norway are generally of a high standard. Norwegians are among the world's largest users of mobile phone services; from a population of 4.8 million, there are around 5 million mobile phone subscriptions. The use of the Internet is also common; households as well as companies regularly access the Internet and send e-mails. The leading telecommunications company is the former state-owned enterprise, Telenor. It offers a wide range of specialist services. Payphones accept cash, Norwegian phone cards and most credit cards.

PUBLIC TELEPHONES

There are two types of payphones in Norway, both operated by Telenor. The red telephone boxes found in most large towns accept phone cards *(telekort)*, a range of credit cards and Norwegian coins. Phone cards can be purchased in the Narvesen kiosks located throughout the country. The green telephone kiosks only accept phone cards and credit cards, not cash.

Telephone kiosk

It is possible to be called back by the person you are talking to. Ask the person to ring the number given in the telephone box.

MOBILE TELEPHONES

The demand for public telephones has decreased considerably in the wake of the mobile phone, the use of which is particularly widespread in Norway. Generally, visitors from Europe can use their mobile phones in Norway. If you have pre-paid cards, contact your local dealer for information on operating in Norway. Mobile telephones from the USA and Japan cannot usually be used in Norway.

It is worth noting that it is the receiver of a telephone call who pays most of the cost when calls are received from abroad. The person phoning pays only the local rate; the difference in the cost is paid by the receiver.

The GSM network covers 97 per cent of the population and 70 per cent of the country. NMT is a system used in Norway, Sweden and Finland. The system is also known as "the wilderness network" *(villmarkstelefonen)*, as its coverage is wider than that of GSM. But it is advisable not to rely on GSM and NMT to provide a comprehensive nationwide service.

Mobile telephones are useful to have when travelling in wilderness areas, but remember that the coverage is not total, and you should not rely on a mobile phone as a guarantee that you will always be able to call for help.

FAX, TELEGRAM AND E-MAIL

The majority of places offering overnight accommodation will be helpful when it comes to sending faxes, telegrams and e-mails.

Large hotels often have some rooms with ISDN or broadband connections enabling you to plug in your laptop. Request these services – and ask the price – before

USING A CARD-ONLY TELEPHONE

1 Select the instructions in your preferred language.

2 Lift the receiver.

3 Insert phone or credit card and wait for a dialling tone.

4 Dial the number and wait to be connected. If you require assistance or information about charges, ring 80 08 20 65.

5 Remove the card. You will hear a signal if you forget to remove the card.

Telephone card worth 40 Nkr

MAKING A TELEPHONE CALL

- Norwegian telephone numbers have 8 digits; there are no area codes.
- To phone abroad from Norway dial 00, then the country code, area code (minus the initial 0), then the number.
- The country code for Norway is 47.
- Domestic directory enquiries: 1881; international directory enquiries: 1882.
- Telenor customer services: 05000.
- Telenor mobile phone customer services: 09000.
- Netcom mobile phone customer services: 05050.

checking into your room. If you are travelling without your own computer and need access to the Internet, an increasing number of hotels have terminals for the use of guests.

Public libraries and Internet cafés also have facilities for Internet access.

SENDING LETTERS

There are post offices in all towns and nearly all villages. In addition, some shops have postal services.

Post offices are usually open from 9am–5pm on weekdays and 10am–3pm on Saturday. Opening hours for postal services in shops are the same as the retailers' opening hours and vary from shop to shop.

You can buy stamps at post offices, in shops, kiosks and bookstores. The cost to send a normal letter or postcard weighing less than 20 g to a European country is 10 Nkr. Heavier letters, up to 50 g, cost 14 Nkr. Postage to the rest of the world is 12 Nkr for letters weighing less than 20 g and 23 Nkr up to 50 g. To send a letter within Norway costs 8 Nkr and 12 Nkr respectively.

There are postboxes everywhere. They are red and occasionally yellow. When a red postbox is on its own, letters to all addresses can be posted in it. When a red and yellow postbox stand next to each other, the red box is for national and international letters; the yellow box is for local mail and you need to check that the postal code on your letter corresponds to that on the box. Collection times are given on the postboxes.

Norwegian postal codes have four digits and the code precedes the place name. In

Norwegian daily newspapers

addresses, the street number comes after the street name.

It is possible to receive mail via Poste Restante. Addresses should contain the name of the addressee, and the name and postal code of the post office where the letter will be collected. Courier services are provided by a number of international companies.

TV AND RADIO

Almost all hotel rooms in Norway are equipped with colour TV, and can receive both Norwegian and international programmes. The Norwegian channels are NRK1, which is state owned and non-commercial, and NRK2, an auxiliary channel. TV2 is Norway's leading commercial television channel. TV2 transmits weather forecasts periodically in the morning. The other Norwegian commercial channels are TV3 and TV Norge. All channels show foreign films and series in their original language (mostly English).

Hotels often have international channels such as Eurosport, MTV and CNN. The larger hotels also offer pay-TV with a choice of films.

The most popular radio stations are P1 and P2, which broadcast news and weather on the hour. There are a number of other Norwegian stations which broadcast music, classical and modern, 24-hours a day.

Red boxes for national and international post, yellow for local mail

NEWSPAPERS

Norway has an impressive number of newspapers. Most towns have one or more local or regional newspapers while the three national ones are *Aftenposten*, *Verdens Gang* and *Dagbladet*. *VG* is a daily tabloid newspaper with a large circulation. *DN-Dagens Næringsliv* is a daily business newspaper. One newspaper has an English version on the Internet, with up-to-date news and sports, business and feature stories, including upcoming festivals and concerts: www.norwaypost.no. International newspapers are available from **Narvesen** kiosks in larger towns.

DIRECTORY

MAIN POST OFFICES

Posten Norge BA
Biskop Gunnerus' Gate 14, Oslo.
Map 3 E3. **Tel** 81 00 07 10.

Bergen Postkontor
Småstrandgaten 3, Bergen.
Tel 81 00 07 10.

COURIER COMPANIES

DHL Express
Tel 81 00 13 45.

FedEx
Tel 63 94 03 00.

TNT
Tel 81 00 08 10.

INTERNET CAFES

Accezzo Internettcafé
Galleriet, Torgallmenningen 8,
Bergen. **Tel** 55 31 11 60.

Arctic Internet
Jernbanetorget 1, Oslo.
Map 3 E3. **Tel** 22 17 19 40.

FOREIGN NEWSPAPERS

Narvesen
Stortingsgata 24–26, 0161 Oslo.
Map 3 D3. **Tel** 2 42 95 64.

Bystasjonen (bus station),
5015 Bergen.
Tel 55 32 59 06; route info: 177.

Trondheim Central Station,
7491 Trondheim.
Tel 73 88 39 20.

TRAVEL INFORMATION

The majority of visitors coming to Norway by plane arrive at Oslo's Gardermoen airport. Torp in Vestfold and some of the larger towns and cities in western Norway, such as Bergen, Stavanger and Trondheim, also have international airports.There are good car ferry connections to southern Norway and Bergen from Great Britain, Denmark, Sweden and northern Germany. Many visitors also

Scandinavian Airlines (SAS) aeroplane

travel to Norway by bus, car, train and cruise ship. Note that you are entitled to shop duty-free when travelling to and from Norway, as it is not a member of the European Union (see p256). Despite the many natural obstacles such as fjords and mountain chains, travelling around Norway is easy thanks to the many car ferries, tunnels and bridges, and a good road network. Train and bus links are also well developed.

Interior of the new terminal at Oslo's Gardermoen airport

ARRIVING BY AIR

Many European cities and some in the USA have flight connections to Norway. Gardermoen, the country's main international airport, has excellent road and train connections into Oslo. The journey by bus takes 35 to 40 minutes. Flytoget, the express shuttle train to the city centre, departs every 10 minutes, and takes about 20 minutes. Taxis are expensive and take longer than Flytoget.

SAS (Scandinavian Airlines) is the leading airline in the region, with flights to and from Great Britain and other European countries. The services are either direct or

routed via Copenhagen. SAS also has daily flights from the USA and the Far East. **SAS Braathens** is a subsidiary of SAS, with flights from London Gatwick, Manchester, Newcastle and Aberdeen to Oslo, Bergen, Stavanger and Trondheim.

Widerøe, with its Dash 8 planes, operates from Aberdeen and Newcastle to Stavanger and from Manchester to Bergen with connections to a large number of smaller destinations throughout Norway.

International airlines with flights to Oslo include **British Airways, bmi british**

midland, Lufthansa, Finnair and Icelandair. The low-cost airline **Ryanair** operates from London Stansted to Haugesund and Torp near Sandefjord, about 130 km (81 miles) south of Oslo. Ryanair offers discounted tickets for the two-hour bus journey to Oslo.

Norwegian Air Shuttle ASA, know as **Norwegian**, is a low-cost airline operating domestic and international flights across Scandinavia and Europe.

FLIGHT PRICES

Ticket prices to and from Norway vary greatly. In addition to the cut-price deals offered by most airlines, there are large price variations for children, students, families and for booking well in advance.

A rule of thumb is that the nearer the date of departure a booking is made the more difficult it becomes to obtain a discount. Booking just prior to departure often means that only full-price tickets are available.

APEX tickets, which need to be booked well in advance, are reasonably priced, but be aware that they cannot be changed or refunded.

There is stiff competition between the airlines and it can often pay to look into what offers are available; check airline websites for special deals. Charter flights can sometimes be more favourable than individual flights.

Ask your local travel agent about the various package deals to Norway.

SAS

SAS logo

Flytoget, the fastest connection between Oslo and Gardermoen airport

Car ferry docking in Kristiansand harbour in southern Norway

ARRIVING BY FERRY

Norway's coastline is the longest in Europe and ferries have always been an important means of travel to and around Norway.

DFDS Seaways operates between Oslo and Copenhagen, as well as to Gothenburg (Sweden), and from Harwich to Esbjerg (Denmark). **Fjord Line** operates between Newcastle and Stavanger, Haugesund and Bergen.

From Denmark, **Stena Line** sails between Frederikshavn and Oslo; **Color Line** runs services between Hirtshals and Oslo, Hirtshals and Kristiansand, Frederikshavn and Larvik and Kiel (Germany) and Oslo. There are crossings from Hanstholm to Bergen, and Strømstad to Sandefjord.

All crossings are by means of large and comfortable car ferries with various categories of cabins. They usually have a good selection of restaurants and tax-free shops to make the crossing as pleasant and relaxed as possible.

ARRIVING BY TRAIN AND COACH

Oslo is served by good daily train connections from Copenhagen and Stockholm. Trains from Copenhagen follow the route along Sweden's west coast.

From London, **Eurolines** operates a coach service to Copenhagen from where **NOR-Way Bussekspress** runs to Oslo. Nor-Way Bus Express also operates from Gothenburg and Stockholm to Oslo. In Northern Norway

there are bus connections between Skellefteå in Sweden and Bodø, and Umeå in Sweden and Mo I Rana; and from Rovaniemi in Finland to Tromsø, Tana Bru, Lakselv, Karasjok and Kautokeino.

Main entrance, Oslo Central Station

ARRIVING BY CAR

Norway borders three countries and has a large number of border crossings from Svinesund in the south to Grense Jakobselv on the border with Russia in the far north.

All crossings are open to private vehicles. Most travellers by car enter from Sweden via the busiest border crossing at Svinesund.

It is not advisable to drive into Norway from Sweden on a Saturday or Sunday afternoon when traffic is often at its busiest with long queues on both sides of the border crossing. This is because Norwegians regularly travel to Sweden to shop, as the price of many items is lower across the border.

There are customs posts at the border, but if you have nothing to declare you can simply drive through. There are occasions when you may be waved over for a customs

check. You should note that this can also happen a considerable distance from the border crossing.

DIRECTORY

AIRLINES

bmi british midland
Tel 0844 493 0787 (UK).
www.flybmi.com

British Airways
Tel 0870 850 9850 (UK).
www.britishairways.com

Norwegian
Tel 0047 21 49 00 15 (Nor).
www.norwegian.com

Ryanair
Tel 0871 246 0000 (UK).
Tel 0818 303030 (Eire).
www.ryanair.com

SAS Braathens
Tel 0047 05400.
www.sasbraathens.no

Widerøe
Tel 0047 81 00 12 00 (Nor).
Tel 0870 6072 7727 (UK).
www.wideroe.no

FERRY COMPANIES

Color Line
Tel 0047 81 00 08 11 (Nor).
www.colorline.no

DFDS Seaways
Tel 0870 533 3111 (UK).
www.dfds.no

Fjord Line
Tel 0191 296 1313 (UK).
www.fjordline.co.uk

Stena Line
Tel 02 010.
www.stenaline.no

TRAIN AND COACH COMPANIES

Eurolines
Tel 0870 514 3219 (UK).
www.eurolines.co.uk

NOR-Way Bussekspress
Tel 0047 815 44 444 (Nor).
www.nor-way.no

Rail Europe
Tel 0844 848 4064 (UK).
www.raileurope.co.uk

Travelling by Air, Train, Bus and Boat

Distances are so great in Norway that nearly all travel between the north and south of the country takes place by plane. There are comprehensive air services between the major towns with connections to outlying districts. To get the most out of your visit to Norway, it is often a good idea to combine flying with the train and ferry. In Northern Norway in particular, combining air travel with the Hurtigruten ferries *(see p211)* offers the chance to visit the more remote communities that lie outside the airline network. Bus travel is another option.

Widerøe flight calling at Svolvær in the Lofoten Islands

DOMESTIC FLIGHTS

Nearly all the provincial towns have airports with daily domestic flight connections. There is also a good network of smaller airports so you are rarely far from an air strip. Travelling times are relatively short unless you are flying between the north and the south. The flights from Oslo to Bergen, Oslo to Stavanger and Oslo to Trondheim take 50 to 60 minutes. The Oslo-Tromsø route takes about one and a half hours. The longest flight is from Oslo to Kirkenes in the far north, a journey that takes just over 2 hours.

SAS is the leading airline and has taken over **Braathens** and **Widerøe**. However, Widerøe still operates as an independent company. Also there are several small companies with limited scheduled flights.

SAS serves 15 domestic airports and SAS Braathens operates to nearly as many. Widerøe, the third airline company, has 35 mostly smaller destinations. Between them, the three airlines maintain a comprehensive network of flights. Airline tickets can be purchased at travel agents or directly from the airlines. Domestic travel in Norway is not cheap, but if you are flexible with respect to flight times, it is possible to get good discounts. Widerøe's Explore Norway Ticket offers unlimited air travel for 14 days.

Up-to-date flight times and information about delays are continually posted on page 320 of NRK1's *tekst-TV*. SAS also offers a text messaging service for checking arrival and departure times. Be aware that the timetables vary between summer and winter.

TRAVELLING BY TRAIN

From Halden in the south to Bodø in the north there is an excellent train network. Services to the west of the country, such as to Stavanger and Bergen, are also good.

The trains in Norway are operated by Norwegian State Railways, **NSB** (Norges Statsbaner). Both the trains and the railway stations are of a generally high standard. Compartments are always clean and comfortable. There are special facilities for the disabled. Skis and bicycles can be carried as luggage, but on long-distance trains you need to make a reservation for your bike as well as for yourself. Luggage can also be sent in advance. The NSB website has detailed information.

Norwegian trains are divided into three categories. Local trains in the Oslo area, Bergen, Stavanger, Bødo and Trondheim serve the immediate vicinity. InterCity trains operate on medium-distance routes between towns in Eastern Norway. Long-distance trains include Ekspress (express train) and Nattog (night train). For long-distance trains it is necessary to book tickets in advance, with a seat reservation. On regional trains, no seat reservation is required, and unless you wish to book in advance, you can buy your ticket at the station or on board the train (many smaller stations are unmanned).

The most spectacular train journey is that on the steeply

Flåmsbanen, one of Norway's most dramatic stretches of railway line

M/S *Telemarken* at Akkerhaugen wharf on the Telemark Canal

winding Flåmsbanen *(see p182)*. This can be taken as part of the "Norway in a Nutshell" tour, a round trip from Bergen via train and bus, which also includes a fjord cruise. To book, contact Fjord Tours (Tel: 81 56 82 22, www.fjordtours.no).

TRAVELLING BY BUS

Most towns and regions have their own local bus companies, with frequent services in urban areas and less frequent services in rural districts. Oslo airport is served by *flybusser* (airport shuttles) from the towns around the capital.

NOR-Way Bussekspress operates the largest network of buses in the country with domestic and international routes. The company offers a seat guarantee scheme. This makes it unnecessary to reserve tickets in advance. If the bus is full, another bus will be put into service.

Buses offer a range of discounts, such as for children and pensioners, and for return journeys. There are frequent departures; between Oslo and Bergen there are three buses per day in each direction. Coffee and tea are served on board. On night buses the seats can be reclined. Blankets and pillows are available on some services.

Many of the bus companies arrange round trips in Norway and abroad. Ask your travel agent for information.

TRAVELLING BY FERRY

Car ferries and express boats link the islands and fjords along Norway's coast. Not only do they provide a vital means of communication for these areas, but they are also a splendid way of seeing the country.

The famous coastal express, **Hurtigruten**, offers daily cruises between Bergen and Kirkenes in both a northerly and southerly direction *(see p211)*. The boats make 34 stops along the way. The return journey takes 11 days and the route is planned so that the stretches which are covered during the day in one direction are passed at night on the return trip. The ships vary in terms of age and size, but all are of a high standard.

Some of the counties along the coast have their own ferry companies with car ferries *(see p285)* and express boats, providing the opportunity to experience the spectacular scenery of the fjords. On the majority of these, you pay once aboard the ferry. It is often possible to take a day trip, for instance on Sognefjorden, from Bergen to

Boarding a fleet of sightseeing buses in Eidfjord

Flåm, or between Svolvær in the Lofoten Islands and Narvik. Tickets for the Telemark Canal, from Skien to Dalen and Akkerhaugen *(see p148)*, can be purchased through **Telemarkreiser**.

DIRECTORY

DOMESTIC AIRLINE RESERVATIONS

SAS Braathens
Tel 05400.
www.sasbraathens.no

Widerøe
Tel 810 01 200.
www.wideroe.no

TRAIN OPERATOR

NSB
Tel 815 00 888.
www.nsb.no

Airport Express Train
Tel 815 00 777.
www.flytoget.no

FERRY TRAVEL

Hurtigruten (NNDS)
Tel 810 03 030 (Nor).
Tel 020 8846 2666 (UK).
www.hurtigruten.com
www.norwegian
coastalvoyage.com

Telemarkreiser
Tel 35 90 00 20.
www.telemarkreiser.no

BUS TRAVEL

NOR-Way Bussekspress
Tel 815 44 444.
www.nor-way.no/nbeweb

Travelling by Car

"Scenic road" sign

Norway has an extensive road network. Most of the roads are of a high standard. The majority are tarred, but gravel roads may be found in more remote areas. A large number of highways are toll roads. With some planning it is possible to avoid the tolls in most cases. The journey may take a little longer, but almost certainly there will be more to see along the way especially if there is a sign for "Turistveg", indicating a scenic route. Below are details on how to pay the motorway tolls and information regarding the rules and regulations for driving and parking, as well as how to cope with road conditions in winter.

Automatic toll road station with sign displaying fees

TRAFFIC REGULATIONS

Traffic is well-regulated, and Norwegian motorists are law-abiding, possibly because there are stiff fines for breaking the rules.

Be particularly aware of the speed limits. Driving 20 km/h (12 mph) over the speed limit may cost you around 3,000 Nkr. If you exceed the speed limit by more, you risk having your licence confiscated on the spot, in addition to a hefty fine. Most main roads have cameras to catch speeding motorists.

The speed limit on highways is normally 80 km/h (50 mph). On motorways it is between 80 and 90 km/h (50–56 mph) and on certain stretches 100 km/h (60 mph).

You should also be aware of the strict regulations for drink-driving. The maximum legal blood alcohol concentration is 0.2 per mil, which means that you virtually cannot drink any alcohol before driving. Concentrations of 0.2–0.5 per mil will result in a very large fine. Driving with a blood alcohol level in excess of 0.5 per mil warrants an unconditional custodial sentence of a minimum of 21 days, confiscation of driving licence and a big fine.

The use of seatbelts is compulsory, and applies to back-seat passengers, too. Young children are required to sit in special child seats.

Dipped headlights have to be used at all times.

It is advisable to ensure your car is in good order before arriving as there are spot checks, albeit infrequently.

Be aware of the many roundabouts. Drivers entering the junction must always give way.

Traffic lights must always be observed. Under no circumstances should you be tempted to drive through a red light even if the road is clear.

ROAD TOLLS

Several of the larger conurbations are surrounded by toll stations and you are required to pay to enter the town. Make sure you have some Norwegian coins to hand.

Most toll stations are automatic and you simply throw the coins into a special receptacle. There are manned booths, too, for which you also need Norwegian money. Tolls vary between 20 Nkr and 30 Nkr per entry.

Tolls are also payable on a number of main roads and at some tunnels and bridges. A toll is levied in both directions. Most toll stations have both manual and automatic collection.

Certain private roads also charge tolls, particularly over mountain passes or in areas with holiday cabins. This is, however, more the exception than the rule.

Private road tolls are paid by putting a coin in an envelope marked with the registration number of the car, then placing the envelope in a special box. Envelopes are available at the barrier. There are controls to check that the fee for passing the barrier has been paid. The cost of the toll varies from 10 Nkr to 150 Nkr.

PARKING

In most towns and urban areas there are parking meters or multi-storey car parks. In Oslo, if you exceed the allocated time on your meter, you will be fined 500 Nkr – the parking wardens are known for their efficiency. In car parks you pay on departure, so there is no risk of exceeding the time limit.

One of Norway's spectacular bridges connecting islands and skerries

Parking charges vary considerably; in the capital parking can cost 20–30 Nkr per hour.

ROAD STANDARDS

Norwegian roads are divided into so-called Europe roads (*europaveier*), national roads (*riksveier*) and smaller roads. The standard of the *europaveier* is often very high, especially in southern Norway. The *riksveier* are also good. Smaller roads vary in quality. In western Norway there are numerous tight bends, so adjust your speed.

HIRING A CAR

There are a number of local Norwegian car hire companies, as well as the international chains, **Avis**, **Budget** and **Hertz**. Car hire firms can be found at the main airports and in the towns. Bookings can be made either through the international network of the big companies, or directly.

The minimum age for hiring a car is 19 (Avis). For the hire of more exclusive cars and for paying by credit card the minimum age is 25. The hire conditions are more or less the same as in other countries.

Prices, however, may vary significantly compared to other countries. The cost of car hire will often be higher in Norway, but there are a variety of special offers which are worth enquiring about.

CAR FERRIES

The Norwegian coastline is broken up by numerous fjords penetrating deep inland. In places car ferries are an indispensable means of transport. There is an extensive network of ferries, with frequent sailing times.

Usually tickets are bought either just before boarding, or from a ticket collector on board. During the summer months, however, it is best to book in advance for larger ferries to popular destinations, such as Lofoten. Reservations can be made by calling the ferry company OVDS. The

cost of ferry tickets is heavily subsidised, and therefore low. Most car ferries have cafeterias serving simple food.

PETROL STATIONS

As a rule, it is never far from one petrol station to another in Norway. Many towns have manned 24-hour petrol stations and most have automatic credit card payment facilities. If you are driving at night, however, start out with at least half a tank of petrol.

Even though Norway is an oil producing nation, neither petrol nor diesel is cheap.

NAF (Norges Automobilforbund), **Falken** and **Viking** are the main vehicle recovery organisations. Members of the AA and RAC are able to obtain help from NAF in case of a breakdown or accident.

Petrol station run by Norway's state-owned oil company

ROAD SIGNS

International road signs prevail in Norway. There are a few exceptions: a white M on a blue background denotes a passing place.

Don't be tempted to take an elk warning sign home as a souvenir. Elks are common in Norway and the signs serve an important purpose, indicating the risk of an elk crossing the road just ahead of you. You should adjust your speed accordingly. Collisions between elks and cars can result in serious damage and have even been known to cause death.

Beware, elk on the road

WINTER DRIVING AND SAFETY

Driving conditions during the winter vary considerably from one part of the country to another. In Oslo and the coastal areas of eastern

DIRECTORY

CAR HIRE

Avis
Tel 81 53 30 44.
www.avis.no

Budget
Tel 81 56 06 00.
www.budget.no

Hertz
Tel 67 16 80 00.
www.hertz.no

VEHICLE RECOVERY

Falken *Tel 918 02 222.*
NAF *Tel 08505.*
Viking *Tel 06000.*

CAR FERRIES

OVDS *Tel 769 67 600.*

Norway and Vestlandet the roads are normally free of ice and snow all year round. However, they may be slippery, and special winter tyres or studded tyres are strongly recommended for use between November and April. In the mountains and in the north of the country there is a risk of snow and ice for five or six months of the year. Appropriate tyres and sometimes a set of chains may be necessary.

The most exposed roads are fitted with barriers. In case of difficult or impossible driving conditions, these roads are closed. Some mountain passes are shut for most of the winter season. Road closures are usually signed up well ahead. On those mountain passes which are normally kept open throughout the winter, snowfalls may make driving difficult. At such times, a snowplough will drive through at set intervals with cars following in convoy.

It is always advisable to check on conditions before setting out. Take warm clothes and extra food with you when driving in the mountains during the winter.

Getting Around Oslo

It is easy being a tourist in Oslo. Most places of interest are centrally situated, and the various museums, attractions and restaurants are close at hand. The best way to experience Oslo is on foot or by bicycle. From the principal thoroughfare, Karl Johans Gate, it is only a few minutes' walk or cycle ride to the main sights. The capital also has an extensive public transport network that branches out from the city centre. Frequent services mean that even the outskirts of the city are easily accessible. It is advisable to avoid using private cars during the morning and afternoon rush-hour when the roads can become very congested.

Pedestrian crossing on Oslo's Karl Johans Gate

WALKING IN OSLO

There is no better way to enjoy Oslo than on foot. This way you can experience the city from close quarters. Traffic is not a hindrance to pedestrians and in the centre there are several pedestrianized streets.

Note that you are not allowed to cross the road if the light is red, even if there are no cars nearby. In some places you need to press a button to get a green light. When the "green man" appears, you can cross. When crossing at a pedestrian crossing without traffic lights, cars must give way to pedestrians, but do take care.

The streets in Oslo are generally well signposted, and with the Oslo Street Finder (see pp104–07) it is easy to find your way around.

Karl Johans Gate (see p50) is Norway's street for parades and an attraction in itself. It leads from the Central Station past the Parliament building and the National Theatre to the royal palace. The area around it is pedestrianized.

A 10-minute walk from here brings you to the harbour and the commercial centre of Aker

Brygge. The harbour teems with life, with small boats and ferries coming and going. The best view of Akershus Festning, the historic fortress facing Oslofjorden, is from the harbour. Walk up to Akershus for an even more splendid view of the fjord.

DRIVING IN OSLO

If you are used to driving in cities then driving in Oslo should not pose a problem. The traffic density in the capital is no greater than any other city. As in many other

Rush-hour traffic causing long queues on the approach into Oslo

urban areas, however, there is an extensive one-way system in the centre, which might be difficult to negotiate unless you have a map on which it is marked.

As long as you avoid the rush hour (7am–10am and 3pm–6pm) getting around Oslo is straightforward. The speed limit in the centre varies between 30 and 50 km/h (18–31 mph). Near schools and on some residential roads the limit is 30 km/h (19 mph).

Be aware of speed bumps. On smaller roads they are very close together, and if taken at speed the shock can be fierce enough to damage the car.

Tunnels make it easy to drive through the city. The largest tunnels are Rådhustunnel (along the fjord under Rådhuset) and Vålerengtunnelen (from the east going in a northerly direction).

Oslo has numerous large multi-storey car parks, including those at Østbanen, Grønland, Ibsen and Aker Brygge. If you park on a controlled parking bay in the city centre between 8am and 5pm you will need to obtain a ticket from a pay-and-display machine. At other times and on Sunday parking is free. Parking becomes increasingly expensive the nearer the city centre you are. Do not forget to pay during the specified parking times. The fine for failing to pay is high. Private parking places and multi-storey car parks charge at all times.

Always lock your car and keep valuables out of sight, preferably by locking them in the boot.

TAXI SERVICES

Getting a taxi in Oslo is easy, except at the height of the rush hour. Taxis have a sign on the roof. When the light is on, the taxi is for hire.

Official taxis can be hailed on the street or at special taxi ranks. They can also be booked in advance, usually for a small additional charge, up to 20 minutes before the required time. Most taxis can take four passengers, but it is also possible to request a larger vehicle for more people. Oslo has a number of cab companies – **Oslo Taxi**, **NorgesTaxi** and **Taxi 2**.

A market has also grown for so-called pirate taxis in the city, where private people offer to drive for an agreed price. However, they are not to be recommended.

Blue taxi operated by NorgesTaxi

PUBLIC TRANSPORT

Oslo has an efficient public transport system with trams, buses, trains and the Tunnelbane (metro), also known as T-bane, with frequent services between the city centre and the outskirts. There are also routes connecting outlying areas without crossing the city centre. Tunnelbane lines radiate from the city centre *(see map, inside back cover)*. Call **Trafikanten** for information on routes, timetables and connections.

Tickets can be purchased from machines and from staffed Tunnelbane stations, or on buses and trams. If there is no conductor then you must stamp your ticket in the automatic machine. Penalties are high for travelling without a valid ticket.

A single ticket is valid for an hour after it has been stamped, on all forms of public transport within the city. It also allows an unlimited number of changes during this time slot.

You can also buy a ticket that is valid for several trips, a 24-hour ticket, known as a *dagskort*, or a weekly card which gives you unlimited travel for seven days.

The Oslo Pass *(see p273)* entitles the holder to free public transport (except on night buses and trams).

Ferry connecting Bygdøy with Oslo city centre

FERRY SERVICES

A boat service operated by **Nesoddbåtene** runs between Aker Brygge and the peninsula, Nesoddtangen, on the east of Oslofjorden, every hour. In rush-hour the service is more frequent.

From the end of April to early October you can take the **Bygdøyfergene** (Bygdøy Ferry) for a scenic trip across the water to the museums on Bygdøynes *(see pp78–9)*, or to Dronningen Pier for a walk to the outdoor museum, Norsk Folkemuseum.

CYCLING

It is easy, enjoyable and practical to cycle around Oslo, especially if you choose routes that pass through parks and quiet streets. Bear in mind, however, that Norwegian drivers are not particularly well-disciplined

Sign for a bicycle route

with regard to cyclists, so you will need to be cautious and not assume that drivers will stop automatically for you.

You may walk with your bike on the pavement and you may cycle on the pavement if conditions require and you are not causing a nuisance to pedestrians.

Bicycles can be rented at **Kikutstua** or **Oslo Bysykkel**.

SIGHTSEEING TOURS

An alternative to touring the city on your own is to take a guided tour. A typical itinerary for a three-hour guided tour by coach arranged by **Båtservice Sightseeing or HMK**, for example, would include the centre of Oslo, Vigeland-parken, the Holmenkollen Ski Jump and Museum and

the museums in Bygdøy. Tailor-made tours with a personal guide can be arranged by companies such as **Oslo Guideservice** or **Oslo Guidebureau**. They offer traditional itineraries as well as walking, cycling and themed excursions.

There are also cruises on Oslofjorden between May and September. **Båtservice Sightseeing** operates a 50-minute mini-cruise of the harbour every hour, and a 2-hour sightseeing trip around inner Oslofjorden departing three or four times a day. The boats depart from Bryggen in front of Rådhuset (City Hall) *(see pp56–7)*.

General Index

Acknowledgments

Streiffert Förlag would like to thank the following staff at Dorling Kindersley:

Senior Map Co-Ordinator
Casper Morris.

Senior DTP Manager
Jason Little.

Managing Art Editor
Jane Ewart.

Publishing Manager
Anna Streiffert.

Publisher
Douglas Amrine.

Dorling Kindersley would like to thank all those whose contributions and assistance have made the preparation of this book possible.

Main Contributor
Snorre Evensberget, former chief editor at Gyldendal Norsk Forlag and author of *Thor Heyerdahl, Oppdageren (Thor Heyerdahl: The Explorer)*, Norwegian and English Editions 1994, the reference works *Bevingede Ord*, 1967, and *Litterært Leksikon*, 2000. Evensberget has also edited works on Norway, including *Bygd og By i Norge, 1-19, Norge, Vårt Land, 1-9*, and many books on Norwegian nature, hunting and fishing.

Fact checker
Sharon A. Bowker.

Editor, UK Edition
Jane Hutchings.

Editorial & Design Assistance, UK Edition
Emma Anacootee, Catherine Atundi, Claire Baranowski, Julie Bond, Rhiannon Furbear, Phil Hunt, Laura Jones, Toril Lund, Catherine Palmi, Helen Partington, Pete Quinlan, Ellen Root, Susie Smith.

Additional Picture Research
Rachel Barber.

Proof Reader
Stewart J Wild.

Index
Hilary Bird.

Additional Photography
Catherine Atundi, Tim Ridley, Ian O'Leary.

Photography Permissions
Dorling Kindersley would like to thank all the churches, museums, restaurants, hotels, shops, galleries and other sights too numerous to thank individually, for their permission to photograph their establishments.

Picture Credits
Key: t = top; tl = top left; tlc = top left centre; tc = top centre; tr = top right; cla = centre left above; ca = centre above; cra = centre right above; cl = centre left; c = centre; cr = centre right; clb = centre left below; cb = centre below; crb = centre right below; bl = bottom left; b = bottom; bc = bottom centre; bcl = bottom centre left; bcr = bottom centre right; br = bottom right; d = detail.

Works of art have been reproduced with the permission of the following copyright holders: Shaft (1988) Richard Serra ©ARS, NY and DACS, London 2006 70b; Bust of Einar Gerhardsen Nils Aas © DACS, London 2006 75cl; Inner Room (1990) Per Inge Bjørlo © DACS, London 2006 70cl; Winter Sun (1966) Gunnar S. Gundersen ©DACS, London 2006 70tr; The Rubbish Man (1935-95) Ilya Kabakov © DACS, London 2006 71tl; Tilted Form No 3 (1987) Sol Le Witt © ARS, NY and DACS, London 2006 71cra; Without Title (1990) Per Maning © DACS, London 2006 71b; The Night Wanderer Edvard Munch ©ADAGP, Paris and DACS, London 2006 93b; The Scream (1893) Edvard Munch © ADAGP, Paris and DACS, London 2006 52clb; Høstens Promenade Ludvig O. Ravensberg © DACS, London 2006 58br; Winter Night in the Mountains (1914) Harald Sohlberg © DACS, London 2006 53cr; Ibsen Gustav Vigeland © DACS, London 2006 52b; The Monolith Gustav Vigeland © DACS, London 2006 89t; The Little Angry Boy Gustav Vigeland © DACS, London 2006 90tl; Wheel of Life Gustav Vigeland © DACS, London 2006 90ca; The Monolith Gustav Vigeland © DACS, London 2006 90cb; Triangle Gustav Vigeland © DACS, London 2006 90b; Fountain Gustav Vigeland © DACS, London 2006 91cr; The Clan Gustav Vigeland © DACS, London 2006 91t.

Every effort has been made to trace the copyright holders. Dorling Kindersley apologizes for any unintentional omissions. We would be pleased to insert the appropriate acknowledgments in any subsequent edition of this publication. The publishers are also grateful to the following individuals, companies and picture libraries for their kind permission to reproduce their photographs and artwork:

4Corners Images: SIME/ Da Ros Luca 98cla; SIME/ Mezzanotte Susy 268bl; SIME/ Susy Mezzanotte 98bc.

Alamy Images: Adams Picture Library t/a apl/ Mikael Svensson 10tc; blickwinkel/ Baesemann 268cr; blickwinkel/ McPHOTO 10bl; Bryan and Cherry Alexander Photography 257tl; Danita Delimont/ Russell Young 241c; Cody Duncan 11tr; FAN travelstock/ Bildarchiv Friedrichsmeier 102br; Nick Hanna 268tc; Robert Hollingworth 11br; Jon Arnold Images/ Walter Bibikow 11clb; Art Kowalsky 99cr, 102tr; Leslie Garland Picture Library 98tc; Elisa Locci 241tl; Picture Contact/ Jochem Wijnands 100tc; Dave and Sigrun Tollerton 240cl.

All Over Press: 40c, 41br, 156br.

Amarok AB: Magnus Elander, 21bl, 220tr, 221tl 221cra, 221cr, 221br, 267b.

Tom Arnbom: 207br.

Liv Arnessen: 26bc.

AWL Images: Walter Bibikow 88.

Barnekunstmuseet: 95b.

Bergen Kunstmuseum: *Bergens Våg, 1834,* by J. C. Dahl 173bl.

Bergen Museum: De Naturhistoriske Samlinger: 175cl.

Bergen Tourist Board: 272c.

Studio Lasse Berre AS: 5clb, 24tl, 24cla, 24ca, 24cra, 24clb, 24cb, 24crb, 24bl, 24bc, 24br, 25tl, 25tc, 25tr, 25cla, 25ca, 25cr, 25cb, 25crb.

British Museum: Peter Anderson 34bc, 35cb.

Carte Blanche: Erik Berg 263tl.

C. M. Dixon: 34tr.

Corbis: John Hicks 10cr, 100cr.

Den Nationale Scene A/S: Thor Brødreskift 262cr.

English Heritage: 34cl.

Fjellanger-Wideröe: 10cl.

Getty Images: MJ Kim 101tl; Nordic Photos/ Anders Ekholm 269tl; Nordic Photos/ Jorgen Larsson 269cr.

Jiri Havran: 51b, 177tr.

Det Kgl. Bibliotek, København: 36t.

Knudsens Fotosenter: 14t, 14b, 15t, 15b, 17b 25bl, 28cl, 29cl, 29b, 31tr, 31b, 73t, 117b, 141cra, 143cl, 172cl, 181bl, 185tl, 194–195, 199cla, 199cra, 199bl, 205cr, 215tl, 218tl, 218c, 219t, 219b, 220bl, 266cr, 275t, 282t.

Kunstindustrimuseet i Oslo: *Baldisholteppet* 59t, 59crb.

Kviknes Hotell: 225t.

Håkon Li: 183cl, 183cr, 183bl, 183br.

Lunds Historiska Museum: 33t.

Munch-Museet: *Nattvandreren,* Edvard Munch 93b.

Museet for Samtidskunst: *Vintersol* by Gunnar S. Gundersen 70tr, *Indre Rom* by Per Inge Bjørlo 70cl, *Søppelmannen* by Ilja Kabakov 71tl, *Form No 3* by Sol Le Witt 71cra, *Uten titel* by Per Maning.

Nasjonalbiblioteket: 39br.

Nasjonalgalleriet: *Brudeferd i Hardanger* by A. Tidemand & H. Gude 8–9, *Leiv Eirikson Oppdager Amerika* by Christian Krohg 34c, *Fra Hjula Veveri* by Wilhelm Peters 39cl, *Fra Stalheim* by J. C. Dahl 49cra, *Babord Litt* by Christian Krohg 52c, *Portrett av Mme Zborowska* by Amadeo Modigliani 53tc, *Den Angrende St Peter* by El Greco 53cra, *Vinternatt i Rondane* by Harald Sohlberg 53cr, *Stetind i Tåke* by Peder Balke 53b, *Skrik* by Edvard Munch 52clb, *Ibsen* by Gustav Vigeland, 52b.

Nordlysfestivalen: 263cr.

Norgestaxi Oslo AS: 287cla.

Norsk Folkemuseum: 3, 12, 82ca.

Norsk Hjemmefront Museum: 41clb, 66bl.

Norway Designs: 99tl.

Oslo Bymuseum: *Det Konglige Slott 1845* av O. F. Knudsen 9, *Prøvetur på Eidsvollsbanen* 39tl.

Oslo International Church Music Festival: 100bl.

Oslo Spektrum: 75b.

Photolibrary: Photononstop/ Dominique Lerault 257br.

Sametinget: 215br.

Samfoto: Kim Hart 26c.

Scanpix: 27cra, 27br.

Smuget: 201cl.

Mick Sharp: 35cr.

Tiu Similä: 21tr.

Skimuseet: 26tr, 26cl.

Statens Historiska Museum, Stockholm: Peter Anderson 34tl, 35tl, 35crb.

Statens Vegvesen: 19br.

Stenersenmuseet *Høstens Promenade* by Ludvig O. Ravensberg 58br.

SuperStock: Brian Lawrence 256bl.

Tofoto: 211t, 211cla, 211cr, 211cl, 211b.

Trøndelag Teater: 262bl.

Universitetets Kulturhistoriske Museer: Ove Holst 34br.

Universitetets Oldsakssamling: 33b; Peter Anderson 4br, 034bl, 54clb, 84b, 85bl; Ann Christine Eek 54ca; 54tr, 55tl Ove Holst 84tl; Ellen C. holte and Lill-Ann Chepstow-Lusty 55bl; Eirik Irgens Johnsen 49tl, 54b, 76, 84cl, 85tl, 85tc.

O. Væring: *Birkebeinerferden* by K. Bergslien 26clb, *Håkon Håkonsson Krones* by Gerhard Munthe 32, *Bærums Verk* by C. A. Lorentzen 36br, *Sjøhelten Peter Wessel Tordenskiold* by Balthasar Denners 37c, *En Aften i det Norske Selskap* by Eilif Petersen 37t, *Torvslaget i Christiiania 17.5 1829* by H. E. Reimers 38br, *Nasjonalforsamlingen på Eidsvoll 1814* by O. Wergeland 38tl, *Christian Michelsen og Kongefamilien 7/6 1905* by H. Ström 40tl, *Akershus Slott* by Jacob Croning 69tl.

Linda Whitwam: 110–111, 202, 203b, 216tl, 216cl, 216bc.

Staffan Widstrand: 013c, 21bcl, 21br, 220cl.

JACKET

Front – 4CORNERS IMAGES: SIME/ Gräfenhain Günter main image; ROLF SØRENSEN: clb.
Back – DK IMAGES: clb; Jørn Bøhmer-Olsen and Rolf Sørensen cla, tl; ROLF SØRENSEN: bl.
Spine – 4CORNERS IMAGES: SIME/ Gräfenhain Günter t; UNIVERSITETETS OLDSAKSSAMLING: Ove Holst b.

All other images copyright © Dorling Kindersley. For further information: www.dkimages.com

SPECIAL EDITIONS OF DK TRAVEL GUIDES

DK Travel Guides can be purchased in bulk quantities at discounted prices for use in promotions or as premiums. We are also able to offer special editions and personalized jackets, corporate imprints, and excerpts from all of our books, tailored specifically to meet your own needs.

To find out more, please contact:

(in the United States) **SpecialSales@dk.com**

(in the UK) **TravelSpecialSales@uk.dk.com**

(in Canada) DK Special Sales at **general@tourmaline.ca**

(in Australia) **business.development@pearson.com.au**

Phrase Book

When reading the imitated pronunciation, stress that part which is underlined. Pronounce each syllable as if it formed part of an English word and you will be understood sufficiently well. A few sounds, particular to Norwegian, are represented by small capitals in the pronunciation guide. Below is an explanation of these.

ew:	try to say 'ee' with your lips rounded (or the French 'u')	
h:	the 'h' sound as in 'huge'	
i:	the 'i' sound as in 'high'	
ur:	the 'u' sound as in 'fur'	

Norwegian Alphabetical Order
In the list below we have followed Norwegian alphabetical order. The following letters are listed after z: æ, ø, å.

'You'
There are two words for 'you': du (addressing one person) and dere (addressing two or more people). The polite form, de, is seldom used.

In an Emergency

Help!	**Hjelp!**	yelp
Stop!	**Stopp!**	stop
Call a doctor!	**Ring etter lege!**	Ring etter lege
Call an ambulance!	**Ring etter ambulanse!**	Ring etter amboolangsseh
Call the police!	**Ring til politiet!**	Ring til pohliteeat
Call the fire brigade!	**Ring til brannvesenet!**	Ring til brannvesenet
Where is the nearest telephone?	**Hvor er nærmeste telefon?**	vohr er nairmeste telefawn?
Where is the nearest hospital?	**Hvor er nærmeste sykehus?**	vohr er nairmeste sewkeh-hooss?

Communication Essentials

Yes/no	**Ja/nei**	yah/ni
Thank you	**Takk**	takk
No, thank you	**Nei takk**	ni takk
Yes, please	**Ja takk**	yah takk
Please (offering)	**Vær så god**	varshawgo
Excuse me, please	**Unnskyld**	oonshewl
Good morning	**Mor'n**	mawrn
Good afternoon	**God dag**	go-dahg
Good evening	**God kveld**	go-kvell
Good night	**God natt**	go-natt
Goodbye	**Morn'a; (informal) ha det**	morna; hah-deh
Sorry!	**Om forlatelse!**	om forlahdelseh

Useful Phrases

I don't understand	**Jeg forstår ikke**	yi forshtawr ikkeh
Please speak more slowly	**Kan du snakke langsommere**	kan doo snakkeh lang-sawmereh
Please write it down for me	**Kan du skrive det opp for meg?**	kan doo skreeveh deh op for mi
My name is …	**Jeg heter …**	yi hayter
Can you tell me …?	**Kan du si meg …?**	kan doo see mi
I would like a …	**Jeg vil gjerne ha en/et …**	yi vil yarneh hah ayn/et
Where can I get …?	**Hvor kan jeg få …?**	vohr kan yi faw
What time is it?	**Hvor mange er klokken?**	vohr mang-eh ar klokken
I must go now	**Jeg må gå nå**	yi maw gaw naw
I've lost my way (on foot)	**Jeg har gått meg bort**	yi hahr gawt mi bohrt
Cheers!	**Skål!**	skawl
Where is the toilet?	**Hvor er toalettet?**	vohr ar toh-a-letteh

Shopping

I'd like …	**Jeg skal ha …**	yi skal hah
Do you have …?	**Har du …?**	hahr doo
How much is this?	**Hvor mye koster denne/dette?**	vohr mew-eh koster denneh/dehtteh
I'd like to change this, please	**Kan jeg få bytte denne (dette)?**	kan yi faw bewteh denneh (dehtteh)
Can I have a receipt?	**Kan jeg få en kvittering?**	kan yi faw ayn kvittayring
Can I try it/them on?	**Kan jeg prøve den/dem?**	kan yi prurveh den/dem
I'm just looking	**Jeg bare kikker**	yi bahreh Heekker
Do you take credit cards?	**Tar du kredittkort?**	tahr doo kredittkort

antique shop	**antikvitetshandel**	antikvitetshandel
baker	**bakeri**	bak-eree
bookshop	**bokhandel**	bohkhandel
butcher	**slakter**	slakter
cake shop	**konditori**	kohnditohree
cheap	**billig**	billi
chemist	**apotek**	apohtayk
craft shop	**husflidsforret-ning**	hoosfleeds-forretning
department store	**varemagasin**	vahremaga-seen
expensive	**dyrt**	dewrt
fashion	**mote**	mohteh
fishmonger	**fiskebutikk**	fiskehbooteekk
florist	**blomsterbutikk**	blomsterbooteekk
gift shop	**gavebutikk**	gahvehbooteekk
grocer	**dagligvarebutikk**	dahglivahrebooteekk
hairdresser	**frisør**	freesur
market	**marked**	marked
newsagent	**avis-og tobakks-butikk**	aveess aw tohbaksbooteek
post office	**postkontor**	pawstkontoor
sale	**salg**	salg
shoe shop	**skobutikk**	skohbooteekk
supermarket	**supermarked**	soopermarked
toy shop	**leketøysbutikk**	layketoys-booteekk
travel agent	**reisebyrå**	raissehbewraw

Sightseeing

art gallery	**kunstgalleri**	kunnstgalleree
church	**kirke**	Heerke
fjord	**fjord**	fjord
garden	**hage**	hahge
house	**hus**	hews
mountain	**fjell**	fyeall
museum	**musem**	mewseum
square	**plass**	plahss
street	**gate**	gahte
tourist office	**turistkontor**	tureestkontoor
town hall	**rådhus**	rawdhews
closed for holiday	**stengt på grunn av ferie**	stengt paw grewnn ahw fereh
bus station	**busstasjon**	bewss-stashohn
railway station	**jernbanestasjon**	jairnbanestashohn

Staying in a Hotel

Have you any vacancies?	**Har dere ledige rom?**	hahr dereh laydi-eh rohm
I have a reservation	**Jeg har reservert rom**	yi hahr ressarvayrt rohm
double room	**dobbeltrom**	dobbeltrohm
twin room	**tomannsrom**	tohmannsrohm
single room	**enkeltrom**	engkeltrohm
room with a bath	**rom med bad**	rohm med bahd
shower	**dusj**	doosh
toilet	**toalett**	toh-a-lett
key	**nøkkel**	nurkkel

Eating out

Have you got a table for…?	**Kan jeg få et bord til…?**	kan yi faw et bohr til…
Can I see the menu?	**Kan jeg få se menyen?**	kan yi faw say menewen
Can I see the wine list?	**Kan jeg få se vinkartet?**	kan yi faw say veenkarteh
I'm a vegetarian	**Jeg er vegetarianer**	yi ar veggetahreeahnehr
Waiter/waitress!	**Hallo! Unnskyld**	hallo oonskewl
The bill, please	**Regningen, takk.**	rjning-en takk
beer	**øl**	url
bottle	**flaske**	flaskeh
buffet	**koldtbord**	kawltbohr
cake	**kake**	kahkeh
children's portion	**barneporsjon**	barneporshohn
coffee	**kaffe**	kaffeh
cup	**kopp**	kopp
fork	**gaffel**	gaffel
glass	**glass**	glass
knife	**kniv**	k-neev
menu	**meny**	menew
milk	**melk**	melk
open sandwich	**smørbrød**	smurbrur
plate	**tallerk**	tal-ark
receipt	**kvittering**	kvittayring
schnapps	**akevitt**	akevitt

serviette	serviett	sarvi-ett
snack	smårett	smawrett
soup	suppe	sooppeh
spoon	skje	shay
sugar	sukker	sookker
tea	te	tay
tip	tips	tips
waiter	kelner	kelner
waitress	serveringsdame	sarvayringssdahmeh
water	vann	vann
wine	vin	veen
wine list	vinkart	veenkart

Menu Decoder

ansjos	anshoos	anchovies
baguette	bagaitt	French stick
blåskjell	blaw-shayll	mussels
bringebær	bringe-bair	raspberries
brød	brur	bread
dyrestek	dewrestek	roast reindeer
eddik	eddikk	vinegar
elg	ailk	elk
fenalår	fehna-lawr	cured leg of mutton
fisk	feesk	fish
flatbrød	flaht-brur	'flat bread' (leaf-thin crispbread)
flyndre	flewndre	sole
fløte	flurteh	cream
fårikål	fawreekawl	lamb and cabbage stew
gaffelbiter	gahffel-beeter	small fillets of herring soaked in marinade
geitost	geytost	sweet, brown goats' cheese
gravlaks	grahv-lahks	cured salmon
grovbrød	gruuv-brur	wholemeal bread
grønnsaker	grurnn-sahker	vegetables
hellefisk	hellefisk	halibut
hummer	hummer	lobster
hvalbiff	vahlbiff	whale steak
hvitvin	veetveen	white wine
høns	hurns	chicken, poultry
is	ees	ice cream, ice
jordbær	joordbair	strawberries
kalv	kallv	veal
karbonade	karbonahdeh	minced beef steak
kjøtt	hurtt	meat
kjøttkaker	hurttkahker	minced beef balls
kneipbrød	k-neyp-brur	crusty wheaten bread
knekkebrød	k-nekke-brur	crispbread
kokt	kookt	boiled, poached
koldtbord	kawltbohr	cold buffet
krabbe	crahbbe	crab
kreps	krepss	crayfish
kveite	kvaiyteh	halibut
kylling	HEWlling	chicken
laks	lahks	salmon
lam	lamm	lamb
makrell	mahkrel	mackerel
melk	mailk	milk
mineralvann	mineralvann	mineral water
multer	mewlter	cloudberries
mørbrad	murbrur	sirloin
okse	ookseh	beef
oksestek	ookseh-steek	roast beef
ost	oost	cheese
pannekaker	pannekahker	large thin pancakes
pariserloff	pareewser-loff	French stick
pinnekjøtt	pinne-hurtt	salted, dried side of lamb
pisket krem	piskett kraim	whipped cream
poteter	pootaiter	potatoes
pølser	pulser	frankfurter sausages
rakørret	rahk-urret	fermented trout
reinsdyr	rainsdewr	reindeer
reke(r)	rehker	prawns
ris	rees	rice
rogn	rogn	roe
rugbrød	rewgbrur	rye bread
rødspette	rurdspetteh	plaice
rødvin	rurveen	red wine
røkelaks	rurkelaks	smoked salmon
rømme	rurmmeh	soured cream
rå	raw	raw
saus	saws	sauce
sei	saiy	coley
sild	seell	herring
sjokolade	shokolahde	chocolate
skalldyr	skall-dewr	shellfish

skinke	shinkeh	ham
skjell	shayll	shells
smør	smurr	butter
smørbrød	smurrbrur	open sandwich
saus	saws	sauce
stekt	stehkt	fried, roasted
sukker	sookker	sugar
suppe	sooppeh	soup
surkål	sewkall	sauerkraut
svin	sween	pork
syltetøy	sewlte-turj	jam
søt	surt	sweet
torsk	tawshk	cod
tyttebær	trwtte-bair	cowberries or lingonberries
tørr	turr	dry
vafler	vahfler	waffles
vann	vann	tap water
varm	vahrm	warm, hot
vilt	veellt	game
vin	veen	wine
øl	url	beer
ørret	urrett	trout
østers	ursters	oysters

Numbers

0	null	nooll
1	en/ett	ayn/ett
2	to	toh
3	tre	tray
4	fire	feereh
5	fem	fem
6	seks	seks
7	sju/syv	shoo/sewv
8	åtte	awtteh
9	ni	nee
10	ti	tee
11	elleve	elveh
12	tolv	tawll
13	tretten	tretten
14	fjorten	fyohrten
15	femten	femten
16	seksten	sisten
17	sytten	sutten
18	atten	atten
19	nitten	neetten
20	tjue/tyve	HOO-eh/trwveh
21	tjueen/enogtyve	HOO-eh-ayn/ayn-aw-trwveh
22	tjueto/toogtyve	HOO-eh-toh/toh-aw-trwveh
30	tretti/tredve	tretti/tredveh
40	førti/førr	furti/furr
50	femti	femti
60	seksti	seksti
70	sytti	surtti
80	åtti	awtti
90	nitti	neetti
100	(ett) hundre	hoondreh
110	hundre og ti	hoondreh aw tee
200	to hundre	toh hoondreh
300	tre hundre	tray hoondreh
400	fire hundre	feereh hoondreh
1,000	(ett) tusen	toossen
10,000	ti tusen	tee toossen

Time

today	i dag	ee-dahg
yesterday	i går	ee-gawr
tomorrow	i morgen	ee-mawern
this morning	i morges	ee-morges
this afternoon	i ettermiddag	ee-ettermiddag
this evening/tonight	i kveld	ee-kvell
late	sent	saynt
early	tidlig	teeli
soon	snart	snahrt
later on	senere	saynereh
one minute	et minutt	et minoott
two minutes	to minutter	toh minootter
quarter of an hour	et kvarter	et kvartayr
half an hour	en halv time	ayn hal teemeh
Sunday	søndag	surndag
Monday	mandag	mandag
Tuesday	tirsdag	teerssdag
Wednesday	onsdag	ohnssdag
Thursday	torsdag	tawrssdag
Friday	fredag	fraydag
Saturday	lørdag	lurrdag